PATRICK BISHOP has been a war [correspondent for] twenty years, reporting from conflicts all over the world. He is the author of the critically acclaimed and bestselling *Fighter Boys*, his most recent work is *3 Para*. He lives in London.

From the reviews of *Bomber Boys*:

'Superbly written and authoritative . . . the members of Bomber Command now have a fitting commemoration of their heroic deeds'
                                                                                    Observer

'Deeply humane, lucidly written and powerful . . . All this bravery, and the way of life that supported it, are faithfully recorded in Bishop's refreshingly unpretentious account'
                                                    MICHAEL BURLEIGH, *Sunday Times*

'This is a terrific book, so riveting, exciting and moving that it must help bring back the Bomber Boys to their rightful place of honour. A true war memorial'
                                                    MONTAGU CURZON, *Spectator*

'This is the best kind of military history – the kind in which the author never loses sight of the impact of war on its victims, German as well as British, and those who were left behind. *Bomber Boys* will remind the survivors that they and their lost comrades are not forgotten. And it reminds the rest of us what their war was all about'   DANIEL JOHNSON, *Evening Standard*

'Impressive and important . . . Bishop is a fine writer and his feel for the period is outstanding. In this powerful account of the ordeals men went through over Germany, he is at his best'
                                                                                    TLS

By the same author

3 Para
Fighter Boys
The Irish Empire
The Provisional IRA

PATRICK BISHOP

Bomber Boys

FIGHTING BACK 1940–1945

HARPER PERENNIAL

London, New York, Toronto, Sydney and New Delhi

Harper Perennial
An imprint of HarperCollins*Publishers*
77–85 Fulham Palace Road,
Hammersmith, London W6 8JB

www.harperperennial.co.uk
Visit our authors' blog at www.fifthestate.co.uk

This edition published by Harper Perennial 2008
1

First published in Great Britain by Harper*Press* in 2007

A catalogue record for this book is available from the British Library

ISBN 978-0-00-719215-1

Plans of Halifax and Lancaster bombers © Copyright The National Archives.
Plans of Stirling, Mosquito and Wellington bombers © Crown Copyright RAF Museum.

Maps of Cologne and Berlin © Copyright Royal Geographical Society.

Maps of Bomber Command Stations, Targets in Europe, Germany, and
the Ruhr Valley by John Gilkes.

Set in PostScript Giovanni Book with Photina display by
Rowland Phototypesetting Ltd, Bury St Edmunds, Suffolk

Printed and bound in Great Britain by Clays Ltd, St Ives plc

Mixed Sources
Product group from well-managed
forests and other controlled sources
www.fsc.org Cert no. SW-COC-1806
© 1996 Forest Stewardship Council

FSC is a non-profit international organisation established to promote the
responsible management of the world's forests. Products carrying the FSC
label are independently certified to assure consumers that they come
from forests that are managed to meet the social, economic and
ecological needs of present and future generations.

Find out more about HarperCollins and the environment at
www.harpercollins.co.uk/green

To Peter, Margaret, Amelia
and Daniel

Contents

	List of Illustrations	ix
	Maps	xiii
	Prologue: Perkins	xxv
	Introduction	xxix
1	Learning the Hard Way	1
2	Coventrated	19
3	'To Fly and Fight'	33
4	Crewing Up	47
5	Dying in the Dark	67
6	Enter 'Butch'	86
7	The Feast of St Peter and St Paul	113
8	The Reasons Why	130
9	The Battle	154
10	'A Select Gang of Blokes'	182
11	The Big City	199
12	The Chop	219
13	Crack Up	238
14	Home Front	256
15	Love in Uniform	280
16	D-Day Diversion	307
17	Tallboys and *Tirpitz*	326

18   Götterdämmerung   342

19   Forgetting   366

Epilogue: Went the day well?   391

Notes   397
Bombers   405
Acknowledgments   417
Index   419

List of Illustrations

Integrated

p. xxx Potsdam 1945. *Ullstein Bild*

p. 3 Pilot and co-pilot at the controls of a Wellington.
Imperial War Museum (D4737)

p. 26 The Morning After. *SV-Bilderdienst*

p. 40 Leonard Cheshire and opponent, Germany, August 1936.
Courtesy The Leonard Cheshire Archive

p. 58 Plotting a course. *Imperial War Museum* (CH7466)

p. 69 Whitley. *ww2images.com*

p. 96 The shape of things to come: Lübeck, March 1942.
SV-Bilderdienst

p. 128 Aftermath of a firestorm. Hamburg, July 1943.
Ullstein Bild

p. 148 Martha Gellhorn. *Empics*

p.160 'The target for tonight is . . .' 57 Squadron learn their destination, 30 March 1944. *Imperial War Museum* (CH12598)

p. 197 Manser VC. *Imperial War Museum* (CHP796)

p. 204 Me110 night-fighters. *ww2images.com*

p. 222 Tail End Charlie. *Imperial War Museum* (CH9866)

p. 246 A flak battery opens up as an attack goes in. *Ullstein Bild*

p. 269 Leading from the front: WC John Voyce.

p. 288 'Silver wings in the moonlight / Flying high up above,
While I'm patiently waiting / Please take care of my love.'
Science and Society Picture Library

p. 311 An American P-51 Mustang long-range escort.
akg-images

p. 329 A Tallboy, seconds after release. *ww2images.com*

p. 348 Essen, May 1945. *Imperial War Museum* (CL2571)

p. 383 Noble Frankland. *Topfoto*

Plate Section

Guy Gibson and comrades, Coningsby, summer 1942.
Hulton Getty

Wellingtons flying in formation. *Ullstein Bild*

Charles 'Percy' Pickard. *Imperial War Museum* (CH10251)

Lincoln Cathedral. *ww2images.com*

Harry Yates. From *Luck and a Lancaster* (1840370793) by Harry
Yates, *courtesy The Crowood Press*

Aircrew checking kit. *Imperial War Museum* (D6022)

Halifax crews boarding lorries, October 1943.
Imperial War Museum (CH11401)

WAAFs wave *au revoir* to a Lancaster. *ww2images.com*

A Lancaster rear gunner. *Imperial War Museum* (CH12776)

A Lancaster navigator. *Robert Hunt Library*

An Avro Lancaster. *Courtesy Tony Iveson*

A Halifax EY-E. *ww2images.com*

Flak, seen from the ground. *Ullstein Bild*

Bomb doors open: a Lancaster bomb aimer.
Imperial War Museum (CH11540)

Incendiaries tumble down on Duisberg.
Imperial War Museum (CL1405)

Berlin cellar life. *SV-Bilderdienst*

A family in the aftermath of a bombing. *SV-Bilderdienst*

The price of total war: Berlin, 1944. *Ullstein Bild*

Cologne at the end of the war. *Ullstein Bild*

A 90 Squadron crew is debriefed. *Imperial War Museum* (CH10804)

Mary Mileham. *Courtesy Philip Mileham / Imperial War Museum*

Frank Blackman. *Imperial War Museum*

George Hull. *Courtesy Joan Hatfield*

Joan Kirby. *Courtesy Joan Hatfield*

Frances Dowdeswell. *Courtesy Frances Dowdeswell*

Denholm Elliott and Virginia McKenna, 1954. *Hulton Getty*

Tony Iveson in 1943. *Courtesy Tony Iveson*

Don Charlwood. *Courtesy Crécy Publishing*

Ken Newman. *Courtesy Ken Newman*

Reg Fayers' self-portrait. *Imperial War Museum*

Tony Iveson and some of his crew. *Courtesy Tony Iveson*

Setting off for Hamburg, July 1943. *Imperial War Museum*

Arthur Harris with his wife Jill and daughter Jackie.
Imperial War Museum

Leonard Cheshire. *ww2images.com*

Charles Portal and Ira Eaker. *Imperial War Museum* (H27478)

A B-24 Liberator in a daylight raid. *Ullstein Bild*

A B-17 Flying Fortress drops its bombs. *akg-images*

A Grand Slam bursts on Arnsberg Bridge, March 1945.
From Volume III (plate 23) of *History of the Second World War* by
Sir Charles Webster and Noble Frankland

Cyril March and crew. *Courtesy Cy March*

The Dresden raid. *ww2images.com*

VE Day crowds outside the Saracen's Head.
Courtesy of Lincolnshire Echo

Main Bomber Command
stations in the UK

| 0 | 10 | 20 | 30 | 40 | 50 |
miles

North
Sea

O Group HQ
• Airfield

• Middleton St George
• Croft

Leeming •
• Thirsk   • Wombleton
Skipton-on- • • Topcliffe
Swale   • Dalton
Dishforth • • Tholthorpe
• Tholthorpe   Carnaby •
Linton-on-Ouse • • East Moor   Driffield •
Allerton O • Full Sutton   Lissett •
Marston Moor • O YORK
Rufforth •   • Pocklington
Elvington •   • Leconfield
Riccall • • Melbourne   • Leconfield
Breighton • • Holme-on-Spalding-Moor
Burn •
Snaith • • North Killingholme
Elsham Wolds •
Sandtoft •   • Kirmington
Lindholme • SCUNTHORPE
Doncaster • • Finningley   Grimsby •
Bircotes O   • Blyton   • Binbrook
Bawtry • Sturgate • • Hemswell • Kelstern
Worksop • Faldingworth • • Ludford Magna
Ingham • • Wickenby • Strubby
Gamston • Scampton • • Dunholme Lodge
LINCOLN • Fiskerton
Ossington • • Wigsley Skellingthorpe • • Bardney   • Spilsby
Swinderby O • East Kirkby
Winthorpe • • Woodhall Spa
Waddington • Balderton • • Coningsby
Syerston • • Fulbeck   Metheringham •
Newton •   • North Creake
• Church Broughton Langar • Bottesford • • Little Snoring
O Eggington O Grantham   Sculthorpe • Oulton •
• Tatenhill • Castle Donington • Saltby   Foulsham O Swannington •
• Lichfield Wymeswold • • Cottesmore   Great Massingham • Attlebridge •
• Woolfox Lodge West Raynham • Swanton Morley • Bylaugh Horsham St Faith
North Luffenham • Downham Market • Marham • Hall
Nuneaton • Market   • Watton
Bruntingthorpe • Harborough Polebrook • Methwold • • Bodney
Bramcote • Bitteswell • Upwood • Feltwell • • East Wretham
Husbands Bosworth • Desborough • Warboys • Mepal • Witchford • • Lakenheath
• Honiley Harrington • Alconbury • • Mildenhall
Molesworth • Huntington O Wyton • Waterbeach • • Honington
Wellesbourne Graveley • • Tuddenham
Mountford Kimbolton • Oakington • O Exning
• Gaydon Little Staughton • Bourn • Newmarket • • Chedburgh
• Stratford • Chipping Warden Tempsford • Gransden Lodge • • Stradishall • Wattisham
Edgehill • Bassingbourn • Wratting Common • Woodbridge •
Hinton-in-the-Hedges • • Silverstone Cranfield • Steeple Morden • • Ridgewell
Barford St John • Croughton • Turweston
Enstone • Finmere • • Little Horwood
• Bicester O Winslow
Upper Heyford • • Wing
Weston-on-the-Green • • Westcott • Cheddington
O Oakley

Mount Farm •
Benson •
High Wycombe
Hampstead HQ Bomber Command
Norris

LONDON

N
W   E
S

Main Targets in Europe

0   100   200   300

miles

Range circles are measured from Lincoln

⊙ ○ Bomb targets

Stockholm •

E D E N

Baltic Sea

Copenhagen

Sassnitz ○
Peenemünde ○
Warnemünde ○ ○ Swinemünde
○ Stettin

E R M A N Y

Berlin ⊙
Potsdam ⊙

Magdeburg
○ Dessau
Leipzig
⊙ ○ Dresden
Leuna
Chemnitz

Prague •

⊙ Pilsen

C Z E C H O S L O V A K I A

⊙ Nuremberg
Schwandorf
⊙ Regensburg

• Linz   Vienna •   • Bratislava

⊙ Munich
Berchtesgaden ⊙

A U S T R I A

• Budapest

H U N G A R Y

• Trieste

Y U G O S L A V I A

I T A L Y   *Adriatic Sea*

Danzig ⊙

EAST
PRUSSIA

• Warsaw

P O L A N D

• Krakow

• Minsk

S O V I E T
U N I O N

R U M A N I A

Bucharest •

Belgrade •

B U L G A R I A

• Sophia

Germany

Stalag Luft I   POW camp

- - - - -   Siegfried Line

North Sea

DENMARK

Hörnum

Flensburg

Heligoland

Heide   Kiel

Kiel Canal

Brunsbüttel   Stermoor

East Friesian Islands

Wilhelmshaven

Lübeck   Wismar

Bremerhaven   Schulau

Emden   Hamburg/Harburg

Fredeburg

Tarmstedt   Wenzendorf   Büchen

Farge   Rotenburg

Bremen   Hemelingen   Hitzacker

Amsterdam

Aller

Diepholz   Nienburg   Nienhagen

Dortmund-Ems   Dedenhausen

Canal   Misburg   Ehmen

HOLLAND   Salzbergen   Osnabrück   Hannover   Dollbergen

Rotterdam   Ibbenbüren

Waal   Münster   Brunswick

English Channel   Dülmen   Ems   Salzgitter

Emmerich   Killwinkle

Rhine-Herne   Hamm   Biedefeld

Eindhoven   Canal   Paderborn

Duisburg   Kamen   Königsborn   Bernburg

Antwerp   Krefeld   Ruhr   Rüthen

Essen   Göttingen

BELGIUM   Düsseldorf   Kassel

Reisholz   Fredeburg   Eschwege

Brussels   Cologne   Monheim

Waterloo   Wesseling   GERMANY   Efurt   Weimar

Louvain   Aachen   Gotha   Bad Berka   Jena

Liège   Bonn

ARDENNES   Dulag Luft

Schmidt   Neuwied   Wetzlar   Thuringian Forest

Koblenz   Limburg   Fulda

Lutterade   Rhine

Moselle   Wiesbaden   Frankfurt   Coburg

LUXEMBOURG   Mainz   Hanau   Schweinfurt

Trier   Kreuznach   Darmstadt   Bamberg   Bayreuth

Worms   Würzburg   Pegnitz

Neunkirchen   Oppau   Mannheim   Erlangen

Verdun   Merchweillen   Ludwigs-   Nuremberg

hafen   600 miles from Foggia

Metz   Karlsruhe

Pforzheim

FRANCE   Baden-Baden   Stuttgart

Strasbourg   Offenburg   Damube   Neuburg

Rhine

Breisach   Munich

0   25   50   75   100   Freiburg   Freiham

miles

The Ruhr Valley

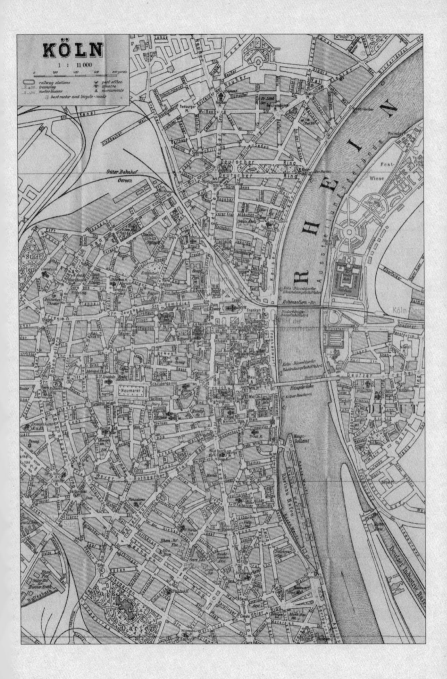

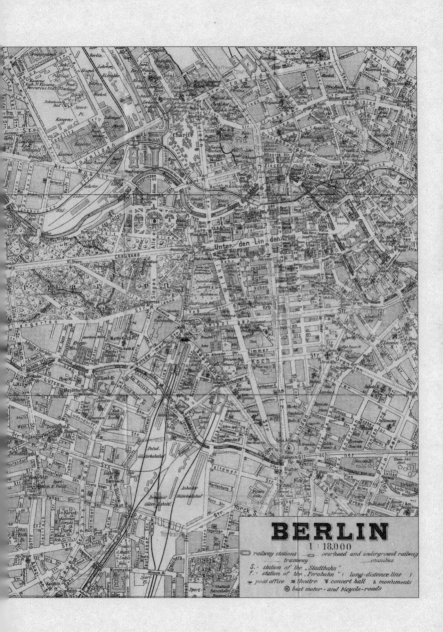

BERLIN

1 : 18,000

railway stations   overhead and underground railway

  tramway   omnibus

S. - station of the „Stadtbahn"

F. - station of the „Fernbahn" (long-distance line)

post office   theatre   concert hall   monuments

best motor - and bicycle - roads

Prologue

PERKINS

In the early summer of 1961, sophisticated Londoners were laughing at an entertainment brought to them by four young Oxbridge graduates. *Beyond the Fringe* had been a great hit at the Edinburgh Festival the previous year. Now, night after night, smiling audiences in the capital left the Fortune Theatre feeling they had witnessed something fresh, audacious and above all very funny. The excitement that comes with the anticipation of sudden and unpredictable change was in the May air. The old, hierarchical Britain personified by the prime minister, Harold Macmillan, appeared to be tottering to an end. The shape of the future was hard to make out but it surely belonged to the young, the daring and the irreverent. Alan Bennett, Peter Cook, Jonathan Miller and Dudley Moore were the incarnation of all that.

One of the sketches was called 'Aftermyth of War'. It made fun of legends created during wartime and already planted deep in Britain's consciousness. There was quite a list. It mocked Neville Chamberlain and his 'piece of paper', stoical working-class Londoners and the Blitz spirit and even the Battle of Britain. Then it was the turn of the men who flew in the aeroplanes that bombed Germany.

The sequence opens with Peter Cook, in the uniform of a senior RAF officer, entering to the sound of airmen singing heartily around a piano.

> COOK: Perkins! (Jonathan Miller breaks away from the singing.) Sorry to drag you away from the fun, old boy. War's not going very well, you know.

MILLER: Oh my God!

COOK: . . . war is a psychological thing, Perkins, rather like a game of football. You know how in a game of football ten men often play better than eleven?

MILLER: Yes, sir.

COOK: Perkins, we are asking you to be that one man. I want you to lay down your life, Perkins. We need a futile gesture at this stage. It will raise the whole tone of the war. Get up in a crate, Perkins, pop over to Bremen, take a shufti, don't come back. Goodbye, Perkins. God, I wish I was going too.

MILLER: Goodbye, sir – or is it – *au revoir*?

COOK: *No*, Perkins.

The last lines got one of the biggest laughs of the night. In the stalls, sitting with his wife Margery Baker, Tony Iveson tried to laugh along with the rest. They both worked in the new world of television and were part of the emerging Britain. But not very long before he had been Squadron Leader Tony Iveson DFC of 617 Squadron, and at the front of the bombing war. 'I didn't like it,' he said forty-four years later. 'I remember being upset. I probably wouldn't be now but at the time it seemed unnecessary, in view of how many we lost.'[1]

Of the 125,000 airmen who passed through Bomber Command during the war, about 55,000 were killed. Twenty-one of the dead were called Perkins. The first to die was Flying Officer Reginald Perkins of 54 Squadron who was killed on the night of 14/15 November 1940. He was the pilot of a Hampden which took off from Waddington in Lincolnshire to bomb Berlin. Little is known about his death or those of his three crew mates. Their aircraft is 'believed to have exploded in the air and crashed on the outskirts of Berlin'.[2] The last to die was Flying Officer Robert Perkins of 49 Squadron, the pilot of a Lancaster who was killed with the rest of his crew while bombing the Lutzkendorf oil refinery on the night of 8/9 April 1945, a month before the end of the war in Europe.[3] Nothing at all is known about how they were lost.

As far as I am aware, no Perkins died bombing Bremen, but one might well have done. From 18 May 1940 until the end of the Second World War it was attacked some seventy times. As a result, about 575 aircrew were killed. So too were 3,562 residents.[4] It is this aspect of Bomber Command's war, the death of German civilians, that has preoccupied historians in the years since the *Beyond the Fringe* sketch. All the myths that were the butt of its jokes have since been re-examined and turned out to be remarkably resilient. It is Bomber Command's reputation that has suffered the most. Re-evaluations have found the crews' efforts to be at best misdirected and at worst little better than war crimes.

This last accusation is false and insults truth and justice. Bomber Command, as I have said, attacked Bremen frequently. The first bombs killed thirteen people. They also burned down two warehouses full of furniture confiscated from Jews who had understood what fate awaited them in Germany and fled. Bombers were busy over the city on the night of 17/18 January 1942. Only eight of the eighty-three aircraft dispatched found the target and little damage appears to have been done. The Nazi newspapers in the days following denounced the raiders as 'terror fliers'. As they did so, sixteen Nazi bureaucrats met on 20 January in a villa at Wannsee outside Berlin to co-ordinate the extermination of the entire Jewish population of Europe.

The Nazis were to good as a black hole is to light. The effects of British and American bombing on Germany and the lands the Germans conquered were dreadful and it is right that they should be recorded and remembered. But the Allies' real crime would have been to hold back from using any of the means at their disposal to destroy Hitler and those who sustained his war.

The argument over exactly what Bomber Command achieved will never be settled. One undeniable success, an awkward one to acknowledge nowadays, is that it altered Germany's personality. Saturation bombing may not, as intended, have broken the Germans' spirit. But it helped powerfully to bring about their post-war conversion to peaceful democracy.

History in its current mood has paid limited attention to the ethos and character of the men who fought this most extraordinary war. This book sets out to correct that imbalance. It is for, and about, Perkins. In the process I want also to redress a wrong. There is no national memorial to the men of Bomber Command, no one place where their sacrifice and contribution to victory are properly and thankfully commemorated. I hope that *Bomber Boys* will mark a first step in changing that.

Introduction

After the Whirlwind

No one who saw what Allied bombing did to Germany forgot it. A traveller in an official delegation passing through Berlin two months after the German surrender noted in his diary: 'Berlin . . . is ghastly. I could never have believed how complete the destruction is. We covered [about five miles] and saw less than a dozen undamaged houses and not one in ten was anything more than a burned-out shell.'

Soon afterwards he visited Potsdam, less than twenty miles to the west. 'Bert Harris removed the town of Potsdam in half an hour one night in April,' he wrote. 'I have never seen anything so complete . . . the usual procession of handcarts, prams etc. and the same slab-faced people as in Berlin.'

The sight, he felt, was the finest possible lesson to the Germans of the folly of initiating wars. Yet he 'came away feeling very sorry for these people and when I eventually said so I found all the others felt just the same.'[1]

The man who wrote these words had played a central part in creating the scenes he witnessed. He was Marshal of the Royal Air Force Sir Charles Portal, who as Chief of the Air Staff had overseen the bombing campaign. 'Bert Harris' was his subordinate, Air Marshal Sir Arthur Harris, the head of Bomber Command who had put Allied strategic theories into devastating practice.

A little afterwards, a veteran pilot who had taken part in many of the raids flew over some of the areas he had bombed. 'It was a fine clear day and we flew at 4,000 feet,' wrote Peter Johnson, 'a good height for an overall view and we saw as we passed something of what had happened to, amongst others, Hamburg, Lübeck, Hanover, the Ruhr towns, Cologne, Aachen and Düsseldorf and so south

Potsdam, 1945.

to Stuttgart, Nuremberg and Munich . . . the general devastation was almost unbelievable. In town after town hardly a building seemed to be intact, hardly a house seemed to be habitable. All that showed from the air were rows and rows of empty boxes, walls enclosing nothing . . . the whole area was, for the time being at least, dead, dead, dead.'

Johnson could not help wondering 'whether this truly dreadful sight represented a degree of overkill, whether such destruction had really been necessary to stop the production of arms for the Nazis in the greatest industrial complex in Europe.' He reassured himself with the thought that even when the Ruhr was encircled by Allied forces the German people 'were still obeying Hitler's frenzied calls for resistance to the last man'.[2]

The debris was to hang around accusingly for years. In March 1949 the American diplomat George Kennan returned to Hamburg where he had served in pre-war days. He visited the large residential districts east of the Alster. 'Here was sweeping devastation, down to the ground, mile after mile,' he wrote. 'It had all been done in three days and nights in 1943, my host told me. Seventy-five thousand persons had perished in the process. Even now, after the lapse of six years, over three thousand bodies were estimated to be buried there in the rubble.'*

These sights demanded reflection, and justification or judgement. The natural response of most of those who planned or carried out the attacks was the same as Portal's. The Germans, unquestionably, had started it. They had, as Harris predicted in a much-repeated proverb, sown the wind and reaped the whirlwind. Kennan, however, felt differently. For the first time since the war ended, he wrote, 'I felt an unshakeable conviction that no momentary military advantage – even if such could be calculated to exist – could have justified this stupendous, careless destruction of civilian life and of material values, built up laboriously by human hands over the course of centuries for purposes having nothing to do with this war. Least of all could it be justified by the screaming non-sequitur, "They did it to us."'³

The debate over the morality of all-out aerial bombardment had been under way long before the strategic air campaign began and would rumble through the post-war years to the present day. But the first reaction of those who gazed across the haunted mounds of rubble that were all that remained of scores of German city centres was simple awe at the destruction that had been wrought. The onlookers thought they knew what a blitzed town looked like. The results of what bombs did were on display in many of Britain's major cities. But none of them looked like this.

During the war Bomber Command had been a priceless asset to government propaganda, as a symbol of Britain's resolve and its willingness and ability to take the war to the enemy. Its actions were thoroughly publicized and its pilots and crewmen ranked as heroes. It fought a continuous campaign from the first day of the war to the last, interrupted only by the weather. The enormous effort and the great sacrifice of life this entailed were honoured and the destruction done to the enemy was presented as a vital element

* The actual number of victims of the raids carried out on Hamburg between 27–30 July 1943 was closer to 40,000 dead.

in the victory. In peacetime, the wrecked towns and the grave pits filled with the bones of civilians became an embarrassment and the Bomber Boys faded from the official legend. On the afternoon of 13 May 1945 Churchill broadcast his Victory in Europe speech. There was praise for everyone who had contributed to the war effort. But apart from an allusion to the damage done to Berlin, the main activities of the bomber crews were barely mentioned. There were campaign medals for those who had fought in Asia, the Middle East and Europe. There was to be no specific award for the men who had set about dismantling Hitler's empire from the air.

The public memory of the air war was selective. People seemed inclined to consign the bombing campaign and those who had fought it to the past. The pilots of Fighter Command, however, had a special place in the post-war consciousness. Scores of books were written by them and about them. Men like Douglas Bader, Bob Stanford Tuck and 'Sailor' Malan were celebrities. They were The Few and the battle that they fought was relatively short, roughly four months from the beginning of July to the end of October 1940. The men who crewed the bombers were The Many and their struggle went on and on. Of the 125,000 who passed through the fire, only Guy Gibson and Leonard Cheshire won any lasting fame. Gibson had led the Dams Raid of May 1943, a feat of dash and daring, quite unlike the demolition work which Bomber Command conducted every night. Cheshire was known not so much for damaging people as for healing them, in the homes he set up after the war.

Nobody, it seemed, wanted victory to be tarnished by reminders of the methods that were used to obtain it. Harris had a simple explanation for the ambivalence. 'The bomber drops things on people and people don't like things being dropped on them,' he remarked after the war. 'And the fighter shoots at the bomber who drops things. Therefore he is popular whereas the bomber is unpopular. It's as easy as that.'[4]

There was much in what he said. In the United States, which was never touched by aerial bombardment, there was no such uneasiness and the crews of the Liberators and Flying Fortresses were honoured alongside the rest of America's fighting men and their deeds praised in films like *Twelve O'Clock High*. The official assertion that Americans were engaged in precise bombing, rather than the area bombing practised by the British, was widely accepted, even though the distinction often meant little to the people underneath.

The strategic air campaign fought by the RAF and the USAAF was a terrible novelty. For the first time, aeroplanes were used in huge numbers against large population areas to smash an enemy's capacity to make war by destroying its industry and demoralizing its civilians.

The German Blitz of British cities over the winter of 1940–41 provided the campaign's initial justification. Bomber Command's subsequent *raison d'être* was that it was the main means of exerting direct offensive pressure on Germany, within its own territory. At first the crews flew smallish aeroplanes carrying negligible bomb loads and were guided by primitive navigational aids. In the month of February 1942 when Harris took over his men dropped 1,001 tons of bombs. Better aircraft, new technology, cleverer tactics, Harris's ruthless style and – above all – the courage and skill of the crews, turned the air force into the most potent proof of Britain's will to win. In the month of March 1945, with Allied troops closing on Berlin, they dropped 67,637 tons and the Americans 65,962. By the end, the hurt the Luftwaffe had done to Britain had been repaid over and over. German air attacks against the British Isles, including those by V weapons late in the war, killed just over 60,000. Estimates of the deaths caused by Allied bombing of Germany range between 305,000 and 600,000. The cities touched by the Blitz were scarred but not devastated. In 1945 Germany's seventy biggest towns and cities were in ruins and one in five dwelling places destroyed.[5]

This disproportionality caused very little anxiety at the time. Germany had struck first and deserved the retribution the RAF was meting out. What concern might have been felt at the suffering of German civilians faded in the knowledge of the price the Bomber Boys were paying to deliver this vengeance. It was impossible to hide the losses and the government did not try.

This was a home-front war and civilians along the outbound and inbound routes to the Continent were present at the opening and closing scenes of the action. During the war years the RAF in Britain grew into the most visible of the services. In the bomber station-cluttered east and north there seemed almost as many airmen and -women as there were civilians. 'By the time I got there Lincoln had turned blue,' remembered Reg Payne, a wireless operator who was based at Skellingthorpe just outside the city.[6]

Bomber Command grew and grew as the volunteers arrived in numbers that never slackened even during the darkest hours of its campaign. Behind each man flying, there were many more keeping them in the air. There were fitters and riggers and armourers maintaining the huge aeroplanes. There were WAAFs who drove the crews to their hangars and staffed the operations rooms when ops were on. There were the women who served them their dinner before they took off and, with luck, their breakfast when they returned home. RAF men met and mingled with local women in dance-halls and pubs, flirting with them, sometimes sleeping with them, often marrying them. Homesick young men were adopted by families and would slip away for an afternoon in front of a coal fire in a front parlour that reminded them of the family life they had left behind.

The many Britons who had seen the RAF going into action, droning overhead on their way to and from Germany and France and Italy, relished the sight. They learned of what they did there from the newspapers and BBC radio for whom Bomber Command's actitivies provided the main source of good news for much of the war. The tone of the reports was exultant. 'The Vengeance Begins!' was the strapline on the *Daily Express* front-page story of Monday 1 June 1942 announcing the first thousand-bomber raid on Cologne. The sky over the city was 'as busy as Piccadilly Circus'. One bomber passed over every six seconds and 3,000 tons of bombs were dropped in ninety minutes*. It was particularly pleasing to report that the official communiqué from Berlin admitted that 'great damage' had been done. 'Germans squeal "havoc, misery"' was the headline on the story of how the Nazis had reacted to the raid.

The RAF had saved the country from invasion by winning the

---

* The real figure was 1,455 tons.

Battle of Britain. It had failed, it was true, to prevent the Blitz. But now, night after night it was carrying the war to the Reich, paying the Germans back in kind and contributing mightily to the downfall of Hitler and the Nazis.

That was how it was seen by British civilians as they read accounts of devastating attacks on previously obscure towns such as Essen, Duisburg and Gelsenkirchen and great cities like Hamburg and Cologne and, above all, Berlin. This was how it was presented by Harris, a natural propagandist, who strove to create the impression that with each raid the road to victory and peace was one step shorter. This was what was believed by the majority of the men who were flying the aeroplanes. They tended to be bolder and more imaginative than the rest of their contemporaries. Flying was dangerous but they preferred its perils and the relative informality of RAF life to the drudgery of existence as a soldier. In letters and diaries they reveal a high degree of idealism and optimism and a strong sense that they were fighting not only to destroy a present evil but also to lay the foundations of a future good.

In a letter to the father of his friend Andrew 'Paddy' Wilson, who was killed during a raid on Düsseldorf in June 1943, Sergeant John Lobban, the sole survivor of the crew, wrote: 'They died for the greatest of causes, the freedom of the peace-loving nations and I only wish that fate could have let us play a greater part in bringing the war to a close.' It had been their first operation.[7]

Such idealism is found mainly in the young. Many of the Bomber Boys were barely out of their teens, though the almost constant strain they lived with made them seem older. They were called Dougie and Ron and Ken and Reg and Bill. They came from the middle reaches of society and were strongly marked by their time. In their short lives they had felt the numb emotional pain left by the last war and sensed the mounting dread among their elders as the next one approached. They knew what poverty was and had witnessed the cruelties of interwar capitalism. If there was a dominant political outlook among the crews it was a mildly sceptical socialism and belief in social justice. But overlying it always was a profound sense of duty. None of them set out to destroy German cities and few cared to reflect too closely on the effects of their bombs. But like the rest of their generation, they possessed a patriotism and respect for authority that had barely been dented by their knowledge of the First World War. It was easier for them to do what they did because they tended to believe what they were told about the purpose and progress of their struggle. It was an outstanding peculiarity of the strange new conflict they were engaged in that there was no real measure of gain. Armies could gauge success by the amount of ground taken or the number of enemy killed or captured. Navies could do so by the quantity of enemy tonnage sunk. But how did you judge the achievements of a bombing campaign?

The authorities continually proclaimed the effectiveness of Bomber Command's actions. Early communiqués created an illusion of extraordinary efficiency, of bombs slanting down on strictly military targets with scientific precision. This optimistic view was based largely on the reports of the pilots dropping the ordnance, an unreliable measure as it was to turn out. It was only after two years of war, when a report based on an analysis of aerial photographs revealed the hopeless inaccuracy of most bombing, that tactics and equipment improved and the gap between reality and propaganda began to close. By the end of the war Bomber Command could obliterate any target it wished to and did so, sometimes flattening towns whose military importance was minuscule. But the value of such destruction was always open to question and afterwards there was disagreement over what it was that Bomber Command had achieved.

Harris lived another forty years after the last bomb was dropped. Right until his death he fought to persuade the world that his Command's contribution to victory had been decisive. His arguments were based not so much on the data provided by the American and British official surveys of damage conducted after the war, but more on the word of Hitler's munitions minister, the silky and self-interested Albert Speer. The surveys themselves failed to settle the arguments that raged throughout the war over how bomber power should be applied and started a new round of controversy.

The questions of how much material harm bombing did to the German war effort, and whether the energy and sacrifices involved were worth it, have never been fully answered and never will be.

It was even more difficult to determine the psychological effect of bombing. Bombs were spiritual as much as physical weapons. Air strategists had been arguing since aeroplanes were invented that the *moral* power of bombing was as great as anything it did to factories or homes, perhaps much greater. By destroying the will of workers to work, air attacks could do as much effective damage as they did when they smashed up a steelworks or assembly line.

This convenient belief grew as it became clear that pre-war assumptions about bombing accuracy were absurdly optimistic. The first bombs were aimed at small targets and hit nothing. Better then to aim at a large target and hit something – anything – for in a built-up area no bomb would be wasted. Even if a bomb missed the factory it was aimed at, the chances were it would hit the home of someone who was employed there. It might kill him and his family. Death or fear of death would keep him away from work. If enough bombs were dropped, so the theory ran, workers might eventually turn against their rulers and force them to stop fighting.

Even before the war the evidence available from the German and Italian bombardments of Madrid and Barcelona suggested that this was not necessarily so. Britain's own experience of the Blitz pointed to a more startling conclusion: that aerial bombardment could actually toughen resolve and deepen resistance. For much of the war, there was a prevailing belief that Germany would crack if only it was hit hard and often enough. The RAF's pre-war professional judgement that in a totalitarian state, coercion trumped public opinion, was soon forgotten in the desperation to achieve results.

The lack of any accurate understanding of what the campaign was achieving was characteristic of the oddly disconnected way in which the war was waged. Even those dropping the bombs felt they were engaged in a surreal exercise. Looking down from a Lancaster or Halifax at Essen or Berlin from 20,000 feet you saw nothing that connected you to the earth you knew, only a diabolical *son et lumière* of smoke and fire. 'I would try to tell myself . . . that this was a city,' wrote Don Charlwood, an Australian navigator with 103 Squadron. 'A place with the familiar sights of civilization. But the thought would carry little conviction. A German city was always this, this hellish picture of flame, gunfire and searchlights, an unreal picture because we could not hear it or feel its breath. Sometimes when the smoke rolled back and we saw streets and buildings I felt startled. Perhaps if we had seen the white, upturned faces of people, as over England we sometimes did, our hearts would have rebelled.'[8]

Harris liked to call the successive phases of the air war 'battles'. There was a Battle of Hamburg, a Battle of the Ruhr, a Battle of Berlin. But they were not battles as most people understood the word. There was not one enemy, waiting and visible, but many. The crews were constantly at the mercy of the weather and mechanical failure. On the approach routes and over the targets they faced searchlights, flak and night-fighters. There was no relaxation on the way home. The last minutes were sometimes as dangerous as the time over target as the skies above the base filled with aircraft, many of them sieved with flak and cannon holes, clinging to the air with their last few gallons of petrol, praying for the signal to touch down.

Flying in bombers was an extraordinarily dangerous activity. Harris, with his usual harsh honesty, asked people to bear in mind that 'these crews, shining youth on the threshold of life, lived under circumstances of intolerable strain. They were in fact – and they knew it – faced with the virtual certainty of death, probably in one of its least pleasant forms.'[9]

Altogether 55,573 Bomber Command aircrew – British, Canadian, Australian, New Zealanders and others – were killed. That is out of a total of 125,000 who served. Another 8,403 were wounded and 9,838 taken prisoner. In simple terms that means 44.4 per cent of those who flew, died. The real picture was rather grimmer. Many of those included in the overall aircrew figure were still training when the war ended and never saw action. According to one study, the true figure is closer to 65 per cent. The chances of death then, were appallingly high, far higher than those facing soldiers and sailors. The life expectancy of an airman was considerably shorter even than that of a junior infantry officer on the Western Front in

1916.[10] To Peter Johnson who swapped a cushy instruction post for operational flying, the enterprise sometimes seemed like the Charge of the Light Brigade, over and over again.

It was no wonder that crews discussed obsessively the odds on their survival and tried to discern some pattern in the tapestry of death. It was very confusing. Some 'sprog' crews fresh from a training unit got the 'chop' first time out. But so did veterans on their last but one trip of their thirty-operation tour. Good pilots died inexplicably and poor ones blundered through. It was all down to luck and Lady Luck, capricious tart that she was, had to be wooed and cosseted constantly. The modern young men in the bombers were as superstitious as mediaeval peasants. Final preparations would be thrown into chaos if someone lost his lucky silk stocking or remembered he had forgotten a pre-operation ritual. They also developed a mediaeval fatalism. Flying was 'dicing' and death was 'the reaper'.

But despite death's towering presence, it could still seem curiously remote. It was a common experience to see an aeroplane just like your own, ahead of you in the bomber stream, suddenly explode as flak ignited hundreds of gallons of petrol and thousands of pounds of explosive. It was not unusual to watch as a night-fighter nosed upwards beneath the pregnant belly of an unsuspecting neighbour and with one squirt of its vertically-directed guns sent it screaming down.

After witnessing these dreadful sights, crews were often struck by the complexity and selfishness of their feelings. 'Suddenly,' wrote Harry Yates, a Lancaster pilot, 'ahead of us in the stream a vic of three kites was consumed in a prodigious burst of flame which immediately erupted outwards under the force of the secondary explosion. The leader had been hit in the bomb bay, the others were too close. No one could have survived, I knew. There was no point in looking for parachutes. I flew on straight and level, Tubby standing beside me, both of us dumbstruck by the appallingly unfair swiftness and violence of it all. But there was still that deeply-drawn breath of relief that somebody else, and not oneself, had run out of luck. And hard on the heels of *that* was a pang of guilt. One grieved for whoever was in the kites and wondered if friends might not be coming home . . .'[11]

For all the danger, operations involved little that could be described as exciting or could later be interpreted as glamorous. There were stretches of tedium. For wireless operators and bomb-aimers there was little to do for much of the time. Only the navigator and the pilot were kept permanently occupied and there was not much fun in flying bombers. Piloting a Lancaster was nothing like skidding across the skies in a Spitfire. It was a task rather than a pleasure, requiring endless tiny adjustments and constant vigilance. Guy Gibson, the leader of the Dams Raid, compared bomber pilots to bus-drivers.

There was a complete absence of comfort. The rear gunner, stuck at the 'arse end' of a Lancaster, froze. The wireless operator, stuck next to the port inner engine, often roasted. Everyone was swaddled in multiple layers of clothing surmounted by parachute harness and Mae West lifejacket. It was hard work moving around the cramped, equipment-stacked interior, where every edge was sharp and threatened injury.

On the ground life was far removed from the ease of the RAF's pre-war existence and there were few of the comforts or entertainments available to the fighter pilots of 1940 when they touched down at the end of the day. Writing to his wife from his first squadron, Flying Officer Reg Fayers was anxious to dispel any idea that the organization he had joined resembled 'Max Aitken's RAF'. Aitken, Lord Beaverbrook's son, had fought in the Battle of Britain and was a model of style and sophistication. 'You are fastidious and sweetsmelling cleanliness,' Fayers declared. 'You are gentle, you are comfort . . . the RAF is opposite in all respects.'[12]

The defining sound of Bomber Command life was not the cheerful blare of the mess gramophone but the patter of rain on a Nissen hut roof. The pervading smell was not the whiff of expensive scent but the reek of coke from a smoky stove. Opening the doors of their quarters the crews looked out not at the green, upholstered Sussex hills or the fertile fields of the Weald but the vast skies and watery steppes of Lincolnshire.

Fighter pilots went to the pub by car. Bomber Boys travelled by bike or bus. They drank flat, weak beer in drab pubs and dance-halls where they competed for the favours of young women war-workers. Sex was in the air but when it took place it was often urgent and utilitarian. What they really wanted was love and it flared up often, as fierce and incandescent as the pyrotechnics that marked the targets they bombed. Sometimes it was just as ephemeral.

But once on 'ops', the world of lovers, friends and families beyond the base dwindled and faded, to be replaced by a different reality. The future stretched no further than the next few hours. Life was reversed. Night became day and day became night, the time when the crews went to work. Then, to each crew member the only people who mattered were those around him. There were only seven people in existence and the universe had shrunk to the size of a bomber plane.

1

Learning the Hard Way

On the morning of Sunday 3 September 1939, at bases all over Britain, ground and air crews stood by for the announcement that after many false alarms they were finally to be launched into battle. At Scampton, 'Sunny Scampton' as it was wryly nicknamed on account of the usually dismal Lincolnshire weather, the men of 'A' Flight, 89 Squadron, were smoking and chatting in the flight commander's office while they waited for the prime minister to speak on the radio. At 11 a.m. the talking stopped and the room filled with the low, apprehensive voice of Neville Chamberlain telling them that, as of that moment, a state of war existed between Britain and Germany.

Until then, the flight commander, Anthony Bridgman, had been a study in unconcern. Now he took his feet from his desk, exhaled a slow stream of cigarette smoke and spoke, 'quietly and rather strangely' according to one who was present, to his men. 'Well boys, this is it,' he said. 'You had better all pop out and test your aeroplanes . . . there will probably be a job for you to do.'

There was. In the early afternoon they were called to the lecture room where the squadron's CO, Leonard Snaith, a distinguished pilot whose gentle manner set him apart from the boisterous, public-school ethos of the pre-war RAF, announced 'we are off on a raid'. The targets were German pocket battleships, believed to be lying in Wilhelmshaven harbour, the great heart-shaped North Sea inlet. Their orders were to bomb them. If the ships could not be found, they were allowed to attack an ammunition depot on the land. The six crews detailed to the task were warned that 'on no account' were they to hit civilian establishments, either houses or dockyards, and that 'serious repercussions' would follow if they did so.

They surged to the crew room to climb into their kit and wait for a lorry to take them to the aircraft. They were flying in Hampdens, up-to-date, twin-engined monoplane medium bombers with a good range and a respectable bomb-carrying capacity. They had a bulbous but narrow front fuselage, only three feet wide, and a slender tail that gave them an odd, insect look. It was cramped for the four men inside, but the speed and handling made up for it.

Before they could leave, news came through that the initial take-off time of 15.30 had been put back. The men lay outside on the grass, smoking and thinking about what lay ahead. Another message arrived saying there had been a further delay, provoking a chorus of swearing. By now everyone's nerves were fizzing. One pilot, despite a reputation for cockiness, found his 'hands were shaking so much that I could not hold them still. All the time we wanted to rush off to the lavatory. Most of us went four times an hour.'

At last the time came to board the lorry and just after 6 p.m. the engines rumbled into life and the Hampdens bumped down the runway. For all their training, few of the pilots had ever taken off with a full bomb load before. The aircraft felt very heavy with the 2,000 pounds of extra weight but they lumbered into the air without mishap and set course over the soaring towers of Lincoln cathedral, over the broad fields and glinting fens and rivers of Lincolnshire, and out across the corrugated eternity of the North Sea for Germany.

As they approached Wilhelmshaven, the weather went from poor to atrocious. The gap between the grey waves and the wet cloud narrowed from 300 to 100 feet. Gun flashes could be seen through the murk but there was no telling where they came from.

Eventually, Squadron Leader Snaith's aircraft swung away to the left. The appalling conditions and the impossibility of knowing precisely where they were had persuaded him there was no point in carrying on. The initial disappointment of one pilot gave way to the realization that Snaith was right. 'For all we knew,' he wrote, 'we were miles off our course. The gun flashes ahead might have been the Dutch Islands or they might have been Heligoland.'

They dumped their bombs into the sea and headed for home. By the time they crossed the coast at Boston it was dark. Most of the

Pilot and co-pilot at the controls of a Wellington.

crews had little experience of night flying and one got hopelessly lost. Luckily, the moon picked up a landmark canal and they followed it back to Scampton, landing tired, and rather disillusioned, at 10.30 p.m. 'What an abortive show!' wrote the captain of the errant aircraft. 'What a complete mess-up! For all the danger we went through it couldn't be called a raid, but nevertheless we went through all the feelings.'[1]

But at least everyone had got back alive. If Bomber Command's first offensive operation was a disappointment, the second was a disaster. On 4 September more attacks were launched against German warships off Wilhelmshaven and further north, at Brunsbüttel, in the mouth of the Kiel Canal. A force of fourteen Wellingtons and fifteen Blenheims set off. The weather was dreadful. Ten aircraft failed to find the target. The Blenheims managed to reach the pocket battleship *Admiral Scheer* and the cruiser *Emden* at Wilhelmshaven. They even landed three bombs on the *Scheer*. The bombs failed to explode. The *Emden* was damaged when a stricken bomber crashed on to it. But five of the attacking aircraft were destroyed, most by flak from the fleet's anti-aircraft guns.

Some of the Wellingtons claimed to have located targets to bomb at Brunsbüttel but if they did they caused them little harm. Four aircraft were shot down by German fighters. A gross navigational error meant that two bombs were dropped on the Danish town of Esbjerg, 110 miles to the north, killing two innocents. The day's efforts had achieved nothing and resulted in the loss of nearly a quarter of the aircraft dispatched.

These initial efforts displayed many of the myriad weaknesses of Bomber Command as it set out to justify the extraordinary claims that had been made in its name in the years between the wars. The operations were based on sketchy intelligence and preceded by only the most perfunctory of briefings. The aircraft were the best the RAF could offer but the navigation equipment available to guide them to their targets was primitive, and some of the bombs they dropped were duds. The training the crews had received, long and arduous though it had been, had still not properly prepared them for the job. And the tactics they were following were clearly suspect, given the losses that had been sustained.

On the other hand, the episode did provide a demonstration of the potential of Bomber Command's underlying strength. The crews had shown a powerful 'press on' spirit, with fatal results in the case of most of those trapped in the seven aircraft that went down. Despite the paltry results, nothing could be inferred about the quality of the airmen. The man whose memoirs provide the basis for the account of the first raid, the pilot of the Hampden who got lost, was the twenty-year-old Guy Gibson, who three and a half years later was to lead the triumphant Dams Raid. At the time, though, these first operations served mainly to expose the RAF's weakness and to reveal the huge gap between what a bomber force was supposed to do and what it could in fact achieve.

In their short life, bombers had gained an awesome reputation for potential destructiveness. The prospect of unrestricted air warfare tinged the mood of the interwar world with quiet dread. It cast the same shadow of fear and uncertainty over life as the thought of nuclear holocaust did in the post-war years. The sense of doom was fed by a tide of alarming articles and books.

A novel, 1944, published in 1926 was typical of the genre. The fact that its author, the Earl of Halsbury, had served on the Air Staff's Directorate of Flying Operations in the First World War appeared to lend particular weight to its arguments. The tale was told in the brusque, conventional prose of contemporary thrillers, but the message was revolutionary. Its hero, Sir John Blundell MP, is regarded by his colleagues as a crackpot for his insistence that another world war is inevitable. The next conflict, he believes, will bring about 'the total obliteration of civilization not more nor less. Total obliteration, phutt, like a candle.'

He warns anyone who will listen that in 'not more than twenty years' fleets of bombers will be roaming the skies of Europe, dropping poison gas. The country's air defences will prove useless. The government will be paralysed. Lacking leadership or a militaristic tradition to maintain discipline, people will turn on each other. When the first raid occurs, Sir John's son Dick is sitting down to dinner at the Ritz with his girlfriend Sylvie. 'Above the night noises of a great town could be heard the faint but unmistakeable hum of aeroplanes. Presently they became louder and there was an uncomfortable hush throughout the restaurant. To Dick ... the noise seemed to be coming from everywhere. Trained to appreciate such things, he knew there must be an immense number of machines. Somewhere to the south came the sound of a futile anti-aircraft battery ... like a swarm of locusts a mass of aeroplanes was just discernible, lit up by the searchlights, as yet mere specks in the sky. More anti-aircraft guns were heard coming into action, somewhere down the river. Bursting shells winked like fireflies in a tropical forest . . . the raiders were through and over London . . . they had easily broken through the carefully-prepared but utterly inadequate defence that met them.'[2]

Dick and Sylvie manage to escape the capital. On their way west-wards they see anarchy and cruelty everywhere. A band of pro-letarian refugees from Plymouth turn cannibal, preying on stragglers who stray near their Dartmoor hideout. Almost everyone behaves badly. In a country mansion, upper-class loafers meet death in a last orgy of drink and drugs. At one point the pair run into a crowd of scavengers. '[It] was not made up of the English [Dick] had known. They were a new race, a hard, grim, cruel race, changed completely by days of want, total lack of discipline and above all by the complete dissolution of the bonds which knitted their civilization into a kindly, altruistic society.'

Halsbury was serious. He claimed his assertions were based on current scientific fact.[3] Official projections of what unrestricted air war might mean were scarcely less alarming than his lordship's imaginings. They took as their starting point the results of German air raids on Britain in the Great War, which started with Zeppelin attacks in January 1915 and continued with raids by Gotha and Giant bombers. Altogether, they killed 1,413 people and injured 3,407. The great majority of the casualties were civilians. From this data it was calculated there would be fifty casualties for every ton of bombs dropped. In 1937 the Committee of Imperial Defence, which brought together the country's most senior airmen, soldiers, sailors and bureaucrats, was informed by its experts that the Germans had the means to maintain an all-out air assault on Britain for sixty days. This would result in the deaths of up to 600,000 people and serious injury to 1.2 million.

A year later the Ministry of Health estimated that between 1 million and 2.8 million hospital beds would be needed to deal with casualties. The huge numbers of dead would have to be interred in mass graves. In April 1939 a million burial forms were sent out to local councils.

Like Halsbury, the government also assumed that the public's nerve would fail. The scattered bombing of the previous war had produced flickers of panic and despondency. Concentrated attacks were expected to trigger widespread hysteria. A report to the Committee of Imperial Defence in 1931 proposed throwing a police cordon around London to prevent a mass exodus and discussions began in 1937 to recruit 20,000 reserve constables to keep order in the capital. It was thought that the first duty of the army, should Germany attack, was to 'maintain confidence, law and order among our civil population before attempting to fulfil any other role'. In the spring of 1939 the War Office warned army commanders of the sort of work their men might be expected to carry out. In one scenario, 'crowds without food have taken refuge in the open land in the suburbs. Civil authorities have organized soup kitchens which are being rushed by hungry people. Troops are required to restore order and organize queues.'

It was suggested that psychiatric casualties might outstrip physical casualties by three to one. In 1938 a committee was formed of senior psychiatrists from the London teaching hospitals and clinics to plan wartime mental health requirements. Its report to the Health Ministry proposed a network of centres providing immediate treatment in the bombed areas, outpatient clinics and roving teams of adult and child counsellors.

These dire predictions were a reflection of a fear that gripped everyone. 'We had entered a period,' Churchill wrote later, 'when the weapon which had played a considerable part in the previous war had become obsessive in men's minds. Ministers had to imagine the most frightful scenes of ruin and slaughter in London if we quarrelled with the German dictator.'[4]

Much of the alarm had been generated by the man who was regarded by both politicians and the public as the country's greatest authority on air war. Hugh Trenchard had risen to be head of the Royal Air Force during the First World War. He was known as 'Boom' to his colleagues, a reference to his foghorn voice. They regarded him and his utterances with what now seems like extraordinary reverence. 'What a character he is!' declared Sir John Slessor, one of his many disciples and a wartime bomber group commander. 'The enormous lanky figure; the absent-minded manner, shot with sudden flashes of shrewd and humorous insight; the illegible handwriting; the inarticulate speech – always a lap or two behind his racing brain; his wonderful capacity for getting people's names mixed up. Boom was a constant source of joy to those who were lucky enough to serve under him.'[5]

Lord Trenchard, as he became, was forceful and confident and contemptuous of ideas that were not his own. He had been head of the first separate bombing force, created in 1918 to repay the Germans for having bombed England. He had started out, though, as a doubter, sceptical of what aircraft could achieve on their own. His conversion to the value of strategic bombing, when it came, was absolute. Through the Twenties and Thirties he became the foremost advocate of using aeroplanes to smash the enemy into submission on their own territory. He was to exercise a powerful influence over RAF and government policy right into the early years of the war, with dogmatic assertions which were seldom backed up by data.

An early and often-repeated dictum was that 'the moral effect of bombing industrial towns may be great, even if the material effect is, in fact, small.' Later he refined this into the doctrine that 'the moral effect of bombing stands undoubtedly to the material effect in a proportion of 20 to 1', an observation that had no basis in measurable fact. After the slaughter of 1914–18, the prospect of any war, let alone one that promised annihilation of civilians from the air, was horrifying to governments and populations alike. In the pre-Hitler years there were several international attempts to outlaw the bomber: at Washington in 1922, The Hague in 1923 and Geneva in 1932. They all ended in failure, undermined by pessimism, cynicism and the impossibility of uninventing the machine that defined the century.

Britain had been at the forefront of attempts to ban the bomber and had held back from spending on the development and production of bomber aircraft in the hope that they would not be needed. The rapid rearmament of Nazi Germany after Hitler's victory in 1933 forced the abandonment of this policy and the start of a scramble for military parity.

The hope was that a sizeable bomber fleet might deter a German attack. If not, it would provide the means, and given Britain's geographical position and dearth of soldiers, the *sole* means of striking back if Germany dared to attempt an aerial 'knock-out blow' at the start of hostilities.

By the end of the First World War, Britain was already committed to a policy of strategic bombing. The main work of the air force between 1914 and 1918 had been tactical: to support the army, flying reconnaissance missions, spotting the fall of artillery shells and attacking German soldiers in the field. Later, bigger aeroplanes and heavier bomb loads raised the possibility that the air force could play a strategic role in defeating the enemy, by attacking the factories and foundries and power plants that turned the engines of modern industrial war.

The possession of a long-range bombing fleet suited British needs. A Continental power like Nazi Germany saw aeroplanes largely as an adjunct to its land forces who would carry out the main work of conquest. This was reflected in its choice of versatile, medium-sized aircraft which could blaze a trail of destruction to clear the path for its advancing armies, as well as carrying out conventional bombing.

Britain's case was very different. It had no plans to invade anyone and saw air power chiefly as a means of defence – but a defence founded on aggression. Trenchard had stimulated the offensive spirit among his pilots on the Western Front, rarely flinching from the losses that that policy inevitably entailed.

Some in the RAF argued that Germany could be defeated by bombing alone. That was always an extreme view. However everyone, including the chiefs of the other services, agreed that the air force had a major role to play in destroying Germany's war industry, demoralizing its population, and preparing the ground for the army to finish the job.

This was the essence of strategic bombing, and in the interwar years it was the RAF's ability to wage a strategic bombing campaign that provided the chief justification for its existence. Everything was geared to attack, with only minor consideration given to the defensive role of aircraft. Bombers outnumbered fighters by about two to one through the period. There was a brief, fortuitous diversion from this path in 1937 when the Air Staff was forced to accept the argument of Sir Thomas Inskip, brought in as Minister for the Co-ordination of Defence, that Britain needed a strengthened fighter force to ward off the immediate threat from the German air force. But the RAF's resultant triumph in the summer of 1940, when the Battle of Britain swirled in the sky over southern England, did nothing to subvert the doctrinal orthodoxy that it was attacks that won wars.

Despite this preoccupation, the RAF started the war with a bomber fleet that was totally inadequate to carry out its own stated aims. The machines of the early Thirties were ungainly and saddled with uninspiring names. The Boulton Paul Overstrand, the Fairey Hendon and the Handley Page Harrow did not sound likely to strike fear into the enemy. They were stop-gaps, filling the ranks until the arrival of the new generation of aircraft. The programme to re-equip with giant, four-engined aircraft, which eventually produced the Stirling, Halifax and Lancaster, was launched in 1936, but it took until 1942 for them to start arriving on the squadrons. Bomber Command's heaviest bombers at the start of the war were two-engined Wellingtons, Hampdens and Whitleys, which were reasonably advanced for the time but plainly insufficient for the task that the air force had set itself.

The RAF's blueprint for waging war was contained in the Western Air Plans, first drawn up in 1936. They rested on the belief that bombers could find and destroy the factories, oil installations, roads and railways that were the object of a strategic force's attentions. This was to turn out to be a hugely mistaken assumption.

The plans supposed that Germany would start the war either by attacking Belgium and France or by launching an all-out bombing campaign on Britain. In the first case, Bomber Command was to attempt to slow down the advance of the German army by striking its supply lines. In the second, it was to reduce the power of the Luftwaffe assault by attacking aerodromes and other aviation targets. At the same time, the Air Staff who directed the command's efforts were also eager to disrupt the enemy's supply of oil. The dream of bringing the German military to a halt by starving it of fuel would persist to the last days of the war.

In the event the Germans took their time digesting their prey before raising their eyes hungrily westwards. Britain did little to provoke them. Until the invasion of Norway in April 1940, the RAF confined itself to intermittent raids on shipping and leaflet-dropping sorties over Germany and the conquered territories. This was partly a reflection of the scrupulousness that was Britain's official policy. Thirty months before the start of the war Prime Minister Neville Chamberlain announced to the House of Commons that Britain would only bomb purely military objectives and take every measure to avoid civilian casualties. A few days after it began, the RAF's Director of Plans, Air Commodore Sir John Slessor, promised that 'indiscriminate attack on civilian populations as such will never form part of our policy'.

But the caution was also a reflection of reality. The air force was weak and inadequately equipped and in no position to risk its men and machines unnecessarily. The phoney war period provided Bomber Command with a desperately needed space in which to measure its capabilities and build up its strength. The propaganda leaflet drops, which look faintly ludicrous to modern eyes, may have done little to subvert the Nazi regime but they served another useful purpose. They provided crews with crucial experience of night flying over enemy territory, at very little cost.

Night flying, it was to turn out, was a vital skill. The first lesson the RAF learned when tested by wartime conditions was a painful one. The prevailing wisdom was that bombers, if they held to a tight formation, could defend themselves in daylight from attack by German fighters. So great was the faith in this belief that only five of the thirty-three operational squadrons had received any training in flying in the dark.

The theory was thrown into doubt from the beginning. German fighters, directed by radar, savaged the bombers sent off on shipping searches over the North Sea. In two attacks on 14 and 18 December, half of the thirty-four Wellingtons dispatched were destroyed. The myth of the self-defending daylight bombing formation lingered on until the spring when it was demolished by another punishing encounter with reality. Following the German invasion of Norway and Denmark in early April 1940, Bomber Command was ordered to disrupt the advance. On 12 April, nine Hampdens and Wellingtons out of a force of sixty were shot down by fighters while trying to bomb shipping in the Stavanger area. It was the last appearance of the two types in daylight operations. Henceforth bombing at night-time would become the norm for these aircraft and the heavier ones that succeeded them.

Britain held back from launching attacks near population centres for as long as it could. With the German invasion of the Low Countries on 10 May 1940 and the Battle of France that followed, restraint was gradually abandoned. Everyone knew that sooner or later civilians would be killed. The only question was how many. In the early months of the war the Germans had been as anxious as the British not to take innocent lives, fearing it would provoke a retaliation that would make the negotiated settlement that Hitler desired more difficult. But it had happened nonetheless.

At dusk on 16 March 1940, at the hour the locals call the 'grimling', a 27-year-old Orkney Islands farmer called James Isbister heard the sound of aircraft. He left his wife and three-month-old son and went to his cottage door to look. Silhouetted against the northern sky were the broad wings and slender bodies of a fleet of four Heinkel bombers. They seemed to be heading for Scapa Flow, a sheet of sheltered sea, surrounded by low hills, where warships of the British fleet were anchored. As the aircraft closed on the fleet other shapes appeared in the sky. A cluster of small, dartlike machines hovered above the bombers before swooping down among them. What looked like blue electric sparks glittered from under their wings and stitched across the sky. The RAF had arrived. The German formation that had looked so sure of itself held firm for a moment, then wavered and broke. The bombers lunged in all directions, desperate to shed their loads and head for home. One came directly towards Mr Isbister. It flew very low, near enough for him to have been able to notice the camouflage of the fuselage, grey-green like the scales of a pike, and its pale belly and glass snout. On the underside, where the wings met the body, were two cross-hatched panels. They swung open and dark shapes tumbled out. The bombs fell in a stick, sending up fountains of dirt. The shrapnel left a pretty starburst shape in the turf. James Isbister was caught in the blast and earned the sad distinction of becoming the first civilian to be killed by Germans in the British Isles in the Second World War. The following day the people from round about went to survey the damage. Among them was the poet George Mackay Brown. 'We felt then a quickening of the blood, a wonderment and excitement touched by fear,' he remembered. 'The war was real right enough and it had come to us.'[6]

When the German army began its great surge westwards, the RAF at last moved to put its war plans into action. Bomber Command had been engaged from the beginning in trying to stem the flow of armour as it flooded into Belgium, Holland and France, bombing bridges and communications and suffering terrible punishment from mobile flak batteries and fighters in the process.

Initially raids were restricted to targets west of the Rhine. On the night of 11/12 May, an attack was launched on Mönchengladbach, the first on a German town. The thirty-seven aircraft that took part were aiming for road and rail junctions but bombs fell among houses and blocks of flats. They killed three Germans: Carl Lichtschlag, sixty-two, Erika Müllers, twenty-two, and a two-year-old girl called Ingeborg Schley. The dead also included a British citizen. Ella Ida Clegg had been born fifty-three years before to a British father who left Oldham to work as a factory foreman in the Rhineland. Nothing else is known about her. She was listed in official records simply as a 'volunteer'.[7] She will be remembered only as one of the first batch of civilians to die in the air war in Germany. These first corpses had names, but that did not last long. Such tragedies soon became commonplace as aerial war dragged ordinary people on to the battlefield and names gave way to numbers.

Four days later Bomber Command visited for the first time a target to which it would return over and over again in the years ahead. Nearly a hundred aircraft set off to attack sixteen different oil and rail targets in the Ruhr, the smoky, densely-populated agglomeration of steel and coal cities clustered along the Rhine river system, which was the heart of Germany's war industry.

It was a puny raid by the standards of what was to come, but it was later counted by Bomber Command's official historians as the first action of the strategic air campaign. The targets included factories in Dortmund, Sterkrade, Castrop-Rauxel and Cologne. One bomb, aimed at the IG-Werk at Dormagen, landed on a farm and killed Franz Romeike, a dairyman. Local rumour had it that he had switched on a light on his way to the lavatory and attracted the attention of a bomb-aimer. The story revealed an exaggerated notion of the accuracy of bombing, but an entirely realistic understanding of how randomly death could arrive in an air raid.

By attacking industry and communications, Bomber Command was fulfilling its *raison d'être* but the events of the rest of the summer meant it was deflected from concentrating on this activitity. In July, having swallowed France, Germany turned its attention to Britain, launching the Luftwaffe across the Channel in an attempt to clear the skies for a possible invasion. Bomber Command was ordered to weaken the enemy's air strength at its source by destroying aluminium plants, airframe factories and stores. It was also tasked with attacking airfields and sinking the barges appearing in the North Sea waterways to carry the invasion troops. On top of all this, it was expected to continue hitting oil, communications and industrial targets when it could.

The weight of Bomber Command's duties meant there was no concentration of effort and the effects of their bombing, apart from on troop transports, were negligible. Nonetheless, throughout the summer the Air Ministry showered its commander-in-chief, Sir Charles Portal, with directives. Portal was a realist and a sceptic, whose perfect manners and quiet demeanour hid a mind that was as cool and hard as marble. It was he, as much as anyone, who led Bomber Command away from its pursuit of a precision that was, initially at least, unattainable, and towards a policy of annihilation. Portal queried, in his courteous but firm fashion, the wisdom of attacking the German aircraft industry. Many of the targets were sited in remote areas. He pointed out that 'the very high percentage of bombs which inevitably miss the actual target will hit nothing else of importance and do no damage and the minimum amount of dislocation and disturbance will be caused by the operations as a whole.' He also advocated that when initial targets could not be reached because of bad weather, aircraft should be free to dump bombs on alternatives, thus increasing 'the moral effect of our operations by the alarm and disturbance created over the wider area'.

With these observations, which caused some surprise and concern at the ministry, Portal opened the way to a crucial shift in bombing policy. In his view, any damage was better than none and undermining *morale*, the moral effect in the language of the day, was a very important and desirable product of aerial bombardment. The Air Staff felt the need to sound a cautionary note. It felt that 'moral effect, although an extremely important subsidiary result of air bombardment, cannot in itself be decisive'.[8] For the time being, at least, it maintained its faith in what it believed were selective, precise attacks.

Portal was being indiscreet in advocating so frankly the spreading of panic. But he was stating a belief that had been accepted inside the air force from the earliest days. Despite undertaking that the RAF would not attack the civilian population as such, it was understood that any attack on land-based strategic targets would result in civilians dying. Trenchard's independent force had killed 746 innocent Germans in the 242 raids it mounted in the six months of its existence.

Few moral contortions were necessary to justify certain civilian deaths. Many took the view that the factory worker manufacturing shells was as lawful a target as the artilleryman firing them. The killing of women and children naturally caused revulsion. But at the same time it was widely accepted that all bloodshed, or the threat of it, had beneficial results in lowering enemy spirits and undermining the will to sustain the war effort. This was no more than a reflection of Trenchard's dictum that the moral effect of bombing was twenty times that of the material effect. The question was, as the Air Ministry reply made clear, whether the issue of morale could be decisive. And if it could, should morale itself be a primary target of strategic bombing?

The first reports filtering out of Germany suggested that this might be the case. Germans had been led to believe that they would be largely untroubled by air attack, and very well protected if any should occur. The thin evidence available, from neutral journalists and diplomats and a handful of spies, spoke of shock and dismay among ordinary citizens that the war had entered their towns.

Meagre though this testimony was, it reinforced the conviction in some quarters that German nerves were weaker than those of the British. This was Trenchard's belief. It was not Churchill's, who in October 1917, when calls for revenge for the German air raids were at their loudest, had dismissed the idea that a response in kind could produce a German surrender. 'Nothing that we have learned of the capacity of the German population to endure suffering justifies us in assuming that they could be cowed into submission by such methods,' he wrote.[9]

Even if the Germans' pluck was suspect, it was questionable whether this would produce any immediate advantage for Britain and its allies. An influential subcommittee reporting to the Chiefs of Staff had pointed out with some understatement three years before the outbreak of war that 'a military dictatorship is likely to be less susceptible to popular outcry than a democratic government'.[10] This was only common sense, but it was to be very often forgotten or ignored.

The Battle of Britain and the Blitz provided the great test of British morale. In the first two months of the air war, 1,333 people were killed as German bombs missed their targets or were scattered at random when the raiders headed for home. On the night of 24 August the first bombs fell on central London and a fortnight later it experienced its first heavy bombardment. That month 6,954 civilians were killed all over Britain, and a further 6,334 in October. This was death on a hideously larger scale than had been endured in the previous war.

In the capital, the bombs were ostensibly aimed at docks, railways and other locations with an arguable military or war-industrial value. In practice they landed everywhere. They fell on Westminster Abbey, St Paul's Cathedral, Kensington Palace, Lambeth Palace and Buckingham Palace, twice. They hit hospitals and theatres, the London Zoo and Madame Tussaud's. They crashed down on rich and poor alike, the brick terraces of the East End and the stucco squares of Kensington and Mayfair. But the great sprawl of London meant that the violence lacked concentration. As one part of the city was 'getting it bad' another was having a relatively quiet night. The capital adjusted quickly to death from the air. The damage was spectacular but had minimal effect on the war effort. There was little sign of the collapse of morale feared by the authorities, even though the Blitz was to continue, night after night, until the following spring.

Churchill had reacted to the first London raid by ordering an attack on Berlin. It went ahead on the night of 25 August. The city was covered with thick cloud making aiming virtually impossible. The incendiary bombs that did fall within the city limits did little damage, mostly landing harmlessly in open country. There were three further raids on Berlin in the next few days. The prime minister wanted to spread the attacks throughout Germany but faced resistance from the Air Staff who continued to argue for narrow and selective targeting.

But as the German bombardment persisted, such a detached view became untenable. As a concession to the new mood, on 21 September the Air Staff directed Portal to continue the assault on Berlin. The bombers should aim for 'legitimate' targets such as railways and the like. But the object was also to cause 'the greatest possible disturbance and dislocation both to the industrial activities and to the civil population generally in the area'.[11]

To Portal, the directive did not go nearly far enough. Ten days before he had offered a new policy to the staff, based on direct retaliation. He suggested twenty German towns should be warned by radio broadcast that each attack on a British town would be repaid by a heavy, indiscriminate attack by Bomber Command on one of their number. Alternatively, a town like Essen, the home of the arms manufacturer Krupp, which could be regarded in its entirety as a military target, could be subjected to overwhelming bombardment. Another approach was to select a military target, presumably a barracks or suchlike, for an all-out assault in 'the knowledge that the normal spread of such a heavy attack would inevitably cause a high degree of devastation to the town.'[12]

Portal's views, combined with those of the prime minister, forced the Air Staff planners to think again. They had stuck to their view in the belief that precision bombing was attainable and producing desirable results. They regarded the inevitable civilian deaths as incidental to the main aim of destroying strategic targets, not an end in themselves.

Portal's position was strengthened by a German decision to raise the stakes in the air war. On the night of 14 November, a force of 449 aircraft was sent to Coventry in the Midlands. The air raid killed 554 people and seriously injured 865, almost all of them civilians. Its political impact, though, was to prove far greater than the physical damage inflicted. What happened in Coventry would shape the direction of the air war.

2

Coventrated

Coventry was an obvious and, by the standards that Britain had set itself, a legitimate target for aerial attack. Its mediaeval core and fine cathedral and churches did not alter the fact that it was an important centre of war industry, crammed with aircraft and motor-car factories and machine-tool and instrument works.

The people who worked in Coventry liked the place. Many had come from elsewhere to man the production lines and were pleasantly surprised to find themselves in a city of manageable size and that nowhere was far from open country. Rearmament had made it prosperous. By 1940 its population had grown to nearly 240,000, double what it had been thirty years before.

Even with the influx of outsiders, civic pride was strong. 'People were self-disciplined and proudly self-reliant,' wrote Dennis Field, a Coventry schoolboy at the time of the raid who went on to join Bomber Command. There was a marked communal loyalty summed up in the signature tune of the city's favourite entertainer, Sydney James, who appeared every week at the Rialto. As he played the organ, the audience would sing along.

> Looking at life and wearing a smile
> Helping a lame dog over a stile
> Don't mind the rain
> Forget your umbrella
> Or lend it, for once, to the other fella
> Making the best of all that you find
> Leaving your cares and your worries behind
> Laughing at your troubles and your trials and your strife
> Yes, that is the best way of looking at life . . .[1]

An air of complacency seems to have hung over the pleasant streets of Coventry in the early part of the war. Its politics were Labour, a consequence of the strong trade-union movement rooted in the factories. Coventry people made weapons but many were opposed to their use. Pacifism and the disarmament movement were strong. In Coventry, as elsewhere, a strange mood of insouciance, verging on fatalism, was noticeable as the violence grew nearer. When, in the spring of 1939, the authorities offered Anderson bomb shelters at a price of five pounds (free for the lower-paid) there were few takers. Those who accepted had their legs pulled for being 'windy'.

In June 1940, when the first bombs dropped on Ansty aerodrome just outside the city, they were seen as a novelty. People set out in cars and on bicycles to gawp at the craters. The thrill soon wore off. Between 18 August and the end of October Coventry was attacked seventeen times, killing 176. As the casualty list lengthened, people started leaving the city at night, 'trekking' to the safety of the surrounding countryside. The better off went by car, the less affluent by bus. The very poorest piled bedding on to prams and walked out, sleeping under bridges.

By the time of the big raid people had grown accustomed to the howl of the sirens and the nuisance of shifting down to the basement or heading to the nearest public shelter. For the workers of the fire service and Air Raid Precautions, the attacks provided good practice. They had seen mutilated bodies and knew what an air raid felt like.

Despite the acknowledged threat, Coventry's defences were weak, with only thirty-six anti-aircraft guns protecting the city. There were searchlights and fifty-six reassuring-looking barrage balloons wallowed over the city, but they were not much of a deterrent on the fatal night. RAF night-fighters found tracking intruders in the dark an almost impossible task and their success rate was to remain pitifully low until enough aircraft were fitted with radar.

A shelter-building programme had been accelerated as the raids continued and there was room inside them for most of the population but many of them were damp and cheaply built. The council's emergency committee kept an informal log of what was being said in bus queues and pubs. The state of the shelters, the feebleness of the anti-aircraft defences and the absence of British fighters were consistent themes of complaint.[2]

Coventry's transformation from an obscure Midlands city to an international symbol of civilian suffering and the inhumanity of modern war started at dusk on Thursday 14 November when crews of the Luftwaffe Pathfinder Force Kampfgruppe 100 boarded Heinkel 111s and took off from a base at Vannes, north of Saint-Nazaire. Coventry was one of three targets that night. The others were Wolverhampton and Birmingham.

The moon began to rise over Coventry at 5.18 p.m. Everyone would later recall its extraordinary brightness. It gleamed on the cobbles of the old city and the lead roof of the cathedral. The sight made people nervous. The citizens had come to fear a bomber's moon. At 7.10 p.m. the sirens sounded. This was early for a raid to be announced and the apprehension deepened. Ten minutes later the Germans were overhead and the bombardment began. It started with small incendiaries. They made a curious swishing noise as they fell. By now people had learned how to deal with them, picking them up with a long-handled shovel and dropping them into a bucket of water or sand.

But they came down in huge numbers and the emergency services and volunteer firewatchers were soon overwhelmed. At 9.31 p.m. the first high explosive (HE) bombs hit the ground. A firewatcher's log recorded at 9.40 p.m.: 'Cathedral blazing fiercely. HEs all around the city centre.' The sirens had sent women and children hurrying out into the blacked-out streets to seek the public shelters, or down into their basements or back-garden Andersons. 'When the sirens sounded I was doing homework in our front room,' Dennis Field remembered. 'The continual drone of engines and falling bombs made it quickly obvious that the raid was unusually heavy and Mum and I soon decided to go to next-door's shelter where we had an open invitation when things looked sticky. It was cold and we took extra coats ... the bombs rained down ... many times we crouched down expecting the worst ... occasionally there were colossal bangs and blasts which blew open the door. I wanted to go out and see what was happening and to help if I could but demurred to Mum's pleadings and restricted myself to occasional peers outside. The sky seemed aglow with the brightest huge conflagration lighting the sky in the direction of the city centre.'

After the initial fire-raising attack lit up the city the main force of bombers converged on it in three streams, crossing the English coast at Lincolnshire, Portland and Dungeness. The raid had been planned in considerable detail. Each of the eight bomber units involved had been assigned an objective. Their targets included the Alvis aero-engine factory, the Standard Motor Company, the British Piston Ring Company, the Daimler works and the Hill Street Gasworks. The greatest destruction was done to the Daimler factory to the north of the city centre, which produced among other things rotating gun turrets. The site was struck by up to 150 HE bombs and 3,000 incendiaries. The Alvis factory was bombed flat. Altogether twenty-seven war production factories including twelve engaged in making aeroplanes were hit.

The raid reached a climax around midnight. A survivor remembered 'a night of unforgettable horror – the scream of falling bombs – the shattering explosions – the showers of incendiaries, literally thousands, and then . . . perhaps the most horrifying sight of all – the sudden fires leaping up, their flames, fanned by the wind, rapidly spreading and enveloping all within reach.'[3] The smell of the burning city reached up to the bombers. A crewman, Hans Fruehauf, who had taken part in the first London raids, looked down on the lake of fire and wondered what he was doing. 'The usual cheers that greeted a direct hit stuck in our throats. The crew just gazed down at the flames in silence. Was this really a military target, we all asked ourselves?'[4] A 'Front Reporter' for the German propaganda service was a passenger in one of the aircraft. He had no doubts of the legitimacy of what he witnessed. 'We could see enormous fires raging, some white and brilliant, others dark red. Then came the high spot of the raid, the dropping of the bombs . . . a tremor went through the machine as the bombs dropped . . . our bombs had hit their mark; the fires extended . . . it is the nerve centre of the British armament industry which had been hit, and I am proud that I witnessed this.'[5]

The anti-aircraft guns soon ran out of ammunition and there was no sign of RAF night-fighters so the Germans were free to bomb as they pleased, swooping in low to improve accuracy. As mains were shattered and hydrants buried under rubble, the firemen's hoses ran dry. Crews drafted in from outside watched impotently as Coventry burned. The fire was fiercest in the old city centre. John Shelton who owned a stables in Little Park Street described the din of 'falling walls, girders, pillars, machinery crashing four storeys, the droning of the planes as they let go their bombs and the rattling of shrapnel on corrugated sheeting'. It seemed to him that no one caught in the open could possibly have survived.[6]

The fire created weird effects. In Broadgate, in the heart of the city, the smell of roasting meat from burning butcher shops mingled with the scent of fine Havanas from the tobacconists, Salmon and Gluckstein. Inside the shelters, the air was thick with plaster and brick dust shaken loose by the pounding, and the stench of filth from the primitive or non-existent latrines. The overwhelming feeling was of powerlessness. It was better to be outside doing something. The ARP and Auxiliary Fire Service workers, the ambulancemen, doctors and nurses found they were too busy to be afraid. The urge to not let oneself down, to be seen to be coping and doing one's best was a strong antidote to fear or at least a help in suppressing it. 'Everyone was working as a member of a team,' said a student nurse at Gulson Road Hospital which was inundated with casualties after the Coventry and Warwickshire Hospital suffered heavy damage. 'Even the consultants who were normally treated like little gods and who to us poor nurses never seemed to be in the best of moods became human.' During her training she had dreaded having to assist at an amputation and had arranged to be off duty when such operations were scheduled. 'The blitz on Coventry changed all that for me. I didn't have time to be squeamish.'[7]

Despite the ferocity of the attack, rescue workers struggled on. Instead of reducing the value of life, the scale of the slaughter seemed to increase it. Every death averted, every existence saved, was a small victory. The hope of preserving a life drove the rescue teams to extraordinary lengths of selflessness. Les Coleman, an air-raid warden, heard a baby crying from beneath the rubble of a demolished house. He and his mates scrabbled for hours at the pile of bricks, fearful of using picks and shovels in case they hurt the child. Overhead the Luftwaffe were busy and the bombs fell steadily. They only stopped digging when the crying faded to silence.[8]

The all-clear sounded at 6.16 a.m., eleven hours after the first warning. Few heard it. Most of the electricity cables that powered the sirens were cut. Gradually people crept from the shelters into a drizzly morning and a changed world. The first thing they did was to look for their houses. Dennis Field found his, 'like most around, with windows out and roof damaged and clearly uninhabitable.' At least it was still standing. Whole streets had disappeared and landmarks vanished. The town seemed to have dissolved. The survivors walked through mounds of smoking debris flickering with flame, around craters big enough to swallow a bus. The most shocking sight was the cathedral. It lay open to the sky. The roof and the pillars had collapsed and everything inside the nave had burned to ash, piled up within the sagging external walls. All that remained was the spire and tower.

Coventry had been hit by 503 tons of high explosive, 56 tons of incendiaries and 127 parachute mines. The city was like others which had expanded during the Industrial Revolution. The workers' houses were huddled along the flanks of the factories they worked in. It was inevitable that the German bombs, no matter how well aimed, would hit them. Altogether 42,904 homes were destroyed or damaged, 56 per cent of the housing in the city. The number of dead was put at 554. Another 863 were seriously injured.

This was the most concentrated attack of the Blitz to date. To Britain and its allies it seemed that the Germans had set a new standard in ruthlessness. Those who took part in the raid believed they were engaged in a respectable act of war. At the pre-operation briefing, crews were told by their commander that Coventry was 'one of the chief armament centres of the enemy air force and has also factories which are important for the production of motor vehicles and armoured cars.' If the raid succeeded, he said, 'we shall have dealt another heavy blow to Herr Churchill's war production'.[9]

The raid was indeed a great success. Eight hours after it ended, German radio listeners were told that bombers had 'inflicted an extraordinarily heavy blow on the enemy' and that Coventry had been 'completely wiped out'. In the broadcast a notorious word was heard for the first time. What the bombers had done was to *koventrieren*, to Coventrate, the city.[10]

Until now civilian spirits had held up well in air attacks. Coventry provided a new and sterner test of morale. The raids on London so far had been heavy but scattered. The attacks on places like Liverpool and Southampton had been limited and of much shorter duration. The violence against Coventry seemed more focused and therefore potentially more traumatic than anyone else had experienced. It was here that the question of whether Britain could take it might be answered.

The first evidence was troubling. As people struggled to recover, a feeling of numb hopelessness appears to have set in. By now there were reporters around to record the city's mood. Hilde Marchant, a thoughtful and courageous *Daily Express* correspondent who had witnessed the war in Spain, arrived while fires still burned and buildings toppled. She came across a dazed-looking group standing helplessly in the street, 'occasionally asking when bread was coming into the city. There was no clamour, just sullen resentment at the inconvenience. They had patience because they were too weary to be angry.' Outside the Council House, the municipal headquarters, she saw a long queue. 'Men without collars and still in their carpet slippers. Women in woollen dressing gowns and slippers just as they had come from the shelter . . . asking for food and money.'

When an aeroplane appeared overhead there was a wild scramble and women hauled their children to the nearest shelter. The aircraft shifted in the sky to reveal RAF roundels, but it was some time before anyone was persuaded to come out. Some people had never left the shelters after the all-clear. Peering into one, Marchant saw two adults and two children 'with greenish faces, so still that they looked dead'.

The Morning After.

A team from the pioneering social study group Mass Observation, veterans of bomb attacks on London and elsewhere, arrived in Coventry on Friday afternoon less than a dozen hours after the raid finished. Their report claimed the attack had caused 'unprecedented dislocation and depression', compared with what they had seen before. 'There were more open signs of hysteria, terror, neurosis observed than during the whole of the previous two months together in all areas,' it said. 'Women were seen to cry, to scream, to tremble all over, to faint in the street, to attack a fireman and so on. The overwhelmingly dominant feeling on Friday was the feeling of utter helplessness. The tremendous impact of the previous night had left people practically speechless in many cases. And it made them feel impotent. *There was no role for the civilian. Ordinary people had no idea what they should do* (original emphasis).'[11]

The lack of organization or direction was unsurprising given the power of the attack. The mayor and his officials, the men who ran the city's services, had all suffered the same experience as everyone else. An individual report by a Mass Observation representative suggested that Coventry's relative smallness meant the 'shock effect of the bombing was much greater than in London . . . everybody knew somebody who was killed or missing . . . everybody knew plenty of people who had been rendered temporarily or permanently homeless. And these subjects occupied literally 90 per cent of all conversation heard throughout Friday afternoon and evening. Even in Stepney at the beginning of the Blitz there was not nearly so much obsession with damage and disaster.'

This was to be expected and no indication of despair. But the observer also noted that people seemed anxious to leave Coventry behind, reporting that 'the dislocation is so total in the town that people easily feel that *the town itself is killed* (original emphasis).'[12]

This was the reaction that the authorities had feared, opening the way to anarchy. It was particularly disastrous if it happened in Coventry. If the city descended into chaos and flight, who would man the war factories when they were rebuilt, as they would have to be if the struggle was to continue?

Senior government figures rushed in to test the mood themselves. The Home Secretary Herbert Morrison, the Minister of Health Aneurin Bevan and the Minister of Aircraft Production Lord Beaverbrook converged on Coventry. The city officials who met them were angry. They demanded to know why there had been no night-fighters to protect them and so few guns. Morrison wrote later that he found 'an almost total lack of will or desire to get the town moving again' and detected an 'air of defeatism'. This was desperately unfair. The men in front of him were still in shock from an experience that was unknown to the men from London. The chief fire officer, who showed up covered in grime from the smoke, fell asleep at the table.

Lord Beaverbrook, the Canadian-born press baron and crony of the prime minister, seemed particularly unsympathetic. Instead of offering any apology for the absence of fighters he made a florid speech, reminding the officials of their duty to get Coventry working again. This was the brutal truth. Coventry was essential to the war effort and the resumption of production was given precedence over easing the plight of survivors. The first major decision was to set up an organization under the chairmanship of a powerful local car manufacturer, William Rootes, to oversee the restoration of gas, water, electricity and transport so that the war factories could function again.

Apprehension rather than defiance was the prevailing sentiment in Coventry's shattered streets on the morning after the Blitz. There was no reason to doubt that the Germans would be back again that night and no expectation that anyone would be able to stop them. The story went round that they had deliberately left the cathedral spire intact to provide an aiming point for the next bombardment.

As the short day wore on the city emptied. It reminded Hilde Marchant of what she had seen in Spain and Finland. 'Yet this was worse . . . these people moved against a background of suburban villas, had English faces . . . they were our own kind.' Both sides of the road were filled with 'lorries, cars, handcarts and perambulators . . . the lorries were packed with women and children sitting on suitcases or bundles of bedding . . . the most pathetic of all were those who just leaned against the railings at the roadside, too exhausted to move, their luggage in heaps around them and a fretful tired child crying without temper or anger . . .' Those with relations round about were hoping they would have room to take them in. Those without were looking for cheap or free lodging with strangers and often they found it. Church halls and Scout huts opened up to supplement the existing emergency centres. Some gave up looking and slept under hedges or against walls.

But over the following days, people began to drift back. Many spent the day in town then trekked back to the country in the evening. There was no real choice but to return. Coventry was where their lives were. There, they joined a significant number who had stayed put, either because their duties demanded it or out of a refusal to be driven out. The pride involved in having endured quickly asserted itself. Tom Harrisson, one of the founders of Mass Observation, arrived on Friday afternoon and found the city in low spirits. 'It would be an insult to the people of Coventry to ballyhoo them and exaggerate their spirit,' he said in a talk broadcast after the BBC *Nine O'Clock News* the following night. The most common remark he had heard from people as they first surveyed the mess of their city was 'poor old Coventry'. But by Saturday, he found the mood had changed. 'I was out in the streets again before daylight. It was a mild clear morning and the first thing I heard was a man whistling. Soon people began crowding through the town but today they were talking, even joking about it. Instead of the despair I heard them say "we'll recover – life will go on, we can get used to it." People still felt pretty helpless but no longer hopeless. The frightened and nervous ones had already left. Those left behind were beginning to feel tough – just as the people of London had felt tough before them.'

A week later a visitor noticed a card in the window of a half-wrecked baby-clothes shop.[13]

BUSINESS AS USUAL

KEEP SMILING

There will always be an ENGLAND

It was the spirit of Sydney James, the Rialto troubadour.

The story of what had happened in Coventry was played down in the BBC's first big news broadcast of the day at 8 a.m. By 1 p.m. it was being given unusually full treatment. For the first time, the Ministry of Information allowed a blitzed city other than London to be mentioned by name. This was gratifying for those who endured the raid but the official version of what had happened differed sharply from what they had experienced. According to the BBC 'the enemy was heavily engaged by intensive anti-aircraft, which kept them at a great height and hindered accurate bombing of industrial targets.' It did admit heavy casualties – a figure of a thousand was given – and that many buildings had been destroyed and damaged. The attack, it emphasized, was an 'indiscriminate bombardment of the whole city'. This account was repeated in the following day's newspapers. T. S. Steele of the *Daily Telegraph* described the operation as a 'terror raid'. He accused the Germans of seeking 'to reproduce the Spanish tragedy of Guernica on a larger scale', a reference to the Condor Legion's destruction of the Basque capital in 1937.

Steele repeated the line that a fierce anti-aircraft barrage had kept the raiders five miles above the city. 'There was not even a pretence at an attempt to select military targets,' he wrote. 'For ten hours raider after raider flew over at an immense height and dumped bombs haphazard (sic) at the rate of nearly one a minute on the town. The result is that factories which are legitimate military targets have escaped comparatively lightly. The brunt of the destruction has fallen on shopping centres and residential areas – hotels, offices, banks, churches and – no Nazi raid is complete without this – hospitals.'

Much of the information contained in the reports came from a Ministry of Home Security communiqué. Faced with the magnitude of the raid, the government had chosen to play the story up. The wisdom of publicizing the attack was questioned at the War Cabinet meeting on Monday 19 November. The Secretary of State for War, Anthony Eden, had listened to Harrisson's Saturday night talk on the BBC and felt it had 'been a most depressing broadcast'. The prime minister disagreed. The effect of the publicity had been considerable in the United States and in Germany he said.

American correspondents indeed covered the raid in detail and seized on the city's ordeal as a symbol of British steadfastness and Nazi barbarity. The Germans responded by claiming that 223 had been killed by the RAF during a raid on Hamburg carried out the night after the Coventry attack (the true number was in fact twenty-six who died when bombs hit the Blohm and Voss shipyard). The assumption was that transatlantic indignation at what had been done to Coventry had stung Germany into insisting that its civilians were also suffering. To one watching American, it seemed clear what was coming next. Raymond Daniell of the *New York Times* told his readers that people in Britain now found it difficult to escape a feeling that a 'war of extermination is beginning. Each bomb that falls intensifies hatred and stimulates the demand for retaliation in kind.'

The note of the all-clear siren had barely faded before calls for retribution began. When King George visited the city less than two days afterwards a man in the crowd called out to him: 'God bless you. Give them what they gave to us! We can take it.'[14] The intelligence reports reaching the city's emergency services during the raids that preceded the big attack suggested that people had thought bombing attacks would be worse than they in fact were. As a result, 'more people than hitherto now feel that indiscriminate bombing of Berlin would be an unwise policy.'[15]

That attitude had now changed. Hilde Marchant had been one of the first to report the calls for revenge. She had issued one of her own. 'The Nazis added one more word to the English language – "Coventrated",' she wrote. 'Let us add one more – "Berliminated".' Her observations had been contradicted by Harrisson in a throwaway remark at the end of his broadcast. 'I see some reporters stressing the fact that Coventry is clamouring for reprisals,' he said. 'That wasn't borne out by my own observations . . . it only makes Coventry realize that this sort of thing doesn't end the war and only makes it more bitter.'

This judgement was not supported by the findings of his own teams. A fortnight after the raid they asked people in the streets of the city what they would like the government to do. 'Knock bloody hell out of them,' said a forty-five-year old man, described as middle class. 'For every one he gives us, we ought to give him twenty,' said a sixty-year-old working-class male. Another, youngish man replied. 'We're fighting gangsters, so we've got to be gangsters ourselves. We've been gentlemen too long.'[16]

Whatever gentlemanly attitudes lingered among those making Britain's war decisions were about to disappear for the duration of the war. It was a month before the government moved to avenge Coventry. The attack took place on the night of the 16/17 December and the target was Mannheim, an industrial town that straddles the Rhine in south central Germany. There were 134 aircraft on the raid, the biggest force to be used so far. At first sight there is nothing in the operations book or subsequent intelligence reports to suggest that the purpose of the raid was any different to many that had preceded it. The order was to attack the industrial centre of the town and the primary targets were the Mannheim Motorenwerke and naval armaments factories. The clue to the special nature of the raid lay in the bombs that the aircraft were carrying. There were a few 1,000-pound bombs and many more 500- and 250-pounders, packed with high explosive and designed to knock down walls and collapse roofs. But by far the largest number of bombs were incendiaries, weighing only four pounds each but capable when dropped in sufficient numbers, as Coventry knew all too well, of setting a city ablaze.

The raid was led by eight Wellingtons which carried nothing but incendiaries in their bomb bays, flown by the most experienced crews available. The aircraft that followed them were to use the light of the fires they started as their aiming point and in the words of Sir Richard Peirse, who succeeded Portal as commander-in-chief of Bomber Command, 'to concentrate the maximum amount of damage in the centre of the town.' It was a perfect moonlit night over Mannheim and the returning crews thought they had done well. More than half the aircraft claimed to have hit the town. Some reported later that when they flew away at 3.30 a.m., the target area was a 'mass of fires'.

In fact the raid was only a partial success. The first Wellington 'fire-raisers' failed to accurately identify the centre of the city and many incendiaries fell in the suburbs which were then bombed by the following aircraft. Other bombs fell on Ludwigshafen on the western bank of the Rhine. The city authorities reported 240 buildings destroyed or damaged by incendiaries and 236 by high explosive. They included thirteen shops, a railway station, a railway office, one school and two hospitals. The total casualty list was thirty-four dead, eighty-one injured and 1,266 bombed out of their homes. Of the dead eighteen were women, two were children, thirteen were male civilians and one was a soldier.

The Cabinet had given their approval for the plan three days before. If they had hoped for destruction to match that done to Coventry the reconnaissance photographs told another story. It was a disappointment and the exercise was not repeated for some time. But it was the shape of things to come.

3

'To Fly and Fight'

Bomber Command was poorly equipped to face the challenges of this new and vulnerable phase of its existence. In one respect, though, it was extraordinarily rich. The quality and quantity of men available to it were the best Britain and its overseas Dominions could provide. The Bomber Boys were all volunteers and the supply of aircrew candidates never slackened, even when losses were at their most daunting.

They were an extraordinarily varied bunch. Most were British. There was a sprinkling from the diaspora of the defeated nations, Poles, Czechs, Norwegians, French and Belgians, wanting their revenge on Germany. They were outnumbered by large numbers of Canadians, Australians, New Zealanders and South Africans, the 'colonials' as they were mockingly but affectionately called, whose lands were not directly threatened by Nazism but who, driven by a sense of adventure or fellow-feeling for their British cousins, none-theless offered themselves for what it was soon understood were among the most dangerous jobs in warfare.

For imaginative boys growing up in the 1930s, the prospect of going to war in an aeroplane carried an appeal that the older services could never match. Aviation was only a generation old and flying glowed with glamour and modernity. In the years before the war Peter Johnson, languishing in a hated job as a breakfast-cereal sales-man, looked at this world and longed to join it. 'I read aviation magazines,' he wrote, 'watched the activities at an RAF aerodrome from behind a hedge and even once penetrated into a flying club on the pretext of finding out the cost of learning to fly. That, needless to say, was well out of my income bracket but the contact with the world of flight, the romantic instructors in their ex-RFC leather coats, the hard, pretty girls with their long cigarette holders, the rich young men boasting about their adventures, fitted perfectly with my picture of a dream world to which, if I joined the Air Force, I could find a key.'[1]

By the time the great wartime expansion began, the RAF's aura of chic had faded. There was little that was dashing about Bomber Command. The new aircraft were big, blunt and utilitarian and the men who flew in them were unmistakably sons of the modern age.

The pre-war professionals were, on the whole, skilled and conscientious fliers, but they masked their seriousness behind a show of pseudo-aristocratic insouciance. The new boys were much less sophisticated. They came from all backgrounds and classes, and the prevailing ethos was democratic and popular. In their writings, in their work and play, they seem sterner, more earnest and more grown-up. The white flying-suited paladins of the RAF of the 1920s and early 1930s had joined to fly rather than to fight. The newcomers had signed up to do both.

On the outbreak of war, young men flocked to join the air force. In the initial rush, the recruiting staff were sometimes overwhelmed. Edward Johnson, who went on to fly as a bomb-aimer on the Dams Raid, was working for J. Lyons, the bakers, in Leeds when war broke out. 'I tried very hard to join up but in the initial stages they kept sending me back because they had nowhere to send people that were volunteering . . . it was a case of calling regularly to see if they'd made up their minds they were going to let us join.'[2]

As an eighteen-year old trainee surveyor, Arthur Taylor joined the Territorial Army before the war and was called up on the day war was declared. Within a few months he was bored and responded eagerly to an official circular announcing the RAF was looking for volunteers. So too did many of his companions. 'About twenty-two applied immediately,' he wrote. 'Understandably our colonel took a poor view of this and pointed out that few of us were bright enough to be accepted. The number of applications then dropped dramatically to fifteen.'[3]

In the month of September 1939, the Aviation Candidates Board at Cardington near Bedford interviewed 671 young men. The recruiting officers were delighted at the quality of the applicants. The board could afford to be choosy. Of the 671 who presented themselves, 102, or 15.2 per cent, were rejected.

The surplus of suitable manpower persisted throughout the war. In the first quarter of 1944, when Bomber Command was suffering terrible losses during the Battle of Berlin, the board still felt able to turn away 22.5 per cent of the volunteers who applied. The great majority of applicants had not waited for an official summons before stepping forward. A much smaller proportion had chosen the RAF after being called up. There were also a number seeking a transfer from the army. The general standard of education of the army candidates tended to be lower than that of the pure volunteers, the board's head, Group Captain Vere Bettington, observed, and a higher percentage of rejections was to be expected. RAF personnel working on the ground also responded well to appeals to 'get operational'.

At first, candidates were required to hold the School Certificate, the multi-subject examination taken by sixteen-year-olds before going on to higher education, but by August 1940 this proviso had been dropped. Nor was leaving school before the age of sixteen considered a bar. The initial test included intelligence, mathematics and general knowledge papers. But Bettington never rejected an applicant on educational grounds alone. 'A candidate's desire to fly and fight,' he declared, is 'of primary importance.'[4]

The old RAF's sensitivity about its *arriviste* origins had given it a tendency to snobbery. This was dissolved in the flood of men from modest and poor homes taking up the flying duties that had formerly been the preserve of the sons of the military, clerical, medical and colonial middle classes. Harry Yates, who left school at fourteen and worked as a junior clerk in the offices of a printing company in the south Midlands, wondered as he waited for a reply from the RAF whether his lack of education would disqualify him. 'Could it be,' he wrote, 'that, in reality, becoming one of these pilot types required a university education or even an old school tie? Was it the preserve of the sons of the well-to-do? But this, as I was to discover, was far from true. Terrible thing though it was, the war brought opportunity. The great British class system counted for surprisingly little. I saw nothing of it in all my RAF days.'[5]

The impulse to fly had been stimulated in many applicants by an early encounter with aeroplanes. Brian Frow went to the 1932 Hendon Air Show with a friend from his south-London prep school. 'I was spellbound,' he remembered. 'A hostile fort was bombed with live missiles; balloons forming life-sized animals were chased by big game hunters in fighter aircraft and eventually shot down.' In the school holidays he cycled to Croydon aerodrome with an aircraft recognition book in his satchel, identifying and recording everything that flew. The fact that his eldest brother, Herbert, had been killed in action flying in the First World War did not dent his enthusiasm. Herbert's loss was commemorated by a shrine in the family home made out of the wooden propeller of his doomed aircraft.[6]

Ken Newman, another south-London boy, also made regular pilgrimages to Croydon, which was only a mile or so from his home. 'As a boy, and like so many others of my generation, I had been fascinated by aeroplanes,' he recalled. 'They were seldom seen in the sky and caused open-mouthed surprise when they were . . . I used to go and watch, from the roof of the airport hotel next to the terminal and flight control building.' Sometimes an hour or more would pass between the arrivals of the Imperial Airways and KLM airliners 'but every take-off and landing was exciting, particularly when the aeroplanes came close to the hotel building.'[7]

In opting for the RAF, volunteers were exercising a choice, and choices were rare in wartime. By doing so, they avoided being drafted into a less congenial branch of the services, and in 1939, there was no more unattractive option than the army.

The young men arriving at the recruiting centres had been born during, or just after, the end of the First World War. They had heard tales of the Western Front from their fathers and male relations. Dennis Field, the Coventry boy who had witnessed the Blitz from his back-garden shelter, had an uncle who had been in the trenches. 'His pugnacity and bitterness were apparent even to a youngster,' he wrote. 'My friend's father was a signaller in France and only reluctantly talked of the moonscape devastation, or mud, barbed wire, shell holes, bodies and rats and lice and drownings in mud and filth. My youthful picture was overwhelmingly one of revulsion.'[8]

In the streets, the sight of men who had lost limbs, the wheezing and hacking of gas-damaged lungs, told young men what they could expect. Aeroplanes were intrinsically dangerous, everyone knew that. But they were also exciting. And death in an aeroplane seemed quicker and cleaner in comparison with what they would face on land.

Jim Berry, who became a Pathfinder pilot, used to look with fascination and a tremor of fear at a German bayonet which his father had brought back from the trenches. '[He] used to tell us stories about the first war and it sounded horrific to me,' he said. 'The mud and the mess. It was something we looked at with a fair amount of horror as children. I thought that's not for me at any price. If I had been made to go I would have had to go but I thought, well, I'm going to volunteer so I volunteered and (went for) aircrew.'[9]

The RAF, as Group Captain Bettington said, was looking for people who were eager not only to fly but to fight. The First World War had generated a hatred of conflict and yearning for peace that was evident in the great popularity of the pacifist movement. Yet the hope amongst the young that they would not be called on to take part in another great war seldom hardened into a determination not to do so. Charles Patterson, born in 1920 and brought up in middle-class comfort by his mother and sister after his parents separated, found that his early childhood 'was overshadowed by the terrible First World War and the appalling suffering and sacrifices which were implanted in me not just by my mother but by all the grown-ups with whom I came into contact.' It was 'something so appalling that it just could not be ever allowed to happen again, because if it did, it would be virtually the end of the world.'

He felt, nevertheless, that 'if another war came I would inevitably have to join up as soon as it began, to try and fight. It was very firmly implanted in my mind that the greatest sacrifices in the first war had been endured by the ordinary Tommy. What I believed and was taught was that if these young, working-class boys could show such courage it made it absolutely imperative on me to not let them down, or at least make an effort to live up to what they had done should another war come.'

As the war approached Patterson considered his choices. It was quite simple really. 'I could never have stood up to the rigours of fighting on land and in dust and heat and dirt and so on. That simply would have been quite beyond me.' He knew something about flying from his brother-in-law, an RAF pilot who had taken him up in a Gypsy Moth when he was ten. Like many others he had seen *Dawn Patrol*, a remarkably bleak and unidealized story of First World War aviators which nonetheless pushed many adolescent boys into the arms of the RAF. '[It] had a tremendous influence on me. It struck me that although the casualties were very heavy it was much the most exciting and wonderful way to go to war.'[10]

The decision to fight was made easier by the seeming inevitability of the conflict. The Germans had left Britain with no choice. To the older airmen, this came as no surprise. Peter Johnson, who was nearly five when the first war broke out and whose naval officer father was killed in 1914, felt that 'mass hatred . . . was inoculated into my generation against the Germans'.[11] He was at least ten years older than most of his comrades in Bomber Command. The writings and recollections of the younger men do not reveal much evidence of instinctive loathing for the Hun.

A surprising number of them had some direct or indirect contact with events in Germany. When he was about fourteen, Ken Newman made friends with a German boy called Erich Strauss who had come from Stuttgart to visit his grandmother. 'It was during one of our walks around Mitcham Common that he told me he and his family were Jewish and that the Jews in Germany were being given a very hard time by the Nazis,' he wrote. 'I was not quite sure whether he was telling the truth or was exaggerating to impress me.' In 1938 he visited Germany with a school party, travelling by boat and train to Cologne then sailing up the Rhine to Mainz, staying in youth hostels along the way. 'In every one were parties of Hitler Youth who marched about in military-style uniforms, and every morning and evening attended a flag raising or lowering ceremony with arms raised and shouts of "Heil Hitler!"' Even so, they seemed friendly enough to the English visitors. Every young person he met 'repeated again and again that the last thing they wanted was another war with Britain and France.' [12]

Informal attempts had been made to forge friendly links with Germany in the years between the wars through school trips and exchanges. Sometimes they were too successful. In the spring of 1936 thirteen-year-old Ken Goodchild went on a visit with some schoolmates from No. 6 Central School in Morden, Surrey. They were in the Rhineland when the Germany army marched in, and visited Cologne, which he was to pass through seven years later as a prisoner. On their return their families were surprised to see they were wearing swastika lapel badges. In 1937 Ken went again and was present in Düsseldorf when Hitler arrived to open an exhibition. The Führer exchanged some friendly words with the master accompanying the boys and patted some of them on the head. Goodchild was perhaps the only Bomber Command airman to have stared the enemy leader in the face.[13]

In the same year, Leonard Cheshire, a restless, rather wayward eighteen-year-old, who had just left Stowe public school, went to stay with a German family in Potsdam before he went up to Oxford. The head of the household was a retired admiral called Ludwig von Reuter. He was not a supporter of the Nazis but shared some of their opinions, telling Cheshire that 95 per cent of humanity were worthless and war was a valuable means of keeping them down. Cheshire went on to become one of the most dedicated and ruthless pilots in Bomber Command.[14]

Before the war it was still possible to differentiate between Nazis and 'decent' Germans. 'How I loathed the Nazis,' wrote Guy Gibson. 'How could the common people of Germany allow such a world-conquering crowd of gangsters to get into power and stay in power? Ruthless and swaggering, domineering brutality, that was their creed.' His anger was directed with almost equal vigour against British politicians, the 'rotten Governments, the Yes men and the appeasers' as well as those who voted for them.

Leonard Cheshire (*left*) and opponent, Germany, August 1936.

Gibson blamed the older generation for allowing another war to happen. But he was also concerned about the willingness of his contemporaries to fight it. On 1 September 1939, having been called back from leave to rejoin his squadron, he passed through Oxford with his friend Freddy Bilbey who had been studying biology there. After a lengthy session in a pub they went to have dinner. 'It was fairly late and we were pretty hungry, and fed like kings with some excellent 1928 burgundy, but what a rotten crowd to be seen at that place – drunken, long-haired, pansy-looking youths, mixed with foppish women. They so disgusted me that I asked Freddy if they were undergraduates . . . "Good Lord, no!" he said. "They are the types who try to look like undergraduates."'[15]

Gibson's doubts about some 'varsity men may have stemmed from the Oxford Union debate of a few years before in which the motion that the house would not fight for King and Country had been carried. The event had been treated as if it was a genuine barometer of young, privileged opinion. It turned out to be utterly misleading.

Robert Kee, a handsome, rather bohemian history undergraduate, might possibly have attracted a suspicious glare from Gibson had he encountered him in an Oxford pub. But Kee was as contemptuous as Gibson was of the appeasers and as eager to get to grips with the Nazis. 'At the time of Munich all of us at Oxford hated what was going on,' he said. 'We all thought [the politicians] were doing exactly what the Nazis wanted them to.' He was in France with his tutor A. J. P. Taylor when war was declared and rushed back to sign up for the RAF.[16]

Whatever subtleties of feeling might have existed towards the Germans in 1939 faded with the end of the phoney war, and they became, simply, the enemy. Soon they were all too visible, in the skies over Britain. The Battle of Britain provided the most effective recruiting sergeant the RAF could have hoped for. Michael Beetham was a seventeen-year-old schoolboy in the summer of 1940. At the start of the holidays he went to stay with his father, a company commander with the York and Lancaster Regiment then based on the hills just outside Portsmouth at Hillsea barracks. 'It was a lovely summer and the Battle of Britain was just beginning with the German bombers bombing Portsmouth naval base,' he said. 'God, it was spectacular. We went outside and saw the bombers going in and the Hurricanes and Spitfires diving in and having a go at them. I said to my father, that's what I want to do. He obviously wanted me to join the army. I couldn't put my name down until I was eighteen but I did it as soon as I could. I joined the air force to be a pilot. I'd never flown in my life but I wanted to do what those chaps were doing.'[17] At the same time Edward Hearn, a young estate manager, was watching dogfights in the skies over his home in

Folkestone, Kent. 'I thought at that time that if I've got to go to war then I'll go in an aircraft.' He decided to keep his decision from his parents in order not to add to their burden of worry. All his siblings were in the process of joining up. He signed on in Maidstone. 'When I got back my mother said why aren't you at work? I told her, and she said well, I suppose it had to happen sooner or later.' Eddie ended up serving as bombing leader alongside Michael Beetham in 50 Squadron.

Bruce Lewis was standing with his friends outside the tuck shop during mid-morning break at Dauntsey's School in Wiltshire when 'we heard the grinding growl of unsynchronized German aero-engines . . . the Battle of Britain was at its height and schoolboys knew all about these technical matters. The twin-engine Luftwaffe bomber flew low over the school, and then, thrill of thrills, came the shapely little Spitfire in hot pursuit, the distinctive whistle from its Merlin engine sounding almost like the wind itself.' Later they heard the bomber had been shot down. Amazingly, the victorious fighter pilot was an old boy of the school, Eric Marrs, who destroyed six German aircraft before being killed the following year.

At that moment Lewis jilted the Royal Navy, his first preference, and chose the RAF. It was two years before he could join up. He had a talent for drama and got a job as a radio actor with the BBC. His father, a professor who had been badly wounded at the Somme, wanted him to go to university which would gain him exemption from war service for three years. To Bruce, 'such an existence would have been impossible – to sit studying in complete safety while others of my age were dying for their country was not on.' [18]

The start of the Blitz reinforced the realization that the air was now a crucial battlefield as well as the belief that it was in the sky that the war would be decided. Bill Farquharson, who had been raised in Malaya where his father was in the colonial service and was awaiting call-up, was serving with Air Raid Precautions in Birmingham when he was ordered to rush to Coventry to help out after the raid. The experience made him 'angry and yet dead scared'. He felt no particular desire for revenge. He had already made up his mind to go into the air force and the experience 'confirmed the fact that I preferred to be up [in the air] rather than down there'.[19]

Len Sumpter, a Corby steelworker and former Grenadier who had been recalled to the colours at the start of the war, was training recruits at the Guards Caterham depot when it was hit by German bombs. 'We took a real hammering,' he said. 'A lot of people were killed there.' When advertisements appeared calling for volunteers for aircrew he applied, impelled by the thought of 'a little bit of excitement' and 'a bit of personal anger'.[20]

Britain's vulnerability was brought home to Ken Newman when in August 1940, a month after his eighteenth birthday, he watched Croydon airport being attacked by waves of Stuka dive-bombers. When the Blitz began he made his way each day from his home in Norbury to the City where he worked in the accounts department of a mortgage company. One Sunday night in October, the sirens sounded and he hurried his parents to their air-raid shelter. He was 'just closing the door when I heard bombs screaming down towards us. There was no mistaking they were about to hit us or fall very close indeed and I must admit that I was very frightened and thought our end had come. Crump went the first bomb, quite near . . . accompanied by the sound of splintering wood, smashing glass and falling masonry . . .' So it went on. When quietness returned he opened the shelter door. The air was swirling with brick dust and the house was gone. There was 'no sleep for us at all that night. My mother was weeping in a corner of the shelter, partly over the loss of her much-loved home and also in relief that we had survived.' Later, when asked for his reasons for wanting to join the RAF he told the chairman of the selection board that he was 'keen to become a bomber pilot in order to have my revenge'.[21]

Those who had already joined up were glad they had done so when they heard the news from home. Doug Mourton, a wallpaper salesman before the war, was undergoing his RAF training at Abingdon when on 17 September his mother wrote to him from south London. 'Things are very uncomfortable here at present but we are getting used to it . . . they don't give us five minutes' peace. [Aunt] Beat's house was bombed and they have come to live with us. There [are] fourteen of us living in the cellar . . .'[22]

The recruits went off to war in a spirit of optimism. Joining up dispelled the feeling of impotence that aerial bombardment generated and the air force provided the most immediate means of hitting back. There were some restless spirits who welcomed the excitement and openings that war has always offered.

When the storm finally broke Leonard Cheshire was leading what would seem to many an enviable existence, studying law, none too diligently, at Oxford. He was easily bored and game for challenges, which had led him to join the University Air Squadron. His log book recording his flights paused at the end of August 1939. Under the heading WAR he wrote: 'a heaven-sent release . . . a magic carpet on which to soar above the commonplace round of everyday life.'[23]

By the end of 1940 every Briton was faced with an unavoidable truth. There could be no accommodation with the Nazis. If Britain was to remain Britain it would have to fight and after the fall of France the RAF was the only force in the world that was directly attacking the Germans on their own ground.

Thousands of miles away, across oceans and hemispheres, this conviction was felt almost as deeply as it was at home. Imperial attitudes and arrangements were changing. Colonies had become Dominions and were taking their first steps to independence. Yet the cultural and emotional fabric of the empire was still densely woven and strong. At the start of the war, the official instinct of Canada, South Africa, Australia, New Zealand and Rhodesia was to rally to Britain, even though their interests were, for the time being at least, unthreatened by Hitler's foreseeable ambitions. They immediately offered their young men to bolster the ranks of the RAF.

Altogether 130,000 men from the Dominions served as airmen in the RAF, almost 40 per cent. One in four of the Bomber Command aircrews was from overseas and 15,661 lost their lives. Of those, 9,887 were from Canada. Canada's cultural ties with Britain were less established than those of other Dominions. Volunteers tended to think of themselves as answering a call to fight for their own country, rather than going to the aid of a faraway mother nation. Ralph Wood came out of church in Woodstock, New Brunswick, on the morning of Sunday 11 September to find newsboys hawking special editions of the local newspaper, the *Telegraph-Journal*, announcing that Canada was at war with Germany. As he walked back to the home of the parents of his girlfriend Phyllis he confronted the choices before him.

> I knew I had fear of being labelled [a] coward or yellow if I didn't volunteer my services to my country. I knew also that I had fear of losing my life if I did volunteer. There was no contest. All that remained was to choose the service I would join. The Navy? No way! I'd probably be seasick before we left the harbour, let alone battling those thirty-foot waves at sea . . . The Army? Well according to stories of World War I, which was the only reference we had to go by, this meant mud, trenches, lice, bayonets, etc. This was definitely not my cup of tea. Air Force? This was more appealing as it presented a picture of your home base in a civilized part of the country accompanied by real beds with sheets, fairly good food, local pubs with their accompanying social life with periodic leaves to the larger centres and cities. The hour of decision was at hand but it didn't take me an hour to decide on the Royal Canadian Air Force. Being a fatalist, I was pretty sure my number would come up, and in the air it would be swift and definite.[24]

Wood was volunteering out of a sense of duty to Canada and it seems that, at first, he expected to be doing his fighting at home. If the discovery that he was to be sent to England caused him or his comrades any concern there is no mention of it in his frank and cheerful memoir.

Australians and New Zealanders seem to have had a more developed feeling of kinship with Britain and a stronger sense of a shared destiny. Don Charlwood was proud of his English ancestry. His great-grandfather had been a bookseller in Norwich until 1850, when he transferred the business to Melbourne. As soon as Charlwood was able, he volunteered for the Royal Australian Air Force, in the knowledge that it meant crossing the world to go to the rescue of a country he had never visited.

Like Charles Patterson he felt that his generation 'never really emerged from the shadow of the shadow of the First World War . . . the rise of Nazism was a lengthening of the same shadow over our youth. When this threat was faced by Britain in 1939, the response in Australia was not only that we, too, must face Nazism, but that we must stand by the threatened "Homeland".'[25]

The Dominion airmen sometimes appeared to feel an attachment to the British Empire that was stronger than that of the British themselves. One of Bomber Command's great leaders, Air Vice-Marshal Sir Don Bennett, raised in the Great Dividing Range town of Toowoomba in Queensland, spoke of the 'true British, of . . . Australia, of Canada, New Zealand, South Africa, Rhodesia and the Old Country itself.'[26]

By the end of 1940, then, the push of the war and the pull of the air was driving tens of thousands of young men towards Bomber Command. They were rich, middling and poor and they came from every corner of Britain and its empire. They were the best of their generation and they were heading for one of the worst tasks of the war.

4

Crewing Up

The process by which these disparate and largely unskilled young men were moulded into effective members of a bomber crew was one of the great achievements of the wartime RAF. It was thorough, on the whole efficient, and surprisingly imaginative, qualities which seemed quite out of keeping with the prevailing pre-war service ethos of myopia and conservatism. Noble Frankland, who had joined the University Air Squadron on going up to Oxford in 1941 and went on to join Bomber Command and co-write the official history of its war, reckoned that by the end of operational training 'most crews [had] a reasonable basis upon which to test their fortunes and their courage.'[1] The instruction period certainly lasted long enough. Ken Newman, who volunteered in May 1941 and was selected for pilot training, did not fly his first operational mission until the spring of 1944. A gap of about two and a half years between joining up and going into battle became the norm.

The strategic air campaign was, essentially, made up as it went along. Circumstances changed rapidly in the early days and it was some time before a regularized training programme evolved. With the coming of the four-engined heavies, the Stirlings, Lancasters and Halifaxes, the system settled down to produce a continuous stream of competent and well-prepared airmen.

The long journey to an operational squadron began with a visit to the RAF local recruiting station. Applicants were given a medical, an academic test and a brief interview after which the most obviously unsuitable were weeded out. Volunteers were applying simply to join the RAF and had no idea in which branch of the service they would end up. In the early stages, many dreamed of becoming fighter pilots. But by the end of 1940 Fighter Command's hour had passed. The air war now belonged to Bomber Command and it was there that most volunteers would be sent. Even while the Battle of Britain was at its height, Churchill told the Cabinet and the Chiefs of Staff that 'the fighters are our salvation, but the bombers alone provide the means of victory.'

Official propaganda emphasized their vital role. The first successful film of the war, *Target for Tonight*, which came out in July 1941, was a drama-documentary which used no actors, only RAF personnel who played themselves. It followed the crew of a Wellington, F for Freddie, preparing and executing a typical raid on a typical target in Germany, piloted by Charles 'Percy' Pickard, a blond, impassive, pipe-smoking paradigm of the pre-war RAF. The flying scenes, although spliced with authentic footage, look amateurish and unreal now and the airmen act their parts with a touching diligence but an almost total absence of technique. It was nonetheless a wild commercial success and was seen by audiences all around the free world.

Recruiting posters portrayed the crews as gallant and spirited, the natural successors to the Fighter Boys. Noble Frankland needed little convincing that Bomber Command was the place to be. 'I thought that the defence of Great Britain was over and the next step was to smash the Germans up. I was quite keen to take part in smashing up the Germans, which I think was a fairly common sort of instinct, but I actually had an opportunity to do it.'[2]

As the war progressed, it became clear that bombing was drudge work, tedious and repetitive, and with the added disadvantage of being highly dangerous. Some volunteers who were chosen to fly were dismayed when they heard what it was that they would be flying. Dennis Field had done his initial instruction on single-engined Harvards and was looking forward to going on to fighters. As he moved to the next stage of his training 'a special parade was called and the CO announced that the whole course would be trained for multi-engined aircraft and, we inferred, four-engined bombers. I felt totally deflated at the news. The very little I knew about them gave the impression that I should become a glorified bus-driver.'[3]

For Harry Yates, the ex-clerk who had worried that he was too humble for the RAF, distaste for the grim, mechanical nature of the work over-rode appeals to duty. In early 1943, after a spell serving as an instructor, he decided that he wanted to go to the front line of the air war. 'My expectations were quite specific and they were high: night fighting in Mosquitoes or Beaufighters or, failing that, ground-strafing in Beaufighters. Flying a bomber didn't figure any-where. Indeed the whole point was to avoid it.' The RAF's priorities dictated otherwise and he was sent to Bomber Command.[4]

At the beginning of the war Bomber Command's most pressing need was for pilots. As aircraft grew in size and complexity, its requirements became much broader. The bombers in service in the early period contained an assortment of crews. The Whitley and the Wellington carried five men, including two pilots. The cramped and narrow body of the Hampden held four and had room for only one pilot. All types had an observer who acted as both navigator and bomb-aimer as well as a wireless operator and one or two gunners. The observer role was eventually split into the separate categories of navigator and bomb-aimer.

In August 1940 the first of the new generation of bombers began to appear, starting with the Stirling and followed by the Halifax and then the Lancaster, which by the end of the war was flown by 75 per cent of Bomber Command squadrons. It had been decided late in 1941 that a second pilot was superfluous. He rarely gained any flying experience and was little more than a passenger. Second pilots were dropped and replaced by flight engineers, highly trained tech-nicians who monitored the running of the aircraft during flight. This was an important decision. Pilot training took longer and cost more than the other aircrew roles. With only a single pilot needed, more aircraft could be put in the air. If the practice of using two pilots had persisted, the great raids of 1942 that announced the opening of the main offensive would not have been possible.

By spring of 1942 there were six aircrew jobs for which volunteers could be considered: pilot, navigator, engineer, bomb-aimer, wire-less operator and air gunner, of which there were two. After the initial vetting stage candidates were sent to an Aircrew Selection Centre. On the first day they faced a fairly demanding set of academic tests which were marked on the spot and the failures sent home. The following morning there was a rigorous medical. To pass 'Aircrew A1' required a higher level of fitness than was demanded by the other services. Next came an interview, typically by a panel of three senior officers. Dennis Steiner, a confectioner's son from Wimbledon, who passed through the Oxford selection centre in August 1941, found it 'more of a friendly chat than an interview. I knew that I had been accepted when it was remarked that I would like flying. As I left the room one called out "good luck lad".'[5] Successful candidates were sworn in, issued with their RAF number and then, anti-climactically, told to go home and wait to be summoned. This period of 'deferred service' could last many months.

Eventually they were called to an Air Crew Reception Centre where basic training began. The newcomers marched, saluted, went on endless runs and listened to hair-raising lectures from the medical officer. These, wrote James Hampton, who was the youngest of three brothers who volunteered for aircrew and the only one to survive, warned the new arrivals, virgins almost to a man, about 'some of the shocking and terrifying diseases that abounded and of which they had previously been unaware. These diseases had certain things in common. They could not be caught from lavatory seats and they invariably ended with General Paralysis of the Insane followed shortly by death.'[6] Venereal diseases were a service obsession. At his training centre in Babbacombe near Torquay, Brian Frow's sheltered, middle-class innocence was shaken by lectures given at 'great length, complete with slides lurid enough to frighten even the bravest from casual intercourse for life.'[7]

The RAF was adapting as fast as it could, but no one had told the pre-war regular NCOs who served as drill instructors and were not about to change their rough old ways. Cyril March, who went down the pit straight from his school in Durham, was told after a wait of more than a year to report to the reception centre at Lord's Cricket Ground in London. The NCOs 'let us know in no uncertain manner that we were now in the RAF. They had one thing in common. They were fatherless to a man. There was the sergeant who told me to get my hair cut twice in one day, the sergeant who said he would cure our stiff arms after various inoculations [then] gave us a scrubbing brush, a bucket and a long flight of stairs to scrub down.'[8]

Institutionalized, low-level sadism was not uncommon. Bruce Lewis, who volunteered on his eighteenth birthday, early in 1942, regretted that 'a fine service like the Royal Air Force should have tolerated such an unworthy reception camp' like the one he passed through at Padgate near Warrington. 'Enthusiastic young volunteers entered this gateway to their new career only to be cursed at, degraded and insulted by the low-quality types on the permanent staff.' He felt 'well prepared for all this bullying nonsense having tasted the rigours of life in public school. But some of those lads were away from home for the first time. I used to feel sorry for the ones I heard sobbing in our hut at night.'[9]

After a month, cadets moved on to one of the Initial Training Wings (ITWs) which had been set up in universities and requisitioned resort hotels, where they spent six to eight weeks. There was classroom instruction in airmanship, meteorology, mathematics, Morse code and aircraft recognition. Drill and PT accounted for four hours a day of a six-day week. The courses were tough and the standards high. An 80 per cent success rate was needed to pass.

There was leave at the end of the course and a chance for the cadets to return home to show off their uniforms. Cyril March had spent the worst part of a bitter winter at Bridlington, billeted in the attic of a run-down boarding house. He set off, 'not being sorry to leave frozen "Brid" and feeling very grand in our new uniforms with the distinctive white Air Crew Cadet flash in our hats. I got off the train in Durham to be surrounded by my young brothers and all their mates, all wanting to carry my gear. When we got on the bus to go up home they wouldn't let me pay; I felt like a conquering hero instead of a comparative sprog.'

By the end of the ITW course the cadets had been sifted into the categories, 'trades' in RAF parlance, in which they would fight their war. The path to an operational squadron now diverged as trainees proceeded to specialist flying, engineering, navigation, bombing, gunnery and wireless schools. There was some room for further adjustments. Pilots 'washed out' in the testing conditions of ever more advanced training were often re-assigned as navigators or bomb-aimers. But most would stay in the occupation to which they had been assigned until the end.

The British climate made it one of the worst places in the world to train airmen. In another act of surprising foresight, the Air Ministry had come to an agreement with the Dominions to make use of the blue skies they possessed in abundance. The result was the Empire Air Training Scheme which began operating in April 1940. At its peak in 1943 there were 333 training schools outside the UK, ninety-two of them in Canada with most of the rest in Australia, South Africa, Rhodesia and India. There were five in the United States. Over the war years they turned out more than 300,000 aircrew for all branches of the RAF.

To leave wartime Britain for North America was to move from monochrome to Technicolor. The transformation began on the boat, often one of the great passenger liners that in peacetime had plied the transatlantic route. Dennis Steiner sailed from Gourock on the Clyde to America on the *Queen Elizabeth* to continue his training. As Ireland slipped away he sat down for his first meal. 'We had pork chops and snow-white bread. We hadn't realized how grey our wartime bread had become.' The film stars Merle Oberon, Edward G. Robinson and Douglas Fairbanks who were sailing back to the United States added an extra touch of glamour. The liner docked at New York where the cadets boarded a train for a twenty-seven hour journey to the main receiving centre at Moncton in New Brunswick, Canada.

Dennis Field arrived in Canada in May 1942 to carry on his flying training. 'The lights, lack of civic restrictions, unrationed goods and food, hospitality of the folk of the small town suddenly flooded with servicemen and the novelty of our new surroundings was appreciated,' he wrote. At cafés and drugstores they wolfed down 'huge T-bone steaks covered with two eggs sunny side up and chips, followed by hefty helpings of real strawberry flan and ice cream.'

Those coming the other way found England welcoming and even sophisticated compared with puritanical provincial Canada. Ralph Wood, now trained as a navigator, arrived at the Uxbridge receiving depot in the spring of 1941. He was on his way to the Operational

Training Unit (OTU) at Abingdon, Berkshire, before joining 102 Squadron, a Royal Canadian Air Force unit. 'It was here that we were introduced to English food, Engish pubs and English girls – in that order,' he wrote. 'The pubs were happy new experiences for Canadians used to the dingy taverns of home where one was made to feel uncomfortable, if not immoral . . . the food was plain, palatable and rationed. The girls were friendly and good company . . .'[10]

Training was fun, by and large, whether at home or abroad. It was a time of instant friendships and hard, satisfying work relieved by horseplay, laughter and mild excess. Young men who in peacetime would have been rigidly separated by class and circumstances were thrown together and found that they got along fine. Henry Hughes, who was one of eleven children of a poor but happy family in Bolton, Lancashire, was waiting for a Morse test while training in Blackpool when 'suddenly an airman at our table started to sing "A Nightingale Sang in Berkeley Square" in a really posh Noël Coward-type voice.'[11] The singer was Denholm Elliott who went on to become one of Britain's best-loved post-war actors. Elliott was at RADA when the war began and had volunteered for the RAF on his eighteenth birthday. He found service life 'rather exciting. I was mixing for the first time with many different types of men from different strata of society and I found that I was [getting] on really quite well with them. I had been living in a fairly monastic world since the age of nine, in prep and public schools and had never till now seriously rubbed shoulders with such a spectrum of different classes of people. I hardly realized that they existed. I found myself making great mates with all sorts of people I would probably never have met had it not been for joining up to meet the national crisis.'[12]

Discipline was more flexible now. It needed to be. The trainees were individually-minded and, if not for the war, would have been unlikely to have chosen a service career. They were some of the most adventurous spirits of their generation and tended to chafe at unnecessary restrictions and unearned authority. That did not mean they lacked discipline. Rules, they knew, could be broken. But orders had to be obeyed.

Once the trainees arrived at their specialist schools, flying became part of their daily existence, and so inevitably, did death. There was no system which could take the danger out of learning how to operate a bomber. Walking back to Abingdon after a night in the Red Lion pub, Ralph Wood and his fellow-Canadians watched a Whitley which was practising take-offs and landings crash into the commanding officer's house killing all the crew. It could happen to anybody. Sergeants McClachlan and Iremonger shared a billet with Dennis Field during advanced flying training at South Cerney. They were a worldly pair who seemed to exude confidence. One morning they failed to turn up after night-flying training. They had been killed colliding with each other. When Brian Frow and seven other trainees arrived at the OTU at Cottesmore, they were told by the chief instructor that he had a 'little job' for them before they started. 'This was to act as escort officers at the mass funeral in Cottesmore village for five students who had crashed on the airfield during the week before. We subsequently learned that there had been four fatal crashes in the previous week.' By the end of the war 8,090 Bomber Command personnel had perished in training accidents, roughly one seventh of all who died, and 4,203 were wounded. The suspicion that many of these deaths had been avoidable created some anger and resentment.

At the end of specialist training everyone was promoted. The majority, about two thirds, became sergeants. The rest were commissioned as pilot officers. The criteria used to award commissions were vague. The logic that leaders were automatically officers was not always followed. The captain of a bomber was the pilot, and it seemed sensible that the captain should hold the senior rank. But it was not unusual for a sergeant pilot to be outranked by his navigator or bomb-aimer. Operating a heavy bomber involved shared responsibility and intense mutual dependence. The anomalies and injustices of drawing distinctions of status, as well as pay and conditions, between men who fought and died inside the same claustrophobic metal tube grated particularly on the Canadians who were providing so many men.

The matter surfaced in May 1942 at an air training conference in

Ottawa. It seemed to the Royal Canadian Air Force that there was 'no justification for the commissioning of some individuals whilst others are required to perform exactly the same duties but in NCO rank.' The Canadians pointed out the inequities of pay, transportation and travel allowances. Dividing crews into commissioned and non-commissioned officers meant, in theory at least, the end of socializing on an equal footing. Sergeants would go to the sergeants' mess, officers to the better-appointed officers' mess. They argued that it could only be bad for team spirit if 'the crew, as an entity is not able to live and fraternize, the one with the other, during leisure and off-duty hours.' A radical solution was proposed. Everyone flying in a bomber should be an officer.

The RAF avoided answering the Canadians' detailed points, but did try to define the qualities that made an officer. Commissions were granted, 'in recognition of character, intelligence (as distinct from academic qualifications), and capacity to lead, command and set a worthy example. Many aircrews (*sic*), although quite capable of performing their duties adequately, have no officer qualities.' The debate fizzled out.

Despite the relative absence of awkwardness about class in the RAF, there was plenty of evidence to suggest that being educated at a public school was no handicap when it came to obtaining a commission. Arriving at Brize Norton Flying Training School in April 1941 Brian Frow and his fellow-trainees were addressed by the chief ground instructor, a squadron leader aged about fifty, with First World War medals on his chest. After a welcoming speech he told his charges he was going to select flight commanders and deputies from among the cadets who would act as leaders and principal contacts between students and staff.

'We were all sitting in the hall and he started. "Stand up all of those who were in the OTC (Officer Training Corps) at a public school." About twenty stood up. "Any of you who failed to pass Cert A, sit down." This left some ten standing. "Sit down those who failed to reach the rank of corporal." Two more sat down. "Failed to reach sergeant." Three more sat down. (He) then said, "You five airmen report to my office for interview."'

When Frow arrived, 'The first question was "Do you have any close relations who were commissioned in the Royal Air Force?" I had two brothers, and when I said that one was a squadron leader . . . that was sufficient.' He was 'amused and somewhat embarrassed by this method of selecting the cadet flight commanders and their deputies . . . By a process of elimination, he had dismissed all cadets who had not attended public school, who had not been in the OTC, who had failed to pass Cert A and who had no close relations commissioned into the RAF.' Frow was duly appointed commander of 'A' Flight.

At the same time as they were graded by rank, the cadets earned the right to wear the brevet appropriate to their aircrew category. To outsiders there seemed something unformed about the single wing and circle insignia. It prompted an article by Godfrey Winn, a star writer of the day. 'Don't ask the man with one wing when he will finish his training and get the other half of his wings,' he advised. 'Don't ask him anything. Just shake his hand and offer him a drink.'

Aircrew members were proud of their trades. Many had started out hoping to be pilots. Few of those who were reassigned resented for long the new roles they had been allotted. It was the crew that mattered more than one's individual part in it.

Flying a big bomber was entirely different from flying a Spitfire or a Hurricane. It was the difference, it was sometimes said, between a sports car and a lorry. A four-engined bomber was an immensely complex machine, whose systems needed constant checking. It was a responsibility rather than a pleasure. Tony Iveson who flew Lancasters with 617 Squadron believed that bomber pilots needed 'a steady personality, and you could tell that from what you heard about how they behaved off duty . . . I was a natural bomber pilot. I was patient. I liked precise flying.'[13]

Fighter pilots wrote about flying in the language of love and passion. There are no descriptions in letters and memoirs of the joy of flying a Halifax or a Lancaster. In fighter squadrons it was considered disrespectful to refer to your aircraft as anything other than an aeroplane. Bomber Boys called theirs 'kites'. Operational flying over Germany could mean trips of seven, eight, nine hours. These journeys involved high drama at take-off and landing and intense fear over the target area. But between these peaks of feeling there were long passages of boredom and fatigue, especially on the journey home, even though the danger was far from over.

Crews were organic entities and the prevailing atmosphere was egalitarian. Nonetheless, there was no doubt that it was the pilot who ultimately was in charge. He was responsible for the lives of the other six members of the crew, to the extent that if the aircraft was irretrievably damaged or on fire and about to explode he was expected to stay at the controls until the others had baled out.

The pilot, together with the navigator and the bomb-aimer, were essential for a bomber to be be able to bomb. It was extremely desirable to have a flight engineer, wireless operator and mid-upper and rear gunners. But a sortie could succeed without them.

The pilot's concern was to reach the target. The navigator's job was to find it. Don Charlwood, a navigator himself, felt that 'as a group [they] tended more to seriousness than the men they flew with'.[14] The job, and the training it required, were demanding and exhausting. Noble Frankland, like many navigators, had started off wanting to be a pilot but failed to make the grade. Despite his high intelligence he found the course at his elementary navigation school 'academically the most difficult thing I had ever tackled'. Astronavigation required an ability to think in three dimensions, 'a very, very difficult concept for somebody who is not mathematically gifted or trained'.[15] In the early days navigators had no radio aids to guide them to targets. Even with the advent of *Gee*, *Oboe* and *H2S*, which used radio and radar pulses to direct aircraft on to targets, the navigator's job was the most mentally testing of aircrew tasks, requiring constant alertness at every stage of the journey.

Once the navigator had guided the aircraft to the target area the bomb-aimer took over. As the aircraft went into its bombing run, he became the most important person aboard. He lay face-down in the Perspex nose, exposing the length of his body to the flak bursting all around. Pressing his face to the lens of the complicated bomb-sight, he called course corrections to the pilot as they went into the

Plotting a course.

final run, ordered the bomb doors open and, when he was satisfied, pressed the button that sent the bombs tumbling into the night. In those final moments, every man aboard was clenched in expectation, pleading with him to finish the job and let them head for home. Good bomb-aimers possessed an almost inhuman sangfroid which allowed them to divorce all feelings for their own safety and that of the crew from the necessity of getting their bombs on the target, or the colour-coded pyrotechnic markers dropped by the leading aircraft to highlight the aiming point. On his debut trip with 49 Squadron to Hagen, in the eastern Ruhr, Donald Falgate, who had defied his parents' wishes to join up, was 'determined I was going to get my bombs slap-bang on the target and there was no way I was going to release them if I couldn't get the markers in the bombsight.'

The pilot tried to weave to avoid the bursting flak as they went in, toppling the gyroscope that kept the bombsight level, making it impossible for Falgate to aim accurately. He ordered the bomb doors closed and insisted on going round again. 'I won't repeat what was said over the intercom by various crew members,' he said when telling the story later. It was only on the third run that Falgate was satisfied and pressed the bomb release. 'I was unpopular, very unpopular,' he recalled many years afterwards.[16]

The complexities of four-engined bombers created a need for an extra crew member to assist the pilot. Many flight engineers were ex-groundcrew airmen who already had mechanical skills. Their training included a spell at an aircraft factory producing the type of bomber they would fly in to ensure that they were fluent in all the systems of the huge new machines. In a Lancaster they sat next to, and slightly behind the captain. Their duties included monitoring the panels of dials and warning lights, one for each engine, which were situated on the side of the fuselage out of the pilot's line of sight. This left him to concentrate on his flying instruments. Their most important responsibility was nursing the fuel levels to ensure there was enough petrol to get home. Engineers received elementary flying training and could theoretically fly the aircraft in an emergency. In practice, if the pilot was dead or too badly hurt to function, the engineer was likely to be in a similar condition.

The wireless operator had, according to Bruce Lewis, who served as one, 'a lonely existence, mentally isolated from other members of the crew for long periods of time while he strained to listen through the static in his headphones for faint but vital signals.' These told him the aircraft's position which he passed on to the navigator. He also manned the radar monitor which warned of the approach of night-fighters.

The gunners had what appeared to be the worst job of all. They lived in metal and Perspex turrets that poked out of the top and the back of the aircraft, washed by whistling winds that could freeze them to their guns. They carried the huge responsibility of defending their mates, constantly scanning the night for flak and fighters. Yet the long hours of staring into darkness meant it was all too easy to lose concentration, even fall asleep. If a night-fighter was spotted a decision that could mean the difference between life or death had to be made. You had seen him, but had he seen you? There was one sure way of ensuring he had, which was to pour glowing tracer fire in his direction. If you got it wrong, your end was particularly lurid. Everyone had a story of seeing the rear gunner being hosed out of a shot-up bomber that had hobbled back to base.

Yet some chose the job. It was the quickest way to an operational squadron with the actual gunnery course taking only six weeks. The training, though, was thorough. By the end, many could manipulate the turrets so well they could trace their names on a board with a pencil wedged in a gun barrel. Cyril March had seen an RAF recruiting poster in the window of Stanton's furniture store in his native Durham appealing for Tail End Charlies and 'decided there and then that I would become an air gunner, none of the other trades appealing to me.' For all the privations and dangers of the job it was possible to get used to it or even enjoy it. 'In the end you learned to love it, strangely to say,' said Peter Twinn, who had abandoned a safe job in a reserved occupation to join up. 'You were the king of your own castle, right back there on your own. You never spoke to anybody unless the pilot gave you orders, so there you were sixty feet from the rest of the crew, all together at the front of the aircraft. They could see each other, they were near each other and they had that bond of being together. But the rear gunner, no, he was right out on a limb, down the other end looking the other way. Many of the raids lasted seven, eight, eight and a half hours . . . you never left your turret at all. It was lonely but you got used to it. And you were there for the crew's protection and they were a lovely crew.'[17]

After finishing their specialist training pilots, navigators and bomb-aimers had a further spell at an advanced school before finally arriving at an OTU. Wireless operators and gunners went there directly.

At the OTUs the British came together with their Australian and New Zealand counterparts from the Empire schools (the Canadians formed their own, separate group of squadrons). It was here that one of the most crucial processes in the training programme took place, the welding of individuals into crews. For each member, the crew would from now on be the centre of his existence. Life beyond the base, the world of parents and family and home, drifted to the margins of their thoughts. The six men you would share your bomber with were now the most important people in the world.

The process of selection was called 'crewing up'. In devising it the RAF departed from its strictly utilitarian selection and training methods and took an enormous leap of faith. Instead of attempting a scientific approach to gauge compatibility they put their trust entirely in the magic of human chemistry. The crews selected themselves. The procedure was simple. The requisite numbers of each aircrew category were put together in a large room and told to team up. Jack Currie, who reached his OTU at the end of 1942, 'hadn't realized that the crewing-up procedure would be so haphazard, so unorganized. I'd imagined that the process would be just as impersonal as most others that we went through in the RAF. I thought I would just see an order on the noticeboard detailing who was crewed with whom. But what happened was quite different. When we had all paraded in the hangar and the roll had been called, the chief ground instructor got up on a dais. He wished us good morning . . . and said: "Right chaps, sort yourselves out."'

Currie stood among the other sergeant pilots and, trying not to stare at anyone in particular, looked around him. 'There were bomb-aimers, navigators, wireless operators and gunners and I needed one of each to form my crew. I didn't know any of them; up to now my air force would have been peopled by pilots. This was a crowd of strangers. I had a sudden recollection of standing in a surburban dance-hall, wondering which girl I should approach. I remembered that it wasn't always the prettiest or the smartest girl who made the best companion for the evening. Anyway, this wasn't the same as choosing a dancing partner, it was more like picking out a sweetheart or a wife, for better or for worse.'

Like most pilots, the first thing Currie looked for was a navigator. He saw a knot of them standing together. But how was he to pick one?

> I couldn't assess what his aptitude with a map and dividers might be from his face, or his skill with a sextant from the size of his feet. I noticed that a wiry little Austra-

lian was looking at me anxiously. He took a few steps forward, eyes puckered in a diffident smile and spoke: 'Looking for a good navigator?' I walked to meet him. He was an officer. I looked down into his eyes, and received an impression of honesty, intelligence and nervousness. He said:

'You needn't worry. I did all right on the course!'

I held out my hand. 'Jack Currie.'

'I'm Jim Cassidy. Have you got a bomb-aimer? I know a real good one. He comes from Brisbane, like me. I'll fetch him over.'

The bomb-aimer had a gunner in tow and while we were sizing each other up, we were joined by a tall wireless-operator, who introduced himself in a gentle Northumbrian accent and suggested that it was time for a cup of tea. As we walked to the canteen, I realized that I hadn't made a single conscious choice.[18]

At some OTUs new arrivals were given up to a fortnight to team up. Harry Yates, having got over his disappointment at not being posted to a fighter squadron, arrived at Westcott with the ambition to 'skipper a well-drilled crew, the best on the squadron, every man handpicked, utterly professional at his job and dedicated to the team.' He started his search in the officers' mess where he found himself at the bar next to Pilot Officer Bill Birnie, a stocky New Zealander navigator who 'seemed to be the sort of tough-minded chap who knew the score'. During the evening's socializing he noticed a young pilot officer wearing a wireless operator's badge. For a wireless operator to be commissioned so early in his career suggested exceptional ability. So Rob Bailey, 'tall, slim and blessed with the dark, aquiline looks that women tend to admire', was in.

The following day the 220 men of the intake assembled in a hangar to finish off the process. They were mostly formed into twos and threes now and there was 'a lot of movement and noise', as they scrambled to complete their teams. Bill Birnie disappeared into the crowd and returned 'with a bronze-skinned giant in tow. This was Flight Sergeant Inia Maaka, the first Maori I'd ever met and I knew the bomb-aimer for me.' Mac, as he immediately became known, 'was a stranger to the inner tensions and vanities that make liars of the rest of us'. He had wanted to fight the war as a pilot and had won a place at elementary flying school but had not been selected to advance and been reassigned to bombing school. 'He clearly loved the job,' Yates recorded, 'there wasn't a hint of second best.' It was Mac who found the gunners: Geoff Fallowfield, an extrovert eighteen-year-old Londoner and Norrie Close, a taciturn Yorkshireman, who was a month younger still. 'So there they were,' Yates marvelled later, 'my crew: a straight and level Kiwi, a ladykiller; a Maori warrior; and two lads as different as chalk from cheese.'[19]

Such assorted crews were the norm. The mysterious chemistry that had brought them together was durable. Many crews forged bonds of affection and respect that, if they came through the war, lasted until the grave. It was rare for an Englishman to have met a Canadian or an Australian, yet when crewing up they seemed drawn to each other, confirming the wisdom of the process. Group Captain Hamish Mahaddie, who was tasked with finding talent for the Pathfinder Force, which was formed to lead the main bomber force to the target, believed that 'the best crews were a mixture'.[20]

The system was not perfect. At Bruntingthorpe OTU Cyril March teamed up with an Australian skipper, navigator and wireless operator. The rest of the crew were English. 'We did our job and had one or two good thrashes but we were never all together and to my mind we didn't gel.' Their first training trip was a fighter affiliation exercise in which the pilot was expected to throw the Wellington around the sky to shake off the 'attacker'. After a row with the navigator, he appeared to lose control and ordered the crew to crash positions. The bomber landed but overshot the runway coming to a halt in the grass. The next trip took place in clear sunshine but the captain still managed to lose his way. March 'felt so bloody helpless. I was doing my job, telling them when we were passing over airfields and such. I couldn't help thinking [what] if this were Germany on a black night with duff winds etcetera – Christ!' Word of the crew's failings reached the station authorities. It was split up and its members redistributed. This time March was lucky. The first of his new comrades was Ken Ford, a Londoner, who with the rest of the crew, became his lifelong friends.

> Ken took me to meet my new skipper, a tousle-haired fair Aussie with steady blue eyes and a friendly grin. 'I'm Neville Emery,' he said, 'Bug to my mates.' I had noticed he had been eyeing me up and down and asked him why. 'Oh nothing mate,' he said laughing. 'Kenny was telling me that you were an old married man.' I was just twenty-one. I met Des Gee the Aussie wireless operator, again blond and blue-eyed; then Ray Brooker, a dark Englishman from Cambridge, the bomb-aimer with a ready smile. Then I met Terry Sayles, a Yorkshireman from Doncaster, the navigator. I told him my name was Cyril. 'Hi Cy,' he said and that was my name thenceforth. Des got me a bed in their Nissen hut and helped me move my gear in. That night they weren't flying and they said, 'Coming down the village for a jar?' 'Sure,' I said.
>
> 'Where's your bike, Cy?' Terry asked. 'Bike!' I replied, 'I haven't got one.' He got one, I don't know where and I didn't ask. Off we went in formation. I knew I was in a crew at long last.

They came back in high spirits, yelling 'Bring out your dead' as they wobbled on their bikes over rickety planks bridging the Leicestershire ditches. Cyril was happy and content. 'I knew then that with these lads we would survive, no doubt about it.'

This, in the end, was what the airmen were searching for as they milled around the hangars looking for kindred spirits. An efficient air, a friendly manner were all very well. But in the end, the most attractive quality anyone could possess was to seem lucky.

Inevitably, when the mating ritual finished, a gaggle of wallflowers remained. 'At the end of the day there were some odd bods left around who . . . had no choice but to take the leftovers,' said Tom Wingham, who flew with 102 Squadron. '[You] had a feeling that they weren't going to make it and inevitably they didn't. They didn't have that same sort of "gel". I suppose you could say they had the smell of death about them and it was not funny.'[21]

The men that would lead them through the final stage of training and into the daunting world of 'ops' seemed old, even though many were only in their mid-twenties. These were the veterans, 'tour-expired' survivors of thirty operations or more. 'It was our first close contact with people who had completed operations, surviving against unlikely odds,' wrote Dennis Field. 'Gongs were common, almost part of the dress, and worn without flamboyance. Although we were keen to hear and learn all we could, in off-duty hours they stayed detached and there was little line-shooting in our presence. We realized that within a few months we should all meet some ultimate experience.'

Instructing posts were the reward for survival. Not that such jobs were free of risk. Half of the flying done at OTUs was at night. The darkness, and the sometimes clapped-out machines which were used for training meant that deadly accidents were routine. After agreeing to fly with one captain, Dennis Steiner was approached by two other pilots whom he had to turn down. Subsequently, one flew into the ground for no discoverable reason, killing himself and all his crew. The other developed engine trouble during a flight and ordered the crew to bale out. 'Their luck ran out soon after when at night a practice bomb from another aircraft fell on them and they crashed,' he wrote. 'None of the crew survived. The line between surviving or not was becoming very thin.'

It seemed to Ken Newman that at least some of the accidents were due to criminal recklessness rather than the demands of war. In February 1944 he went to a Heavy Conversion Unit for a month's training. This was where crews familiarized themselves with the types that they would be flying on operations. Newman was learning his way around the Halifax. 'The aircraft were old, poorly maintained and in the most part barely airworthy. But it was constantly drilled into us that complaints would not be entertained and if we refused to fly because we thought a Halifax was not airworthy, or for a reason that the staff decided was trivial, we would be treated as LMF [Lacking in Moral Fibre, the RAF bureaucratic euphemism for the accusation of cowardice].' This was very much the view of the chief flying instructor who Newman held responsible for the death of one of his best friends and all his crew.

He had met Alec, 'a tall, likeable chap' while training in South Africa and caught up with him at RAF Lindholme where the HCU was based. One night he was detailed for a high-level cross-country flight, even though the weather forecast had warned of heavy cloud and severe icing conditions. To reduce the risk, it was essential to fly at maximum altitude. 'Alec took off and after a while found that his aircraft would not climb above 15,000 feet. Consequently he returned to RAF Lindholme. Wing Commander X heard about this and ordered Alec to continue the exercise, refusing to believe that the aircraft could not reach a safe height and accused him of being LMF. Intimidated, Alec and his crew went off. The following day we heard that his aircraft had crashed into a Scottish mountain and all were dead.' The instructor was to die in an accident a few months later.[22]

The road to the operational squadrons was long and expensive. It cost on average £10,000 to train each crew member, the equivalent, according to one indicator, of about £850,000 in today's money. This was a lot to pay to get each Bomber Boy into battle. It did not, however, mean that when they got there, their lives would be worth very much.

Dying in the Dark

Bomber Command lost 4,823 men and 2,331 aircraft on operations in the first two years of the war. There was very little to show for it. In that time it dropped only 35,194 tons of bombs. That was two thousand tons *less* than it dropped in the single month of May, 1944. Despite the great effort, the resulting destruction was often small and the casualties inflicted were minimal. A typical night's work was that of 29/30 August 1941. More than 140 aircraft were sent to attack railways and harbours in Frankfurt. They reached their target successfully and began bombing. They managed to do some damage to a gasworks, a barrel warehouse and a few houses and to kill eight people. In the course of the operation one Hampden was lost without trace. Another crashed in France killing all on board. A Halifax crew baled out over England after running out of fuel but two men died in the process, one after his parachute got caught in the tailplane. A Whitley was forced to ditch off the Essex coast. All in all, the operation resulted in the loss of sixteen lives – two for every German killed – and seven aircraft. Despite the sacrifice, the attack barely bothered the Frankfurt authorities who nonchalantly recorded the raid as 'light and scattered bombing'.

The perils of each trip mounted as the German fighter and flak defences adapted and improved. In March 1941, Doug Mourton arrived at 102 Squadron to fly as a wireless operator on Whitleys. One night his crew were detailed to attack Hamburg. Initially, it seemed 'a comparatively easy trip'. They took off in bright moonlight and as the target approached Mourton could see another Whitley flying a parallel course. 'Suddenly it exploded. What had been an aircraft a few seconds before, was now a mass of debris, flying through the air. It had apparently been hit by an anti-aircraft shell, most likely in its bomb bay . . .' He learned later that the pilot had been Alec Elliot, his best friend on the squadron with whom he had passed many nights in the pub and played innumerable games of crib while waiting in the crew room.[1]

After enduring such experiences the crews were reluctant to believe that their efforts were being wasted. To be able to carry on it was necessary to persuade oneself that the risks were worth it. From the air it was impossible to know whether or not a raid had succeeded. The sight of big fires burning below was taken as a measure of success. But they could not know what these blazes were. The Germans soon suspected that the attacking aircraft had often only the haziest idea of their whereabouts. They developed a system of decoy fires which they hoped the arriving aircraft would mistake for the target. It worked very well. Many a crew returned home satisfied they had carried out their mission after bombing empty countryside.

A different sort of deception was being perpetrated on the home front. Government propaganda painted a picture of continuous success. A broadcast by Flight Lieutenant J. C. Mackintosh, a bomb-aimer in a Hampden, made night bombing sound like a cool, precise science. His script started with the bold assertion that 'when the war began we were well-trained in finding targets in the dark and were therefore never compelled to bomb indiscriminately through the clouds.' He went on to describe a recent attack on an oil refinery. At first, the crew thought it a tricky target. But the fact that it was sited near a bend on a river which would provide a useful navigational reference caused them to decide that 'perhaps, after all, it would not be such a difficult job to find.' As they entered the target area they located the river but after three runs through anti-aircraft fire had still not spotted the objective. Mackintosh gamely called on the skipper to go round once more. Then, 'there it was. The dim outline of an oil refinery wonderfully camouflaged. It was getting more and more into the centre of the sights. I pressed the button and my stick of bombs went hurtling towards Germany's precious oil. The rear gunner watched the bombs burst and in a very few seconds those thousands of tons of valuable oil had become hundreds of feet of black and acrid smoke.'[2]

Whitley.

This was strategic bombing as dreamt of by the Air Ministry planners. But it was rare indeed that events followed Mackintosh's script. A more typical experience was that of Eric Woods, who had joined the RAF before the war as a reservist and qualified as a navigator before being sent to 144 Squadron. His first operation was on the night of 9/10 October 1940 and the target was the Krupp factory in Essen, one of the first of many that would be launched against this citadel of German military industry. At the briefing the crews were told they could expect only scattered cloud over the target. But 'from the outset it was obvious that the Met people had got it wrong as a solid mass of cloud was clearly visible below and as we progressed eastwards we saw that the cloud was becoming denser ahead. We pressed on but two ominous developments took place: a film of ice appeared on the windscreen and an opaque mass of rime ice began to spread out along the leading edge of each wing.' His Hampden's twin engines started to run rough as ice found its way into the fuel inlet system. 'There was a hurried conference since it was pretty obvious that the target was unlikely to be identifiable, so the decision was taken to fly on and see what happened when we reached our ETA (Estimated Time of Arrival). In the event at that time we were still in dense cloud, the whole mass being lit up by searchlights sweeping below, with frequent bright flashes which could have been anti-aircraft fire or bomb bursts, I certainly knew not what.' With no sight of the ground and dreadful weather conditions a decision was made not to bomb but to seek some alternative target on the way home. As they headed homewards 'the cloud began to break up to the west, quite the opposite to what the weatherman had said . . . we did in fact fly along the Scheldt estuary and as we passed over the port of Flushing the navigator let go with our total load and I clearly saw bomb bursts though I wasn't sure precisely where they landed.'³ Only three of the aircraft that set out reached their target.

The basic problem remained navigation. There was no accurate means of directing the bombers to faraway targets and none would arrive until March 1942. In the meantime, navigators relied on dead reckoning and the main instrumental aid was the sextant. This was still the pioneer age of bombing. 'The aircraft were without heating and the cold was appalling,' wrote Doug Mourton later. 'The crews flew clothed in layers of silk, wool and leather and yet they were still bitterly cold. Vital systems jammed, wings iced up for lack of adequate de-icing gear [and] guns froze . . .' The navigator gave his pilot a course on take-off and then, if he was lucky and the skies were clear, looked out for landmarks to check if they were on track. When visiting Germany they left England's shores over Flamborough Head then scoured the sea below for the Friesian Islands off the Dutch coast, where German night-fighters lurked, straining to get at the raiders. If the conditions were right, the navigator might use his sextant to obtain a fix from the stars, but only if the pilot was willing to fly straight and level long enough. The crews were given a weather forecast before leaving, but they were notoriously unreliable. Predicted winds failed to blow and unpredicted ones drove the bombers hopelessly off course. It was no wonder that German targets were sometimes unaware that they had been the subject of an attempted attack.

The gap between what was expected of the RAF and what it could in fact deliver was enormous. The man whose task it was to narrow it was Charles Portal, appointed to the top air force post of Chief of the Air Staff (CAS) in October 1940 at the young age of forty-seven. The promotion came after a brief, six-month stint as the Commander-in-Chief of Bomber Command. He was to stay in his post for the rest of the war. Portal was short and stocky, with a lean, creased face, hooded eyes and a large, hooked nose which gave him the look of one of the falcons he had reared when a schoolboy at Winchester. He was at Christ Church, Oxford, when the war broke out in 1914, and immediately suspended his studies to go to France as a motorcyclist with the Royal Engineers. In 1915 he joined the Royal Flying Corps and finished the war as a lieutenant-colonel. His intellectual gifts and boundless capacity for work ensured that his subsequent climb was sure and fast. His character and demeanour contrasted sharply with that of Arthur Harris. He hid his feelings behind a mask of scrupulous courtesy and expressed himself quietly and subtly. Whereas Harris was capable of rough bonhomie, Portal never unbent. Those around him noticed that beyond his family he had no close friends, gently repelling company when he dined at the Travellers' Club at the end of his long working day.

Portal's part in the policy of attacking whole cities, 'area bombing' in the bureaucratic euphemism of the day, is little known or remembered nowadays, while Harris's name will be linked to it for ever. But his enthusiasm for the project was, at the outset at least, just as great as that of his subordinate and he was prepared to express himself forcefully in support of it even when Churchill's faith faltered.

As head of Bomber Command at the start of the Blitz he sympathized with the public desire for revenge and had joined Churchill in urging reprisals on a reluctant Air Staff. On arriving at the top, he stressed the need to destroy the resolve of the German people by smashing their towns and cities. The rhythms of Bomber Command's activities would vary from time to time as it was diverted to deal with various threats and crises. But, until the run-up to D-Day, this was to be the central theme of the air war.

In successive directives Portal continued to point his men towards industrial and military targets. But great emphasis was given to the will-sapping potential that he claimed would result. On 30 October

1940, as London prepared to endure its 53rd night of continuous bombardment, he wrote to Sir Richard Peirse who had replaced him as C-in-C, Bomber Command, that

> the time seems particularly opportune to make a definite attempt with our offensive to affect the morale of the German people when they can no longer expect an early victory and are faced with the near approach of winter and the certainty of a long war ... if bombing is to have its full moral effect, it must on occasions produce heavy material destruction. Widespread light attacks are more likely to produce contempt for bombing than fear of it. I am therefore directed to say that as an alternative to attacks designed for material destruction against our primary objectives, it is desired that regular concentrated attacks shall be made on objectives in large towns and centres of industry with the prime aim of causing heavy material destruction, which will demonstrate to the enemy the power and severity of air bombardment and the hardship and dislocation that will result from it.

Berlin was put first on the list for Bomber Command's attentions. If it was clouded over, other towns in central and western Germany were to be considered. Aircraft industry and oil targets might also be selected, as long as they were 'suitably placed in the centres of the towns or populated districts'. The directive envisaged sending greater numbers of aircraft, carrying a mix of bombs. The first to arrive would drop incendiaries to set the target area ablaze. The following force would then 'focus their attacks to a large extent on the fires with a view to preventing the fire-fighting services dealing with them and giving the fires every opportunity to spread.'[4] This amounted to an explicit announcement that the strategic aim now was to achieve blanket destruction, disruption and death.

In reality, Bomber Command lacked the resources to carry out such an apocalyptic plan. Even if it had the aircraft and equipment, it would never be able to mount a concentrated and relentless campaign while it was subject to the apparently insatiable calls on its services from the War Cabinet, navy and army.

On top of the strategic targets, oil and now cities, Bomber Command was supposed to support the navy by laying mines at sea. In March 1941 another great responsibility was loaded on to its shoulders. German submarines and bombers were wreaking terrible damage on the transatlantic convoys carrying the cargoes that kept Britain alive and threatening to sever Britain's vital ocean links with America. Churchill ordered Portal to concentrate on attacking the yards that built the U-boats and the pens where they sheltered, as well as the factories and bases which produced and housed the maritime bombers. Bomber Command did its best against these targets, and the great German warships *Gneisenau* and *Scharnhorst* in their haven at Brest, but the effects were limited. Its aircraft were withdrawn after four months and it was left to Coastal Command and the Royal Navy, aided by improvements in technology and resources, to turn the Battle of the Atlantic Britain's way.

The diversion deflected Peirse from his intention to use the improved conditions of spring to systematically pursue oil targets. The 'oil plan' had many powerful supporters inside the Air Staff and among civilian specialist strategic advisers. They saw the destruction of synthetic oil plants, which transformed Germany's rich coal reserves into liquid fuels and lubricants, as a quick way of bringing the enemy to its knees. The plan would swing in and out of favour throughout the war. But the prescription was easier than the practice. Despite the claims of official propaganda, when oil targets were attacked, the results were often miserable. The plants were sited away from the big towns and were hard to find and even harder to destroy or damage. If the bombers missed them, as they usually did, their bombs hit nothing but fields and forests. The new practice of using high-flying Spitfires for photo reconnaissance the morning after a raid allowed an operation's success to be assessed scientifically rather than relying on the visual reports and blurry night-time images submitted by the crews from onboard cameras. In the absence of hard evidence, optimism about the progress of the campaign had remained high in the upper reaches of the RAF.

The daylight pictures showed it to be misplaced. No assumptions could be made about bombing accuracy. The truth, according to Sir John Slessor, who had taken over 5 Group of Bomber Command in May 1941, was that the crews were 'failing to find and hit any but the most obvious targets on the clearest moonlight nights'.[5]

It became clear to Portal that, as things stood, the only target that Bomber Command could be guaranteed to find was a largish town. The attacks on London, Coventry, Southampton, Plymouth and elsewhere had provided more than enough justification for retaliating in kind. Britain had suffered an unprecedented loss of innocent life. By the time the Blitz petered out in May 1941, more than 41,000 civilians had been killed and 137,000 injured. Such a policy, Portal now believed, was not simply *faute de mieux*, but a logical and desirable course of action.

The new, or rather resumed, thinking was spelled out in another Portal directive to Bomber Command dated 9 July 1941. It stated that a comprehensive review of Germany's political, economic and military situation disclosed that one of 'the weakest points in his armour' lay in the morale of the civilian population. It called for 'heavy, concentrated and continuous area attacks of large working-class and industrial areas in carefully selected towns'. At the end of August the formula was extended to smaller towns so that they too could experience 'the direct effect of our offensive'.[6]

This marked another important step in the shift from scrupulousness to ruthlessness. Before the war the British government had assured the world it had no intention of bombing civilians. Now the RAF had been nudged on to a heading which made the mass killing of civilians inevitable. The faith that was put in the belief that this would produce beneficial results by undermining the Germans' will to fight on was puzzling. Nothing that had happened in the war to date supported Trenchard's dictum that the moral effect of bombing was twenty times greater than the material effect. If anything, the experience of Coventry, London and other blitzed towns like Plymouth and Liverpool, suggested the opposite. Yet in the absence of any immediate alternative, what was an ill-founded opinion began to take on the solidity of an iron law of war.

Trenchard was an old man now but he was still regarded with reverence by the military establishment and his views were treated with respect. In May 1941 he sent a memorandum on the current state of the air war to the Chiefs of Staff. He reduced the complexities of the problems facing the RAF to one simple proposition. It was, he reiterated, all a question of national morale and who could stand their losses best. There was no doubt about the answer. For Trenchard, the 'outstanding fact' of the current situation was 'the ingrained morale of the British nation which is nowhere more strongly manifest than in its ability to stand up to losses and its power to bear the whole strain of war and its casualties.' History had proved 'that we have always been able to stand our casualties better than other Nations.' As for the enemy, 'all the evidence of the last war and of this, shows that the German nation is peculiarly susceptible to air bombing. While the A.R.P. services are probably organized with typical German efficiency, their total disregard to the well-being of the population tends to a dislocation of ordinary life which has its inevitable reaction on civilian morale. The ordinary people are neither allowed, nor offer, to play their part in rescue or restoration work; virtually imprisoned in their shelters or within the bombed area, they remain passive and easy prey to hysteria and panic without anything to mitigate the inevitable confusion and chaos. There is no joking in the German shelters as in ours, nor the bond which unites the public with A.R.P. and Military services here of all working together in a common cause to defeat the attacks of the enemy.' This, he concluded 'is their weak point compared with ourselves and it is at this weak point that we should strike and strike again.' Such a policy would mean 'fairly heavy casualties' for those doing the bombing, but Trenchard had faith in their toughness. In his judgement, 'the pilots in the last war stood it, and the pilots in this war are even better and, I feel, would welcome a policy of this description.'[7]

Where Trenchard got his information from was a mystery. At least one pilot had a very different appreciation of the morale question. In the early winter of 1942 when Bomber Command was beginning to bring the war to the German people Guy Gibson was still unconvinced that domestic morale would collapse. 'We are dealing with the mass pyschology of a nation and a bad nation at that,' he told Charles Martin, the adjutant of 106 Squadron. 'It is run, organized and controlled by Gestapo and SS Police . . . the fact still remains that if they were to give in they would have everything to lose and nothing to gain. I think myself they will fight to the end.' Gibson had little time for 'people who go around talking so much bull about the crack appearing and once the crack has appeared the foundation will weaken etc., etc.'[8]

Most people who were running the war agreed with Trenchard. It would have seemed defeatist to say otherwise. Identifying morale as the main target also provided some hope of progress at a time when there was little to show that Bomber Command was achieving anything. Any scrap of evidence was seized on as proof of the wisdom of this course. In September 1941 the American correspondent William Shirer who knew Nazi Germany well, wrote a piece in the *Daily Telegraph* saying that attacking war industries was not enough. 'What [the RAF] must do is to keep the German people in their damp, cold cellars at night, prevent them from sleeping and wear down their nerves. Those nerves are already very thin after seven years of belt-tightening Nazi mobilization for total war. The British should do this every night.' The cutting was reverently placed in an Air Ministry file. The Ministry of Information maintained its own survey. It had concluded as early as December 1940 that 'the Germans, for all their present confidence and cockiness will not stand a quarter of the bombing that the British have shown they can take.'

In the middle of 1941 support for the bombing offensive was sustained by faith rather than evidence, but the absence of a rational foundation for belief meant only that the flame of conviction burned all the brighter. It was not only Portal and the Air Staff who believed. The heads of the navy and the army became fervent converts. At the end of July 1941 they had produced a statement on general British strategy in which they declared their support for Bomber Command's mission and admitted they were relying on an all-out attack by the RAF to create the conditions for a land invasion and victory. Inter-service jealousy over resources, hitherto a genetic condition, was forgotten as the air force was offered everything it wanted.

They approved the building of heavy bombers as a first priority 'for only the heavy bomber can produce the conditions under which other offensive force can be employed.' They endorsed the view that the focus of attack should be 'on civilian morale with the intensity and continuity which are essential if a final breakdown is to be produced.' If the plan was pursued 'on a vast scale, the whole structure upon which the German forces are based, the economic system, the machinery for production and destruction, the morale of the nation will be destroyed.' This was just the 'bull about the crack appearing' that Gibson had found so unconvincing.

Soon afterwards an attempt was made to translate what were instinctive suppositions into hard formulae. In September 1941 the Directorate of Bomber Operations at the Air Ministry began working on a new plan. In an important departure from previous practice it was based not on what Bomber Command might do, but on what the Luftwaffe had already done. By analysing the damage caused by German air attacks on London, Coventry, and other English towns, the planners came up with a yardstick of what was needed to mount an all-out offensive on German towns.

They used an 'index of activity' to gauge the effects of bombing on a town's ability to function. Coventry, it was reckoned, had suffered a 63 per cent reduction in its index of activity the morning after the raid. The calculation included not just physical destruction but also psychological damage; fear and demoralization. It had taken Coventry thirty-five days to recover. Four or five follow-up attacks on the same scale, it was reckoned, would have crippled the city's ability to operate. A sixth raid would have put it 'beyond all hope of recovery'.

Using the same encouraging extrapolations that were always employed with such calculations, it concluded that if 4,000 bombers were directed against forty-three towns with populations of 100,000 or more, Germany would be finished. At the time, the average daily availability of bombers was just over 500. Portal approved the plan and passed it on to the prime minister promising 'decisive results' in six months if he was given the aircraft required.

But Churchill's initial enthusiasm was faltering. A minute study of reconnaissance photographs ordered by Churchill's scientific adviser Lord Cherwell had revealed in undeniable detail the blindness of the bombing effort. The work was carried out by D. R. Butt, a civil servant with the Cabinet secretariat. His job was to analyse photographs taken on one hundred night attacks during June and July 1941. The results, published in August 1941, were dismaying. The essential finding was that of those crews claiming to have attacked a target in Germany, only one in four got within five miles of it. Over the Ruhr the proportion was one in ten. The statistics related only to aircraft recorded as attacking the target. One third of the crews failed to get within five miles of it.

These figures, if true, were shocking and at Bomber Command, Sir Richard Peirse and his senior officers tried to dispute them. Churchill, however, had been persuaded. He was in no mood then, to give a positive reception to another plan based on the unverifiable. His view was summed up in a pessimistic minute of 27 September that contradicted everything he had previously said as prime minister on the subject of bombing. 'It is very disputable whether bombing by itself will be a decisive factor in the present war. On the contrary, all that we have learnt since the war shows that its effects, both physical and moral, are greatly exaggerated.'

These words caused great anxiety to Portal and his men. Churchill appeared to be saying that he had no confidence in their approach to the air war. Portal took several days thinking about his response. His reply, when it came, was robust. He told the prime minister that it was too soon to come to such a definite conclusion as a serious bombing campaign had yet to begin. It was difficult to believe that any country could withstand indefinitely the scale of attack contemplated in the new plan. German air raids in the previous year caused death or serious injury to 93,000 British civilians. This result had been achieved with a small fraction of the bomb load Bomber Command hoped to employ in 1943. He repeated what had now become an article of faith. 'The consensus of informed opinion,' he declared, 'is that German morale is much more vulnerable to bombing than our own.'

Portal was calling Churchill's bluff. The prime minister's doubts had come very late in the day. The whole bomber programme, aircraft production, aircrew training and technical developments were based on the understanding articulated by the Chiefs of Staff back on 31 July that bombing on an unprecedented scale was the weapon Britain had to depend on to bring victory. He pointed out that if Churchill had 'ceased to believe in the efficacy of the bomber as a war-winning weapon' then a new plan would have to be produced. This would mean a complete reshaping of the RAF's main effort and remove it from the battlefield for many months to come. Britain would be denied its only means of waging war on the enemy's own territory.

Churchill had no real choice but to back down and he did so, but not before sounding a sour cautionary note. 'I deprecate,' he wrote on 7 October, 'placing unbounded confidence in this means of attack and still more in expressing that confidence in terms of arithmetic.' In the end, he concluded, 'the only plan is to persevere'.

This period marked the lowest point in Bomber Command's war, a demoralizing period of costly experimentation. In its short life, aerial warfare had gained enormous importance in the minds of politicians, soldiers and the public. But no one yet understood exactly what it was for. Defending the failures of the early years Slessor reminded a post-war audience that 'this was the first air war (his emphasis.) . . . we had embarked upon it, not only with totally inadequate weapons and woefully incomplete intelligence about our enemy but with vitually no experience whatever to guide us.'[9] Operations had never achieved a consistent tempo as the emphasis shifted from target to target and even, as the Battle of the Atlantic broke out, from land to sea with squadrons being transferred temporarily or permanently to Coastal Command. Throughout the year preconceived expansion plans had to give way to the constant diversion of aircraft and crew to other theatres.

During 1941, 1,341 aircraft were lost on operations, meaning that the average first-line strength had been destroyed roughly two and a half times over. These great sacrifices failed to make any significant impression on Germany. The ports of Hamburg, Kiel and Bremen had suffered some damage, but the Ruhr, the heart of Germany's war industry, remained almost completely intact. Bomber Command's main achievement had been to give heart to the Blitz-battered British people. As it did so, its own morale was beginning to fray. In 106 Squadron, where Michael Wood was piloting a Hampden, 'there was a story going around that the accounts related by one of our crews were suspect and did not tie up with the accounts of the target area put forward by the rest of the squadron. The CO became suspicious and arranged to plot the course of the aircraft in question. From the information gathered, it transpired that the aircraft was flying up and down the North Sea dropping their bombs in the drink and, after the necessary time lapse, flying back to base.' Wood never verified the story. But the fact that it was doing the rounds was indicative of the low mood.

One pilot from 144 Squadron was court-martialled for a similar-sounding incident. Sergeant W, a married man with two young children who had been a grocer in civilian life before joining the RAF in 1938, was accused of 'failing to use his utmost exertions' to carry out orders. He had been detailed to attack Frankfurt on the night of 22/23 July 1941. On his return, he reported that the mission had been successful. A few days later, the navigator on the trip informed a senior officer that they had never reached Germany at all. The pilot maintained that the navigator, who had been borrowed for the operation, was incompetent and had failed to provide the correct headings to reach the target, resulting in them flying around the North Sea for nearly seven hours. The navigator maintained that the skipper was 'windy' and had never intended to carry out the attack. Sergeant W was backed up by three other members of his crew. He was an experienced pilot who had spent seven months on the squadron and whose conduct had until then satisfied his CO. Had he reported the failure to complete the mission it was unlikely that matters would have developed as drastically as they did. As it was, he told the court-martial, 'after landing and thinking back over the trip, I decided to say nothing about getting lost. In consequence the personal experience report was made out as for a successful trip.' The worst interpretation was put on his actions. He was found guilty and sentenced to be reduced to the ranks, imprisoned with hard labour for two years and discharged with ignominy from the service. The sentence was cut to six months on appeal.[10]

For all the institutional belief in British resilience, no one in authority was going to tell anyone, civilian or airman, how little the campaign was really achieving. 'Fortunately,' wrote Slessor, ' I think the crews were for the most part sustained by the belief that they were hitting the enemy harder than they actually were.'[11]

The futility of the effort was starkly revealed on the night of 7/8 November. The weather forecast was abysmal, with thick cloud, storms, ice and hail predicted. Sir Richard Peirse nonetheless ordered 392 aircraft, a record number, into attacks on Berlin, Cologne and Mannheim, as well as smaller operations against Boulogne and Ostend. The weather was particularly atrocious along the North Sea routes leading to Berlin. Of the 169 bombers sent to Berlin, less than half got anywhere near it. Those that did, barely scratched the city. The official survey reported damage to one industrial building, two railway premises, a gasometer, two administrative buildings, thirty houses (fourteen of which were destroyed), sixteen garden sheds and one farm building. Eleven people were killed and fourteen injured. Bomber Command however lost twenty-one aircraft, 12.4 per cent of those dispatched. Eighty-eight airmen died; eight for every German killed by their bombs. All together thirty-seven aircraft were lost, 9.7 per cent of the force. This loss was double what had been suffered in any previous night operation. Peirse had gone ahead despite protests, notably from Slessor who had been allowed to withdraw his 5 Group aircraft from the force and send them instead to Cologne. His refusal to cancel the operation seems to have been driven by a desperate desire to achieve results when faith in his leadership was dwindling. It was a gamble rather than a calculated risk and it was taken with the lives of men whose fate he held in trust.

Some of those taking part in the raid had sensed disaster from the beginning. Sergeant John Dobson, only nineteen years old but already one of 218 Squadron's most experienced pilots, was woken at 6 a.m. on the morning of 7 November, an unusually early hour that suggested that a daylight operation was planned. Half-asleep, crotchety, some of them mildly hungover, the squadron slouched to the briefing room. Dobson sat down and his crew grouped themselves on the chairs around him. There was 'no greeting, just a plain and dismal silence'. He pulled out his cigarettes from his pyjama pocket and 'exercised the Skipper's prerogative of offering each crew member a fag. A sharp, grating sound, puff, puff, puff and then silence once more. The whole room was silent and pent up with a fierce concentration. No celluloid sallies here, no carefree chatter which film-struck spinsters associate with an operational briefing . . . we were all in the bluest of blue funks so that no one dare speak for fear of voicing with his eyes or gruffness his innermost, uppermost fear of the unknown. More especially today it was felt, because of the unusual hour, which [preyed] heavily on the superstition of fliers.'

Wing Commander Kirkpatrick climbed the three steps to the dais. He was a pre-war regular and his crews liked and trusted him, 'just the man for any job which would get this damned war over quicker,' in Dobson's view. The order of the day that he read out was unlike any other the audience had previously heard. Instead of being given a routine railway junction or gasworks to aim at, the squadron's mission was directed against a factory twenty miles south-east of Berlin which was believed to be researching experimental weapons. The target was to be be completely demolished 'at all costs'. Should the bombs fail they were to strafe the factory at low level. The success of the mission, he stressed, would obviate great loss of life in the future.

The 'met' reports were read out which predicted three storm fronts and blanket cloud over the continent, though this might clear to eight-tenths cover by the time the aircraft arrived giving the captain the option of bombing through the holes in the murk or risking flying below it. The wing commander then went on to confirm what Dobson's gut had told him. The heavy bomb load meant that it would be touch and go whether there was enough fuel to get them back. The squadron sat 'entranced and dumb-founded as the words ate like acid into their brain, numbing all senses but that awful emptiness of fear in the stomach.' They spent the rest of the morning trying to lose themselves in 'doing those hundred and one . . . things to keep the mind from death.' The music on the mess gramophone did nothing to lighten the gloom. Even the liveliest tunes were simply a reminder of a world they might never return to.

At lunch Dobson could not bear to eat. He slipped away early to look over his Wellington, K-Kate. It was raining heavily but he 'did not pause to collect a greatcoat, feeling somehow that it was superfluous and not in keeping with the dread feeling all around . . .' But the weather provided a spurt of hope. 'I gazed upwards at the lowering clouds whilst the increasing rain stung my pupils and made tiny, salty tears run into my face and aggravated the soreness of my cheeks where I had shaved. Could it be . . . that ops were scrubbed?'

He ran back to the mess where he met his crew who told him that ops were still very much on. They were coming to the end of their tour and shared his fear of what lay ahead. Speaking on behalf of the rest, the navigator informed Dobson they had decided 'we are certainly not going to chuck our lives away on this damned death but no glory stunt.'

Dobson went to tell the CO, who came straight to the point. Was Dobson going to join the mutiny? He replied, 'not without certain trepidation, "no sir." To see the relief shining in his eyes . . . was gratitude enough but he rose and patted my shoulder gently, almost fatherly, and said, "Thank you, Dobson."'

He was allotted a new crew and learned to his dismay that they were 'sprogs' straight out of training and virgins when it came to operational flying. He was further alarmed by the discovery that the man flying as 'second dickey' or assistant pilot, was an Australian. The prevailing superstition had it that Australians were prone to disaster on their first show.

Dinner was even more depressing than lunch. When they reached the aircraft 'the rain was falling in an ever-increasing tempo, drumming like bullets on the fuselage.' Dobson's misgivings were well-founded. Before they had even crossed the English coast they came under fire from a German intruder. He dived into cloud to escape, emerging in time to see the sky in front twinkling with red stars as the first coastal flak batteries opened up. Dead ahead there was a huge sheet of flame as a bomber exploded. Then it was their turn. Dobson threw the Wellington this way and that 'but more flak concentrated on us until it seemed as though the whole sky was a mass of flaming, eye-scarring bursts. And the smell like the smell of death itself; cloying, foetid, lingering in . . . nostrils wide with fear.' A heavy burst plunged the Wellington into a downward spiral. 'Completely out of control isn't fun at any time but in a welter of up-coming flak our predicament was terrible. The crew were in a frenzy, yelling and screaming over the intercom.' They levelled out at 3,200 feet but were now pinned against the sky by searchlights. Dobson felt 'the intensity of the beam on one's face simply sapped the strength from one . . . the eyes burned like all the fires of hell as I strove to penetrate the terrific vista of light.'

Eventually they left the searchlight batteries behind. They crossed the Dutch border and set course for their objective. Long before they reached Berlin they could see the flak barrage glowing above it. Their target was to the south. As they turned away, two night-fighters bore in on them from ahead and below, riddling the fuselage with tracer. Dobson, a former Hurricane pilot, threw the Wellington into a violent turn, a manoeuvre which had the lucky effect of bringing one attacking Messerschmitt into the front gunner's sights, just as he was climbing away. 'Bits began to fly from the fighter as the murderous hail of bullets from the two Brownings, so ably wielded, bit into his fabric, his engines and his tanks . . . the last we saw of him he was spinning down in a death dive and no pilot got out.' The other fighter was shaken off in the turn.

They went on. Dobson had to drop through a thick layer of clouds, 'so solid, so absolutely like a new earth that one wanted to step out on them and walk,' to have any chance of finding the target. By the time the Wellington emerged only 2,000 feet were showing on the altimeter. Ahead they could see parachute flares, and artillery flashes lit up the target area. Bert Faltham, the navigator-cum-bomb-aimer now took charge. As he led them in the flak increased in intensity until 'the sky around and ahead was a vast, twinkling maelstrom of light.' At last Faltham called out, 'Bombs gone Skip!' and the Wellington's 3,500-pound load fell away. Dobson climbed, taking 'what seemed like a leaden century' to reach 18,000 feet where he levelled off.

About an hour and a half from home Dobson allowed himself to start thinking that they might just make it. Then the sky ahead reddened with a flak barrage which flared up and died away before he could identify its location. Suddenly there was 'a terrific crack, like a whip going hard against naked flesh, whilst a gale roared through the hole the flak had created . . . a nucleus of bursts held us in their thrall, smashing into the fuselage at every point, tearing huge gaps . . .' For the next forty-five minutes Dobson fought to keep the aircraft steady but it started to slide into what seemed like a final descent. He gave the order to bale out. 'One by one the crew filed past my seat and dropped through the opening at my feet. When the last one . . . had vanished I trimmed Kate, tail heavy, so that in a few moments her nose would come up and she would spin in to her complete destruction. Then, still holding the stick, I slid from my seat and as the aircraft swayed slowly backwards I fell forward through the hole in the manner approved. The time was 05.00 . . . Height 1,500 feet.'[12]

Such was the end of K-Kate, one of thirty-seven aircraft lost that night. Peirse's determination to restore his and his command's reputation had brought disaster. Two months later he was removed. The Berlin calamity prompted the War Cabinet to put an end to big raids for the rest of the winter to preserve lives and aircraft and allow the new policy to take shape. In the coming months only limited operations with small numbers of aircraft were sanctioned. It was to be another fourteen months before Berlin was attacked again.

6

Enter 'Butch'

Though it might not have appeared so to despondent crews that winter, Bomber Command's overall prospects were slowly improving. The Bomber Boys rarely caught a glimpse of the big picture. But during the second half of 1941 the wider war had taken on a new and encouraging direction. The German invasion of Russia in June had transformed the Soviet Union from an enemy to an ally. With the entry of the United States into the conflict after the 7 December attack on Pearl Harbor, all the riches of America were unlocked for use in the fight against the Nazis.

The pause in major operations ordered after the Berlin disaster gave an exhausted, depleted and dispirited force the chance to catch its breath and gather its strength. Over the months that followed the recent volunteers started to arrive in force at their operational squadrons. The first of the new generation of four-engined heavies, the Stirlings and Halifaxes, began to replace their two-engined predecessors. On Christmas Eve, 1941, the first of the Lancasters landed at RAF Waddington in Lincolnshire. Soon its blunt, menacing lines would be seen everywhere. Some of the new aircraft carried desperately-needed new electronic navigation aids. By the time Harris took over Bomber Command at the end of February 1942 the force was approaching a position where it could start applying the policies on which those running the war were now agreed.

Shortly before his arrival there was an event which gave heart to the battered squadrons. One day in early March 1942, Peter Johnson visited a bomber station in Nottinghamshire to have lunch with the base commander. Entering the mess he found a group of young officers in the middle of a raucous party. His host explained they were celebrating a 'wizard prang' the night before. 'Come and look at the photos,' he said. 'They're the best ever. Teach those bloody Frogs to play along with the Boche.'

Johnson examined the pictures taken during the raid and agreed they were 'remarkable indeed'. They showed the Renault works on an island in the Seine just outside Paris, overlaid by a mass of explosions, flares and fires. It looked as if 'the factory was a complete write-off and that it would hardly be worth the enemy's while to try to recover significant production from the chaos.'

A shout of 'NEWS' cut through the triumphant hubbub. The 'din of laughter and talk was followed by a chorus of "Ssssshh, ssssshh." Tankards in hand, everyone gathered round the radiogram . . . "I bet we're on first," said someone. "Unless they've murdered ole Hitler!" The cool tones of the BBC announcer gave this, the most outstanding success of Bomber Command in two and a half years, pride of place.' Johnson was reluctant to drag the CO away from the party and excused himself, pleading an appointment with a visitor from the staff. Ignoring shouts of 'Fuck the staff!' and 'Teach them to fly!' he departed. He drove away deep in thought. 'What I had seen was, I realized, something of a "one-off" born of the exceptional success of the night's operation. But I was very conscious that the camaraderie, the sense of being an exclusive band of brothers, in this, the first wartime bomber squadron I had known was something quite apart from the rest of the service.' He applied immediately to leave his post commanding the Ossington Advanced Flying Training School and get on to operations.[1]

The Renault factory at Billancourt had been chosen by the Air Staff on the direction of the War Cabinet. It was turning out an estimated 18,000 lorries a year, most of which went to the German military. This was thought to justify the risk of French civilian casualties. The attack went ahead on the night of 3 March 1942. The results, for the time, were devastating. The operation involved 235 aircraft, the greatest number so far sent on a raid, which arrived in three waves. The attack was opened by a vanguard of the most experienced crews who dropped large numbers of pyrotechnic markers. This was the first, full-scale attempt to use flares to identify targets which the main force could then use to aim at. The bombers went in very low at between 1,000 and 4,000 feet to increase accuracy and minimize the danger to locals. The works were only lightly defended by anti-aircraft guns. A record tonnage of bombs went down and the damage they did was considerable. About 40 per cent of the buildings were destroyed and production was halted for four weeks at a loss of nearly 2,300 trucks.

The precautions against spilling French blood, however, had little effect. Blocks of flats housing the workers were clustered around the factory and 367 people were killed. This was twice as many as had died in any RAF raid on a German city so far. This did not detract from the feeling that the Renault attack was a great success. Heavy damage had been done to a precise target with minimal losses. Only one Wellington failed to return.

But the episode was, as Johnson had realized, far from the normal run of Bomber Command operations. There was no cloud below 10,000 feet and almost full moonlight. Most importantly, all the crews had enjoyed a practically flak-free outing which enabled them to make low-level attacks. These conditions made a reasonable degree of precision possible. This was never going to be the case in Germany and it was in Germany that the big battles would have to be fought.

The man now leading the offensive had an ideal service background for the job. Arthur Harris had joined the Royal Flying Corps in 1915 and flown on the Western Front before being given command of a home defence squadron where he acquired a reputation as a pioneer of night flying. Between the wars he served in Iraq, helping keep rebellious tribes in line by bombarding them from the air. He knew how Whitehall worked from stints at the Air Ministry, notably as director of plans in the crucial mid-thirties period. He also understood and got on with Americans, having served as head of the RAF delegation in Washington during 1941.

It was Harris who bore the brunt of post-war revulsion at the destruction of Germany. But no matter how enthusiastically and unswervingly he may have pursued the policy, the idea of pulverizing cities had not originated with him. As he pointed out in his memoirs: 'There is a widespread impression that I not only invented the policy of area bombing but also insisted on carrying it out in the face of a natural reluctance to kill women and children that was felt by everyone else. The facts are otherwise. Such decisions are not in any case made by Commanders-in-Chief in the field, but by the ministries, the Chiefs of Staff Committee and by the War Cabinet. The decision to attack large industrial areas was taken long before I became Commander-in-Chief.'[2]

The first directive from the CAS to greet Harris had indeed confirmed the direction that had been set. 'The primary object of your operations,' it said, 'should now be focused on the morale of the enemy civil population and in particular, on the industrial workers.' Portal was concerned that perhaps the meaning of his orders was not clear enough. He wrote to Air Vice-Marshal Bottomley who had drafted the directive: 'I suppose it is clear that the aiming points are to be the built-up areas, *not*, for instance, the dockyards or aircraft factories . . . this must be made clear if it is not already understood.' He need not have worried. Harris knew very well what was expected of him.

It was Harris's bad luck to look and sound like a bully whose determination to win took little account of the lives of German civilians or indeed his own men. He was broad, short-sighted and bad-tempered and wore a small, bristling moustache which added to the impression of porcine belligerence. He was easily angered by anything he perceived to be criticism and seemed to relish using the most wounding language in crushing it. He seldom saw any validity in views that did not chime with his own. In the words of the official historians, he had 'a tendency to confuse advice with interference, criticism with sabotage and evidence with propaganda.'

Harris spent his early years seeking his fortune in Rhodesia, a part of the world he loved, and the crack of an invisible sjambok could often be heard in his dealings with his subordinates. The accuracy of this impression appeared to be confirmed by the nickname bestowed on him by his men. The public might know him as 'Bomber' Harris, his peers as 'Bert' but to the crews he was 'Butch', short for 'butcher', in reference to his willingess to spend their lives. Very few of them had a chance to form an opinion based on direct knowledge. Jack Currie and his companions at Wickenby 'never met our Commander-in-Chief, never saw him, never heard his voice . . . he was in fact distanced from us by such far echelons of rank and station, that he was a figure more of imagination than reality. Uninhibited by any bounds of truth, we were able to ascribe to him any characteristic that our spirits needed. It pleased us to think of him as utterly callous, indifferent to suffering, and unconcerned about our fate.' There was, he thought, 'a paradoxical comfort in serving such a dread commander: no grievance, no complaint, no criticism could possibly affect him . . . we chose to believe that Harris lived in utter luxury at Claridge's, and that with his morning beverage a servant brought him a jewelled dart, which he casually cast at a wall map of Europe above his dressing table. He would then take up the silver scrambler telephone and call High Wycombe. "This is the Commander-in-Chief. The target for tonight is . . ."'[3]

As a pilot in 617 Squadron, Tony Iveson felt that the gap that separated him from his chief served to reinforce Harris's authority. He was 'a colossus, up there running the show, like Zeus from Olympus.' He accepted, as most airmen did, the explanation for his decision not to tour bases. 'If he'd gone to one station he would have had to go to them all and if he was coming they'd be painting stones and parading and all this lark and taking them away from their proper job.'[4] This was a deferential age and service life inculcated a reflex respect for seniority. 'At twenty-two years of age, Harris to me was a God,' said Jim Berry, another pilot. 'We used to refer to him in all sorts of ways, but there was an underlying respect for Harris [that] everybody had, I think.'[5]

On the occasions when he did drop in on the crews he had a galvanizing effect. Reg Fayers was one of the minority who saw and heard him in person. Harris visited Holme-on-Spalding-Moor on 15 September 1943 to talk to 76 Squadron. It was at a time when it was suffering from a worrying incidence of 'early returns', the term used for when crews arrived back having failed to bomb. After a forceful speech he asked the crowd for their questions. Fayers, an independent-minded man inclined to scepticism, wrote to his wife that he felt 'privileged, really, to hear . . . the boss of the whole show. I even asked him a question. I've always been for his ideas . . . his faith in the efficacy of our bombing is terrific and catching altho' I'd already caught it. I still think [Bomber Command is] winning this war more certainly than anything else. I pray God I may see peace in six months.'[6] The following day Harris went to Elsham Wolds where the crews greeted him with sustained cheering.

Harris understood the value of a touch of menace. But he also knew it was wise to show a softer side from time to time and he could be charming and even gentle with his favourites, such as the *beaux idéals* of Bomber Command, Cheshire and Gibson. Leonard Cheshire described being summoned shortly after he had been awarded his VC. 'He sent for me . . . I thought I'd done something wrong . . . he was very nice and fatherly and very friendly and I liked him very much.'[7]

Harris arrived at Bomber Command at a good time. From March 1942, aircraft began to be fitted with a new navigation system called *Gee*. With *Gee*, the great problem that dogged Bomber Command's efforts and limited and defined its activities started to be solved. It worked on a system of radio pulses. Three stations strung out over 200 miles transmitted radio signals which were picked up by a *Gee* box on board the aircraft. Measuring the time difference between the pulses provided co-ordinates which were displayed on a cathode ray tube in the navigator's cabin. A competent 'nav' could get a fix which, within a few minutes, gave the aircraft's position to an accuracy of between half a mile and five miles. There were drawbacks. Because of the curvature of the earth, the range of *Gee* was limited to 350 miles. The Germans soon learned how to jam it, making it unreliable once over the Dutch coast. But *Gee* set the bombers on a true course on the outward journey and was a great help in bringing them home to base on their return.

Gee was later joined by *Oboe*, which came into service on 20 December 1942. It also operated on transmissions from ground stations in England but was more accurate. It was claimed that at its best it could hold an aircraft to within sixty-five feet of its position. *Oboe* got its name from the musical pulse it emitted which was audible to the pilot. Variations from the course were marked by variations in the pulse. As the target approached, a second signal was heard, a series of dashes followed by a series of dots. When the dots stopped, the bomb-aimer pressed his button. The big advantage of *Oboe* was that it allowed targets to be marked and bombed even in cloudy conditions. Initially, however, the *Oboe* ground stations could communicate with only a limited number of aircraft.

These aids were supplemented in January 1943 by *H2S*, a radar device which was carried on board and did not rely on external signals. A transmitter in the aircraft's belly reflected a picture of the ground below on to a TV screen in the navigator's cabin. The blips of light that appeared could be difficult to interpret, especially over big cities.

These were great improvements, but they did not mean that Bomber Command was now capable of bombing precisely. What the new technology did was to get aircraft to the target area, rather than pinpoint the target to be hit.

The new aeroplanes, though, were the best any commander could wish for. The faithful but outmoded aircraft of the first, disappointing years of the air war, were disappearing to be replaced by four-engined machines, far bigger than anything that had been seen before.

The first to appear was the Short Stirling which went into service in August 1940. It was eighty-seven feet long and stood very tall, slanting upwards sharply so that the cockpit was nearly twenty-three feet above the tarmac. But the Stirling was also slow, with a maximum speed of 260 mph and its unimpressive 740-mile range and 19,000-feet altitude limit meant it was the poor relation of the bomber fleet. The Avro Manchester made an appearance at the end of 1940 but its underdeveloped Vulture engines made it lethally unreliable and it was soon phased out.

The crews felt happiest in a Halifax or Lancaster. The Handley Page Halifax began operating in March 1941. It suffered from severe initial design faults but eventually evolved into a fine and trust-worthy aircraft. To the Canadian Ralph Wood, who switched from Whitleys in May 1942, the 'Hallybag' was a 'beautiful four-engined bird'. It had three gun turrets, front, mid-upper and rear. It could cruise at 280 mph and carry a bomb load of 8,000 pounds or three and a half tons. It took seven to fly a Halifax; a pilot, navigator, flight engineer, bomb-aimer who was also front gunner, wireless operator, mid-upper gunner and tail gunner.

Wood inhabited the 'dinky little navigator's compartment [which] was below and in front of the pilot's cockpit. You went down a few steps and entered a small section with a navigator's table down one side, ahead and below the pilot's feet.' Wood doubled as the bomb-aimer/front gunner. A curtain in the nose hid 'the even smaller compartment where I would huddle with my Mark Fourteen bombsight . . . when we got reasonably close to the target.' The gun he was supposed to operate when needed was a Vickers gas-operated .303 machine gun, which was mounted on a swivel and stuck out through the Perspex nose, high above the bombsight. They were 'popguns' in the eyes of the crews, a poor defence against an attacking night-fighter armed with cannons and, Wood had been warned, notorious for jamming. 'All you had to do was look at it the wrong way and it would plug up on you.'[8]

The Avro Lancaster was a masterpiece of military aviation design. It was capable of carrying great loads of up to 14,000 pounds. Later special aircraft were adapted to deliver the monstrous 22,000-pound Grand Slam bombs. Despite its phenomenal lifting power it was fast and manoeuvrable. It could reach nearly 290 mph and was nimble enough to corkscrew out of trouble when under attack from a night-fighter, though the technique was far from infallible. It was reliable and safe, with the lowest accident rate of the bombers. Tony Iveson had already notched up about 1,800 hours flying time in many different types when he first flew one. 'The Lanc was a lovely aircraft,' he remembered. 'It was splendid, day or night.' Ken Newman 'liked the Lancaster from the first moment that I climbed aboard.' The cockpit layout 'was much more sensible than that of the Halifax' with everything within easy reach. It was only in an emergency that the main design fault became apparent. The thick spar that lay across the fuselage supporting the wings was very difficult to negotiate when moving forward and aft and was a significant impediment in emergencies.

The heavies conveyed a feeling of strength and menace that inspired confidence in those who were to fly them. To the trainee bomber crews seeing them for the first time they looked huge and threatening. Noble Frankland thought them 'incredibly sinister and powerful', an impression that was deepened by their glistening black surfaces. They were huge, bigger than anything the Germans had, and as impressive as the American Liberators and Fortresses that would soon appear. The Halifax was seventy feet long and had a wing span of 104 feet, long enough for forty men to line up on in group photographs. They were as fast as the Americans and they carried heavier bomb loads. No one looking at them could doubt that they meant business.

Harris's first major change in operational procedures was to end the practice of splitting up the force and sending it to bomb two or three targets over a protracted period. His study of the German air attacks on Britain convinced him that the Luftwaffe had squandered a great opportunity by not focusing its attacks. The principle now was concentration. Henceforth the pattern was to dispatch as many aircraft as could be mustered against one target. Attack times were shortened which increased the chances of collisions but reduced the time in which the flak gunners had the bombers in their sights. They were aiming for saturation, swamping the defences and overwhelming the emergency services by sheer weight of violence. The method of destruction favoured by Harris was fire. Incendiaries were at least as important as high explosive. It was easier to burn down a city than to blow it up. The purpose of bombs was to rip off roofs and knock down walls, choking the streets with mounds of brick and stone and timber that would cripple the movement of firemen and rescue workers. Then the four-pound incendiaries would float down into the shattered buildings and start blazes that would feed on the winds whipped up by the blasts. The aim was, he said, to start 'so many fires at the same time that no fire-fighting services, however efficiently and quickly they were reinforced by the fire brigades of other towns, could get them under control.'[9]

The first major demonstrations of the new technique came with attacks on Lübeck and Rostock. Lübeck, as Harris admitted, was not a vital target, although it housed a a medium-sized port and a U-boat building yard. It was chosen because it was relatively simple to find and, given the part-wooden construction of many of the houses, 'easier than most cities to set on fire'. The raid was launched on the night of 28 March, and the aiming point was the centre of the *Altstadt*, the old quarter where the streets were narrow and crooked and the buildings were highly flammable. A separate attack was mounted on a machine-tool works. Two thirds of the 300 tons of bombs that were dropped were incendiaries. As well as the small magnesium incendiaries, the load included a thirty-pound bomb designed to fling benzol and rubber in a ten-yard radius from the point of impact. In mounting the attack Harris was testing a theory. The main object 'was to learn to what extent a first wave of aircraft could guide a second wave to the aiming point by starting a conflagration.' He ordered 'a half an hour interval between the two waves in order to allow the fires to get a good hold before the second wave arrived.'[10]

The fact that Bomber Command was now engaged unapologetically in area bombing was acknowledged by a change of terminology so that it now gauged success in terms of acres destroyed. Analysis of reconnaissance photographs suggested that 190 acres of Lübeck had been devastated, or 30 per cent of the town's built-up area. Most appeared to have been consumed by fire. This reckoning was an overestimate but not a wild one. The German survey counted 3,401 buildings destroyed or seriously damaged. Of those, all but 331 were houses and flats. The attack destroyed a factory which made oxygen equipment for U-boats. But it also ruined the Marienkirche, a church of great religious and architectural importance. Up to 320 people were killed, the heaviest death toll in a raid on Germany so far, but still far short of the 1,500 who had been killed in London on the night of 10 May 1941. The weakness of the town's defences meant Bomber Command's losses were relatively light, twelve aircraft out of the 234 sent out, most of which appear to have been knocked down *en route*. Harris was delighted with the

The shape of things to come: Lübeck, March 1942.

results. He had, he wrote later, 'conclusively proved that even the small force I had then could destroy the greater part of a town of secondary importance.'[11]

A month later four raids were aimed in quick succession at Rostock, culminating on the night of 26/27 April. Rostock was a town much like Lübeck, on the water and with a combustible old centre. Incendiaries made up most of the bomb load. All together, by Bomber Command's calculations, the attacks destroyed 60 per cent of the main town area. Again the crew losses had been low. About 200 Germans were killed, a figure that would have been considerably higher if many had not fled after the first raids. A Heinkel factory on the southern edge of town was singled out for special attention by separate forces, including Guy Gibson's 106 Squadron. This double-thrust combining an attempted high-explosive precision attack, Billancourt-style, with a general area attack with incendiaries was to become common practice.

The main weight of the raids, though, fell on the town itself. Josef Goebbels tried to salvage what propaganda advantage he could from the devastation by describing the action as a *Terrorangriff*, a terror attack. The term would stick and those who were carrying them out soon became *Terrorflieger* or terror flyers. Germans suffering these attacks or hearing about them agreed. But far away in California, one German had no doubts about the brutal justice of the raids. 'I think of Coventry, and I have no objection to the lesson that everything must be paid for,' said Thomas Mann, the great novelist and son of Lübeck in a radio broadcast. 'Did Germany believe that she would never have to pay for the atrocities that her leap into barbarism seemed to allow?'[12] Harris calculated that the two attacks had devastated 780 acres. He reckoned that Bomber Command had now 'about squared our account with Germany'.[13] By that he meant that it had inflicted as much destruction and death on Germany as the Luftwaffe had on Britain. German bombing had wrecked about 400 acres of London and 100 acres of Coventry, apart from the damage done to other blitzed cities.[14]

The Lübeck and Rostock raids had been relatively small. By the end of May, Harris was ready for his first spectacular. He knew the value of publicity and the prestige it could bring to him and his command. He wanted to demonstrate to the world the growing power of the bombing fleet. He set out to mount an operation that would impress his superiors, attract the admiration of the Americans and Russians who were now Britain's allies, bring cheer to British civilians, and frighten Germany. The logic of concentration suggested that the more bombers that could be dispatched on one mission the better. The figure of one thousand carried a certain poetic potency.

He took the idea to Churchill and Portal who gave enthusiastic approval and the planning began. Harris had only a little over 400 fully operational aircraft and crews at his immediate disposal and struggled to reach the magic number. Many machines and men came from operational training and conversion units.

This was essentially a huge and risky experiment which if it succeeded would set the pattern for the future. To handle the huge number of aircraft, it was decided they would fly in a 'bomber stream'. This, theoretically, would bring important defensive and offensive advantages. Every aircraft would follow the same route at staggered times, flying in different air corridors to reduce the risk of collisions. Thus, it was hoped, the vulnerability of the fleet to the German night-fighters who were growing increasingly active, operating in defensive boxes on the main approach routes, would be limited. It would also reduce the time over target and exposure to the defending flak batteries. At the same time, the bomber stream would deliver a continuous torrent of bombs that would overwhelm the defences and cause maximum disruption and terror creating the best conditions for apocalyptic conflagrations.

The first 'thousand' raid took place on the clear, moonlit Saturday night of the 30/31 May 1942 . The target was Cologne, Germany's third largest city. It had been subjected to many raids, most recently in March when, in the first successful *Gee*-led raid, 135 aircraft had attacked the city doing considerable damage and killing sixty-two people. Now seven times that number were launched against it. Harris's message to the departing crews left no doubt about the significance of the operation. 'The force of which you form a part tonight is at least twice the size and has at least four times the carrying capacity of the largest air force ever before concentrated on one objective,' he declared. 'You have an opportunity therefore to strike a blow at the enemy which will resound, not only throughout Germany, but throughout the world.' All together, 1,047 aircraft took part in the raid including seventy-three of the new Lancasters. They carried 1,455 tons of bombs of which two thirds were incendiaries. The aim was to set Cologne ablaze. The city's configuration with broad streets and modern buildings meant that fires did not take hold with the same hungry energy as they did in the old Hanseatic towns. The damage was still impressive. According to local records 3,330 buildings were destroyed, 2,090 seriously damaged and 7,420 lightly damaged, almost all by fire. The flames were indiscriminate. The conflagration devoured 13,010 homes, mostly apartments, and seriously damaged 6,360 more. Nine hospitals, seventeen churches, sixteen schools and four university buildings as well as numerous other premises that could not be considered military or industrial targets were burnt or blasted down. Ralph Wood, looking down from his Halifax, saw what seemed to be the 'red hot embers of a huge bonfire'. The German records list damage being done to seventeen water mains, five gas mains, thirty-two electricity cables and twelve main telephone routes. The only military building mentioned is a flak installation.

The death toll established a new record. At least 469 people were killed. Of these 411 were civilians and 58 military, most of whom had been manning flak batteries. The RAF traumatized Cologne in the same way that some eighteen months before the Luftwaffe had traumatized Coventry. Some 45,000 people had been 'bombed out'. As in Coventry, many fled the city, about a fifth of the 700,000 population according to local estimates. As in Coventry, the raid created a symbol of destruction and suffering in the form of a ruined cathedral.

Brian Frow was now a pilot with 408 Squadron which was charged with dropping parachute flares to light up the target for the main force. 'At briefing we were told that the aiming point for 5 Group was the square in front of Cologne Cathedral,' he wrote. This was 'a bow to realism; it was well known that in area attacks against cities at night, the bomb pattern followed the design of a triangle, with the apex at the aiming point, widening and falling back along the inbound track of the raid.' After the first bombs landed the aiming point was covered by dust and smoke, making accurate aiming impossible. There was also a tendency for anxious crews to release their bombs early. By taking the cathedral as a landmark the bomb load would fall into the densest part of the city where the maximum destruction would be achieved. Afterwards, Konrad Adenauer who had been the anti-Nazi mayor of the city, wrote that 'there was no gas, no water, no electric current and no means of transport. The bridges across the Rhine had been destroyed. There were mountains of rubble in the streets. Everywhere there were gigantic areas of debris from bombed and shelled buildings. With its razed churches, many of them almost a thousand years old, its bombed-out cathedral, with the ruins of once beautiful bridges sticking up out of the Rhine, and the vast expanses of derelict houses, Cologne was a ghost city.' The damage was light compared with what was to come. It was, in Frow's words, merely 'a foretaste of what was to befall the Hun'.[15]

These attacks met with noisy approval from the British press and public. Even George Orwell's tender conscience was untroubled by what was going on. The Germans, he warned, in a radio broadcast a few days after the raid, deserved no quarter. 'In 1940, when the Germans were bombing Britain, they did not expect retaliation on a very heavy scale,' he said. '[They] were not afraid to boast in their propaganda about the slaughter of civilians which they were bringing about and the terror which their raids aroused. Now, when the tables are turned, they are beginning to cry out against the whole business of aerial bombing, which they declare to be both cruel and useless. The people of this country are not revengeful, but they remember what happened to themselves two years ago, and they remember how the Germans talked when they thought themselves safe from retaliation.'

It was not until the following spring that mammoth raids became routine. Bomber Command was still growing and simply did not have the strength to maintain a tempo of heavy attacks. Cologne, was, in the opinion of Hamish Mahaddie, then a pilot with 7 Squadron who was to go on to be a leading figure in the foundation of the Pathfinder Force, something of a 'con trick', whose main purpose was to establish the feasibility of such an exercise and by extension the value of the strategic bombing campaign.[16] If so, the ruse worked. Cologne and the raids that preceded it went a long way to silencing the doubters and establishing strategic bombing solidly at the heart of Allied war planning.

The successes of the first phase of the Harris era were, however, relative. *Gee* had improved navigation but not transformed it. The bomber fleets still had difficulty finding the target. The arrival of the Pathfinders brought a further, important improvement. The Pathfinder Force was not a Harris invention and he opposed it with all the considerable vigour he could muster against ideas which were not his own. The principle was that to aid accuracy an elite unit formed from the best crews would fly ahead of the main force and illuminate aiming points with target-marking bombs for the following aircraft to aim at.

The concept had been raised inside the Air Ministry at the end of 1941 before Harris took over and was promoted by a powerful Air Staff lobby. It was led by Group Captain Syd Bufton, the director of bomber operations at the Air Ministry. He had commanded 10 Squadron early in the war and pioneered a technique of using his best crews to locate targets with flares. The Australian Don Bennett, who was to command the force, remembered Harris fighting 'tooth and nail to try and stop it'. He 'argued that the best crews were too valuable and that putting them out in front to lead the rest . . . would also expose them to greater risk. The losses amongst your best crews would be so high that it would be prohibitive. In other words you'd lead all the force with a good bunch of people in front but not for long because the leaders would be shot down and lost.' Bennett's solution to this problem was to surround the half a dozen or so Pathfinder Force (PFF) crews with a phalanx of 'supporters' to help bear the brunt of the flak. The system worked and PFF losses were no worse and in fact slighly better than those of the main force. The other objection, a valid one as Bennett admitted, was that skimming off outstanding leaders would weaken squadrons as well as denting their morale. 'Naturally they all looked to their squadron commander and to have their squadron commander whisked away down to headquarters Pathfinder Force . . . may have been a great honour to the person concerned but it was a tremendous loss to the squadron.'[17]

Harris's opposition was supported by all his group commanders. But it was clear to Portal that despite the recent technological improvements and successes, Bomber Command's efficiency was still severely limited and anything that offered the hope of improvement should be tried. He backed the Air Staff view and Harris was ordered to drop his objections and form the new force. He did not concede quietly. He insisted that instead of selecting the best crews, the PFF would be made up of four ordinary squadrons, one from each night bomber group. Portal, knowing when to cede ground, agreed.

The Pathfinder argument shone a light on the battle of ideas about how the strategic air campaign should be fought. Those who backed the PFF regarded area bombing as a temporary measure which could be dropped once improved technology and expertise allowed the RAF to perfect the technique of precise attack. Those who opposed believed city-battering was an end in itself which, if pursued hard enough, was the surest path to hastening victory. It was a debate that was to continue until the end.

At this point, Portal was firmly on the side of obliteration. The entry of America into the war had greatly increased the potential assets available to conduct a massive strategic bomber campaign. The first American aircraft and crews arrived in Britain at the beginning of 1942 and in August began their initial, tentative sorties, bombing rail yards, not in Germany but in France. American bombing doctrine was very different from that of the RAF. The United States Army Air Force believed firmly in the achievability of precise bombing on carefully chosen military and industrial targets. To maximize accuracy, they were organized chiefly to bomb in daylight.

These factors were to complicate the evolution of a harmonized Anglo-American approach. For a time, though, it seemed to Portal that it would soon be possible to muster giant air armadas against the Reich. In the autumn of 1942, he told the Chiefs of Staff that if the bomber force could be greatly expanded to between 4,000 and 6,000 aircraft, devastating results could be achieved. Scientific analysis of the impact of bombs on Britain had produced some plausible-seeming projections of the effects on Germany of an all-out campaign. Portal claimed that if 50,000 tons of bombs could be delivered each month in 1943, rising to 90,000 tons by the end of 1944, the effects would be catastrophic for Germany. Twenty-five million Germans would be made homeless, 900,000 would be killed and one million seriously injured. By the middle of 1944 these tonnages were indeed being achieved, and with far fewer aircraft than had been thought necessary. The results were less catastrophic than predicted. But there was no doubt that Portal regarded such imagined destruction would speed victory.

There was to be no question of Bomber Command suspending

its activities until ideal force levels had been achieved. In between the peaks of its campaign there was almost continuous activity as crews dropped mines in the sea and carried out minor raids on secondary targets. These activities could be as dangerous as any other, as Denholm Elliott, the young RADA hopeful turned wireless operator, found out on the night of 23/24 September 1942.

He had recently arrived at 76 Squadron and on his third operation was ordered off with the rest of his crew in their Halifax, K-King, to bomb the submarine base at Sylt, a spit of land poking into the North Sea. The trip, he remembered, got off to a bad start. 'As we were walking out to the plane the engineer who had been servicing it said "What are you?" I said, "I'm wireless op for K for King." He said, "Oh dear, oh dear," and I asked "Why?" "Well [he replied] the last wireless operator for K for King got a cannon shell up his backside." That didn't encourage me too much.' Elliott did not improve morale by telling his crewmates that he had had a dream the previous night in which they were shot down.

They came in low over the target at 1,000 feet. 'This was the first time I was actually encountering anti-aircraft fire and it really was a most unpleasant sensation,' – he remembered. 'A shell bursting beneath you lifts the plane about fifty feet upwards in the air. You certainly find instant religion.'

Then Elliott felt 'the most enormous explosion . . . the port outer engine was on fire . . . all the lights went out. I was fumbling desperately to find the wire clippers to send a distress signal on the automatic SOS but the plane was going down and there just wasn't time. I just jumped out of my seat which was at the very front of the plane and tore to the middle of the aircraft, as it was going down, and got into the ditching position with your feet up against the central spar and your hands behind your neck to take the shock.' As he passed the navigator, who was also taking up crash stations, 'he sort of grinned in a sickly way . . . that was the last time I saw him.'

Elliott's skipper, Squadron Leader Barnard, managed to put K-King down on the North Sea with the smallest of bumps. But water immediately flooded into the fuselage as they fought to get the escape hatch open. 'I'm afraid I was very ungentlemanly,' Elliott confessed. 'I was scrambling over everybody else to get out. As far I was concerned there was no question of a polite "after you, my dear Charles . . ." '

Five of the crew managed to struggle out. Floating in the moonlight, buoyed up by his lifejacket, rescue seemed very far away and Elliott assumed he was doomed. He found himself thinking of his friends in the squadron whom he would never see again. But his hopes rose when he saw they were only about a mile from land. The aircraft was still afloat. The survivors clambered on top but it was clear that K-King would soon sink. The inflatable dinghy which was supposed to be released in emergencies had failed to emerge. Somebody volunteered to slither back inside and pull the switch. The dinghy shot to the surface. They pulled themselves on to it one by one. A debate began about what to do next. There was a suggestion they try to paddle to neutral Sweden, a mere 300 miles away. It was Elliott who talked them out of it and proposed firing off the distress flare and heading for shore. The signal fizzed into the night sky and not long afterwards a tug pulled up alongside and took them aboard. On dry land they were met by 'a picture postcard Nazi officer with a monocle and a long cigarette holder' who announced that for them the war was over.[18]

It would be some time before Bomber Command could bring its full weight to bear on Germany. During the winter it was diverted to bombing industrial targets in northern Italy. Early in 1943 it was called in again to attack the French ports of Lorient, Saint-Nazaire, Brest and La Pallice from where German submarines were once again threatening the Atlantic sea lanes. Lorient was hit eight times between mid-January and mid-February. By the end the town was ruined and deserted and many of its civilian inhabitants were dead. The U-boats and their crews, however, were virtually unharmed. The Germans had been left alone since the raids of 1941 and had used the time to build pens encased in thick concrete which conventional bombs were unable to penetrate.

The attacks shifted to Saint-Nazaire. On 28 February 427 aircraft bombed the port destroying two thirds of the town and killing twenty-eight inhabitants. Having seen what had happened to

Lorient, most of the population had fled. The almost total lack of positive results led to the cancellation of further operations, sparing Brest and La Pallice.

By the spring of 1943 the elements for an all-out attack on German cities were at last in place. In February 1943, Harris had more than 600 heavy bombers available to him and the numbers were growing. On the grand strategic front, the war was swinging the Allies' way. At Stalingrad, the German army was on the verge of defeat and surrender. Between 14 and 26 January 1943 Churchill and Roosevelt, along with the combined British and American Chiefs of Staff, met in the weak sunshine of Casablanca, to seek agreement on how their campaign should proceed and what part the RAF and the United States Army Air Force (USAAF) should play in it.

The role of Bomber Command was spelled out in what became known as the Casablanca directive. Harris was told: 'Your primary object will be the progressive destruction of the German military industrial and economic system, and the undermining of the morale of the German people to a point where their armed resistance is fatally weakened.'

Harris thus had the highest official approval to proceed with a campaign of all-out destruction. He chose to devote the rest of the spring and summer to hurling Bomber Command's greatly expanded destructive power against the Ruhr. Between March and the end of July, Bomber Command launched forty-three major operations, two thirds of which were aimed at the area. The RAF used the geographical designation 'Ruhr' loosely. It took in not only the Ruhr area itself but the whole industrial conglomeration along the Rhine and the Lippe. It was one of the great productive regions of the world, providing Germany with most of its coal and almost half its electricity. It was ugly even in peacetime, overhung with a perpetual haze, a de-natured monochrome sprawl of mills and factories churning out iron, steel and chemicals to feed the ravenous Moloch that Hitler had called to life. This was the heart of Germany's might. The aim of the Battle of the Ruhr was to stop it beating.

The Ruhr had been attacked many times before but with little effect. The innacuracy of navigation techniques, the perpetual blanket of smog and the strength of the defences combined to protect it. The crews, with their habitual dark humour, called it 'Happy Valley'. The news, at briefing, that it was the target for that night, provoked groans of dismay. But at least the journey was short, usually less than a six-hour round-trip, which reduced exposure to flak, fighters and bad weather.

The Battle of the Ruhr was an exhausting and bloody slog, in which night after night, large forces of up to 800 aircraft pitched themselves against the heaviest flak defences in Germany and the most experienced and best-equipped units of the Luftwaffe to deliver ever greater weights of bombs. The levels of killing and destruction soared. The same cities were attacked over and over again until, after studying the reconnaissance photographs that he pasted into 'blue books' for the enlightenment of important guests, Harris was satisfied. Essen, in the very centre of the Ruhr and the home of the Krupp steel works, was bombed five times. The raids killed nearly a thousand people, destroyed about 5,000 homes and damaged Krupp's, but not so badly as to seriously reduce production. The actions cost Bomber Command ninety-five aircraft.

In the midst of this grim catalogue of demolition and loss, one operation stands out. The Dams Raid of 16/17 May gave a much more positive demonstration of Bomber Command's abilities and the technological advances that had been made since the beginning of the war. It was carried out by 617 Squadron which had been formed in March from selected crews under the leadership of Wing Commander Guy Gibson, by now the pre-eminent operational leader in Bomber Command. The main targets were the Möhne, Eder and Sorpe dams. They were to be attacked with bouncing bombs designed by Barnes Wallis, the scientist who had invented the geodetic construction technique used in the Wellington.

The dams had been selected for attack by the Air Ministry before the war. They were a prime example of the sort of targets a strategic bombing force should be going after. The Möhne dam, south-east of Dortmund, held back nearly 140 million tons of water and was the main source of supply to the Ruhr valley, twenty miles away, as well as a provider of hydro-electric power. The even larger Eder reservoir south-east of Kassel supplied the water for an important canal which linked the Ruhr to Berlin. A successful attack on these targets could do severe damage to the German war economy.

The crews were the cream of 5 Group. For six weeks they trained intensively under Gibson's critical eye, practising the low-level approaches which were necessary to release the bombs at the right height. Harold 'Hobby' Hobday, a trainee insurance worker in pre-war life, had just completed twenty-six operations with 50 Squadron as a navigator and was preparing to go off on an advanced naviga-tion course when his skipper Flight Lieutenant Les Knight was approached by Gibson and asked if he was willing to join 617. Knight agreed, leaving Hobday with a dilemma. He decided to ditch the course and stick with his mates. 'I didn't want to let my crew down,' he remembered later, 'and I was quite keen on bombing. I loved the life . . . I liked the idea of the crew staying as one integral part of the set-up. I wouldn't have liked the thought that another navigator would have taken my place in my own crew.'

At 617 Squadron's base at 'Sunny Scampton' he met Gibson and quickly formed an impression of a man who although friendly 'would not stand any nonsense'. If anyone drank before flying 'he'd be down on them like a ton of bricks . . . one chap had a pint of beer before he was going on training and he was severely reprimanded.' Gibson delivered his rockets personally and with withering effect. 'He'd do it in front of the squadron and, of course, that made you feel about two inches high.'

Day and night the crews skimmed Scottish lochs and Welsh lakes at fifty to a hundred feet with no idea what they were preparing for. The first thought was they were to be sent against the battleship *Tirpitz*, a menace to shipping and the subject of numerous unsuc-cessful attacks. They also practised synchronizing the beams of two searchlights fitted to their Lancasters so that they harmonized at one spot, sixty feet above the ground, at exactly the right height at which the bombs should be released.

On Saturday 15 May, the day before the raid, pilots and navigators were finally told the target. The following morning all 133 crew of the nineteen aircraft that would take part gathered in the huge airmen's dining room to be briefed. The first to speak was Ralph Cochrane, the 5 Group commander. 'Bomber Command,' he told them, 'has been delivering the bludgeon blow on Hitler. You have been selected to give the rapier thrust which will shorten the war if it is successful.' Then Gibson outlined the plan before handing over to Barnes Wallis. He struck Hobday as 'a very kindly man, obviously very dedicated, frightfully clever ... but a fatherly type ... we thought he was a marvellous man. Everybody did.'

Wallis described how his bomb, if delivered correctly, would hit the water and skip along before exploding just below the parapet of the dam. Models of the dams were unveiled and studied. Hobday recalled a hum of animated chatter after the briefing closed. The crews 'were confident. There was no doubt about that. [This] was a marvellous thing to be on. It was so different from any bombing we'd ever done before and much more exciting. We thought it was a great effort.'

The squadron began taking off just before 9.30 p.m. One aircraft had to return after it struck the surface of the sea and lost its bomb. Another was so badly damaged by flak that it abandoned the mission. A further five were shot down or crashed before they reached the target. That left twelve. Hobday's crew had a trouble-free flight until they reached the Möhne dam where they held off while Gibson and four other aircraft launched their attacks through a blizzard of light flak. On the fifth attempt the dam wall crumbled.

Gibson now led four other crews on to the Eder. The dam was in a deep valley and surrounded by wooded hills. The Germans regarded the daunting terrain as sufficient protection and had not bothered with flak batteries. The first attack was made by Flight Lieutenant David Shannon's crew. Lying in the belly was Len Sumpter, a former guardsman who had switched services and become a bomb-aimer after seeing his comrades die in a Luftwaffe air raid. He was unhappy with the approach and told Shannon to go round again.

Gibson ordered Squadron Leader Henry Maudslay, a highly experienced pilot and the holder of the DFC, to go next. His bomb left the aircraft late and struck the parapet, exploding as the Lancaster passed overhead. Hobday 'saw the bomb go up in a huge flash . . . Gibson called the pilot and there was a very faint reply, very faint indeed . . . it was obviously someone who was in a great deal of trouble.' Maudslay struggled to keep the aircraft flying for another forty minutes before it was brought down by flak near Emmerich. There were no survivors.

Shannon's aircraft went in for another run and this time Sumpter was satisfied with the height, distance and speed. The bomb bounced twice and sank at the dam wall before exploding, sending a tower of water climbing 1,000 feet into the night sky. A small breach was seen in the dam but Gibson had to be sure.

At last it was the turn of Knight's crew. They attacked at 1.52 a.m. with the moon on the starboard beam lighting up the lake. After an initial dummy run they went round again, this time in earnest. Hobday 'wasn't tense. I was excited. It was a great thrill.' The only distraction was another pilot who came over the VHF radio offering tips on how to succeed. He was brusquely cut off. Gibson, who was flying alongside, watched the bomb bounce three times, hit the dam and explode. This time 'the thing broke . . . we watched the water billowing down the ravine from the dam . . . I could see cars going along and being overtaken by this wall of water . . . It really was fantastic, a sight I shall never forget.'

They headed for home and 'a very nice reception'. After debriefing and many celebratory drinks Hobday fell off to sleep in an armchair in the mess. The only unhappy man at Scampton was the inventor of the weapon who had made possible the success. Hobday thought Barnes Wallis 'looked shattered, because so many planes were missing. We were used to it of course, although it was rather more than average.'[19]

In fact eight out of the nineteen aircraft dispatched had been lost and fifty-three crew members killed. The raid had been an enormous success, though it failed to fulfil the more extravagent hopes of the planners. Two great dams had been destroyed. The breaching of the Möhne caused widespread flooding and disruption of railways, roads and canals and reduced the water and electricity supply to the

Ruhr. The destruction of the Eder dam caused considerable damage to waterways in the Kassel area. Houses were wrecked, bridges swept away and 1,294 people drowned, 493 of whom were foreign workers and prisoners of war. This was a new record. At least as important was the propaganda success that resulted. The Dambusters legend was created. Their feats showed Bomber Command as it preferred to be seen, wielders, in Cochrane's words, of the rapier rather than the bludgeon.

But it was with the bludgeon that it did most of its work. An operation that took place on the night of 13/14 May was far more typical of Bomber Boys' efforts at this time. Just after midnight on 14 May 1943, Arthur Taylor, who was now a bomb-aimer with 218 Squadron, took off with the rest of his crew from Downham Market in their Stirling, I-Ink, to attack Bochum in the dead centre of the Ruhr. He was setting off with more than his usual share of anxieties. Arthur had begun to lose confidence in his skipper, Bill, whom he suspected of being 'windy'. They were carrying an all-incendiary load. Arthur was 'determined to get there at all costs, with or without Bill.'

It was a beautiful moonlit night and he found his way quite easily until sometime before the target area, 'the *Gee* went u/s (unserviceable)' and they found themselves separated from the bomber stream and alone over Düsseldorf. 'Being the only kite there, they gave us all they'd got,' he wrote. 'Bill panicked and circled about in a frantic endeavour to get out, losing height all the time. Before we left Düsseldorf we were at 6,000 feet, picked up by immense cones of thirty to forty searchlights at a time, and a sitting target for light, medium and heavy flak.' It was at this point that Bill gave the order to bale out. Taylor replied that 'if we did we would never reach the ground in one piece. Bill then said, "You bloody well fly it then" and I ran up the steps and grabbed the second pilot's controls. I steered a straight course and in a few minutes we had left Düsseldorf behind.'

Bill recovered his composure and took over again. The respite did not last long. To get to Bochum they passed over the southern outskirts of Essen where 'for several minutes we were fired at continuously. There was a clap like thunder when flak hit the aircraft and a strong smell of cordite.' At last they arrived at the target. 'The place was ablaze. Immense fires covered the ground reflected red on a great pall of smoke that hung above the town.' They launched their bombs into the inferno and turned homewards.

A check on the intercom revealed that Jock the rear gunner was in desperate trouble. Arthur went back to help. He found he 'had obeyed the order to bale out but had pulled the ripcord too early and his parachute had partly opened, jamming him in the hatch. He had received the full blast of the explosions and was in a dazed condition when I pulled him back into the kite.'

Arthur struggled back along the fuselage, clambering laboriously over the centre spar and into the cockpit. 'I sat next to Bill to quieten him down and in case he was hit . . . I had to hold the throttles all the way as I-Ink was shaking badly.' Between them, they nursed the aircraft back, crossing the Dutch coast at the Zuyder Zee, and arrived over Downham Market in the half-light of dawn and with only a few gallons of petrol to spare.

This was not the end of the drama. The radio was wrecked, so they decided to land without permission. 'Just as I thought everything was OK I looked at Bill to find that he had let go of the controls and had both hands over his eyes. The kite swerved suddenly to port and the next thing I knew we had pranged into the control tower.' Arthur headed for the escape hatch but the way was blocked by Paddy, the flight engineer, who was wielding an axe, trying to hack his way through the fuselage. 'I remember tapping him on the back and asking him if he had tried the hatch . . . with that everyone tore hell for leather out of the kite.'

The starboard wing of the aircraft had ploughed through the briefing room demolishing much of it but mercifully only injuring a few of the people inside. But I-Ink had also careered into a lorry bringing back crews from the raid, cutting it in half and killing Sergeants Denzey and Lancaster.

The kite had had it. The turret of Len, the mid-upper gunner, was sieved with shrapnel, a splinter of which had grazed his nose on the way through. The Perspex astrodome observation point which bulged from the top of the fuselage had been whipped away by blast while Paddy had been looking through it.

They traipsed off to see the medical officer. Jock was sent to the sick bay with a deep cut to his head. The doctor gave Arthur and the rest 'two little yellow pills each which all but knocked me out before we reached the billet'.[20]

Shortly afterwards the crew announced they were sacking Bill. The crew was split up and Arthur was posted to a new station.

Bochum had been a costly operation. All together sixteen aircraft had been lost, killing sixty-four airmen. Another twenty-one were taken prisoner. So it was to go on all through the summer. Between the start of the campaign in early March to the end of July, when the battle was suspended after Harris chose to switch the attack to Berlin, Bomber Command lost just over a thousand aircraft. But it had also dropped more than 57,000 tons of bombs, often with devastating effects. On the ground, after three and a half years of the air war, the apocalyptic fate that Bomber Command's leaders had promised German cities was becoming a reality.

The Feast of St Peter and St Paul

In Germany's big towns the people watched the havoc and waited their turn. During the spring and summer of 1943 civilian casualties rose steadily. In an attack on Essen on the night of 5/6 March, 482 died. A few weeks later, on the night of 20/21 April, the Baltic city of Stettin was bombed and 586 were killed. Three weeks afterwards 693 died in Dortmund. A new record was set on the night of 29/30 May when 710 aircraft attacked Wuppertal in the heart of the Ruhr. They were aiming for the Barmen district, one half of the long, narrow town. The Pathfinder marking was deadly accurate and the bulk of the main force's bomb load tumbled into the narrow old streets. The fire that followed swallowed 80 per cent of the buildings. Some 3,400 people were killed, five times more than in any previous area raid.

Cologne had the unwanted distinction of having been the target of the first thousand-bomber raid, in May 1942. In that attack 469 people were killed. A year on, such a death toll had become commonplace. There had been several subsequent raids on the city, none of which came near to matching the trauma of that night. That was to change in the early hours of 29 June, a day which the fervently Catholic inhabitants celebrated as the feast of St Peter and St Paul.

Catholicism contributed greatly to Cologne's strong and idiosyncratic identity. Of the pre-war population of 770,000, around 600,000 were of the faith. It was a northern city but with a southern outlook and way of doing things. It prided itself on its open-mindedness and humour, displayed in the annual carnival, the biggest and most celebrated in Germany, a theatre of the absurd in which an elaborate procession of floats mocked the authorities.

Enthusiasm for Hitler was muted in Cologne. In the Reichstag elections of 5 March 1933, the Nazis gained 33.1 per cent of the votes, considerably less than in other parts of Germany. They fared better in the local elections, winning 39.6 per cent. By forming a coalition with two other right-wing parties, this was enough to give them control of the city council. The existing mayor, Konrad Adenauer of the Catholic *Zentrum* party, who had vigorously opposed the Nazis and snubbed Hitler by refusing to receive him at the local airport, was deposed. Dr Günther Riesen was installed as the Nazi mayor.

So began the Nazification of Cologne. It proceeded as in the rest of the country, propelled by the enthusiasm of the true believers, and the opportunism or passivity of the rest. With Nazi rule came a gradual degradation of trust. Dr Hans Volmer watched the moral corrosion set in among the 600 staff of the Cologne employment exchange where he started work in 1936. 'It was a conglomerate of the diligent and the indolent,' he wrote, '[the] oppressors and the oppressed, of those who were or wanted to be National Socialists and others who weren't or didn't want to be. Officials, SA and SS people busily kept each other under surveillance . . . the greater part of the employees were very anxious about possible measures being taken against them on account of the political attitudes. An incredible mistrust was spreading. The slogan was "not a word too many . . ."'[1]

Much of such anti-Nazi feeling as existed was caused by the regime's treatment of the Church. Anti-Catholic measures began in the 1930s but slackened after Hitler proscribed any further action against Catholics or Protestants to avoid unrest. The local party seized on the emergency created by the thousand-bomber raid to resume its campaign of persecution, however. The celebration of religious public holidays was banned and the Gestapo took over all confessional kindergartens and orphanages. The greatest uproar was caused by the seizure of eighteen convents and monasteries in the archbishopric of Cologne, an episode known as the *Klostersturm*. Nuns were turned out of their convents overnight and set to work in munitions factories. The theological college was also closed down.

Resistance to the moves was determined and courageous. The Church was led by Cardinal Joseph Frings. His predecessor, Cardinal Schulte, suffered a heart attack during a bombing raid on 10 March 1941 and died shortly afterwards. Unlike Schulte, who had tried to find compromises with the Nazis, Frings was tough, humane and charismatic. He was a popular figure in the air-raid shelter in the hospital at Cologne-Hohenlind. 'The Cardinal would borrow our Karl May books [German children's literature] to take his mind off things and to forget the fear,' remembered Gerhard Uhlenbruck, a teenager who went on to become a professor of medicine. 'I was fascinated by [his] extraordinary composure and his fine sense of humour.'[2]

He was leading a dedicated flock. Despite the repression of Catholic youth organizations, Cologne cathedral would be packed with young people on great Church holidays. 'On the feast of Christ the King, to disturb the service, the Hitler Youth would sometimes march round the outside of the cathedral playing drums and trumpets,' said Albert Roth who was sixteen in 1942. 'The older ones amongst us would go outside and a fight with the Hitler Youth would ensue.'[3] Although religious youth organizations were banned, the teaching of the faith was still allowed in classrooms. Some priests used religious instruction periods to preach against the regime. 'Often these sessions were used to take a critical stand against the political situation,' wrote Wilhelm Becker. 'I remember our chaplain, Otto Köhler saying that Hitler was the Antichrist . . .'[4]

But as much as the Church protested against its own persecution, it did almost nothing to protect the Jewish or Roma and Sinti gypsy people of Cologne. Many Jews had fled by the time the war began but in 1940 there were still 6,044 registered in the city. The campaign of oppression, humiliation and dispossession began almost immediately the Nazis arrived in power. Within a month of the takeover, stormtroopers forced their way into the regional court in Reichensperger Platz. They dragged out Jewish judges and lawyers in the middle of proceedings, placed signs declaring 'I am a Jew' around their necks and paraded them around town on dustcarts.[5] At the end of September 1938, all remaining Jewish lawyers and doctors in Cologne lost their right to practise. Jews were not allowed to leave their buildings after 8 p.m. and were only permitted to shop in certain stores. They became exiles in their own city. In the wake of the law prohibiting Jews and non-Jews from sharing dwelling space, certain buildings were designated as 'Jew houses' into which the outcasts were crammed. Erna Schoenenberg, who was deported to Theresienstadt concentration camp in 1942 and murdered in Auschwitz in 1944, wrote to her brother Julius who had escaped to Shanghai: 'The married couple Steiner live in our former dining room, and our former sitting room accommodates the two Levys. The two of us live in your former bedroom and the store room.'[6]

As Bomber Command's attacks took their toll, Jewish homes were seized to shelter those who had been bombed out and Jewish property was systematically stolen. The first deportation to the death camps took place on 21 October 1941. Jews were permitted to take fifty kilograms of luggage each. They were told to chalk a number on each suitcase so it could be reclaimed when they reached their unknown destination in the east. In fact all the baggage was immediately taken to the customs administration where it was auctioned off to the citizens of Cologne.

After the thousand-bomber raid the city authorities set up a special department to offer seized Jewish goods to the homeless. Regular auctions were held to dispose of heaters, vacuum cleaners, cooker hobs, cooking utensils, irons, hair dryers, gramophones and records, opera glasses, cameras, sofas, cupboards, beds, lamps, chairs, crockery, clocks, sewing machines, picture frames, mirrors, curtain rods and more. They were offered to Cologne's citizens as 'non-Aryan property' and thousands of people flocked to the sales.

For the Nazis it was an easy way of deflecting the grumbling and resentment that had come in the wake of the bombing. The legalized looting also had the effect of widening the circle of those who benefited from the persecution of the Jews.

There was another deportation on 30 November 1941, and a further spate after the thousand-bomber raid. Of the 6,000 Jews living in Cologne in August 1941, only half remained at the end of the year.

The deportations were carried out openly. The Jews left from the Cologne-Deutz station, jeered on their way by the SS and the SA who sang insulting, anti-Semitic songs. Crowds of curious citizens stood by. The Swiss consul in the city, Franz-Rudolf von Weiss, reported to Berne that he had heard people complaining about the 'bad taste' of the spectacle. But there was no protest on any scale from the public or the Church.[7]

Individual, courageous acts of help towards the Jews are hard to quantify. There were, however, some. A schoolgirl, Anne Winnen, recalled how 'once a week, my mother would prepare a parcel for them in our butcher's shop. In the evening, when it was dark, she would let them in by the back door. One noticed how one by one they stayed away. We knew exactly what was happening but what could one do individually? Everybody was afraid.'[8]

The people of Cologne had begun the war in a mood of light-hearted stoicism similar to that displayed in Coventry before the big raid. At a midsummer night's party in 1940 the programme included a firework display 'courtesy of Tommy and Flak, London and Cologne'.

By the night of 28 June 1943, all such levity had long disappeared. Cologne was the nearest big German city to the British bomber bases. It was in the first trench of the very front line of the air war. Already it had been bombed fifty-eight times with varying degrees of intensity. The previous raid had come only twelve days before but a large part of the force had been recalled because of bad weather and thick cloud over the target. About a hundred aircraft struggled on to the city, destroying 400 houses and badly damaging a chemical works.

Apart from the attacks, the inhabitants also had to contend with the disruption and nervous wear and tear caused by the frequent blare of public air-raid warnings which sounded whenever there were Allied aircraft in the vicinity. So far there had been twenty-seven that June. The signal sent everyone trudging to the air-raid shelters. The noise of the sirens induced resignation rather than panic. By now, the population had become well used to life underground.

Public bunkers were built from reinforced concrete and were

relatively robust but access to them was controlled and party not-
ables and their families got first call on the space. Most of the
population had to make do with the cellars of their own homes or
apartment blocks. Few regarded them as secure refuges. 'We sit in
the cellars, defenceless, almost every night,' wrote one Cologne
resident. 'I have reinforced the ceiling so that it will withstand the
rubble above, but ceilings are no protection against even medium-
sized bombs. It is a terrible feeling when the engines drone above
us and when we hear the whine of the falling bombs.' They learned
to identify the progress of the raid from the sounds outside. 'First
there was the rattle of incendiaries . . . then blow by blow, the heavy,
heavy impacts. As our cellar was not deep, we were crouching on
mattresses on the floor by the opening. Everyone had a wet cloth
over their head, a gas mask and matches. When the heavy bombs
fell, we pressed the cloth to our face and kept our ears and nose
shut with our fingers because of the blast.'[9]

Each cellar was connected to its neighbour by a hole in the wall,
knocked through so that people could move from one to the other
if the shelter collapsed. The feeling of insecurity was well founded.
Of the 20,000 people killed by air raids in Cologne during the
war, three out of five died inside shelters, asphyxiated by carbon
monoxide as fire devoured the oyxgen in the air, crushed by falling
brick, stone and timber, scalded by bursting hot-water pipes or
battered by blast. Nonetheless, public shelters were always packed,
so that the authorities imposed restrictions on who had the right
to enter. Jews, gypsies and foreign slave labourers were naturally
excluded on the grounds of their *Untermenschen* status. But such was
the overcrowding in the bunkers of the Rhineland in the summer of
1943 that the bar had to be extended. Able-bodied men between the
ages of sixteen and sixty and 'uniform wearers' were only allowed in
at the highest level of alert when a raid was imminent.

The rules in the public bunkers were enforced by wardens re-
cruited from the local party. In the private shelters a member of the
house community was in charge. As well as their policing duties,
they were expected to fight fires, removing the incendiaries that
crashed through roofs and into attics before a blaze could take hold.

Public bunker wardens seemed to relish their power. There were numerous stories of their bullying, arrogance and eagerness to punish those under their charge for the most trivial infractions.

For all the drawbacks, it seemed better to be in the shelters than outside them. In bad periods people went to them and stayed put. Bunker life was vile.'Just a few days in the bunker are making people dulled, coarse and indifferent,' wrote a male ambulance worker. 'Initially they are overwrought, then they become grumpy and monosyllabic. They steal things, show no respect for women and children. Any sense of order and cleanliness disappears. People who were formerly well-groomed don't wash or comb their hair for days. Men don't shave. They neglect their clothes. They come [to see me] dirty and stinking. They don't use the lavatories in the bunkers any more but find some dark corner.'

The women, it appeared, were as bad. 'Mothers are neglecting their children ... About 70 per cent of bunker inmates have the so-called "bunker disease" [scabies] and there is no water, hardly any heating, no opportunities to delouse. I am horrified when I see children, ill with scarlet fever or diphtheria and wrapped in blankets.' From his own observations and the reports of his fellow medical workers it seemed that everyone had lost their dignity and humanity. 'Decent people become like animals after losing house and home, dwelling like cave men in the bunker night and day to escape with nothing but their lives.'[10]

On the night of the great raid, the people of Cologne could feel reasonably confident as they went to bed that they would still be alive in the morning. The sky was overcast which would make life difficult for the *Oboe*-equipped Mosquitoes leading the Pathfinder crews. They would have to drop their target indicators so they lit up above the cloud, a less accurate method than if they ignited on the ground. In fact the cloud cover offered no protection at all.

All together 608 aircraft – Lancasters, Halifaxes, Wellingtons, Stirlings and Mosquitoes – took part in the raid. The Mosquitoes arrived over the target at around 1 a.m. By the time the bombers had departed they had dropped 162,038 incendiaries and 1,084 high explosive bombs, a ratio that increased the chances of creating an inferno. The sixteen heavy flak batteries around the city, supported by the light and medium flak guns on the east bank of the Rhine put up a strong defence but were eventually overwhelmed.

Heinz Pettenberg, a forty-three-year-old journalist, married with three young children, recorded in his diary that the alarm announcing imminent attack sounded at 1.12 a.m. 'Suddenly they are there,' he wrote. 'Engine noise, flak. We had just taken the children into the cellar and had brought the suitcases down and suddenly the raid is in full swing. The air is trembling with the thunder of the four-engined bombers . . . It's 1.30 a.m. and the following fifty-five minutes are an eternity.'[11]

The Pettenbergs lived in the relative safety of the suburb of Lindenthal. In the centre of town, Albert Beckers and his family were cowering in their cellar shelter directly beneath the bombardment. He too noticed the way 'the aircraft engines made the air vibrate. We were like rabbits in a warren. I was worried about the water pipes. What would happen if they burst and we would all be drowned? The air shook with detonations. Stuck in the cellar we hadn't felt the hail of incendiaries but above us everything was ablaze. Now came the second wave, the explosives. You cannot imagine what it is like to cower in a hole when the air quakes, the eardrums burst from the blast, the light goes out, oxygen runs out and dust and mortar crumble from the ceiling.'

As the cellar roof sagged they scrambled through the breach in the wall to the neighbouring shelter. In the midst of the terror there was a moment of grotesque comedy. 'A corpulent woman got stuck and we had to push and pull to get her through. She wailed, and some people were laughing, even in this potentially fatal situation. I prayed loudly, repeatedly. The "Our Father".'

It was clear that if they stayed underground they would be entombed. But at street level they faced incineration. The Beckers family made their choice. They struggled up the cellar steps and outside into the Waidmarkt, a square in the old town overlooked by the church of St Georg. It was a 'dreadful spectacle. Showers of sparks filled the air. Large and small pieces of burning wood floated through the air and landed on clothes and hair.' The fire was eating oxygen. They found a restaurant, crammed with refugees from the flames. Someone found some beer and people were gulping it down to slake their parched throats. A dog was whimpering with fear. It seemed to Beckers that this was no better than what they had escaped from. They set off again, finally staggering into the concrete public bunker on Georgsplatz, 'half blind and poisoned by smoke. It was completely full and wounded were being carried in all the time.' They stayed there until dawn. Then, with the all-clear sounded, they stepped out to look for another refuge, passing on the way 'the shrunken, charred corpses piled in a heap by the tower of St Georg.'[12]

In the panic and the chaos, children were easily separated from their parents. Hans Sester, a fourteen-year-old schoolboy, followed his mother and father, younger brother and sister after they smelled phosphorus smoke from incendiaries seeping into their cellar and ran outside. In the street 'it seemed that the tarmac had caught fire and melted from the phosphorus. Across the street a part of the old orphanage was ablaze and it seemed as if the high wind would whip up the flames even further.' There was a howling in the air, like a hurricane. It was, he learned later, the sound of the blaze devouring the oxygen.

His father, a postman, led them away, carrying his two-year-old daughter, Karin. Stumbling through the smoke they came across a group praying loudly, imploring Jesus to show them compassion. After a few dozen yards Hans became separated from the rest of the family. He was in a street called the Perlengraben, site of the old orphanage. He 'fled down some dark stairs into the air-raid shelter of the orphanage where I was given a drink of water and was able to press a wet hankerchief to my smarting eyes.' The next morning he went out to look for his family and found his six-year-old brother, who had also got lost but had been rescued by a woman. They comforted each other and after fruitlessly looking for their parents on the corpse-strewn Perlengraben, set out across the smoking rubble in the direction of the outlying district of Weiden where their aunt lived. Hans was still blinded by smoke. His little brother led him by the hand.

They waited at Weiden for the rest of the family to show up but they waited in vain. They were all dead. Their mother's body had been found in a wing of the orphanage. Her time of death was given as 2 a.m. The bodies of their father and sister were never identified. Sester never saw his mother's 'charred remains, thank God'.[13] An adolescent schoolgirl, fifteen-year-old Gertrud L, was not so fortunate. She was one of a number of girls asked by the authorities to record their experiences in essays written in the autumn after the raid. She too became separated from her family during the attack and spent the following day searching hopelessly. The next day she tried again. 'A man told me me that my mother and my sister were dead. I could not believe it. Then the man showed me where my mother lay. She was lying on her front, one hand holding her hair. Beside her there were others, headless, charred.' Her sister, whom she had last seen with her mother and who had an infant son, was not there. 'Another man told me that as they lifted my sister out, her child was drawing its last breath. They tried to revive him with oxygen but it was to no avail.' Gertrud tied a piece of paper with her mother's name to the body but it came loose when she was carted away. She was buried as an 'unknown'.[14]

The raid ended at 2.45 a.m. It had lasted ninety-five minutes. A few hours afterwards, Heinz Pettenberg, the journalist, left the safety of the suburbs to survey the damage. Walking in, he passed large numbers of rescue workers drafted in from outside. He soon realized that 'something terrible had happened'. He was 'walking through a destroyed city'. The fires were still burning and the heat was unbearable. Everything he knew and loved in his home town seemed to have been destroyed. His newspaper's office had disappeared. 'At the Bollwerk lie the collapsed ruins of the ancient inn "Zum Krützchen", where we spent so many happy hours . . . there is not one house left on the Heumarkt and the house of my grandparents, Rheingasse 5, has gone . . . on the Waidmarkt, the irreplaceable St Georg in ruins. The Blaubach – rubble, the Postrasse, the Waisenhausgasse, rubble, rubble. One can hardly see anything. The smoke, poisonous, blue-black, drags through the streets . . . from time to time people with swollen eyes appear amidst the clouds of smoke, gasping refugees, holding a few saved possessions. The swollen cadaver of a dead horse lies on the street, and then – a picture of horror – corpses, twisted, barely covered up.' Remembering the thousand-bomber raid of a year before he asked himself, 'What was the thirty-first of May . . . compared with this! I will never forget this terrible walk.'[15]

The city records show nearly 6,500 buildings were destroyed. Of these, 6,368 were houses and apartment buildings, underneath which the population was cowering. A further 3,515 suffered heavy damage. Two hospitals, seventeen churches, twenty-four schools, two theatres, eight cinemas, seven post and telegraph offices, one railway station, six banks and ten hotels were also swept away. The list also includes twenty unspecified 'official buildings,' four 'military installations' and forty-three 'industrial installations'.[16] Given the great breadth of the violence done to Cologne it is hard to see them as anything other than incidental targets. The Gestapo headquarters, in the Appellhofplatz in the middle of town, by some malign miracle, remained intact. The back yard was equipped with a gallows where towards the end of the war civilians and many slave labourers were hanged for petty offences like stealing a cooking pot. The death toll from the bombing established another record. This time 4,377 were killed, nearly ten times more than in the 'thousand' raid, and probably another 10,000 wounded.

Harris was relentless. The people of Cologne were still numb with shock when bombers appeared again. Four days later another major operation was mounted against the industrial areas on the east bank of the Rhine. Some twenty factories were hit along with the homes of the workers who laboured in them. More than 580 were killed and 70,000 bombed out. There was a further attack on 8/9 July in which another 502 civilians died.

As a result of these three raids in a little over a week, 350,000 lost their homes. Some were rehoused in the few inhabitable buildings remaining in Cologne. Many more were evacuated or fled the city and the surrounding area under their own steam. The exodus was desperate and chaotic. Evacuees who had fled to the surrounding countryside had to return to the city to get a train that would take them to safety. 'In Opladen [a small town north of Cologne] the train stops,' a male traveller, Herr Roemer, recorded in his diary entry for 6 July 1943. 'The journey is to continue in buses and after a long wait they finally arrive. Hundreds of people storm [the first] vehicle. Squashed children and women scream, men curse. Everyone is laden down with luggage and boxes. Many are carrying bedding. A few soldiers are sitting on the roof. We drive for an hour to Cologne. Here are thousands of people at the station, on the platform. Next to me is a heavily pregnant woman with two children and luggage. She is weeping bitterly. A train arrives. There is a surging back and forth. The train is overloaded. The platform is still packed with people bickering. The transport police remove some people from the running boards and the locomotive.' When the train reached Bonn a fight broke out in Roemer's compartment. On the wall of another he noticed 'a chalk drawing. A gallows from which hangs a swastika. Everybody sees it but nobody wipes it away.'[17] Many of those who fled the city did not return until the war was over. In 1940 it was the home of 770,00 people. By March 1945, the population was 40,000.

The authorities paid close attention to the mood of the city. The material gleaned by the army of informants who cocked their ears to conversations in streets, shops and workplaces was disquieting. A survey by the SS security service, the *Sicherheitsdienst* (SD), delivered nine days after the attack, reported widespread defeatism and bitterness and cynicism towards the regime.

In the immediate aftermath the Hitler salute was rarely seen. The leaflets that the RAF had showered by the million on Germany finally had a readership. People picked them from the rubble, read them and discussed their contents with their family, friends and workmates, disregarding the dire penalties that could result if they were caught.

Caution was fraying. Suffering made people bold. The authorities were amazed by the lack of circumspection. The strength of the attack was a profound shock to a nation that had been told that the enemy was weak and victory was inevitable. 'Many people are under the impression that [the enemy], in the future development of the war, are actually much stronger and will overcome us,' ran one passage of the report. 'They [think] the outcome of the war is in doubt and people are nervous and feel weighed down by this.' The fear showed in the sour, unfunny jokes: Hitler's favourite singer Zarah Leander has been summoned to Berlin. She is going to sing her most famous hit for the Führer – 'I Know One Day A Miracle Will Come'.

But the Nazis could take some comfort from the fact that the raid had created anger as well as despondency. The attack on Cologne cathedral had provoked particular indignation and vengeful feelings. The fact that the thirteenth-century Gothic masterpiece had only been damaged rather than destroyed made little difference. For many a devout *Kölner*, the sight of the smoke-blackened spires provoked rage. 'This is the worst thing they have done yet,' a labourer was quoted as saying in the SS report. 'I don't know much about culture but I want to smash the heads of the English for this.' It was just the sentiment on the lips of people in Coventry nearly three years previously when their cathedral had been blitzed.

For others, the damage done to this great symbol of faith seemed like a portent. It was a sign that 'God had turned his face away from the Germans' or a punishment for the destruction of the temples of the Jews.

The fear caused by the St Peter and St Paul raid rippled outwards across Germany. The refugees who fled Cologne to all corners of the Reich took their stories with them. The SD reports from Franconia, far away in the south, spoke of a 'panic-like fear of the Anglo-American air war and its expected consequences'. They noted 'growing nervousness and anxiety at the fact that the enemy seem to have the upper hand in the air and at our own powerlessness'. The utterances of the Party high-ups were given little credence. People preferred to get their news now from Swiss radio rather than official broadcasts. Around Stuttgart, morale was said to be 'under pressure'. Overflights by Allied aircraft increased the sense of dread amongst those below and the feeling that it would be their turn next.[18]

The raids, then, seemed to be having the desired effect. Factories were being flattened and vast acreages of housing reduced to blackened rubble. The long rows of coffins laid out for the official mass burial ceremonies left no one in the Ruhr in any doubt that the war had arrived on their doorstep and they were as exposed to death as their husbands, brothers and fathers on the Eastern Front. People were frightened. More than 28,000 fled Aachen after a raid in mid-July that killed only 294 people. Seven weeks later most of them had failed to return.

As the Battle of the Ruhr progressed the area's defences inevitably improved making operations increasingly dangerous. By the end of May, Harris had 800 aircraft at his immediate disposal, four fifths of which were four-engined bombers. Germany was full of attractive targets. Concentrating on the Ruhr meant that much of the rest of urban Germany was having a quiet time. To preserve his resources and to maintain the principle that all Germany should feel the lash of the bomber offensive, it was necessary to move on.

Hamburg was an obvious target for another spectacular. It had been chosen for the first 'thousand' raid until the weather forecast ruled it out. It was the second-biggest city in Germany with a population of 1.8 million and the country's most important port. Ships were built there including U-boats. Despite all this, and the fact that it was reasonably easy to identify due to its proximity to the Baltic coast, it had so far got off lightly. It had been attacked ninety-eight times by Bomber Command since the beginning of the war but with little serious effect.

At the end of July the Battle of the Ruhr was over and the Battle of Hamburg was about to begin. The plan envisaged four major raids over ten nights in which 10,000 tons of bombs were to be dropped. The first came on the night of 24/25 July. Practice had intensified the concentration of aircraft in the target area and re-duced their time in the danger zone so that on this night the 728 aircraft which reached Hamburg were able to drop 2,284 tons of bombs in fifty minutes. Defences were baffled by the use for the first time of *Window*, bundles of aluminium foil which were dumped out of special chutes cut in the bombers' fuselages and which, for a time at least, baffled the radar operators who could not decide whether or not the blips they made on their screens represented aircraft.

The city was well beyond the range of *Oboe*. This may have reduced the accuracy of the bombardment. By now there was a well-established tendency for the bombing to 'creep back' as crews dropped their loads into the first fires and smoke they saw, spreading the zone of destruction backwards from the target. On this raid it was six miles long. The central and north-western districts of the city suffered badly and 1,200 people were killed.

The following day there were more aeroplanes over the smoking city. These were the B-17 Flying Fortresses of the American Eighth Air Force making their first appearance in support of an RAF operation. The huge plumes of smoke hanging in the air made it impossible for them to identify the industrial targets they had been ordered to destroy. They returned the following day but then withdrew from the battle, leaving it to the Lancasters, Halifaxes, Stirlings and Wellingtons.

The second raid followed seventy-two hours after the first. The Pathfinders' marking was slightly off the city-centre aiming-point but the bombing was tightly concentrated and the 2,326 bombs dropped fell within a small radius.

The bomb load was made up of 50 per cent incendiaries, less than normal, but the effect it created was extraordinary. The night was hot and dry and the fires that sprang up charged through the working-class areas of Hammerbrook, Hamm and Borgfeld, devouring everything combustible. The exhausted fire services could do nothing to slow them and the blazes only began subsiding when there was nothing left for them to consume.

The death toll dwarfed anything yet achieved by Bomber Command. Some 40,000 people died, most of them asphyxiated by carbon dioxide after the fire leached all the oxygen from the air, sucking it from the shelters. The two following raids on 29/30 July and 2/3 August killed only 387. Almost everyone else had fled.

This was by far the most terrible blow suffered by German civilians since the beginning of the war. In his report on the catastrophe, the police president of Hamburg abandoned bureaucratic prose and admitted his difficulty in finding words to describe what had happened. 'Speech is impotent to portray the measure of the horror,' he wrote. Each night of attack was followed by 'a day which

Aftermath of a firestorm. Hamburg, July 1943.

displayed the horror in the dim and unreal light of a sky hidden in smoke ... the streets were covered with hundreds of corpses. Mothers with their children, youths, old men, burnt, charred, untouched and clothed, naked with a waxen pallor like dummies in a shop window they lay in every posture, quiet and peaceful or cramped, the death struggle shown in the expression on their faces.' The picture inside the shelters was 'even more horrible in its effect, as it showed in many cases the final distracted struggle against a merciless fate. Although in some places shelterers sat quietly, peacefully and untouched as if sleeping in their chairs, killed without pain or realization by carbon monoxide poisoning, in other shelters the position of remains of bones and skulls showed how the occupants had fought to escape from their buried prison.'

In the minds of the authorities, at least, the victims of the raids were martyrs. 'Posterity,' wrote the police chief, 'can only bow its head in honour of the fate of these innocents, sacrificed by the murderous lust of a sadistic enemy.' If the British had hoped to create chaos and despair they had not succeeded as 'the conduct of the population, which at no time and nowhere showed panic or even signs of panic . . . was worthy of the magnitude of the disaster.' Instead there was 'an irresistible will to rebuild'.[19] German civilians suffered terribly in the summer of 1943. The RAF had achieved a scale of destruction that far surpassed anything that been seen in the history of aerial warfare. But whether or not the population was approaching a state of paralysing moral collapse was impossible to tell and the question was not about to be settled.

8

The Reasons Why

In the course of their tours, airmen seldom talked about the value of bombing or the morality of what they were engaged in. If they had doubts, they tended to keep them to themselves. They were fighting a sharply focused war. They had a public obligation to carry out the duty they had volunteered for. They had a duty to themselves to survive. These realities created a cast of mind that could make them seem impervious to all other considerations.

A few hours before his first mission, an apprehensive Peter Johnson joined a large crowd in the briefing room. They were addressed by a WAAF intelligence officer, 'a formidable lady who minced no words'. The target, yet again, was the Krupp works in Essen.

'Yes, they've been damaged,' she shouted over the chorus of groans and expletives. 'But make no mistake, they're still turning out guns and shells aimed at you.' She predicted that the defences would be stronger than ever, giving details of the known searchlight and flak dispositions. '"They're going to give you HELL," she spat. "See that you give it them back!"' She sat down 'visibly affected by her own vehemence'.

Johnson found this performance distasteful coming from a non-combatant but he was impressed by the dangers she had so forcefully described. Looking around at the others he was surprised to see that they seemed 'almost totally untouched by what they had heard'. Many had their eyes closed. Their concerns were simply 'the details of route and navigation, which colour of target indicator they were to bomb and what they could do to make sure they arrived on time and got home safely.' He concluded that 'while the fierce lady was probably convinced that she was striking a significant blow in the great struggle, for the bulk of her audience she was whistling in the wind.'[1]

The face the Bomber Boys showed to the world was sardonic and displays of patriotic enthusiasm were considered *infra dig*. It was an ethos that did not encourage self-regard. The contrast with the Americans was marked. One Sunday night in the autumn of 1944 Ken Newman and his comrades sat down to watch a film in the anteroom of the officers' mess at Little Staughton. A few USAAF officers were also present. The movie celebrated the fictional feats of a band of American aviators who volunteer to fly B17s in Europe. 'All the RAF officers present were nearly doubled up with laughter at this rubbishy Hollywood propaganda,' he wrote. 'But when the lights were put on the faces of the USAAF aircrew were a picture – it was all too clear that they had taken the film completely seriously and identified themselves with the actors. They were visibly moved and tears were streaming from their eyes; ours too but for a very different reason.'[2]

Their studied coolness did not mean that the crews did not think about what they were doing. The reserve masked a solid belief in the virtue of the cause. With a very few exceptions, the men of Bomber Command accepted that Germany had wantonly provoked a war then prosecuted it with a ruthlessness and fanaticism that justified almost any amount of retaliation in kind. By the end of 1943, German civilian casualties far outstripped those that the Luftwaffe had inflicted so far on Britain, but any notion of proportionality had long disappeared.

It was one of Hitler's great negative achievements that he succeeded in hardening the hearts of men to whom violence was unnatural and repellent. The sense that what they were doing was essential pervaded Bomber Command. Like many others, Michael Scott, a navigator with 110 Squadron, recoiled at the idea of killing yet he had volunteered for the RAF knowing that he was putting himself in exceptional danger. He was a sensitive, music-loving intellectual who taught at Cheam, where the children of the elite were prepared for the best public schools. He wrote short stories and thought of himself as an anarchist. He was sceptical about

Britain's motivations, believing that the desire to 'retain our spoils from foreign conquests' outweighed the commitment to freedom. The spectre of a Nazi-ruled world dispelled his doubts. He set out his reasons for joining up in a letter to his father, to be opened in the event of his death.

'Dear Daddy,' he wrote. 'You know how I hated the idea of war and that hate will remain with me for ever. What has kept me going is the spiritual force to be derived from music, its reflections of my own feelings and the power it has to uplift the soul above earthly things . . . now I am off to the source of music and can fulfil all the vague longings of my soul in becoming part of the fountain whence all good comes. I have no belief in a personal God but I *do* believe most strongly in a spiritual force which was the source of our being and which will be our ultimate goal. If there is anything worth fighting for it is the right to follow our own paths to this goal and to prevent our children from having their souls sterilized by Nazi doctrines . . . And so I have been fighting.' Scott was killed during a daylight minelaying trip near Texel on 24 May 1941.[3]

Not many of those taking part talked or wrote like Scott. Even though they might have shared his conviction that they were engaged in a fundamental struggle between good and evil, they were unlikely to express such sentiments in public. In the pubs and the canteens the conversation was more likely to be about girls and beer than death and war. It was part of an RAF culture of studied light-heartedness. Reg Fayers lamented the lack of discussion about the aims of the campaign. 'I feel we should all be alight . . . with a flame to inspire us on this crusade to save whatever-it-is. But nobody is.'[4]

Even Fayers did not claim to know precisely what it was they were fighting for. If anything, it was a desire to maintain a way of life that the Nazis were dedicated to destroying. 'I'm fighting so that in the future people will have the chance to live as happily as we did all together before the war without interference,' wrote Eric Rawlings, a twenty-one-year-old from north London, to his parents before his death in 1942. 'Where young 'uns like myself could make the most of the marvellous opportunities which you gave me for twenty years and for which I know you made many, many sacrifices. God bless you all and may everything turn out right in the end.'5

Everyone knew what they were fighting against. The memory of the Blitz persisted as a bitter inspiration long after the German assault had faded out at the end of May 1941. Roy MacDonald, a mid-upper gunner with the PFF, was doing his basic training at Uxbridge when the attacks began. 'One night I got caught up in it and had to sleep down on Piccadilly platform. The raid was tremendous. Then . . . I was posted up to West Kirby just in time for the Blitz on Merseyside and so I saw plenty of what they were doing to us . . . the idea was that if we could keep on doing it back they would pack up or finish the war . . . I'd no conscience about what we were doing, none at all. I don't think anybody did. It had to be done. That was the way we looked at it anyway.'6

After the invasion of the Soviet Union in June 1941 the Luftwaffe was able to mount only occasional raids against Britain. These, together with the V1 and V2 rocket attacks of 1944 and 1945, did little damage to the war effort or morale, but they kept the spirit of revenge sharp and bright. Sergeant Bernard Dye, an air gunner with 622 Squadron, lost his best friend in a German raid in April 1942. 'Nick was my best pal,' he wrote afterwards.

> We were brought up together and played together. We joined youth organizations and had some good fun. He was liked by all. It was a bright and sunny morning . . . my pal was on his way to work. He probably was whistling or humming a tune to himself. He was always happy in life. Then it happened, out of the clear blue sky [came] the Nazi bombers . . . then came the whistle of bombs, red-hot shrapnel was flung far and wide, people fell to the ground and got up no more. My pal Nick was hit in the back, he died some six hours later a lingering death. Nick was a good pal the best you could get. I cannot realize he is gone. When I'm sitting behind my guns I will remember Nick. Nick couldn't hit back, he

was helpless. But I will hit the Huns, hit hard too. I will get my revenge for my dear Pal Nick who was buried today.[7]

For George Hull and his crew the violence they were inflicting on Germany was meant personally. Writing to brown-eyed, brown-haired Joan Kirby on 16 February 1944 after returning from Berlin he told her that they always dedicated their 'cookie', the biggest bomb in a normal load, 'to someone or something. There was the first on Berlin, reprisals for John [Joan's brother killed in a bomber training accident], with an extra on Frankfurt for both John and his Dad. There have been cookies from the people of Australia, the people of Manchester the people of London etc. But tonight's effort was dedicated to all the brown-eyed brunettes we know (don't ask me for all their names!).'

Ten days later he was on his way to Schweinfurt when the route took him over London while a raid was in progress. It made him 'burn with rage . . . I thought of your folks and mine underneath it all and I would not have turned back if we had caught fire.' Hull's decency caused him to reflect on the 'ultimate futility of all this slaughter'. But such thoughts were stifled easily by his hatred of the German regime. 'I never lose sight of the fact that if our feelings rule our judgement we might suffer terrible consequences. Think of it. Nazis in Britain, desecrating our land, destroying those beautiful things that you and I hold dear, fouling our women in brothels, wholesale slaughter – perhaps your dad shot for not obeying an order or my mother forced to billet German officers while suffering insults. It's true. Can you see the Nazis sparing Britain, the country above all which held out against them and turned the tables?'

He was writing having just landed and was suffering from a 'post ops headache'. He felt 'washed out completely and as usual fed up to the back teeth.' But glowing through the fog of weariness there is a burning determination to carry on. 'Of course I hate the job but idealism is not enough. I am fighting for the people I love and the boys who have already paid the full price. To give in to matters on ideological grounds is to let them all down.'[8]

The campaign could, in one sense, be regarded as a continuous act of retribution for those who had died, on the ground and in the air. The survivors felt a strong impulse to avenge dead comrades. By striking back they were exacting a price for their loss and investing it with value and meaning. 'There was [this] feeling that those who were left would carry on,' said Jim Berry, a Pathfinder pilot.[9] One bomber from 467 Squadron was named 'Jock's Revenge' after a flight engineer who had been killed while flying in her. As he dropped his bombs on Duisburg on his first mission, Ken Newman thought of his 'brother-in-law Victor and his now fatherless son'. Victor had been killed in a Halifax over Magdeburg, leaving behind a wife who was five months pregnant.[10]

Berlin's heavy defences and great distance away made it an unpopular target. But there was some satisfaction in knowing that they were bringing the war to the Führer's front door. 'There was something special about attacking the Big City,' wrote Peter Johnson. 'The feelings were partly ... fuelled by the picture of Hitler himself, cowering there below in his bunker.'[11]

But it was not Hitler who was suffering. Looking down from his rear gunner's turret at the towns and villages of Lincolnshire as he headed off to bomb Böhlen, Cy March could not help comparing the tiny figures in the streets below to those he was going to attack. 'We took off ... vowing to do as much damage to Germany as we could. We set course to the East and I noticed that over this [part of the] country the blackout wasn't so good, doors opening etc. I got to wondering about the people below us, going for a pint, meeting a bird for the flicks, and the people we were going to. Probably doing the same, but in for a nasty shock.'[12]

By the end of 1942 no one was in any doubt about the effect the bombs were having. It was not hard to imagine how the victims felt. Tom Wingham, a navigator with 102 Squadron, remembered looking down on his first trip to the Ruhr. 'It was quite a ghastly sight to see the amount of flame and explosions ... I made up my mind that if ever I had to bale out over the target, I wouldn't. I would rather go down with the aircraft because I was sure that if you landed in that, the populace would tear you to bits.'[13]

Some commanders, like Harry Yates's New Zealander CO Jack Leslie, seemed to revel in the damage they were doing. 'I want you to really burn this place,' he told 75 Squadron before an operation on the Lens marshalling yards in the summer of 1944, signing off with: 'See you in the smoke.' These last five words, Yates remembered, 'were to become very familiar to us. Some of Jack Leslie's more gung-ho briefings could be strong meat. Exhortations to blast this and burn that and descriptions of the enemy as vermin or bastards left no doubt about the CO's fighting spirit or the commitment he required from his men.'[14]

Some crews appreciated the bloodthirsty approach. Doug Mourton of 102 Squadron remembered that 'the first time we were given a civilian target to bomb I must say that the majority of the aircrew there raised a cheer because I suppose so many of them had come from towns that [had suffered]. Many of them probably had relations that had been killed in the indiscriminate German bombing and they were very pleased to be doing the same thing.'

Mourton did not share this attitude. As his tour progressed he grew increasingly uneasy about what he was doing. At one point he thought of refusing to fly 'because I hadn't volunteered to incinerate women and children.' He was persuaded to carry on by the argument that 'this type of bombing . . . would make the war end quicker and . . . more lives would be saved than sacrificed.'[15] Willie Lewis was also tempted to revolt when on 29 May 1943 he learned that the target for the night was Wuppertal, thirty miles south of Essen. The briefing officer did not disguise the fact that it was crammed with refugees from the Battle of the Ruhr. According to his account he informed his skipper John Maze that he had 'a good mind not to come'.

He told him that 'up to now, I've kidded myself that I was fighting a man's war risking my neck killing men and being shot at in return but what the hell do they call this? It's deliberate murder of the sort that we've called the Jerries names for for the last three years.' He felt strongly the 'confounded hypocrisy' of the situation. 'There's that Air Marshal type talking on the radio telling everyone what brutes the Germans are and how we wouldn't dream of doing anything like it ourselves and yet we arrange a trip like this.' Maze, with his usual pragmatism, replied that by refusing to go he would be 'branded as yellow, that's all' and declared to be lacking in moral fibre. Lewis bowed to his skipper's worldly logic, blustering that he would 'never pretend that we are nice clean little boys doing a respectable job from now on. We are only mean bastards taking orders from a bunch of hypocrites.'[16] Lewis's premonitions about Wuppertal were well founded. The town was only lightly defended. The PFF marking was excellent and the incendiaries that whistled down on the flares sparked a minor firestorm which burned down 80 per cent of the built-up area. About 3,800 people were killed, almost all of them civilians.

Lewis's finer feelings were eclipsed by the horrors of the trip. At one point T-Tommy was coned by searchlights but managed to wriggle free. Another Halifax half a mile in front was not so lucky. Watching the flak bursting around the doomed aircraft as a fighter hosed it with cannon fire Lewis felt a guilty thrill of relief that they had escaped, then foolish as he remembered that only that morning he had 'been feeling sorry for the Germans'.[17]

As he had pointed out, it was sometimes difficult to overlook the similarities between the crimes with which the Germans were constantly charged and some of Bomber Command's activities. Charles Patterson, now flying a Mosquito for the RAF Film Unit, was tasked with taking cine pictures of the immediate aftermath of a daylight raid on a steelworks at Denain in northern France. At his group commander's suggestion he also dropped some bombs of his own. There were different delays on the fuses from half an hour to twenty-four hours. 'If a German had done it to us,' he said later, 'we would have said [it was] frightfully caddish and wicked and unsporting. But when we did it to the Germans it was considered rather clever and imaginative.'[18]

The demands of operational life did not encourage reflection. Johnny Jones, a rear gunner with 467 Squadron, found his conscience stirring as he bombed Munich on the night of 7/8 January 1945. 'It must have been hell on earth for the poor devils down below,' he wrote in his dairy. 'Mass murder. Whole families wiped out no doubt. I could not help but think when the bombs left the a/c [aircraft] what a terrible thing I am doing. It must be *wrong*.' Five weeks later he took part in the great raid on Dresden. On this occasion his diary records only that the 'damage done must have been colossal'.[19]

Sitting in a prisoner of war camp with almost nothing to do, protracted contemplation came more easily. Geoffrey Willatt, taken prisoner after being shot down on his way to Mannheim on the night of 5/6 September 1943, ended up in Stalag-Luft 3 near Bremen. In the spring of 1944 he noted in his diary the deteriorating behaviour of one of his friends. 'Suddenly George seems much worse and I hadn't realized how bad he was till one day he took me to a secluded place and burst into tears! It appears, or at least he says, that at the beginning of the war he nearly turned conscientious objector and now worries about all the women and children he's killed ... he began by being vague and preoccupied, then was unable to concentrate on anything, had a short period of religion which did him no good at all and then a period of self-persecution (cold showers, running round the circuit till exhausted etc.).'

Willatt diagnosed an acute case of 'barbed wire psychosis' and asked him why the deaths he had caused weighed on his mind 'when there are thousands of other aircrew prisoners who don't worry. I tell him he must live a useful life after the war but his mind won't now function enough to argue it all.'

Despite the well-intentioned interventions of the other prisoners in his hut George's mental condition continued to deteriorate. 'No one dare look at him because it gives him a hunted feeling & yet everyone is being too kind to him – an embarrassing feeling for him I know and no help.' He spent a few days in the camp hospital but seemed even worse on his return. 'He walked up and down the room five steps each way for half an hour with his head in his hands. We take it in turns to follow him when he goes out – so afraid that he'll jump over the wire and get shot.' Eventually George was taken away to the German mental hospital at Lamsdorf with two other prisoners.

Willatt's recipe for staying sane was exercise and the suppression of barren reflection. 'I haven't yet heard of a person going "round the bend" who took part regularly in games,' he noted after George was taken away. As for guilt, it was pointless debating the rights and wrongs until the war was over.[20]

Peter Johnson was in a persistent anguish of doubt about what he was doing. He was born in 1909, joined the RAF in 1930 and lived through the fear and moral confusion that accompanied the rise of the dictators. He had struggled against the anti-German feeling that gripped Britain in the pre-war years, an attitude that survived even the invasion of Poland, but not the attack on the Low Countries. After that he 'hated Hitler and hated the Germans who loved him'.

Nonetheless the first 'thousand' raids made him uneasy. They seemed to have more in common with the Blitz than the precision attacks like the raid on the Renault works at Billancourt, the event that had inspired him to volunteer for ops. A book of drawings by a Polish refugee, Joseph Bato, tugged at his conscience. They were simple, understated sketches of London districts just after the Germans had visited. One showed a terraced house whose front had been torn away, 'exposing to the street the shattered remains of the quiet, decent life that went on in [it].'

Writing to his girlfriend Shelagh in the summer of 1943 Johnson voiced his hesitation in language that revealed the depth of his doubt.

> Of course the Royal Air Force aims for military objectives, but . . . I swear to you my sweet, that nothing that ever happened in London in any way approached what I saw in Dortmund . . . no German pilot ever looked down on London and saw the obscene red mass of flames that was Dortmund last month or Hamburg last week. And this is only the beginning, for nothing can stop us now. Nothing but the end of the war can stop the destruction of practically every city in Germany, destruction that will make Bato's drawings look like the record of a peevish child bored with its bricks.

On one occasion Johnson let his feelings slip in public. Shortly after taking over 49 Squadron in April 1943 he was summoned to 5 Group headquarters near Grantham to look after a VIP guest. The visitor was Sir Kingsley Wood, the chancellor of the exchequer, who had served as secretary of state for air before the war. Johnson's job was to take him through each step of a raid. Wood was to stay at the base until the aircraft had returned and the crews were debriefed. During the evening he was shown some reconnaissance photographs taken after an attack on Düsseldorf a few weeks previously. The chancellor, a cheerful, Pickwickian figure, seemed very satisfied with what he saw. Johnson had viewed a few post-ops photos but nothing like these. 'Seen through the stereoscopic glass the detail was staggeringly clear, showing just rows and rows of apparently empty boxes which had been houses. They had no roofs or content. This had been a crowded residential area, long streets of terraced houses in an orderly right-angled arrangement, covering virtually the whole of the six-inch square photograph. There were one or two open spaces but the chief impression was just those rows and rows of empty shells, a huge dead area where once thousands of human beings had lived.'

Johnson heard himself saying: 'God! The Germans will never forgive us for this.' In an instant the chancellor's cheery demeanour vanished. '"What do you mean, forgive *us*?" he snapped. "Let me tell you, it's we who'll have to forgive the Germans and what's more I hope we don't do it too quickly."'[21]

Wood was only saying what most people felt. That did not mean that there was no controversy about the morality of the bombing campaign. There were politicians and churchmen who shared Johnson's moral discomfort. It was one of Harris's rough virtues that he never tried to disguise the aims or consequences of his strategy. The government, however, consistently avoided admitting the full truth about its policy and persistently refused to acknowledge that one of the main purposes of much of Bomber Command's actions was the destruction of cities themselves. The critics of area bombing were led by Richard Stokes, the loquacious Labour MP for Ipswich. Stokes had no faith in strategic bombing, arguing that the war effort would be better spent in building more ships and fighters, nor in the view that sustained bombing could crush Germany's spirit. As early as May 1942, he told the Commons: 'I have been through practically every raid in London and to most of the places that have been badly blitzed and I do not believe for a single moment that you are ever going to destroy the morale of the people by bombing from the air.' The idea that Germany could be brought down by bombing, he concluded 'is absolutely puerile'.[22]

But the core of his objections to the strategic air campaign bombing was ethical. The bombing of Cologne was not only 'strategic lunacy' but 'morally wrong as no real effort was made to limit the targets to military objectives ... women and little children are women and little children to me, wherever they live.' A further immorality, Stokes, argued was that the architects of the campaign were asking good men to do dreadful things. 'It fills me with absolute nausea,' he said 'to think of the filthy task that many of our young men are being invited to carry out.'[23]

Stokes tried repeatedly to get the government to admit what was going on. On 31 March 1943 he asked the secretary of state for air whether 'on any occasion instructions had been given to British airmen to engage in area bombing rather than limit their attention to purely military targets.' Sir Archibald Sinclair replied that 'the targets of Bomber Command are always military, but night bombing of objectives necessarily involves bombing the area in which they are situated.'[24] When he repeated the question in a slightly different form on 1 December, asking him whether 'the policy of limiting objectives of Bomber Command to targets of military importance has or has not been changed to the bombing of towns and wide areas in which military targets are situated' he was referred to the previous statement.

Concerns about the campaign were also felt at the opposite end of the political spectrum. In November 1943 the Marquess of Salisbury, a Tory grandee, wrote privately to Sinclair in a troubled frame of mind. He was full of praise for the bravery of the bomber crews but was worried by Harris's assertion that the campaign would go on 'until the heart of Nazi Germany ceases to beat'. Salisbury wanted reassurance that this did not give the lie to the government's repeated assertions that only military and industrial targets were being bombed. The letter asserted that 'there is a great deal of evidence that makes some of us afraid that we are losing moral superiority to the Germans . . . of course the Germans began it, but we do not take the devil as our example.' Three days later Sinclair responded. 'Our aim [he wrote] is the progressive dislocation of the German military, industrial and economic system. I have never pretended that it is possible to pursue this aim without inflicting terrible casualties on the civilian population of Germany. But neither I, nor any responsible spokesman on behalf of the government, has ever gloated over the destruction of German homes.' This smooth reply made no mention of the several directives issued to Bomber Command in which the destruction of the morale of the German people was identified as a central objective.[25]

There were dissenting voices from the established Church. The most serious critic was George Bell, the Bishop of Chichester, who on 9 February 1944 used his secular pulpit in the House of Lords to dissect government policy. Bell was a veteran anti-Nazi and no pacifist. He accepted that in attacking military and industrial targets the killing of civilians was inevitable. However, he told his fellow-peers, there had to be a fair balance between the means employed and the purpose achieved. 'To obliterate a whole town because certain portions contain military and industrial establishments is to reject the balance,' he said. Despite the official sophistry, Bell understood what was going on, even if others did not.

'I doubt whether it is sufficiently realized,' he said, 'that it is no longer definite military and industrial objectives which are the aim of the bombers but the whole town, area by area, is plotted carefully out. This area is singled out and plastered on one night; that area is singled out and plastered on another night . . . how can there be discrimination in such matters when civilians, monuments, military objectives and industrial objectives all together form the target?'[26]

Stokes accepted that his was an unpopular view in parliament but insisted that he spoke for a substantial minority outside it. On

27 May 1943 he asked Deputy Prime Minister Clement Attlee if he was aware that 'a growing volume of opinion in this country considers indiscriminate bombing of civilian centres is both morally wrong and strategic lunacy?' This prompted the Labour member for Doncaster, Evelyn Walkden, to disagree. He declared that whatever Stokes might think 'the rest of the country admire the RAF.' Attlee observed that Walkden 'probably more accurately represents the views of [the people] than the hon. member for Ipswich [Stokes].'[27]

If by that he meant that the great majority of people were squarely behind the campaign he was right. Speaking in support of Bell in the Lords debate Lord Lang of Lambeth, who had recently retired as archbishop of Canterbury, deplored the idea that anyone should 'gloat' over the unfortunate necessity of destroying military objectives and their surrounding neighbourhoods, or regard it as 'worthy of almost jubilant congratulations'. However he seemed to see 'a good many signs of the spread of this particular mood . . . amongst some of our people.' He had recently received a 'fairly full correspondence where the language in which this mood is expressed is to me shocking.' The letters were not from cranks and fanatics but from 'apparently, sane and sober citizens. This is the kind of thing – "Let them have it, they did it to us, let us do it to them tenfold, pay them back in their own coin," and all the language with which we are all too familiar.'[28]

Whatever the misgivings of some clerics and brave mavericks like Stokes, most British people felt no guilt about laying Germany waste. They were not inclined to draw a distinction between Germany and the Nazi state. Their attitude was reflected in a parable written by J. B. Priestley which appeared early in the war and was widely and approvingly circulated. 'In the middle of a great civilized continent,' it began, 'far from the sea which brings a breath of the outer world to freshen men's minds, secret people dwell. Ever and ever again they become crazed with a spell of hero worship. A leader arises among them who tells them they are greater than the other peoples of the world.' The secret people of Germany 'are worse than fools in their folly. When the madness comes upon them, out leaps a primitive, barbarian, beast-like instinct. They kill without pity, rejoicing in blood.' It ended with a very un-British exhortation. 'The Hun is at the gate. He will slaughter the women and the children . . . out then and kill . . . the extermination of the wild animal is the plain business of Europe's citizens.'[29]

As the most visible participants in the war against the Germans, the bomber crews had the overwhelming approval of those they were fighting for. It was essential in sustaining their morale. To ordinary people they were bathed in the same heroic light as the fighter pilots of the Battle of Britain who had gone before them and there were few ethical hesitations about the work they were doing. They were regarded as the finest of their generation, noble and self-sacrificing, who were dying in the defence of everything that mattered. 'Andrew will always be remembered by all who knew him as the one of the best of our young men,' wrote the Rev. T. G. Eakins to the parents of Sergeant A. J. N. Wilson, killed on the night of 11/12 June 1943 over Holland, after only two previous trips. 'He was a man of vision and high ideals . . . with a very great love of his home, his parents, his sisters and brother and all the things worthwhile in life. His love of these was so great that he was prepared to sacrifice even himself in order that they might be kept safe.'

Another letter of condolence from Dorothy Courtney Roberts, a family friend, recorded her pride that she 'knew him first as a boy at home and then as a Royal Air Force pilot – manly and with high ideals. That is how I shall always think of him . . . God grant that we shall never forget the sacrifice that he with so many others made for us and our country.'[30]

A waiting father's anxiety and pre-emptive grief could be numbed a little by the thought that if his boy had been killed he had died in a great cause. Writing in February 1945 to Squadron Leader the Rev. George Martin, the Pathfinder Group chaplain who tirelessly corresponded in detail with every grieving mother, father, wife, sibling and sweetheart, Mr Seymour Legge still did not know whether his son was dead or alive. He was prepared for the worst. 'We feel that the country would lose as well as ourselves if this should be the last we ever hear from him,' he wrote. 'He had no need to enter the RAF as he was in a reserved occupation. But after the loss of his wife in the 1940 air raids, he felt he could delay no longer. He is one of those who make this land of ours worth preserving.'[31] His son, Flying Officer K. C. S. Legge, disappeared without trace while on a Mosquito sortie to Berlin.

The RAF had from the beginning been well aware of the propaganda value of its operations. The RAF Film Unit had a staff of cameramen who went along on selected raids and provided dramatic pictures for the newsreels. Newspapers and the BBC covered Bomber Command's work in reverential detail and romanticized those who flew in it. Even the left-wing *New Statesman* magazine presented the crews as 'Glamour Boys', a title previously bestowed on the pilots of Fighter Command whose virtue had been unquestionable. Newspaper and radio correspondents sometimes accompanied the crews on raids taking the same risks and dying the same deaths. On the night of 2/3 December 1943, J. M. B. Grieg of the *Daily Mail* and Norman Stockton of the *Sydney Sun* were killed in separate aircraft with 460 Squadron on a raid on Berlin.

The BBC took a more detached approach than the newspapers, and correspondents were urged to report the bombing campaign in a 'scientific' way. The corporation took its time getting one of its men aboard a bomber. The first to accompany a crew on a Bomber Command raid was Richard Dimbleby, who went with Guy Gibson in a 106 Squadron attack on Berlin on the night of 16/17 January 1943. The capital had not been bombed for more than a year. Despite the BBC's strictures, Dimbleby's broadcast left no doubt about his admiration for the Bomber Boys and the justice of their fight. They took off from Syerston just after 4.30 p.m. 'It was a big show as heavy bomber ops go,' he reported later. 'It was also quite a long raid as the Wing Commander who took me [Gibson] stayed over Berlin for half an hour. The flak was hot but it has been hotter. For me it was a pretty hair-raising experience and I was glad when it was over though I wouldn't have missed it for the world. But we must all remember that these men do it as a regular routine job.'

The journey out was relatively uneventful. But they 'knew well enough when [they] were approaching Berlin'.

There was a complete ring of powerful searchlights, waving and crossing. Though it seemed to me that when many of our bombers were over the city, many of our lights were doused. There was also intense flak. First of all they didn't seem to be aiming at us. It was bursting away to starboard and away to port in thick yellow clusters and dark, smoky puffs. As we turned in for our first run across the city it closed right around us. For a moment it seemed impossible that we could miss it. And one burst lifted us in the air as if a giant hand had pushed up the belly of the machine. But we flew on, and just then another Lancaster dropped a load of incendiaries. And where a moment before there had been a dark patch of the city, a dazzling silver pattern spread itself. A rectangle of brilliant lights, hundreds, thousands of them, winking and gleaming and lighting the outlines of the city around them. As though this unloading had been the signal, score after score of fire bombs went down and all over the dark face of the German capital these great incandescent flowerbeds spread themselves. It was a fascinating sight. As I watched and tried to photograph the flares with a cine camera, I saw the pinpoints merge and the white glare turning to a dull, ugly red as the fires of bricks and mortars and wood spread from the chemical flares. We flew over the city three times for more than half an hour while the guns sought us out and failed to hit us. At last our bomb-aimer sighted his objective below, and for one unpleasant minute we flew steady and straight. Then he pressed the button and the biggest bomb of the evening, our three-and-a-half-tonner, fell away and down. I didn't see it burst but I know what a giant bomb does and I couldn't help wondering whether anywhere in the area of its devastation, such a man as Hitler, Goering or Himmler or Goebbels might be cowering in a shelter. It was engrossing to realize that the Nazi leaders and their ministries were only a few thousand feet from us. And that this shimmering mass of flares and bombs and gun flashes was their stronghold.

In this way Dimbleby linked the attack directly to the possible harm it might do to the certified villains of the war. Few of his listeners could have failed to visualize its likely consequences for ordinary Germans. But nor would they have doubted his support for the 'six brave, cool and exceedingly skillful men' he flew with and the righteousness of Bomber Command's campaign. Dimbleby went on to make another nineteen trips, a remarkable feat of courage by a non-combatant.

'Perhaps I am shooting a line for them,' he finished up, 'but I think that somebody ought to. They and their magnificent Lancasters, and all the others like them, are taking the war right into Germany. They have been attacking, giving their lives in attack since the first day of the war . . . "Per Ardua ad Astra" is the RAF motto and perhaps I can translate it as "through hardship to the stars". I understand the hardship now. And I'm proud to have seen the stars with them.[32]

The crews made a good impression on normally sceptical outsiders. Martha Gellhorn, a stern opponent of the glamorization or sentimentalization of war, softened when she came to write her piece for Collier's after a week with the crews in November 1943. The Bomber Boys touched her well-hidden maternal side. The pilot of one crew she interviewed just before they took off was 'twenty-one and tall and thin, with a face far too sensitive for this business'. The others were 'polite and kind and far away. Talk was nonsense now. Every man went tight and concentrated into himself, waiting and ready for the job ahead, and the seven of them who were going together made a solid unit, and anyone who had not done what they did and would never go where they were going could not understand and had no right to intrude.' She stayed up to await their return and watched the survivors setting off for breakfast 'with mussed hair and weary faces, dirty sweaters under their flying suits, sleep-bright eyes, making humble comradely little jokes, and eating their saved-up chocolate bars.'[33]

Martha Gellhorn.

Gellhorn, a sophisticated and sceptical American, saw the crews in much the same way as they were viewed by the British public. Their gentle image was a total contrast to the grim task they had been set to do. They were waging a war of aggression, but there was little in their demeanour to show it. Portrayals of them emphasized their passivity, tolerance and innate good nature.

This was nothing more than the truth, judging by an RAF internal recording captured during a raid on Essen in April 1943. The names of the men and the identity of their squadron are not known. The

'As great a warrior as these Islands ever bred'. Guy Gibson (*front row, fourth from left*) and exuberant 106 Squadron comrades, Coningsby, summer 1942.

Above The first face of Bomber Command. Charles 'Percy' Pickard was the impassive star of the docudrama *Target for Tonight*, which popularized the work of the crews.

Left Wellingtons flying in formation. The idea that they could defend themselves in daylight was soon shattered.

Above Lincoln Cathedral, Bomberland's most prominent landmark: a welcome sight in the dawn light on return, a melancholy one at dusk.

Left Harry Yates.

Flying kit was bulky and cumbersome but vital to survival. Here a crew gives the kit a last check.

Halifax crews board lorries to be driven to dispersal, October 1943. There are no smiles for the camera – everyone is tense and pre-occupied.

Above The last ritual. A group of WAAFs wave *au revoir* to a Lancaster bound for Hamburg, 1943.

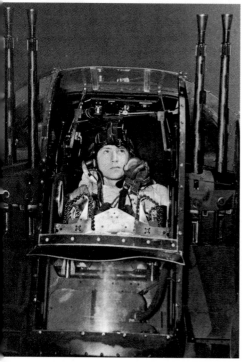

Left The loneliest job on the heavies. A Lancaster rear gunner wedged in his four-gun Frazer-Nash turret. The .303 calibre guns used for most of the war were a flimsy defence against night-fighters.

Below Even with technological advances, navigation remained an immensely demanding task.

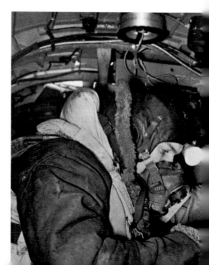

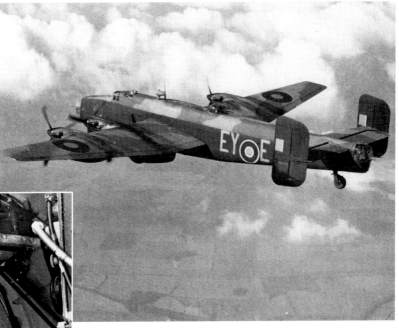

Top A masterpiece of military machinery: an early version of the Avro Lancaster. By the end, sixty of Bomber Command's eighty squadrons flew them.

Above Another fine machine – but the Halifax was always overshadowed by the Lanc.

Deadly light show. Flak, seen from the ground.

OPPOSITE

Above Bomb doors open. All the enormous energy devoted to a bombing raid was focused in the last minutes on a single man.

Below Incendiaries tumble down on Duisberg. Bomber Command delivered nearly eighty million during the course of the war.

Above For the inhabitants of Berlin shelters such as this, cellar life was squalid and demoralizing.

Right A shocked German family stumbles through rubble in the aftermath of a bombing, 1944.

three dominant voices aboard T-Tommy reveal a typical medley of backgrounds and accents. The bomb-aimer sounds what used to be called 'educated'. The navigator speaks in rich Yorkshire. The pilot's genial tones are harder to place but, at a guess, he is from suburban London. The flight engineer, who says only a few words, could be from anywhere. The matter-of-factness everyone displays seems astounding and also rather humbling to modern ears attuned to a risk-free world.

It begins just after they drop their bombs and turn to flee the target area.

BOMB-AIMER: Bombs gone.

PILOT: OK.

NAVIGATOR: Have the bombs gone?

PILOT: Yes.

(In the background can be heard the *thump* of flak, which intensifies and slackens throughout the recording. There is also the harsh ebb and flow of oxygenated breathing.)

NAVIGATOR: OK. Well, I can read my watch in the searchlight. That's 21.54. The idea is to steer oh-two-zero.

PILOT: Oh-two-zero, OK.

NAVIGATOR: Flak directly beneath us. And searchlights underneath us too.

PILOT: Come on T for Tommy. Get cracking.

NAVIGATOR: Watch your height.

PILOT: I'm watching everything. . . How many searchlights would you call that?

NAVIGATOR: Too many, I reckon.

PILOT: Couple of thousand.

NAVIGATOR: Yeah, searching for us. . . bastards.

PILOT (as a searchlight fixes them): Oh hell . . .

BOMB-AIMER: Certainly illuminates things, don't it?

PILOT (breathing heavily): Sure does. (Pause.) I could do with a pint.

BOMB-AIMER: They're firing at us now.

PILOT (mildly interested): Are they?

(There is a big explosion.)

PILOT: That's close.

NAVIGATOR: Well, it's coming close, I can feel it.

PILOT: Yes, I can see it.

BOMB-AIMER: Round to port the heading is, skipper.

PILOT: OK.

BOMB-AIMER: If we press on a bit this way we might get out.

PILOT: Yeah.

(There is a *thump thump thump* from passing flak shells.)

PILOT: You could light your fag on any of those.

(The thumping intensifies.)

UNIDENTIFIED VOICE: Wow, that was a bit close.

NAVIGATOR (matter-of-factly): I think we've been hit, personally.

PILOT: [We'll] lose a bit of height.

NAVIGATOR: That was close.

PILOT: Yeah.

BOMB-AIMER: Searchlights looking for us now. We're pressing on more or less on course.

PILOT: Righty ho.

NAVIGATOR: We'd better press on north until we're clear of this issue.

PILOT: Yes, that's what I'm doing.

(*Thump thump.*)

BOMB-AIMER: Hallo skipper. We've been holed in the front here. There's oil leaking out of the front turret but it's nothing to worry about.

PILOT: OK. . . (To the flight engineer) Could you glance over the temperatures of the engines?

FLIGHT ENGINEER: Could I what?

PILOT: Glance over the temperatures. . . Were we smack on the target today?

BOMB-AIMER: I don't think so. Searchlight on you.

NAVIGATOR: It seemed to be all right to me.

BOMB-AIMER: There's a few searchlights ahead, about a hundred.

NAVIGATOR: It all goes to show, there's only one way to attack this place and that's through cloud.

PILOT: Yeah.

NAVIGATOR: By God, I've never seen anything like this before.

BOMB-AIMER: Neither have I.

PILOT: Four thousand-pounder just gone off, good show.

NAVIGATOR: That's not bad at all.

(The thumping intensifies.)

PILOT: Yes, it's not a bad prang.[34]

The world of Bomber Command was brought to the stage by Terence Rattigan, who left his career as a playwright at the start of the war to join the RAF as a wireless operator/air gunner. *Flare Path* was first performed in London in August 1942 a few months after the first 'thousand' raids. The action takes place in the residents' lounge of the Falcon Hotel in the fictional Lincolnshire town of Milchester, where wives stay to be near their men at the neighbouring bomber base. The play centres on Pat, an actress before the war, and her husband Flight Lieutenant Teddy Graham whom she married in haste during a week-long leave. She is visited by Peter Kyle, a British film star and former lover. Kyle wants her back. She is greatly tempted. Her feelings are tested when Teddy is sent off on a last-minute mission. During the long hours of waiting Pat realizes where her duty lies and in the morning tells Kyle she will not be leaving with him. 'I used to think that our private happiness was something far too important to be affected by outside things, like the war or marriage vows,' she says. 'It may be just my bad luck, but I'm in that battle, and I can't . . . desert.'

The man she is standing by is a refreshing contrast to the Hollywood sophisticate, Kyle. He is gauche, innocent and friendly and totally lacking in pretension, full of Gellhorn's 'humble jokes'. He feels strong affection for his rear gunner Sergeant David 'Dusty'

Miller, a former London bus conductor, and the feeling is returned. But Teddy is more complicated than he seems. After returning from the raid he breaks down, stricken by 'plain bloody funk'. He blurts out to his wife his fear of being grounded for Lack of Moral Fibre which he describes as 'the official phrase for – no guts'. This was probably the first public admission that such a designation existed. The play was also frank about losses. One of the bombers crashes on take-off while the wives are watching from the hotel and the BBC reports a heavy toll on the radio news.[35]

There was no attempt to censor *Flare Path*. The Air Ministry thoroughly approved of its message and when it opened at the Apollo Theatre most of the RAF's top brass were there. The play was ultimately concerned with sacrifice and sacrifice was the positive side of loss, for it suggested that the dying was worth it. This was the theme of Noël Coward, who was proving himself a master at arousing and distilling the nation's sentiments, in a poem that generated a powerful emotional charge. There is no mention of the Germans. The emphasis instead is on the selflessness of the crews, droning overhead as the rest of Britain lies abed.

> Lie in the dark and listen
> It's clear tonight so they're flying high,
> Hundreds of them, thousands perhaps,
> Riding the icy, moonlit sky.
> Men, machinery, bombs and maps,
> Altimeters and guns and charts,
> Coffee, sandwiches, fleece-lined boots
> Bones and muscles and minds and hearts
> English saplings with English roots
> Deep in the earth they've left below,
> Lie in the dark and let them go,
> Lie in the dark and listen . . .

Jack Currie found it 'succinct and stylish but . . . slightly blush-making.' He spoke for many when he recorded later that 'largely unmoved by exhortation, praise or condemnation, I satisfied what need I had for motivation by the companionship of the men from far-off lands around me, and the sight of the cathedral and the wide, green fields.'[36]

Most of the effort to explain Bomber Command to the outside world had little effect on what those within it were thinking or doing. It was as Currie said. The horizons of their universe rarely stretched beyond the crew and the aircraft and the next operation. If they needed an overarching belief to sustain them it was the thought that every successful attack brought victory, and above all peace, a little closer. That gave point to the terrible work they were doing. 'Did you notice what your husband did to Hannover by any chance?' Reg Fayers asked his wife after a major raid on 8/9 October 1943. 'War's end is much nearer 'cos of Bomber Command.'

9

The Battle

Harris liked to present the campaign as a series of 'battles'. It was a commonplace word to describe a strange and completely novel form of fighting. The crews were often struck by the oddness of the war they were waging. They attacked, at night, an enemy they could not see. Their targets were not soldiers or fellow-aviators but buildings, and inevitably, those who lived in them. The engagements were brief and fought far away. There was nothing connecting them to the battlefield. It was a war they visited, then left.

'Life on the squadron was seldom far from fantasy,' wrote Don Charlwood. 'We might, at eight, be in a chair beside a fire, but at ten in an empty world above a floor of cloud. Or at eight, walking in Barnetby with a girl whose nearness denied all possibility of sudden death at twelve.'[1]

Roy MacDonald, a mid-upper gunner with the Pathfinder Force, found it 'a Jekyll and Hyde experience'. After finishing an operation 'it was funny, if you weren't on the night following, to be able to just ride your bike among the fields and think, well it's not many hours since we were in another completely different world, and just thinking once or twice about friends who hadn't come back. It was . . . schizophrenic.'[2]

Even in battle it was possible to feel disengaged. Reg Fayers, the gentle 78 Squadron navigator who had questioned Harris when he visited Holme-on-Spalding-Moor, described the sensation in a letter written to his wife Phyllis in the summer of 1943. 'Lately in letters I've mentioned that I've flown by night and that I've been tired by day, but I haven't said that I can now claim battle honours – Krefeld, Mülheim, Gelsenkirchen, Wuppertal and Cologne. I suppose I've been fighting in the Battle of the Ruhr. But it hasn't felt like that.'

Like many he was surprised at the emotional distance he felt from those he was bombing. 'It's aloof and impersonal, this air war. One has no time to think of [the] hell happening below to a set of people who are the same as you except that their thinking has gone a bit haywire. It's a fair assumption that when Tom [the bomb-aimer] dropped our bombs the other night, women and boys and girls were killed and cathedrals damaged. It must have been so. Were it more personal, I should be more regretting I suppose. But I sit up there with my charts and my pencils and I don't see a thing. I never look out. In five raids all I've seen is a cone of searchlights up by Amsterdam.'[3]

Fayers was shut away in his 'office', curtained off from the sights of the battlefield. As a pilot, Peter Johnson had no choice but to see what was happening but he too found there was something unreal about the spectacle. 'The defences which threatened us were visible enough, the twinkling of innumerable shells exploding in the barrage, the probing fingers of the searchlights, the constant threat from fighters against whom we had little defence. All these we knew but we were not really fighting against them, we were simply trying to evade them. And our own part in the fighting was quickly over. In the glare of searchlights, with the occasional winking of anti-aircraft shells, the occasional thud when one came close and left its vile smell, what we had to do was search for coloured lights dropped by our own people, aim our bombs at them and get away.' The use of target indicators meant that it was easy to forget that the bombs were falling on people and buildings. 'The crux of our every operation,' he wrote, 'lay in the few minutes when the bomb-aimer kept the clear, beautiful colour of a target indicator in his sights, gave his directions and ultimately loosed our load at a firework . . .'[4]

Mounting a raid was a complex business requiring enormous thought, skill and effort. The many variables made each one different. However by the middle of 1943 a routine had been established. Each morning the crews of each squadron woke with no knowledge of what the night would bring. The big decisions were taken far away at Harris's headquarters at High Wycombe, west of London, then passed on to the commanders of the formations that would carry out the attacks.

By now there were seven front-line groups. Number 1 was equipped entirely with Lancasters and operated from South Yorkshire and North Lincolnshire. The light bombers of Number 2 Group were removed from Bomber Command in May 1943 and attached to the American Second Tactical Air Force in preparation for D-Day; 3 Group had Lancasters and was based in Cambridgeshire and Huntingdonshire. The airfields housing 4 Group, equipped with Halifaxes, were in the North and East Ridings of Yorkshire; 5 Group had a mixture of Lancasters and twin-engined Mosquitoes, the sleek, fast beauties of the air war, used for target-marking as well as for precision attacks. It was centred on South Lincolnshire and Nottinghamshire. Airmen of the Royal Canadian Air Force (RCAF) made up the personnel of 6 Group, which operated out of the North Riding and County Durham. The Pathfinder Force was designated as 8 Group and flew Lancasters and Mosquitoes from airfields around Ely in the Cambridge fens. The last group, 100, was sited in north Norfolk and used American Liberators and Flying Fortresses to fly radio and electronic countermeasure missions to jam the German radar during operations.

Crews would hear after breakfast from their flight commanders whether they would be operating that night. If not, an empty day lay ahead. Their job was unlike any other military occupation. Frank Blackman, an Englishman who flew with 429 Canadian Bomber Squadron, explained to his girlfriend Mary that 'aircrew are not like anybody else in the services. They are qualified to fly and damn-all else.'[5] NCOs and junior officers had no men to lead and no other duties but their operational ones. Free days were welcome if they followed a heavy period of raids. But the necessity of completing thirty trips in order to finish a tour and escape from front-line duties meant most were anxious to hurry on and get it over with. Don Charlwood was stationed at Elsham Wolds in the exposed northwest of Lincolnshire when freezing fog shut the airfield down. 'The fog remains,' he wrote in his diary, 'the intense cold and stillness remain; the sun has gone for ever. No ops now for ten days. This is not as pleasant as it sounds. Thirty ops must be done and until they are done the pressure is on. These long gaps give one too much time to think.' There was much to think about. At the time of writing he and his crew had 'still seen no one reach thirty'.[6] In winter, cancellations were routine. Very often they came at the last minute, as commanders hung on waiting for the weather to improve.

Invariably, this deflated crew spirits. An RAF report into operational stress written in August 1942 spoke of 'the disastrous effects upon morale of repeated cancellation of sorties, especially when late in the day.' One of the squadron commanders consulted 'said that "last-minute scrubbing" was the most demoralizing factor with which he had to contend in managing an operational squadron.' He would 'much rather send his squadron on a raid even with 10/10 cloud over the target than subject them to the disappointment, frustration and demoralization of last-minute cancellation due to weather conditions . . .' Frustration was more likely to be generated by a desire to get an ordeal over with than a yearning to have a crack at the enemy. But it was real and damaging enough. A station medical officer quoted in the report told of a freshman who was 'scrubbed seventeen times before he got his first trip. He only lasted three trips after this, and then said he had had it.'[7]

If ops were on, the destination was first revealed to those that most needed to know – the station, squadron and flight commanders and flying control officer. Most of the airmen had to wait until the afternoon to find out where they were going. In the meantime they checked the serviceability of their aircraft, perhaps taking it for a test flight, and passed the time afterwards reading, trying to get some sleep or writing letters. The target was first revealed to the pilots and navigators at a preliminary afternoon briefing. There were specialist briefings for wireless operators and bomb-aimers. Then there was a general gathering for all taking part.

Freshman crews, virgins on their first missions, might feel a thrill of anticipation, even pleasure as they prepared for the evening's events, happy in the thought that all their training was finally going to be put to use. The usual sensation, though, was a low buzz of dread that could only be dispelled by action. Don Charlwood, on hearing that he was about to embark on his first trip, felt an odd mixture of excitement and fear. 'The mood about us changed to something elating but strangely unpleasant, as though suddenly we had been stripped to spiritual nakedness. Half-laughingly men [went off] to write last letters.'[8]

Bomber Command's rapid professional evolution meant that by 1944 preparations were exceptionally thorough. The main briefing took place a few hours before take-off. The 120 or so squadron members taking part in a typical raid filed into the briefing room, usually a utilitarian hut, after being checked at the door by an RAF Police NCO, and sat down in the rows of chairs or forms, each crew clustering around its skipper. Within a few minutes a haze of cigarette and pipe smoke hung in the rafters. They came to attention as the station and squadron commanders strode in and mounted a low dais where a map was propped on a stand, hidden by a blackout curtain. With the announcement 'Gentlemen, your target for tonight is . . .' the CO whipped away the cover and revealed their destination. An ominous red tape on the chart marked the route from base to target. The least welcome objectives were the Ruhr – 'Happy Valley' – and the 'Big City' as Harris called Berlin. Roy MacDonald hated the thought of the Ruhr. 'When they shut the door and pulled the curtain away from the board to show you where you were going I used to die. My heart used to leap out of my chest.'[9]

Bad news was often met by yelled expletives and cat-calls, and sometimes with mournful humour. 'With a deft flick of the wrist, the CO uncovered the wall map behind him,' wrote Harry Yates. '"Gentlemen," he began as always. "The target for tonight is . . . Kiel." As always the gentlemen responded with groans . . . but one bright spark shouted out, "Sir, can we be excused. I promised to meet my girlfriend at eight o'clock."' It was a well-worn joke, but founded in truth. Many an airman had a date he would not turn up to, that or any other night.[10]

The squadron leader then handed over to the senior intelligence officer (SIO) who assessed the importance of the target and explained why it was to be attacked. He, sometimes she, as it was not unusual for WAAF officers to hold intelligence posts, gave details of previous raids and explained why it had been chosen. The SIO also revealed what was known about flak and searchlight positions which were marked on the map with red and green celuloid overlays. Any 'spy' rash enough to use the first person plural when describing the operation ahead was instantly met with shouts of 'What do you mean "we"?'

The squadrons had specialist leaders for each aircrew role who now gave their own briefings. The navigators were taken again over the route and given the turning points. Frequent diversions were commonplace to keep the German defences guessing about the intended target. The wireless operators were reminded of the frequencies of the night. The bombing leader detailed the payloads and the ratio of high explosive to incendiaries and explained the timing and phasing of the attack and colours of the target indicators and aiming point markers. The meteorological officer then gave details of wind speeds, cloud conditions and the weather likely to be encountered over the target.

The RAF had started the war with poor quality bombs that were more metal than charge and that frequently failed to go off. In the spring of 1941 they began to be replaced by a new series of High Capacity (HC) blast bombs, led by the 4,000-pound 'cookie', a fat, green-painted cylinder which appeared to have no aerodynamic qualities whatsoever. They were supplemented with Medium Capacity (MC) bombs which came in sizes of 500, 1,000 and 4,000 pounds. These were mixed with incendiaries. The most common was the hexagonal 4-pound version of which Bomber Command dropped nearly eighty million. As the war progressed, the recipe for the bomb mix changed. In 1940, incendiaries made up only about 5 per cent of the load. During the Battles of the Ruhr and, later, Berlin, the proportion was closer to 66 per cent. The blast bombs blew buildings apart. The incendiaries set fire to the debris. It was this devastating cocktail that caused the Hamburg firestorm and those that followed it.

The CO wound up the meeting with some words of encouragement. In some squadrons, it was the practice for the padre to say a prayer before the final preparations began.

'The target for tonight is . . .' 57 Squadron learn their destination, 30 March 1944.

As the room emptied, the medical officer stood at the door doling out benzedrine 'wakey-wakey' pills to those who wanted them. The crews then headed to the mess for their pre-operational meal. Usually it was bacon and eggs, a treat in a land where rationing had made the mundane exotic. There were a few slack hours before the propellers started to turn. The crews were now sealed off from the world outside. Phone calls to wives or girlfriends were forbidden. Even for someone as practised as Guy Gibson, this was a time of intense anxiety. 'Most people will agree with me when I say that the worst part of any bombing raid is the start,' he wrote. 'I hate the feeling of standing around in the crew rooms, waiting to get into the vans that will take you out to your aircraft. It's a horrible business. Your stomach feels as though it wants to hit your backbone. You can't stand still. You laugh at small jokes, loudly, stupidly. You smoke far too many cigarettes, usually only halfway through, then throw them away. Sometimes you feel sick and want to go to the lavatory. The smallest incidents annoy you and you flare up at the slightest provocation . . . all this because you're frightened, scared stiff . . . I have always felt bad until the door of the aircraft clangs shut; until the wireless-op says "Intercom OK," and the engines burst into life. Then it's all right. Just another job.'[11]

About ninety minutes before take-off they went to the crew room to change. Bomber Command uniform was never standardized. You chose from a haphazard variety of kit, including on occasion the odd civvy item, the gear that made you comfortable. Dennis Steiner wore 'thick woollen long johns and vest, thick knee-length stockings, shirt and electrically heated jacket. This had leads which went down inside your trouser legs to heated slippers. There were also heated gloves which clipped on to the sleeves of the jacket but I rarely wore those. On top of this went a rollneck pullover and a battledress uniform. I had sewn a fur collar on to the jacket. It didn't do much for the warmth but was soft and comfortable. Flying boots were thick sheepskin and I wore three pairs of gloves, first silk, then chamois and finally woollen. I did have a pair of leather gauntlets but they were clumsy and after one was sucked out of [a] chute I never bothered to replace them.'[12]

They wore a whistle on their collars to summon help if they went down in the sea and dog tags stamped with their name and service number. The material used was virtually indestructible and could withstand even the fiercest fire. Steiner also wore a silver medallion with an engraving of two bluebirds and the encouraging message *je reviendrai*, given to him by a girlfriend. Such talismans were central to individual survival routines. Panic could ensue if someone reached the aircraft to find he had left behind the lucky charm that he believed his life depended on. 'Luck and a Lancaster were our daily bread,' wrote Jack Yates. 'We loved the one and couldn't expect to live without a large slice of the other. We all carried a keepsake, a sign of our trust worn around the neck or pocketed next to the heart. It could be the ubiquitous rabbit's foot or a rosary, letter, St Christopher, coin, photograph, playing card . . .'[13]

As a Lancaster skipper Jim Berry was occasionally irritated when he was given a strange aircraft and found its interior festooned with the jujus of the previous occupants. 'Very often there would be rabbits' feet and little things hanging up. I would never have them. I used to say take them down I don't want them. [The crew] said, well they might be good luck. I would say, they might be good luck for somebody [else] but I don't want them . . . it was quite grotesque sometimes, there were so many bits hanging about.' Nonetheless, during the later part of his remarkable stint of sixty-four operations he kept a lucky farthing, given to him by his batwoman, in the finger of his flying glove.[14]

Swathed in multiple layers of clothing airmen waddled rather than walked. The bulk was necessary. It was cold up there, even with the electrically-heated linings that became standard issue by the middle of the war. The aircraft had some hot-air heating but it tended to be erratically distributed. According to Ralph Wood, a navigator, 'a Hallybag was always a deep-freeze proposition, even at the best of times. There were supposed to be pipes giving off heat throughout the aircraft but this was a laugh.'[15] In the Lancaster, however, the heating duct outlet was next to the wireless operator so he and the navigator tended to roast, while in the cockpit the pilot, engineer and bomb-aimer froze. Whatever the aircraft it was the gunners, stuck in the back, who felt the cold the most.

Finally, they struggled into Mae West lifejackets and parachute harnesses. They picked up their parachutes on the way out of the locker room together with a thermos flask of coffee, boiled sweets, chewing gum, and a bar of Fry's Vanilla Chocolate Cream. They were also issued with escape kits in case they were brought down in enemy territory, containing maps of France and Germany printed on scarves and handkerchiefs, phrase sheets, local money and compasses concealed in pens and buttons. The kits contained passport photographs for use in forged documents. They were unlikely to have been very convincing. Base photographers tended to set their subjects in the same rigid pose, cutting them off at the neck to hide their tunics. As a last precaution they left behind anything that might identify their unit or its location. 'We were required to empty our pockets and were given two numbered and differently coloured pouches for the contents,' Ken Newman remembered. 'The contents of one of these would be sent to our next of kin if we did not return but the contents of the others would not . . . some married aircrew had clandestine girlfriends and naturally did not want their photographs or letters to be sent to their wives.'[16] The procedure inspired a poem by the RAF poet, John Pudney.

> Empty your pockets, Tom, Dick and Harry
> Strip your identity; leave it behind.
> Lawyer, garage-hand, grocer, don't tarry
> With your own country, your own kind
>
> Leave all your letters. Suburb and township,
> Green fen and grocery, slip way and bay,
> Hot spring and prairie, smoke-stack and coal tip,
> Leave in our keeping while you're away.
>
> Tom, Dick and Harry, plain names and numbers,
> Pilot, observer and gunner depart.
> Their personal litter only encumbers
> Somebody's head, somebody's heart.[17]

Then it was time to board the lorries that ferried them to the aircraft. At dispersal, the pilot and the flight engineer went over the aircraft with the groundcrew for a final check. There was a pause for a last cigarette, perhaps a piss against the tail wheel for good luck. The remaining minutes on the ground were solemn and unsettling. One summer night in 1943 Willie Lewis, a flight engineer who was to survive fifty-two operations, was waiting to board his bomber for his first trip to Germany. They were going to Essen. 'The dispersal was far remote from the aerodrome,' he wrote, 'set with its back against a wood, in which the final rustlings of the birds could be heard as they settled themselves down to sleep. The leaves crackled in the quiet air and the darkness which was rapidly settling about them had a close warmth, earthy and comforting . . . the realization that there were simple creatures in the undergrowth and trees close at hand, going about their peaceful, age-enduring existence unaffected by, and unaware of war was strangely moving.'[18] It was a relief to climb the ladder and struggle down the fuselage to their positions.

The ignition whined, the propeller blades made a few jerky revolutions then blurred into invisibility as the engines caught. One by one, the pilots edged the aircraft forward, anxious not to stray from the narrow tarmac strip that led to the runway and bog down in the soft ground. The night air throbbed with the confident roar of a hundred aero engines. The lead bomber swung into the runway and as the light on the controller's van flashed green, rolled down the track. When it was only halfway into its run, the next was already on its way. Despite the immense force the Merlin and Hercules engines that powered the Lancasters and Halifaxes could generate, each take-off seemed a struggle. The bombers were often laden with well over their recommended all-up weight and they clambered rather than soared into the air. There was a last little ritual. At the side of the runway, whatever the weather, a small knot of groundcrew and WAAFs waved farewell.

On occasions it was possible to enjoy the sensation of flight and, at the right time of the year, the beauty of the darkening sky. Taking off on a long trip to Milan in August 1943 Lewis and his crew climbed through a thick layer of cloud at 10,000 feet and set course towards the setting sun. As flight engineer, he sat up front with the pilot and could see everything. 'The great sea of cloud underneath turned golden,' he wrote. 'Then it became a huge flood of scarlet which made way for crimson and mauve as the light faded, [then] funereal violet for the last few moments before darkness leapt upon the world. A pallid moon which had occupied one unobtrusive corner of the heavens simultaneously glowed with increased density until from a faded orb it became the dominating feature of the sky.'

The surrounding bombers were slowly swallowed by the dusk so that all that was left was the dim glow of their navigating lights. Aboard their Halifax, T-Tommy, Lewis and his mates sat in silence, listening to the rasp of their breath through their oxygen masks. As they flew south, the cloud disappeared and by the time they crossed the coast the weather was perfectly clear. They were now in enemy territory. The navigating lights were switched off.

'The night sky was beautiful. The splendour of the full moon high above was reflected in a mist over the sea. [We] were suspended in a vast blue dome. The light was so bright that T-Tommy shone silver in it, the roundels on her wings standing out as clear as if it were day . . . ahead lay a completely empty sky.' After twenty trips the crew were now accustomed to the rhythms of the journey. They had 'fallen into the familiar routine. The powerful mechanism of the aircraft had overborne [our] individuality and welded [it] into the machine.' Through their masks they breathed 'the fresh tang from the oxygen tubes and the smells of rubber and oil. A constant flow of hot air gushed into the cockpit . . . warming the forward positions. Outside the barrier of glass in the cold crispness of the atmosphere the exhaust manifold shone against the outlines of the engines. The wingtips swayed gently up and down amongst the stars. The gun turrets turned slowly from side to side, and the face of the mid-upper gunner stared out grimly, his body hunched over his weapons.'[19]

Cy March, the ex-miner now serving as a rear gunner with 467 Squadron, admitted later that when staring out into darkness 'as black as a sheep's bum, I [experienced] something I daren't tell anyone for years in case they thought I was bomb-happy. I could hear the most beautiful singing and music in my earphones . . . none of the crew said anything so I knew it was only me who could hear it. I heard this on many of our trips and could never explain it, but I wasn't complaining for it was really beautiful, barmy or not.'[20]

Over the sea there was no more time for dreaming. The gunners fired a few bursts to test their guns. As sea gave way to land the navigator called out 'enemy coast ahead'. Dennis Field had his 'usual physical reaction' when he heard the words and 'after a bit of a struggle in the confined cockpit . . . managed to relieve myself into my can' which an obliging member of the crew then emptied down a flare chute.[21] Crossing the coast the crews got their first sight of the dangers that awaited them. The shores of the Low Countries and France were fringed with flak batteries and flak ships. Routes were chosen to avoid the main concentrations, but intelligence never kept pace completely with the enemy's ever-shifting dispositions.

By now the Germans were watching, tracking the incoming fleet on their radar system. The crews began the simple but effective counter-measure, shovelling out bundles of *Window*, which created at least temporary confusion on German radar screens.

The defenders would know an attack was coming from the increased radio activity that preceded every big operation as wireless operators checked their equipment. The German radar early-warning system stretched in a thick band from Denmark down the North Sea coast before sweeping south to block an approach from the west across France. It was named after its creator, General Josef Kammhuber. The Kammhuber Line was made up of seventy-four 'boxes' each containing one *Freya* and two *Würzburg* radars. As the radar picked up the incoming aircraft the information was transmitted to a night-fighter control room where controllers directed the defensive battle. They followed the situation on a large screen, assisted by *Luftwaffehelferinnen*, the German equivalent of WAAFs, who shone narrow points of light on the screen depicting the positions of friendly and hostile aircraft.

Once the attack began, German night-fighters took off and circled a radio beacon to await orders. Their positions were picked up by radar and beamed on to the screen as a blue light. The incoming bombers were marked with a red light. The controller's aim was to set the fighter on a course where he could see a bomber or track it down with the *Lichtenstein* short-range radar with which each aircraft was fitted. By the middle of 1943 Germany had about 400 night-fighters, armed with 20 mm or 30 mm cannon. Some were equipped with upward firing *Schräge Musik* cannons. These allowed the fighter to creep up on the bomber from below where it was invisible to the crew and fire a burst into its explosive-packed belly. Along the route the controllers sought to insert twin-engined fighters into the bomber stream.

As the bombers flowed onwards, the eyes of all the crews sifted the darkness for enemy aircraft. But on long trips, fatigue and boredom blunted concentration and attacks usually came without warning. Donald Falgate was peering out of the bomb-aimer's nosecone on the approach to Magdeburg when he saw tracer floating towards him. 'He was on to us before we saw him,' he remembered. 'He made the first attack from the rear and from above which was unusual. He'd obviously come on us quite by mistake. If it was a radar interception they usually picked you up from below.' There was a brief first burst of fire and the fighter, a Ju 88, veered away. The pilot just had time to check that no one was hurt when the German came in for a second attempt. He was too near to focus his guns and the shots went harmlessly by. As he closed in from astern for a third attempt the rear gunner yelled a warning and the captain finally took evasive action. '[He] screamed out: "Corkscrew! Port! Go!"'

The corkscrew was the bombers' only real defence against fighters. It was a testament to the strength and aerodynamic qualities of the heavies that they could be thrown about the sky with a violence that, if they were lucky, could shake off their smaller, nimbler pursuers long enough to escape into the darkness beyond the fighter's limited onboard radar range. The manoeuvre required the pilot to shove the aircraft down into a diving turn until it was screaming through the air at 300 mph. Then he jerked it upwards to climb in the opposite direction. Done properly, it meant the fighter could not hold his quarry in his sights long enough to get in a good burst. It was enough to see off Falgate's pursuer. 'We managed to evade him and get into cloud . . . but it was a very scary time . . . It wasn't until we got back to base that we found bullet holes in the fuselage and two huge holes in the mid-upper turret where the shells had gone through. The poor mid-upper gunner nearly froze to death.'[22]

Leutnant Norbert Pietrek who was based at Florennes in southern Belgium on one of the main routes to the Ruhr gave an account of a night action from the perspective of the hunter. On the evening of 16 April 1943, a warning came in that a double force of British bombers was in the air. They were heading for Mannheim and the Skoda armaments factory at Pilsen.

Pietrek and his Messerschmitt 110 were scrambled to patrol in a box codenamed 'Tomcat'. Before he arrived he was told over the radio beacon by his controller that he had a *Kurier* for him, the Luftwaffe codeword for a heavy bomber. Turning on the course he was given he saw a 'Lancaster, 200 metres to my right and somewhat higher . . . I therefore push the throttles through the gate to catch up with him and then, as I have learned during training, position myself exactly underneath it, adjust my speed to that of the bomber, pull up, and then fire a long burst through a wing between the engines and its fuel tanks.' The move was thwarted when the Lancaster went into a steep dive. Pietrek gave chase. Before he could open fire, however, the bomber flew into a hillside and exploded. It was the first aircraft he had destroyed and he enjoyed the experience. 'Really,' he recalled later, 'it is quite a splendid matter to chase one big *Viermot* [four-engined bomber] into the ground without firing a single bullet.'

His blood up, he was eager to strike again. He headed back towards the beacon, cursing the RAF jamming that was blocking his link with the controller and spoiling his chances of further 'trade' that night. Then, while circling the beacon, he spotted what he described as a 'barn door', a large, easy target in the shape of what appeared to be a passing Stirling. He fired off a few rounds which passed in front of the bomber and alerted the crew to the attack. 'A wild twisting and turning begins,' he recalled later. 'Much too close for comfort, green lines of tracer from the Tommy's tail turret swish past me. We climb and turn, a steep spiral to the left, pull up, the same manoeuvre to the right, up again, and so it goes on and on. Never could I have imagined that one could carry out such wild manoeuvres with a giant [aircraft] like this . . .'

In the frantic exchange of fire Pietrek managed to hit the starboard outer engine. It appeared to ignite but the flames then died down only to flare and gutter again and again. Pietrek thought, 'That pilot must be a madman! He still flies eastward despite one dead engine . . . and is obviously determined to press on and discard his load of bombs on a German city . . . 'Well my dear boy, there is no way that you will pull that off!'

He continued the chase as the bomber sank ever lower. In the back of the Messerschmitt his wireless operator, Otto, slaved to fill the ammunition pans to keep his cannons firing. The stream of tracer from the bomber's mid-upper gunner kept him at bay. Eventually, though, he was able to 'creep up on him from beneath, pull up and level out swiftly and . . . fire a burst exactly over the top of the fuselage. A ball of fire and the turret has disappeared. That's what you get when you cause me so much trouble!'

He put the last, fatal touches to the encounter with a burst that set the port outer engine on fire, only breaking off when he ran out of ammunition. The bomber was by then doomed. Pietrek lined up alongside and watched it slide to earth. He found it a 'strangely beautiful sight, the big black bird . . . well comrade, your fate is sealed. That will be clear to you chaps inside that wounded bird too.'[23]

Sometimes high-flying aircraft dropped flares to help the night-fighters see their targets. The feeling of exposure was appalling. Cy March was well on his way to Böhlen when 'suddenly a string of flares lit up above us, lightening the sky into daylight . . . they continued until there was a double row for miles on our track. We knew fighters were dropping them, but where were they, behind, above or below the flares? Our eyes must have been like saucers looking for them. It was like walking down a well-lit road in the nude.' They were saved by a signal aborting the mission and dived away for the cover of darkness and home.[24] The sky was full of nasty surprises. Some crews reported seeing mysterious bursts of flame. The authorities explained them away as 'scarecrows', designed to frighten crews, though the likelihood is that they were exploding aircraft.

Despite the weight of the German defences it was to possible to reach the target area without encountering fighters. Some gunners completed a tour without ever seeing a German aircraft or firing their guns in anger. It was just as well. The turrets were fitted with Browning .303s which took rifle-calibre bullets and had a short range. They became even less effective after the Luftwaffe improved the armour on its fighters. They offered very little protection to the bombers and perhaps their main value was as a psychological deterrent.

In these unequal circumstances, if a gunner spotted a fighter he was wise to hold his fire. During his tour as a rear gunner Peter Twinn 'never fired a shot because if you did then that immediately gave your position away to other fighters who were in the area who couldn't see you and they would come straight in, pinpoint you and that was it. More often than not if you did open fire it was the last thing you did.'[25]

The first sign that the fighters had found a victim was often a small fire in the blackness ahead, followed by a huge explosion as the bomb load went up. It was an experience that produced conflicting emotions. There was horror, pity, but above all thankfulness that it had happened to someone else.

The fighters posed an intermittent threat all the way out and all the way back and shot down more bombers than did the flak batteries defending the towns. In the last three months of 1943, fighters caused the loss of 250 aircraft whereas flak was responsible for downing only ninety-four.[26] Nonetheless, it was during the twenty or so minutes over the target that the crews felt in the greatest peril.

By the middle of 1943 most area raids ran to a standard pattern. During the raid on Duisburg on the night of 12 May, 238 Lancasters, 142 Halifaxes, 112 Wellingtons and 70 Stirlings took part, led by 10 Mosquitoes of the PFF. They approached the target at staggered heights and intervals. The bottom layer of the stream flew at 15,000 feet, the middle at 18,000 and the top at 20,000–22,000 feet. Each level was two minutes behind the other. On the outward and inward journeys the middle of the bomber stream felt a safe place to be and the turbulence caused by the surrounding aircraft was reassuring. Above the objective the proximity of your comrades became a menace. At Duisburg, all 572 aircraft flew over the target in about twenty-five minutes. Those at the lowest level faced the greatest danger, not only from flak but also from the bombs falling from above. Initially there had been fears that such concentration would lead inevitably to collisions. In practice, the discipline of the pilots meant that mid-air crashes were surprisingly rare.

Arrival in the target area was signalled by searchlights probing the sky, followed by the blossoming of anti-aircraft fire. It was a daunting sight. On the approach to Hamburg and Berlin, it seemed to Doug Mourton that 'the anti-aircraft was so concentrated that from fifty miles away it looked impossible to get through it'.[27] The switch from the cold comfort of the dark to the obscene brightness of the battlefield was shocking. Peter Johnson, approaching Essen on his first operation, noted how alone his aircraft felt, 'suspended in a black vacuum', with nothing to be seen except the yellow flares dropped by the Pathfinders to show where to turn on to the target. But then 'instead of the pitch darkness there was suddenly a mass of searchlights, slowly, methodically scanning the sky over a huge area. At the same time streams of tracer, some white, some coloured, followed the searchlight beams at quite low heights . . . lastly, at levels from well above our height to four or five thousand feet below came a dazzling display of twinkling stars, the Ruhr barrage of heavy ack-ack. There seemed to be hundreds of bursts almost simultaneously. You were quite unconscious of the invisible but lethal load of shrapnel each burst vomited into the sky.'[28]

Doug Mourton, on his first trip to Cologne, could see the flak all too clearly, 'pieces of luminous metal . . . not only luminous but looking as if they were on fire' that thudded into the side of the aircraft.[29] The once empty-seeming sky was suddenly full of horrifying sights. As the Pathfinder pilot Jim Berry began his bombing run over Kiel one night 'the sky got quite a glow on. I felt that we were on fire because I could see this red glow everywhere. I looked around and everything was bathed in this red glow but no one said anything.' Then he noticed the cause of the strange effect. 'Just above and to the starboard side was a Lancaster . . . It was ablaze from end to end. It was a terrible sight and it was not very far away. He was slightly higher than we were and I thought if he falls my way I will have time to get away.' Eventually 'it just fell away to the starboard side and away from me so that was fine. But it was an awful thing to see. I didn't see anybody get out.'[30]

In these last, climactic moments Don Charlwood was sometimes struck by the madness of what he was doing. As he flew, crouched at his navigator's station, into a blizzard of flak above Bremen he 'looked at the commonplace things on my desk – pencils, a scribbling block, a pear ripened in the Staffordshire sun – and suddenly I thought of them as wonderfully sane, inanimate though they were.'[31]

The point of the searchlights was to dazzle the pilot and bomb-aimer and light up the bomber for the flak batteries. Once the radar-guided master searchlight, tinted an unearthly blue, picked up an aircraft it was joined by others so that the intruder was caught in a cone of dazzling light and became the object of the attentions of every gun within range. The effect was hideously disorientating and unnerving for the crews. To Roy MacDonald it was like 'a thousand flashlights going off at the same time. It was blinding.'[32]

Once 'coned' the only way out was to corkscrew. Peter Johnson's first experience of it was over Stettin. 'The near-blindness induced by eight or ten of these very high-powered beams coming from every side produced the frightening sensation of being caged by light. No matter how you struggled the dazzling beams would hold you and you lost all sense of movement. It was as if you were motionless in the sky, shells exploding all around you, waiting for the one which would destroy you, knowing that every fighter in the area had marked you for his prey.'

Johnson warned the crew to stand by to corkscrew. But it seemed the searchlights 'were locked on to us like a vice and, pull and push the control column as I would, taking us into the steepest dives and climbs I dared risk, they clung to us as if they were glued to our shape. The rear gunner warned of an aircraft following us but I was already doing the most violent manoeuvres of which I and the aircraft were capable. Then suddenly one of the searchlights left us and then another and another ... somehow their co-ordination had been upset though three or four still held us.' Sweating, and with his aching arms, forearms and wrists, he ' kept the throttles at maximum and, miraculously, they lost us. Still close, the beams kept brushing over our wings, probing, probing until suddenly, they went out all together. It was a queer sensation to be back in the merciful dark.'[33]

The bomber stream followed the Pathfinder crews whose job was to illuminate the target area with flares, then to drop brilliantly coloured red, green and yellow target indicators (TIs) on the aiming point. The task of the main force was to place their bombs on whichever colour marker they had been allocated by the master bombers, who began to operate from August 1943. The job of the master bomber was extraordinarily dangerous, even by Bomber Command's extreme standards. They circled the bombing zone, observing the fall of the bombs, all the while issuing instructions and corrections to the crews by radio telephone.

Whatever the terrors of the initial approach, nothing matched the dread-filled minutes of the bombing run. To deliver their loads pilots had to fly straight and level allowing the aimer to line up his sight on the marker he had been allocated burning below. The finale was signalled by a blast of freezing air which flooded the fuselage as the bomb doors opened. For the next minutes the bomb-aimer took control, lying face-down in the nose and calling adjustments to the course of the final approach to the skipper over the intercom. The captain, in turn, was taking direction from the master bomber. This was the 'tinny voice' in Willie Lewis's taut description of the climax of T-Tommy's trip to Gelsenkirchen on the night of 9 July 1943.

> In the nose . . . Joe is lying stretched over his bombsight the illuminated cross of which is in line with the town coming up. He is speaking.
>
> Joe (quietly): 'Bomb doors open, skipper.'
>
> John: 'Bomb doors open.' (He pulls a lever on his left. There is a jerk and the aircraft settles down again.) 'I'll put on the radio telephone.' (He presses a switch on the panel and a tinny voice comes over the intercom.)
>
> Voice: 'Come right in, chaps. It's not a bit dangerous. Bomb on the red flare.'
>
> Joe (Cutting across the voice.): 'Left, left, skipper.'
>
> John: 'Left, left.'
>
> (The aircraft jerks slightly to port. The illuminated cross on the bombsight lines up towards a flare halfway down.)
>
> Joe: 'Left, left.'
>
> John: 'Left, left.'
>
> (The aircraft moves again and the flare starts coming down the line towards the centre of the cross. Joe's thumb tenses on the button.)

Voice: 'There's a very good line in yellow just gone down. Bomb on the yellow.'

John: 'Can you see that yellow, Joe?'

Joe: 'Yes, skipper. Straighten up. I think I can manage it.' . . . (Crashing as ack-ack explodes around them, rocking the aircraft violently.)

Joe: 'Right, right, skipper.'

John: 'Right, right.'

Rammy (rear gunner): 'You'll have to get moving full kick as soon as the bombs are gone, skipper. It's getting bloody hot back here. The flak's very close.'

John: 'Shut up.'

Joe: (Presses the button and the aircraft leaps into the air as the load leaves.) 'Bombs gone'.[34]

To be a master bomber required tungsten nerves and supernatural composure. One master bomber who was hit while over the target calmly broadcast that he was on fire and going down. He wished the main force crews good luck before disappearing from the air waves. Their detached interventions were not always appreciated, coming as they did when every member of every crew was straining to get in and out in the fastest possible time. Jack Currie was in one of 300 Lancasters, flying in a concentrated wave over the centre of Berlin on 3 September 1943. As it approached the target, 'the PFF marker flares began to blossom on the ground. On the radio the circling master bomber passed instructions to the attackers. On the whole his words were cool and helpful, but he fell from grace with one slightly patronizing remark, which invited a harsh response and got it.

'"Come on in main force, the searchlights won't bite you!" Few were the transmit buttons left unpressed, few were the bomber captains who did not reply: "F . . . off!"'[35]

As the cookie fell away the bombers performed a great leap upward that sent relief and hope surging through the hearts of the crew. There was still one task left. Harris had insisted on the need for a photograph to be taken over the area where the bombs were supposed to have landed. The six-photograph sequence took another thirty seconds, moments, wrote Willie Lewis, of 'stark, fierce terror'.

With the last click of the camera the job was finally done but several hours of mortal danger still lay ahead. As they left the target area and its umbrella of flak the night-fighters were waiting for a second bite at their quarry. Flying Officer Geoffrey Willatt, a bomb-aimer with 106 Squadron, had only two more trips to complete his tour when on the night of 5/6 September 1943 he was sent to bomb Mannheim.

'At last I said "bombs gone" and the aircraft bounced up as the cookie went,' he wrote in his diary a few weeks later. 'A further period straight and level while the photo is taken and then we turned off. The air seemed full of aircraft and quite near a squirt of cannon fire streamed through the air like a string of sausages and we drift through puffs of smoke from nearby bursts of flak. A Halifax with one wing on fire charged past our nose losing height in a shallow dive.' His skipper, Pilot Officer 'Robbie' Robertson, put the bomber into a corkscrew before levelling out. It was then that the fighter struck. 'The most startling thing about it was the noise. Normally you can hear nothing above the roar of the engines, not even flak unless splinters hit the aircraft, or bombs dropping. This then was a metallic, ripping, shattering, clicking sound repeated three or four times at split-second intervals. The nearest simile I can think of is the noise made by two billiard balls cracked together but magnified a thousand times and loud enough to make my head sing.'

The din made him duck, a reflex that saved his life. He looked up to see 'a foot wide hole in the instrument panel behind and above my head and another in the side of the nose, a few inches above my head as I'd crouched down.'

The engines were still roaring but the nose was dropping and the aircraft seemed to be sliding down the sky. Willatt knelt on the step and peered into the pilot's compartment. What he saw appalled him. 'The seat was empty . . . this was shock enough in itself but then I could see a tangled mass of people lying in a static heap at the side of the pilot's seat and inextricably entangled with the controls. They were all hit and probably dead.' The pilot had been killed instantly by a cannon shell to the head. The flight engineer was mortally wounded. Willatt 'tried to call up on the intercom – it was dead – and it was impossible to climb back over the bodies to speak to anyone.' The aircraft was now well on fire with the port inner engine and wing ablaze and flames licking down the fuselage. He decided there was 'no alternative but to go through the hole.'

He clipped on his parachute, removed his helmet, pulled away the hatch and lowered himself into space, one hand clamped to his rip-cord handle. Almost immediately he felt 'a sickening jerk on my groin as the chute opened. I don't remember pulling the cord. I was practically unconscious from lack of oxygen . . . there was a horrible tearing, burning feeling between my legs where the harness pulled and my fur collar was clapped tightly over my face and ears. Both my boots were tugged off by the wind and my feet were freezing cold.'

Even in this extreme of pain he noticed that 'the target was still burning nicely, bombs thumping, flak cracking and searchlights waving about.' He was suddenly aware of his immense good fortune. 'What a good thing I wasn't dangling in the air in the middle of it!' As he drifted down the intricate parachute drill drummed into him during training kept running through his mind: 'twist if necessary by crossing straps so as to face downwind with knees slightly bent but braced and arm across the face to protect it. Land lightly on the toes and bend the knees.'

Nothing like this happened. The ground came up five minutes sooner than he expected and, with his legs held rigid, he landed with a thump on his heels. Despite following the escape procedure to the letter he was picked up a few hours later. He was lucky, as his captors let him know. He was led to the wreckage of his aircraft. One of the soldiers pointed to a 'grim lump under a tarpaulin' and pronounced the names of the dead men lying under it: 'Robertson, Shadbolt, Hodder, Green.' The rest had fallen elsewhere. Group Captain F. S. Hodder was the station commander at Syerston where the squadron was based. He rarely flew and had gone along for the trip to show solidarity with his men.

Relief at having escaped from a doomed aircraft was quickly overtaken by anxiety of what would happen on the ground. Fear of the reception he would get was very much on Geoffrey Willatt's mind when after his short spell of freedom he emerged from a haystack and came face to face with a farmer. 'There were farm people dotted round the fields in all directions and I was definitely caught,' he wrote in his diary. 'I don't like men with pitchforks, even if they do look scared so I timidly said "RAF" and tried not to look like a Terror-Bomber.' In fact he was treated with politeness by the soldier and policeman who arrested him. When he arrived at a Luftwaffe barracks 'an officer in shiny boots and another in a monocle received me most courteously. I was parked on a bed . . . with some soup, potatoes, sauerkraut and a jug of coffee with sugar . . . some typists giggled and asked me if I was married . . .'[36]

Such amiable treatment was by no means the rule. Passing through Aachen on his way to a PoW camp after being shot down over France, Flight Sergeant Gerry Hobbs of 617 Squadron found himself next to a troop train. The soldiers spotted him and he was 'subjected to a lot of abuse and catcalls. I didn't need to know German to understand their feelings and gestures as they were probably heading for the front.' At Cologne, an elderly lady belaboured another British prisoner with an umbrella.[37]

Some of the prisoners passing through a war-battered Germany on their way to captivity had known it in peacetime. Fate took Ken Goodchild back to Cologne, which he had visited as a schoolboy, after being shot down over Holland in May 1943. He arrived with four other prisoners by train from Brussels and was 'taken off the train by four guards.' When they asked why they needed so many 'they said they had to protect us from the civilians, otherwise they'd lynch us.'

After the war it was reckoned that possibly 350 Allied airmen who survived being shot down were subsequently murdered by Germans on the ground.[38] Civilians who took part likely knew that they had nothing to fear from the authorities. Official policy was to allow them to have their way. In August 1943, Heinrich Himmler had declared that it was 'not the business of the police to get mixed up in altercations between the population and "terror fliers"' who had baled out. As the war progressed and the bombing worsened officials seemed to positively encourage lynchings. In February 1945, Gauleiter Hoffman of South Westphalia directed that surviving aircrew were 'not to be spared from the outrage of the public. I expect the police to demonstrate that they are not the protectors of these gangsters and anyone who ignores this order will have to answer to me.' Indeed, helping survivors was a crime, and several kind-hearted souls suffered for doing so. In the autumn of 1943, two men from Dorsten in the Ruhr were sent to a labour camp for giving coffee and bread to two Allied airmen.

After the war, though, the perpetrators of lynchings sometimes had to face the victors' justice. In one case, six men were put in front of a military court on charges of the ill-treatment and killing of an unknown British sergeant pilot who baled out with his crew during a raid on Bochum, in the Ruhr, on 24 March 1945. He landed in a field watched by a crowd who rushed towards him. The airman was wounded and feebly raised his arms to surrender. Franz Brening, who later served as a prosecution witness, tried to help him by removing his parachute and laying him on the ground. The mob were having none of it and began punching and kicking the victim. One of them, Stefan Weiss, seized a rifle from a German soldier standing passively by and tried to shoot the airman but the gun jammed. Another, Friedrich Fischer, sent a young boy off to fetch a hammer. He then, according to the court records, 'struck the airman a violent blow on the back of his head resulting in the breaking of his skull.' Fischer was heard afterwards 'to boast of what he had done.'

Fischer was sentenced to death. He admitted the crime but blamed 'incitement by the mass' in his appeal. He also asked the court to bear in mind the suffering he had endured as a result of Allied bombing. Weiss cited 'Goebbels propaganda' and 'daily bomber attacks.' Neither was successful as a defence. Fischer was hanged. Weiss was sentenced to twenty years' imprisonment but was released after six.[39]

Ken Goodchild and his comrades made it safely into captivity. Their experience, though, had demonstrated the folly of imagining that the danger in the air diminished the nearer you got to home. They had just been starting to believe they might make it back alive when night-fighters attacked over Holland. It was the end of a nightmarish trip. A flak shell had ripped through their Halifax ten minutes from the target but miraculously failed to explode. A second burst blew off the front turret flooding the aircraft with freezing air and wounding the navigator. Showing amazing resolution they carried on, completed the bombing run and headed homewards.

Without a functioning navigator they were unable to judge the correct course and wandered away from the comfort of the returning bomber stream. They were easy meat for the Junkers 88 and Focke-Wulf 190 which swooped just as the coastline came into view. The starboard wing was soon ablaze and dripping great gouts of flaming petrol from the tanks. The nose went down into a shallow dive and no amount of wrestling with the controls could pull it up. Goodchild

> went to the centre of the aircraft and discovered that the whole middle part of the aeroplane was one ball of flame so there was nothing we could do to get out of the back. The skipper gave the order to abandon the aircraft so the engineer and myself got hold of the wounded navigator and brought him forward to the front escape hatch [and] opened it. There was a safety device there which if you had a wounded member of crew who couldn't operate his parachute then you attached the line to his ripcord, threw him out and that line pulled the ripcord for him. At the same time the bombardier went immediately after him so that he would land somewhere close by and be able to render assistance. The engineer was the next to go and he sat on the edge of the escape hatch. I went back into my cabin to blow up all the radio equipment, destroy all the code lists and [when I came] back the engineer

was still sitting there so I booted him in the backside and out he went. I later discovered that the reason he hadn't gone earlier was simply because he was tied to the aeroplane by his oxygen pipe and by his intercom wire. It all got caught up and when he actually jumped I nearly throttled him.[40]

All the crew, including the wounded navigator Chic Henderson, survived the jump.

Once over the North Sea it felt like the worst was over. To glimpse the lightening sky at the end of a long, rough trip was like slowly waking up from a nightmare. Returning from a raid on Koblenz during which they had survived an attack by night-fighters Harry Yates was finally given the course for Mepal, the crew's home station. 'That precipitated a gradual change of mood. We descended through light cloud and levelled at 6,000 feet. Visibility was good. Moonlight played on the English Channel. We began to feel more relaxed. No, we began to feel good. This had been another demanding raid, a night of the hunter. But we had not been snared . . .'[41]

Jack Currie knew he was not supposed to smoke but 'on the long ride home over the North Sea the temptation was usually too strong for me.' When they had descended below 10,000 feet and oxygen masks were no longer needed he would 'loosen my straps, engage the automatic pilot, sit back and really enjoy that cigarette. At those moments, cruising home on half-power with the darkness, while the dawn began to touch the sky behind my left shoulder with a few bright strokes of gold, the crew cocooned in warm leather and fur, lulled by the gently throbbing metal, the terrors of the night would soon disperse.'[42] In some crews, the wireless operator ignored regulations and tuned the radio to a music station.

There was one more peril to be overcome before the wheels kissed the tarmac. Getting down was harder than getting up. Pilots had to wait for a landing order before they could touch down and the weight of numbers meant that they were sometimes forced to fly circuits until their turn came. Landing and take-off are the most dangerous times in flying. The returning aircraft were often shot up, their controls and surfaces battered by flak and shell and their skippers numb with exhaustion. Severely damaged aircraft were diverted to emergency airfields in Kent, Suffolk and Yorkshire with extended and broadened runways.

The operation ended where it had begun, in the briefing room. Intelligence officers doggedly probed the exhausted survivors of the night about what they had done and what they had seen, eager for any detail that could build their picture of the strength and disposition of the defences. Then, weary and subdued, the crews left to hand in their parachutes, drink a cup of tea and eat a plate of bacon and eggs before crashing into bed, trying to push from their minds the thought that the following night they might have to do it all over again.

10

'A Select Gang of Blokes'

Even by the standards of wartime, when sacrifice becomes the norm, the bombing campaign required extraordinary commitment to sustain it. The motivations that drove bomber crews were complicated but there were certain shared attitudes that bound them together. The most essential was the mixture of devotion, affection and trust that crew members felt for each other.

Serving in a bomber was an intimate experience. As Doug Mourton pointed out, when flying 'each one was directly or indirectly dependent on the other for his survival. There was mutual trust and reliance. This promoted fondness, affection and respect.' Mourton found that 'friendships thus forged, had a depth and unique quality that never existed with friendships before, and for me never after.' There was also a deep personal relationship between aircrew and ground crews. They were 'as one, winning and losing together'.[1]

Bomber Command was staffed with men who in peacetime would have been unlikely to choose a service career, and had no strong feelings of institutional loyalty to the air force. Reg Fayers, a fastidious man who was repelled by the rough side of service life, admitted that after two and a half years in uniform 'on the whole I've disliked the RAF. I doubt I could name six things I've positively liked.' Top of the list were his crew, 'a select gang of blokes, Ken Porter, Joe, Tony, Mac, Ken Brewster, Red and Lofty, than whom I'll never meet better. For those, I wouldn't have missed it.'[2]

The crewing-up technique recognized brilliantly the importance of human chemistry. Crews got together because, instinctively, they felt each other to be competent or lucky. But there was also an element of subliminal mutual attraction. Despite the almost invariable disparities in background and geography, crews tended to like each other. Going to war in a big aeroplane required intense interdependency. Men who functioned competently together in desperate circumstances formed strong bonds of liking and respect. The crew took the place of the family, a little universe whose dynamics were more important and absorbing than those of the world outside. Bomber squadrons were large, with up to 200 operational airmen backed up by hundreds more ground staff, and therefore rather impersonal. The sense of unit identity was much less pronounced than it was in Fighter Command. Its members tended to come together only at briefings and debriefings. Len Sumpter, the guardsman turned 57 Squadron bomb-aimer, found 'you didn't get friendly with other crews. You said "good morning" to them and this and that. But you never really got intimate with them . . . you were your own little band of seven and that was it.'

Sumpter's crew was a typical mix of class and nationality. His pilot was an Australian, David Shannon, who was only twenty years old and looked it yet was already recognized as a superb pilot. The navigator was a Canadian, Danny Walker, the quietest member of the crew. They nicknamed the skinny wireless operator Brian Goodale 'Concave' because when he was working 'he was always bending forward . . . his head was forward and his feet were forward and his bottom was sticking out.' Jack Buckley, the rear gunner, liked a drink and drove racing cars. Bob Henderson, the flight engineer, was a 'tall, staid Scotsman' who only occasionally joined his comrades on their sprees in Lincoln. The front gunner was Brian Jagger whose grandfather had been a portait-painter who had royalty among his clients. All flew with 617 in the Dams Raid of May 1943.

They 'all got on very well together . . . and I think that applied throughout the whole squadron. All the crews were the same I think which was caused by being thrown together so much. You just had to get on with people. You couldn't afford to be indifferent.'[3]

Loyalty to your crew could create conflicts of emotional interest. Cy March should have felt pleased when he was granted fourteen days' sick leave after breaking his finger. It would mean a delirious fortnight with his wife Ellen, whom he had only just married. 'I knew I should have been over the moon but I wasn't, for we knew we were to be posted to 467 RAAF Squadron very shortly.' He went off to the canteen where he knew the 'boys' would be. They congratulated him on his good luck. But March told them miserably: 'I'm worried I'll lose you rotten lot if I go.' The skipper, Neville 'Bug' Emery told him: 'Go home, enjoy yourself, give Ellen our love and don't worry. We will wait for you; we aren't going to break a new bod in.'[4]

The break-up of a happy crew felt as traumatic as the sundering of a happy family. Ken Newman was dismayed to be told that, for reasons that were never explained, his crew were to be split up after only a few operations together. He was 'shocked and upset by this disclosure'. When he complained to a senior officer 'he dismissed my protests out of hand . . . with tears in my eyes I went outside his office and told the other members of my crew who were waiting there.' They were equally unhappy and demanded an immediate interview with the officer. 'This was granted and they all pleaded with him to be allowed to stay together with me as their pilot. He was unmoved and just snapped at them too that a decision had been made and would not be reversed whatever they said.'

Such insensitivity appears to have been rare. Newman learned later that the orders came from his former squadron commander with whom he had fallen out, though 'for what reason we deserved this form of punishment I could not . . . imagine.' The good companions were packed off to other squadrons as 'spares'. The parting was painful. 'I was losing great friends . . . who I had lived with, flown with on training and on operations and had trusted implicitly for the previous nine months.' Newman set off for his new posting 'with a heavy heart and feeling utterly miserable and lonely'.[5]

Of course not all crews were as harmonious. Willie Lewis arrived at his squadron in April 1943 pleased that after all his long training as a flight engineer he was about to put his hard work to use. 'The future held no frightening menace, only the justification for everything which had taken place till then. The sun could not have shone more brightly that day nor the birds in the hedgerow have sung more sweetly.' His captain was John Maze, at twenty the young-

est of the crew. 'The skipper and I immediately made friends. I had
left school at fourteen. The skipper went to university. But on the
squadron I was never made to feel inferior for a moment.' He was
less enthusiastic about two other crew members. Ron, the mid-
upper gunner, was an ex-car salesman who had already done a tour
in the Middle East and been commissioned as a pilot officer. Lewis
resented his haughty manner. 'He wore his uniform with dignity
and enjoyed being an officer. He mixed little with the crew and they
had the unpleasant feeling that he was trying to patronize them.'

Joe, the bomb-aimer, was thirty-six, by far the oldest in the crew.
Before the war he had been a policeman in South London, 'running
in bookmakers' touts and prostitutes'. He 'regarded all the members
of the crew with good-natured contempt. The skipper because he
was a boy of twenty who had a cultured voice, a father who was an
artist and had been to a university. Dave [the navigator] because he
"was only an errand boy" – he had served in a shop in civilian life.
Jock [the wireless operator] went about with Dave so he was just as
useless.' He despised 'Rammy' the garrulous Yorkshire-born rear
gunner 'because, well, he was just Rammy'.

Joe had done some flying and navigation training and was free
with his advice to both pilot and navigator. Maze, despite his youth
had the authority to keep him in his place. But for all Joe's irritating
ways, Willie and the rest of the crew felt there was something comforting about him. He had a self-assurance 'which made him good
to fly with. Looking at him the crew felt that they were safe, for
anybody who loved himself so wholeheartedly must survive and
surely could not come to any harm.' Their hunch turned out to be
justified. Later on when they were faced with emergencies he was
'to prove as capable and resourceful as he was exasperating'.[6]

The crucial element in crew cohesion was confidence. If one
member lost the trust of his fellows, everyone's morale withered.
The system recognized this and in special circumstances agreed to the
removal of the weak link. Bill Farquharson lost a propeller in mid-
flight when piloting a Wellington during training. The crew were
forced to bale out and he crashlanded. Bad luck pursued him to his
squadron, 115, where 'we had the odd mishap, engine failures and

hydraulics failures.' Farquharson's crew were all sergeants. He was an officer. In the sergeants' mess they came across a pilot whose crew had been borrowed by the wing commander. 'They chummed up with him and decided that they would like to fly with him. They came to me and that was that. They put it very nicely. It wasn't that they thought I was a poor pilot or anything like that. They reckoned I was a pretty good pilot to have got them out of [difficult] situations. But they thought I was an unlucky one . . . that happened to lots of chaps.'

When the situation was explained to the squadron commander, Wing Commander A. G. S. 'Pluto' Cousens, he agreed that Farquharson would have to find another crew. 'I was very disappointed indeed [but] Cousens spoke to me and said these things happen, and perhaps for the best, because if the crew is a little dithery it spreads. Perhaps they want to argue with you – "shouldn't you do it this way or that way." And you've no time for arguments. You've got to act.'[7]

If the crew was like a family then the aeroplane was the family home. They were given pet names and there was consternation if the personal 'kite' was unavailable. 'If you had any faults on the plane of course you had to wait until they were fixed, or borrow another one,' said Len Sumpter. 'And we didn't like borrowing planes because you got used to your own plane. It was like when you . . . walk into your own house. If you go into another house, a stranger's house, you've got the feeling that you're not right. But you could always tell when you were in your own plane. I don't know why I'm sure. Whether it was the sound of it, the smell of it or what.'[8]

There was also luck to consider. Don Charlwood always felt happiest in B-Beer, even when it was playing up. During a raid on Essen in January 1943 there was trouble with the port outer engine. The following day the crew was ordered back to Essen again. They learned that though B-Beer had been repaired they were flying in L-London. B-Beer had been given to Sergeant B. E. Atwood, a Canadian pilot who had been attached to the squadron for one night. This, as far as the crew was concerned, was unacceptable and the skipper, Geoff Maddern, went to protest to the CO. 'The Wingco,'

Charlwood believed, 'had intended giving us the better of the two aircraft but to us, L-London was unthinkable.' They had endured two bad experiences in aircraft code-named L. It was an unlucky letter. The CO granted their request. Atwood got L-London and they flew in B-Beer. But that night the port outer engine failed again, catching fire just after take-off. They dropped their bombs into the North Sea and headed back to Elsham. On landing, Charlwood went to see his girlfriend. When he returned to the crew room he found Geoff 'sitting moodily by the fire' talking to the flight engineer, Doug Richards. 'As I came in he glanced up. "Atwood has gone. [he said] L failed to return."

'We were silent for several seconds, then Doug said something we had forgotten in our moment of self-recrimination.

'"I think it might have gone the same way with them if they had taken B. They wouldn't have been prepared for that port outer. We were."

'Geoff was poking the fire. "I suppose that's the way it goes," he said.'[9]

The decision to maintain distinctions between commissioned and non-commissioned ranks within crews meant that they lived different lives when not in the air. Facilities were better for officers than NCOs though sometimes the differences were slight. Sergeants slept up to ten to a Nissen hut whereas officers' quarters offered a higher degree of comfort. Reg Fayers was delighted with the improvement in his accommodation after he was commissioned as a pilot officer. 'I'm sharing with a pilot called Wright who should soon be leaving,' he wrote to Phyllis. 'The room has at least the elements of comfort, including a chest of drawers, a fireplace conspicuously *sans feu*, a table, chairs, and wow, two mirrors.' The habit of dressing for dinner seemed 'a pleasant thing to do'. Even small privileges like the right to wear a soft, Van Heusen officer's collar rather than the stiff, chafing NCO variety were much appreciated.[10]

The quality of life depended on the quality of the station and amenities differed considerably. Fayers was at Holme-on-Spalding-Moor which had opened in 1941 and had been built to reasonably exacting pre-war standards. Dennis Field was based at Tuddenham, in Suffolk, one of the 'pre-fab' bases thrown up hastily in 1943. Promotion meant 'merely a change of Nissen huts . . . there were slightly fewer occupants and occasionally a WAAF swept and cleaned out.' The service in the mess was virtually the same. The main difference he noted, was a sombre one: 'when a crew did not come back, there might be one, or at most two empty beds next morning instead of six or seven.'[11]

The change in status could be unsettling. When Doug Mourton was made a pilot officer he went to Burberry's in London to be fitted with two barathea uniforms and a Crombie overcoat and went on fifteen days' leave 'feeling rather proud, especially as I walked along and acknowledged the salutes of the airmen and soldiers.' But when he returned to duty, he found he 'did not like living in the officers' mess which was so different to the sergeants' mess which I had been living in for several years. The atmosphere was different. I knew no one and felt out of it.'[12]

On base officers had to be formally invited into the sergeants' mess. Away from the station it was easy to mix even though official policy frowned on it. Good skippers took little notice of the rule. 'Officers weren't encouraged to go out at nights with the other ranks,' Reg Payne remembered. 'It was taboo. [But] we did have get-togethers.' Michael Beetham, his captain, organized private dinners for his crew and their wives and girlfriends at the Saracen's Head, the Lincoln hostelry where, during the war years, aircrew drank, flirted and relaxed. 'We had a room upstairs, a room with service. There was a fire in winter time. You rang the bell, the waiter would come to the door and you'd give him your order and he'd go downstairs [then] bring your drinks up.'[13]

As promotion was fairly rapid with many NCOs being commissioned after a reasonable period on operations the social divisions did not seem as irksome or unfair as they might have appeared to outsiders. There were occasions, though, when the distinction rankled. When the King and Queen visited Scampton on 27 May 1943, just after the Dams Raid, Len Sumpter, then still an NCO, was annoyed that they went straight to the officers' mess for lunch. 'All the photographs were taken with the officers in front of the officers' mess. But the flight sergeants and the sergeants didn't see a sign of the King and Queen. They didn't come near our mess. And yet there were more NCOs on the raid than there were officers.'[14]

When it came to medals it did seem that an officer's courage was more likely to be recognized than that of an NCO. The majority of aircrew, more than 70 per cent, were not commissioned. Yet the Distinguished Flying Medal (DFM), for acts of valour, courage and devotion to duty performed by an NCO, was awarded far less frequently than the Distinguished Flying Cross (DFC), which was given to officers. DFMs accounted for less than a quarter of the combined total of almost 27,000 DFMs and DFCs relating to the war.

The men of Bomber Command were among the boldest and most individualistic of their generation. They had been propelled towards the RAF by a sense of adventure as well as duty. It was unsurprising that the rigorous professionalism they showed in the air was not always reflected in their conduct on the ground, so that to some of the more unbending older officers they sometimes appeared more like civilians in uniform than proper servicemen. The pre-war culture of conformism and respect for authority meant that British volunteers were in the end reasonably adaptable to authority, if more apt than their peers in other services to question it. The men from the Dominions came from a less stratified world where rank was not automatically deferred to and discipline was founded on respect. Ken Newman was returning to Wickenby from an operation against oil storage depots in the Bordeaux area in August 1944 when he was ordered to divert to a faraway airfield in Scotland, as the base was about to be blanketed in low cloud. He thought it better to land at Sturgate in Lincolnshire which was much closer to home. This decision got him into trouble when he got back to Wickenby. He was told that as a result of his disobedience the trip might not count towards the crew's total of operations. When he passed this on his men, the Canadians in the crew 'were very angry indeed. This in their eyes was a prime example of the stupidity of senior RAF officers and of the "bullshit" that they had been warned about before arriving in the UK, and which they regarded as intolerable.' They threatened to telephone the Canadian High Commission in London. The authorities relented and let the operation stand.[15]

Everyone, no matter where they came from, was only too aware of the exceptional risks they were taking. They were disinclined to put up with displays of arrogance or attempts to impose mindless pre-war discipline. Flight Sergeant George Hull, a cultured Londoner who emerges from his many letters to his friend Joan Kirby as notably decent and dedicated, had to endure a dressing-down from the station commander at Coningsby after two WAAFs were reported for returning to their quarters after midnight in breach of the rules. Hull and some fellow NCOs had been seen chatting innocently to them earlier in the evening. The group captain accused them of 'disgraceful conduct', and doubled the offence by referring to them as 'errand boys and chimney sweeps'.

'Well feeling ran rather high I can tell you [Hull wrote]. As for the "Errand Boy" remarks, that is the statement of an out-and-out snob . . . Such [are] the antics of the brasshats in the RAF.' The crew retaliated by chalking 'Errand Boys' on the side of their Lancaster when they set off for Berlin the following day. The CO later apologized.[16]

Attempts to get crews to smarten up seemed ludicrous given the dangers they were facing. Cy March once got a 'rollicking' from a senior officer for the offence of allowing his air gunner brevet to come loose. 'He told me to go away and come back tidied up. I went away, put on my best blue, bulled up to death and went back. "That's much better," he said, "go away and keep smart." I could see us saluting before taking evasive action and asking permission to shoot.'[17]

The crews were facing nightly death, engaged in an open-ended struggle the point of which was often hard to discern. Persuading them to carry on doing so required subtle and intelligent leadership. Guy Gibson exemplified one approach to the problem. He was short, with rubbery good looks and a loud, confident manner that hid occasional deep depressions and agonies of self-doubt. He had the power to enthuse and inspire, and was sent by the government to give pep talks to war-workers and on morale-boosting missions to the United States.

Nonetheless many of the aircrew who encountered Gibson felt some ambivalence towards him. He had not been overly-popular among his colleagues in the pre-war RAF who found him boastful and bumptious, and later, after he had proved he had much to be boastful about, some still found his energy, flamboyance and unhesitating opinions off-putting.

He could, as Harold Hobday who flew with him on 617 Squadron noted, be 'the life and soul of the party' at squadron piss-ups, at least with fellow-officers. He also had a fine understanding of the dynamics of crew relationships. 'There was a bit of a rivalry between navigators and pilots. He came up to me and he said "You're a navigator, aren't you? I'll swap jackets with you." So we swapped jackets in the mess. It was rather a nice touch, because it made everybody feel how friendly he was.'[18]

It was his other side that Len Sumpter, who flew with him on the Dams Raid, saw. He only met him once to speak to. 'That's when he tore a strip off me,' he later remembered. Two days before the attack Sumpter took part in a dummy run at Reculver beach but released his bombs too early. 'He had me in the next morning and told me off about it.' There were no hard feelings. His Grenadier background made him appreciate discipline. Nonetheless he felt the faint chill of hauteur when he saw him around. 'He certainly wasn't a mixer down on the floor as far as we were concerned, the NCOs . . . Gibson had just a little bit of side.'

Cheshire however 'had no side or anything. He was one of the best. He wasn't blustering. Some people tell you to do something and you've got to do [it] that way . . . he'd put it in such a way, nicely, that you'd do it without being told to do it. He had a manner with him, softly spoken, quiet, never lost his temper, always smiling. And always joking too. He could be a little sarcastic sometimes but in a nice way . . . he was the best chap I met . . . as far as squadron commanders were concerned.'[19]

Cheshire struck everybody who came across him as remarkable in every way; exceptionally tough, brave and good. He possessed a warmth and humanity that touched all who were fortunate enough to serve with him. When Tony Iveson went to report to him on his first day at 617 Squadron he was greeted with an enthusiasm 'that made you feel he had been waiting to see you all day.'[20] He worked very hard at winning trust and affection and made sure he learned everybody's name, from the crews to the cooks. A story was told of how a wireless operator who had just arrived at Linton where Cheshire was commanding 76 Squadron felt an arm around his shoulder as he was boarding a truck to head out to dispersal. 'Good luck, Wilson,' said the CO, to the pleasant amazement of the new-comer who never imagined he would know his name.

He was without any trace of the snobbery that afflicted some senior officers and was as friendly towards the ground crews as he was with his airmen. Cheshire's manner masked a determination that was as strong as anybody's in Bomber Command. He was every bit as ruthless as Harris and shared his view that the more Germans that were killed the sooner the war would end. The government were quick to spot his potential. Like Gibson he wrote a book and gave morale-boosting lectures in war factories.

Cheshire's outstanding qualities made him a daunting act to fol-low. Many a commander fell short of the ideal he represented. On their way to 76 Squadron in the summer of 1943 Willie Lewis asked his skipper what sort of outfit they were joining. According to Lewis's thinly fictionalized account, Maze replied that it had 'quite a reputation. It was Cheshire's until about two weeks ago and you know what a fine type he is.' If they were expecting similiarly inspirational leadership they were in for a disappointment. His replacement

> stared at them across the table with cold, hard eyes. They were just another crew to him and not an attractive one. A tall, thin pilot with a stoop, an officer gunner and a group of shabby-looking NCOs . . . how long would they last, he asked himself? Not very long! Even the smart crews disappeared in no time. Just the same it was his job to welcome them.

'How long have you flown on Halifaxes?' he asked. His thin, black moustache, set in a white face, made the question appear [like] a sneer.

'Forty-four hours sir,' replied John.

'Hmm. Hardly enough to learn how to land it properly. You fellows are sent on here only half-trained and we have to do our best to make you operational quickly. It's not good enough . . .'

He sighed wearily and glanced towards the side wall where a score of photographs showed the existing crews . . .

'I'm not going to disguise from you that we are losing crews steadily so there won't be much time to give you training flights. You'll get one crosscountry and that's all.'

After telling Maze that he would fly two trips as 'second dicky' with an experienced pilot he dismissed them. Jock, the wireless operator, thought him a 'damn unfriendly type' who 'made me feel as welcome as a leper'. Joe the bomb-aimer remarked that he did not 'look to me as if he would like anybody'. Jock disagreed. 'Oh, he likes himself all right. You can see that.'[21]

The best squadron commanders were those who conveyed an understanding of what their men were going through. On his first day at his conversion unit Don Charlwood reported to 'a pale boyish squadron leader who wore the ribbons of the DSO and DFC over his battledress pocket. Of his words I remember very little but his dark, staring eyes I have never forgotten. I felt that they had looked on the worst: and on looking beyond it, had found serenity. They gazed from an impassive face with a challengingly upthrust chin and firm mouth.' This was David Holford who won the DFC at eighteen and the DSO at twenty-one. He was now only twenty-two but had already completed sixty operations. His men loved him. A year later when Halford was in charge of a Heavy Conversion Unit at Lindholme, Charlwood heard a flight sergeant say that if Halford decided to return for a third tour half the base would follow him. He did eventually go back on operations and was killed in 1943 while landing in fog. In Charlwood's valuable judgement 'he was the personification of all that was best in the RAF.'[22]

Squadron leaders were not required to fly on every operation. But it was essential if they were to maintain their authority to go on some, and they were expected to accompany their men two or three times a month. The crews were contemptuous of those who put themselves down for relatively easy trips to France and Italy and grateful to COs who volunteered to share the dangers of Berlin or the Ruhr. Ken Newman had a particular admiration for his CO at 12 Squadron, Wing Commander John Nelson. He was 'a thick-set New Zealander in his thirties who was liked and respected by everyone. He led the squadron from the front and was often in trouble with the Air Officer Commanding No 1 Group for taking part in too many operational sorties . . . But John Nelson headed the operational order whenever the target was a tough or interesting one. Moreover he seemed indefatigable, as he was always present at briefings and in the debriefing room when the squadron's aircraft returned . . . whatever time of day or night . . .'[23]

Displays of reckless courage were by no means appreciated, however. One night Doug Mourton found himself flying with Squadron Leader Burnett who had just arrived on the squadron but had already established a reputation as a 'press-on type'. The target was Hamburg. It was, Mourton wrote later, 'one of the most nerve-racking flights I had taken part in. The anti-aircraft that night was particularly heavy and on the run up to the target we were caught in about twelve search lights. It was so bright it was impossible to see. If Stevens [an earlier skipper] had been the pilot he would have shouted to the bomb-aimer, "Drop those bloody bombs and let's piss off home," but Squadron Leader Burnett was made of different stuff.' He put the aircraft into a steep dive and jinked and weaved his way out of the searchlights' glare. Then to Mourton's dismay he announced they were going in again. 'The majority of aircraft had now left and once again the searchlights came on us and the anti-aircraft began noisily banging all around us. Somehow we got out of it, but it was only purely by luck, and eventually we left the target area and returned home.'[24]

Many of the Bomber Boys were young, green and away from home for the first time. If they were lucky there was someone on the base who took a fatherly interest in their feelings and concerns. Brian Frow found such a figure when he was posted to 61 Squadron at North Luffenham. Flight Lieutenant 'Cape' Capel was the squadron adjutant and a veteran of the First World War. He was was 'a tower of strength to me personally. He seemed to be aware of matters which were not obvious, and able to advise without being patronizing.' When he discovered that while Frow could pilot a four-engined bomber he could not drive the Hillman runabout allotted to each flight he saved him any loss of face by giving him a few lessons. He then took him for a test drive to a local pub where they spent a pleasant evening talking about everything but the RAF. 'This display of support, so essential to a newly commissioned, very inexperienced skipper was a tremendous boost and had a vital but subtle effect on my development as a Bomber Boy,' he wrote. 'It certainly helped me to face the terrible events that I was about to witness and experience.'[25]

In the air it was on the shoulders of the skipper that the burden of maintaining morale weighed the heaviest. Confidence was the great sustaining quality and Willie Lewis's skipper John Maze had it in abundance. Pilot Officer John Maze was really Etienne Maze. He was the son of Paul Maze, a French painter who became an unlikely but firm friend of Arthur Harris. He seemed unshakeable, cool to the point of numbness. It seemed at times, alarmingly, as if life meant little to him. But there was also an earthiness there and a love of comfort that reassured. Soon after he met Lewis he told him his father had a beautiful young mistress. 'His eyes glowed and he obviously would have loved to go to bed with her.' Maze found the long journeys to and from the target tedious. Hanging around in the air above the base waiting to get down was particularly tiresome. Even though the bombers were free of their loads on the return leg, it still took longer than the outward trip, partly because they were flying into the prevailing westerly wind, partly because they flew slower than their maximum speed to help crippled aircraft keep within the relative safety of the bomber stream. As one of a hundred blips on the German radar screens there was a reasonable chance of slipping through the defences whereas a lone smudge was naked and exposed.

Maze knew this. However he 'was twenty years old, a healthy, youthful animal with all a young man's indifference to such an explanation . . . Let the lame dogs look after themselves as *we* shall if the time comes to do so. Meanwhile *we* live, *our* "kite" is not knocked about and *we* are bored.' Lewis believed that Maze was 'born impatient' and seized by the conviction that 'there was too much fuss in the world. He was prepared to go to any lengths to ensure bombing correctly, but the moment that was over he was desperately anxious to get home in the shortest possible time from a feeling of utter boredom and the knowledge that they had done the job well.'

For the first three operations he followed the flight plan dutifully but on the fourth flew back faster than instructed and was the first bomber to reach the base. After that, T-Tommy was almost invariably the first to touch down. He was in an equal hurry to get into the air. He received regular dressings-down from the squadron commander for breaking the speed limit set on the journey to the runway.

Maze was fun. The ground crews adored him and he held his own at parties. On his twenty-first birthday he took the crew to a pub, 'got hopelessly drunk, broke one of the cues of the billiard table and went on singing a filthy [song] from his schooldays.' He might be little older than a schoolboy, but Lewis recognized that 'there was nothing soft about him.' He seemed to disdain fear. 'Look here, Joe, I'm sick to death of you getting frightened all the time,' he once snapped at the bomb-aimer. 'It's like having an old woman sitting next to me.' When Joe replied that he was 'not frightened, just a bit apprehensive,' he was told: 'Well *don't be.*'[26]

Pilots could feel a responsibility for their crews that transcended their own safety and survival instincts. There were several well-attested cases when skippers had kept a stricken aircraft flying long enough for the others to bale out, even though they knew they would die doing so. Flying Officer Leslie Manser was captain of a

Manser VC.

Manchester during the Cologne 'thousand' raid when it was hit by flak and caught fire. Both pilot and crew could have baled out safely but Manser insisted on trying to get his aircraft and his men home. When it became clear that this was impossible he ordered the others to bale out. The official citation for his Victoria Cross described how 'a sergeant handed him a parachute but he waved it away, telling [him] to jump at once as he could only hold the aircraft steady for a few seconds more.' As the crew floated safely to earth they saw the Manchester 'still carrying their gallant captain, plunge to earth and burst into flames.' They landed in Holland and five of them managed to evade the Germans and make their way back home.

Perhaps even more extraordinary was the fortitude shown by Flight Sergeant Rawdon Middleton, an Australian Stirling pilot during a raid on the Fiat works at Turin in November 1942. He pressed his attack through a storm of flak and delivered his bombs but was hit by shrapnel which tore out his right eye and ripped away his nose. Despite being barely able to see, or to speak without great pain and loss of blood, he managed to nurse the damaged bomber over the Alps. There was a discussion as to whether they should jump. Middleton, according to his citation, 'expressed the intention of trying to make the English coast so that his crew could leave the aircraft by parachute,' even though he knew that owing 'to his wounds and diminishing strength . . . by then he would have little or no chance of saving himself.' When they crossed the English coast there was only five minutes' worth of petrol left. He ordered the crew to jump. Five of the crew left the aircraft safely while two chose to stay on and help their skipper. The bomber crashed into the sea killing all aboard. Middleton too received the VC. The awards were made easier because there were witnesses alive to tell their remarkable tales. There were surely many other stories of amazing bravery and devotion which will remain buried with the dead.

The crew took some of its character from its skipper. But the joint identity was always stronger than the individual. No one in the chain of command was more motivating or inspiring than the collective spirit of seven men engaged in the enterprise of dealing death and trying to cheat it. The crew was where it began and where it ended. Writing to Joan from his dreary base in a mood of self-pity George Hull told her 'Thank God for the crew . . . a fierce bond has sprung up between us . . . we sleep together, we shower together and, yes, we even arrange to occupy adjacent bogs and sing each other into a state of satisfaction.'[27]

It was the crew that dissolved despair and doubt. Don Charlwood had 'little belief in the rectitude of our war or any other war,' when he arrived on his squadron. 'Nor could I believe that more good than evil would arise from our mass bombing.' Yet after a few operations he realized his attitude had altered. 'On the squadron one could not for long admit cynicism, or pessimism, even in the face of the worst. Whatever my frame of mind had been when we had come to Elsham, I realized that now it had changed. Then I had been alone; now I had become one with a crew and a squadron. To demean them was impossible.'[28]

11

The Big City

After almost four years of war Bomber Command had failed to do any critical damage to Berlin. If one of the main objectives of the strategic air campaign was to destroy German morale then the Big City was the best place to attack. Berlin was protected by its distance from the bomber bases, and by its very size which enabled it to absorb much punishment. It sprawled over more than eighty square miles and the townscape was interspersed with lakes, waterways, parks and woods. The centre was designed for victory parades. Broad boulevards led into spacious squares. There were statues everywhere. As the saying went, even the birdshit was marble. There was no *Altmarkt*, no wooden-built mediaeval quarter for Harris to burn down.

Despite these drawbacks, he yearned to attack Berlin. He was convinced that an all-out assault on the heart of Nazidom would bring the war to an end. He had used the short summer nights of 1943 to batter the Ruhr. As the hours of darkness lengthened, he intended to exploit the cover they provided to switch the assault to the capital.

Harris's mission of destroying German cities had been endorsed at the start of the year at the Casablanca conference, when the British and the Americans met to co-ordinate their approach to a war which was now going their way. There, Bomber Command had been told its primary object was the 'progressive destruction of the German military, industrial and economic system, and the undermining of the morale of the German people to a point where their armed resistance is fatally weakened.'

Berlin had been mentioned specifically as a suitable objective for night attack. A few weeks after the conference ended, a directive from the Air Ministry to Harris drew attention to the recent Soviet success at Stalingrad, where, on the last day of January, the bitter siege had ended in German defeat and abject surrender. It passed on the view of the War Cabinet that 'it is most desirable . . . that we should rub in the Russian victory by further attacks on Berlin as soon as conditions are favourable.'[1] This was probably Churchill talking. In 1942 he had sent several impatient memos demanding to know when the dismantling of Berlin would begin.

All this suited Harris very well. It was in line with previous directives which had given him the latitude to develop the technique of area bombing so that attacks were becoming steadily more devastating, and to his mind, more effective. There was nothing to suggest that he would be expected to pay more attention to the doctrines of the Americans who were by now increasingly active in the air war, albeit in a different role to that adopted by Britain. The Americans attacked by day and maintained their faith in precision operations. The British bombed by night, hitting what they could.

Harris was not against precise attacks on specific targets. The Dams Raid was the proof of that and Bomber Command carried out many other less celebrated but no less effective missions like it. But he believed they were only a subordinate part of the main strategy of bombing Germany's major cities flat.

His composure was to be badly disturbed by new orders which superseded the Casablanca directive. The Pointblank directive, issued early in June, threatened to alter the course of Bomber Command's war dramatically.

It reflected a harsh new reality in the air war, and the Americans were feeling its impact painfully. The Eighth Air Force had begun flying from England in August 1942. At first it confined its operations to France. The USAAF believed that to be sure of hitting the target it was necessary to bomb in daylight. It was confident that the firepower that its Fortresses and Liberators could bring to bear when grouped in disciplined formations would provide enough protection to make day-time bombing viable without the protection of escorting fighters.

The Americans' experience in France seemed to justify this confidence. When they started operating in Germany, bombing

Wilhelmshaven on 27 January 1943, the results were similarly encouraging. Out of ninety-one bombers sent, only three were lost. It soon became clear that these figures were freakishly low. As operations continued, losses climbed. In May they rose to 6.4 per cent of all attacking aircraft, a level that could not be sustained. Many were victims of flak. But the main threat came from the German fighter force which grew steadily stronger throughout the year.

As the peril increased in the months after Casablanca, the commander of the Eighth Air Force, Brigadier-General Ira C. Eaker, made a plan to deal with it. He proposed a combined American-British bombing offensive to crush the reviving German air force and win air superiority for the Allies.

Pointblank framed the means of achieving this crucial goal. It reasserted the American belief in precision bombing by concentrating effort on selected targets which if attacked effectively would have a devastating effect on German military operations. To achieve success it was essential to first sweep the German fighters from the skies. This was stated in the first draft of the directive, issued on 3 June, with a clarity that left no room for misunderstanding. It ordered the American and British forces 'to seek the destruction of enemy fighters in the air and on the ground'. That meant attacking factories that made airframes, engines and ball-bearings, repair facilities, component stores and anything else that kept the Luftwaffe flying.

The approach made clear sense. By establishing air superiority, the job of the Allied air forces would become much easier and safer and their efforts more efficient. It was the obvious lesson to be learned from the defeat of the German air force in the Battle of Britain. One of the reasons the Luftwaffe lost was that they switched the force of their attacks away from airfields and aviation factories and on to towns, giving the RAF a lifesaving respite.

Harris did not see it that way. He regarded the Eaker approach as desirable but unattainable and therefore a waste of effort and resources. His response was to mount a slogging, bureaucratic rearguard action of the type he excelled at. In doing so, he had the passive backing of Portal, even though Portal had been party to the drafting of Pointblank. He nonetheless allowed his subordinate to interpret the new orders in a way which contradicted their intention. Portal's indulgent attitude was in part a bow to reality. Harris enjoyed close relations with Churchill and made use of the proximity of Bomber Command's headquarters at High Wycombe to the prime minister's country retreat at Chequers to visit him at least once a week. A head-on confrontation would do no one any good. Bomber Command continued to pursue its mission along the lines laid down at Casablanca and the work of destroying the German air force fell largely on the shoulders of the Americans.

Harris laid out his plans for Berlin in a minute to Churchill on 3 November 1943. They were bold, even by his extravagant standards. Whatever he thought of American methods he was eager to have their aircraft in on the attack. With their help, he declared, 'we can wreck Berlin from end to end . . . it will cost between us 400–500 aircraft. It will cost Germany the war.'[2] The Americans were sceptical, as Harris must have known they would be. He was later to use their negative response to dodge the blame for what was to be recognized by everyone but himself as a dreadful defeat.

Harris's confidence had been bolstered by the successes of Bomber Command's summer campaign culminating in the raids of July and August that destroyed Hamburg and spelled out what 'undermining the morale of the German people' would mean in practice. The Hamburg raids showed what the RAF was now capable of. Two thirds of the population, about 1,200,000 people, were evacuated from the city or left under their own steam, leaving the rubble to a core of heroic defenders. The unsurpassed horror of what happened was beyond the control of even the Nazi propaganda apparatus. Bomber Command had managed to frighten Germany. Adolf Galland, the Battle of Britain Luftwaffe pilot who at the time was inspector of fighters at the German air ministry, wrote later that a 'wave of terror radiated from the suffering city and spread through Germany . . . In every large town people said "what happened to Hamburg yesterday can happen to us tomorrow" . . . After Hamburg in the wide circle of the political and military command could be heard the words: "The war is lost."'[3]

The Nazi leadership was now seriously concerned about how much punishment the population would be able to absorb. Hitler's munitions minister Albert Speer said at his post-war interrogation that 'we were of the opinion that a rapid repetition of this type of attack upon another six German towns would inevitably cripple the will to sustain armament manufacture and war production.' He reported to the Führer his opinion that 'a continuation of these attacks might bring about a rapid end to the war.'[4] But as Speer learned, it was unwise to underestimate the resilience of civilian morale. The majority of workers who fled Hamburg returned soon after. It was calculated later that less than two months of production had been lost.

Gains in the bombing war tended to be temporary. An important element in the Hamburg raids had been the use of *Window* which gave the attackers a strong initial advantage over the German defences. But the brief history of military aviation showed that new developments were quickly neutralized by counter-measures. The rule was to be proved again.

Under the existing system, the Germans' first line of defence had been the curtain of night-fighters based at aerodromes back from the North Sea and Channel coasts. As the incoming bombers passed through the radar 'boxes' of the Kammhuber line, they were picked up on the German radar screens. Ground controllers would then direct individual fighter areas on to their quarry.

'[He] would tell you,' said Peter Spoden, a German night-fighter pilot, ' "We have a target for you five miles ahead . . . turn left now, a little bit more to the left. Higher, higher, speed up. Four miles, three miles, two miles. And if the ground controller was clever he brought the target up above you so that you were in the dark below and you [could] see the British bomber as a kind of silhouette. The first [thing] you saw were the eight flames from the exhaust from the four engines. Then you were closing in . . . ' The arrangements were strictly localized and the night-fighter squadrons were manned by veteran *Experten* who appreciated the decorations and promotions arising from their relatively easy victories.

The method, though, had its limitations. The men flying the

Me110 night-fighters.

Messerschmitt 109s and 110s felt just the same determination to defend their homes and families as had their RAF counterparts during the Battle of Britain. Peter Spoden was an eighteen-year-old student at Hamburg University when the RAF bombed his home town of Essen in 1940. Like many young Germans he had learned to fly gliders at the air schools originally set up by the Nazis to circumvent restrictions on military activity. After the raid he joined the Luftwaffe with the specific intention of becoming a night-fighter pilot. He shared the frustration of the younger pilots at the limitations imposed by the system. He was flying in a box named 'Orion' over Rügen Island when the great Hamburg raid went in. 'I could see Hamburg. I could see the immense fire and I also could see closer to me two or three four-engined planes like moths against the cloud . . . I told my controller, "please let me go" but he did not have any radar reception there . . . I asked him again, "I can see them, I can see them." I was an eager young pilot and I had not had any great success at the time.'5 Permission was refused. For Spoden and his peers, the arrival of *Window* inadvertently created just the freedom of action they sought.

The confusion it had sown was alarming, but temporary. The

Germans responded quickly and cleverly. The controllers learned to follow the cloud of *Window* as it formed on their screens and deduce from that the direction and likely objective of the bomber stream. As the raid developed, fighters were summoned from all over to harass the raiders as they converged on the target. Over the city the fighters would use whatever light was available from the search-lights, fires and marker flares to locate their quarry as they flew straight and level on the last crucial minutes of the bombing run. It was dangerous work. The flak batteries were supposed to keep their fire below a certain height but such instructions could be forgotten in the heat of battle. They harried and struck at the intruders all the way back, with gratifying effectiveness.

The efficiency of the German defences was further improved by the arrival of new aircraft. By early 1944, Junker 88s had mostly replaced Messerschmitt 110s as the standard aircraft of the night-fighter force. Their ability to find their targets was greatly improved by onboard radar and their killing capacity increased by a new armament which arrived in the summer of 1943. These were cannons, known as *Schräge Musik*, which were angled to fire upwards and slightly forward. The tactic was to slink up below the victim and fire a burst into its belly, heavy with high explosive and incen-diaries. The resulting explosion could prove fatal to attacker and quarry alike.

The strengthened German fighter force was therefore as much a danger to the British as it was to the Americans. Once they came within range of a fighter there was little a bomber could do to defend itself. A fully-laden Lancaster could only manage an airspeed of 180 knots on the way out and 210 on the return. Their .303 machine guns were not a serious weapon. The only defence was the corkscrew and that was only intermittently effective against a smaller and more nimble opponent. As Noble Frankland knew from bitter experience, once located, the odds were heavily against the bombers. The truth was that 'outpaced, outmanoeuvred and out-gunned by the German night-fighters and in a generally highly inflammable and explosive condition, these black monsters pre-sented an ideal target to any fighter pilot who could find them, and it was the night-fighters which caused the overwhelming majority of the losses sustained by Bomber Command in the Battle of Berlin.' At this stage of the war the figure stood at about 70 per cent.[6]

Despite the enormous dangers and difficulties involved, Bomber Command entered the battle in an optimistic mood. Hamburg had impressed everybody. Even Harris's critics in the Air Ministry gave their firm support. The mood was buoyed up by two other cheering developments. On 17 August the Americans carried out their first deep penetration operation in Germany. True to their doctrine of precision targeting they sent out 376 B-17 Flying Fortresses against ball-bearing factories in Schweinfurt and the Messerschmitt works at Regensburg. They lost sixty aircraft but inflicted serious damage on both objectives. That evening Bomber Command carried out a precision raid of its own. Nearly 600 bombers set off in the moonlight to blast the German research and rocket production base at Peenemünde on the Baltic coast. The operation set back the programme by several months.

In this positive atmosphere the decision was taken to mount some preliminary raids before the main effort. The first phase opened with three attacks in late August and early September. The results were sobering. The bombs missed the city centre, little serious damage was done and losses were heavy. On the first raid, in which 727 aircraft took part, nearly 8 per cent of the heavy-bomber force was lost, the heaviest toll in one night so far in the war. Most of them were Halifaxes and Stirlings. On the third raid, only the better-performing Lancasters were sent. Even so, out of the 316 despatched, 22 were lost, a rate of 7 per cent.

There was a respite until winter and darkness set in. Given the poor results of the initial attacks, Harris also wanted to wait until the new type of H2S onboard radar arrived. The battle proper began on the night of 18/19 November and was to continue until 31 March 1944. There were sixteen major attacks on Berlin, as well as an equal number of heavy raids on other German cities designed to unbalance the defences and keep the controllers uncertain as to the objective that night.

The Battle of Berlin was the harshest test to which Bomber Command had yet been subjected. The target was far away and was reached by flying long hours through freezing and treacherous skies. Harris wrote afterwards that 'the whole battle was fought in appalling weather and in conditions resembling those of no other campaign in the history of warfare. Scarcely a single crew caught a single glimpse of the objective they were attacking ... thousands upon thousands of tons of bombs were aimed at the Pathfinders' pyrotechnic skymarkers and fell through unbroken cloud which concealed everything below it except the confused glare of fires.'[7]

The brevity of the tactical advantage bestowed by *Window* was apparent in the first few days of the campaign in the weight of losses sustained by the Stirlings and Halifaxes, now the most elderly machines in Bomber Command's line-up. Stirlings were handicapped by their inability to reach the same altitude as the others and were forced to occupy the bottom layer of the bomber stream. This was the most vulnerable position and they suffered accordingly. Between August and the third week in November 109 Stirlings were destroyed, a loss rate of 6.4 per cent. At this point, the decision was taken to drop them from the front-line force. They never took part in operations in Germany again and their squadrons were given less dangerous work until they could be re-equipped with Lancasters.

The Halifaxes moved into the hazardous spot vacated by the Stirlings and suffered an even worse fate. In the eleven weeks from mid-December 1943 to mid-February 1944 nearly 10 per cent of all Halifax sorties to Germany ended in disaster. In January 1944, the worst month of the battle, the Canadian 434 Squadron lost 24.2 per cent of the aircraft it sent to Berlin, 102 Squadron lost 18.7 per cent and 76 Squadron 16.7 per cent. These losses were unbearable and once again Harris was forced on to the defensive. After another painful night over Leipzig on 19/20 February he withdrew a further ten squadrons.

The Battle of Berlin had a shape and chronology that made it easier to follow than Harris's previous 'battles'. In it, he pitted the aircraft available against what he took to be weakened German defenders in an effort to deal a crushing blow to the enemy's heart.

It was a battle of attrition that, as was clear long before the finish, would only end one way.

Harris started out with 700 four-engined bombers, a larger force of heavy aircraft than he had yet had at his disposal. They were capable of carrying bomb loads of 1,500 tons on each raid, quantities that if the targets were correctly marked, would result in the systematic wrecking of the city, district by district. As always, there were grave problems in finding exactly where to drop the bombs. Berlin was 250 miles beyond the range of *Oboe*. It was up to those Pathfinder marker aircraft that were equipped with *H2S* to spot the target. Berlin's vast spread made it difficult to pick out individual features on the blotchy picture painted by the electronic echo. The image was further confused by the lakes, canals and rivers of that watery city.

The Battle of Berlin required new levels of fortitude and endurance from the Bomber Command crews. To sustain their morale they had to believe that they were making progress. Many of those taking part were new to the game. Reg Payne and his crew had arrived at Skellingthorpe to join 50 Squadron just after the battle began. Skipper Michael Beetham and the rest of the crew gathered for the main briefing on the afternoon of 22 November 1943. The last squadron raid had been against the railway line linking France to Italy at Modane, which was widely regarded as a 'piece of cake'. Payne was hoping for a return trip, a nice gentle way of easing into ops. He was to be disappointed. When the CO strode in, 'he drew the curtain straight back and said your target for tonight is Berlin ... on the map there was this red line going up over the Baltic somewhere, towards Denmark and down ... it was a bit of a shaker really ... the crews were aghast. They all went "oooh." They knew it was going to be an eight-hour trip.'[8]

To add to their burden, Harris had ordered that each Lancaster should carry 2,000 pounds of extra bombs. Getting airborne with the standard load was nerve-racking enough. As freshmen, Beetham's crew were spared the extra cargo.

Sixteen of the squadron's twenty-two crews were on that night. It was a big operation with 764 aircraft; 469 Lancasters, 234 Halifaxes,

50 Stirlings and 11 Mosquitoes. It was the largest force sent to Germany yet. Payne sat in his little wireless-operator's den, curtained off from the rest of the crew. As they rumbled down to the runway he looked out at the port inner engine and felt nervous. He could see 'the flames coming off the exhaust . . . after we were given the green light the pilot released the brakes and the engines went full bore so you thought they were almost out of control.' The sight of the two-foot-long flames licking over the top of the wings caused him to remember that 'there were two thousand gallons of petrol in those wings as well as the five tons of bombs on board.' It only needed one engine to malfunction for the take-off to fail. On short runways the pilots would instruct the engineer to remove the gate on the throttle to push up the revs a dangerous little bit higher. The engines could only stand five minutes of it before they overheated and seized up. Sitting powerless at his little desk Payne felt 'that the take-off was more frightening than anything else.'

As a new crew, they were at the back of the bomber stream. The idea was that by the time they got to Berlin the target would be ablaze and easily recognizable. They circled Lincoln cathedral then headed north and east. Payne checked his onboard radar and picked up occasional test broadcasts from base. Close to Denmark they saw a few searchlights and some desultory flak rise from the shores of Sweden. As Germany approached, Payne started shoving bundles of *Window*, lying in the gangway next to him, up to the nose where the bomb-aimer pushed them through a chute.

Nobody troubled them until they approached Berlin. The weather was terrible and many of the night-fighters were grounded. Then, ahead, he could see 'the searchlights in the distance and the glow underneath the clouds. I realized that this was the real thing when the gunners said an aircraft had just been shot down behind us.' Each sighting of a blazing bomber was noted by the navigator in his log to report to the intelligence officer when, or if, he returned.

The mayhem was building outside but inside Beetham's Lancaster there was a weird calm. 'There was no real excitement at all,' Payne remembered, 'it was all very well controlled.' Berlin was covered with cloud. They had been ordered to bomb on the green and red markers, which hung over the murk. The bomb-aimer, Les Bartlett, coaxed Beetham on to the right line. The bomb doors opened. Payne felt the blast of freezing air, a welcome antidote to the heat from the engines. Beneath his feet he could feel the grind and jangle of the shackle holding the cookie as the bomb left its moorings, and the aircraft leapt upwards. For a few more agonizing seconds the Lancaster ploughed on straight and level until the camera flash signalled the end of the immediate ordeal.

They swung away and into the flak. Payne switched out his light and climbed into the astrodome. 'It was about ten-tenths cloud and the searchlights never really got through. All they did was make the clouds glow. They showed the Lancasters up. You could see them going over the top of it like black fish . . . the flak was coming right through the clouds. You could smell it as well. Some of the fumes would get into the aircraft especially on the bomb run when the bomb doors were open.'

On this, his first trip, he felt 'excitement more than anything'. Casualties were light. Bad weather kept the night-fighters on the ground. Only twenty-six aircraft were lost, 3.4 per cent of the force. Despite the appalling visibility, the results were good. The devastation stretched from the centre west across the smart residential areas of Tiergarten and Charlottenburg and out to the suburb of Spandau. Several firestorms were ignited and a huge pillar of smoke towered nearly 19,000 feet the following day. About 2,000 died in the attack and 175,000 were bombed out of their homes. Thousands of soldiers were brought in to calm the chaos.

On the afternoon after the raid, Marie 'Missie' Vassiltchikov was leaving her office in the information department of the ministry of foreign affairs when the hall porter told her another air raid was imminent. She was twenty-six years old, an exiled Russian aristocrat who had been tossed by the fortunes of war into the cauldron of Berlin. There, she had made friends with a small, upper-class group of dedicated anti-Nazis. 'I took to the stairs two at a time to warn those of my colleagues who lived far away to stay put as they might otherwise be caught in the open,' she wrote in her diary. Just after she arrived at the flat where she lived with her father, the flak opened up. It was 'immediately very violent.' Her papa, who scraped a living teaching languages, 'emerged with his pupils and we all hurried down to the half-basement behind the kitchen, where we usually sit out air raids. We had hardly got there when we heard the first approaching planes. They flew very low and the barking of the flak was suddenly drowned by a very different sound – that of exploding bombs, first far away and then closer and closer, until it semed as if they were falling literally on top of us. At every crash the house shook. The air pressure was dreadful and the noise deafening. For the first time I understood what the expression *Bombenteppich* [bomb carpet] means.'

At one point there was a shower of broken glass and all three doors of the basement flew into the room, torn off their hinges. 'We pressed them back into place and leant against them to try and keep them shut.' Missie jumped to her feet at every crash. Her father, however, 'imperturbable as always, remained seated . . . the crashes followed one another so closely and were so earsplitting that at the worst moments I stood behind him, holding on to his shoulders by way of self-protection. What a family bouillabaisse we would have made!'

Before the all-clear sounded they were warned to get out of the house by a passing naval officer. The wind had risen and there was a danger of firestorms. They left the basement and 'sure enough, the sky on three sides was blood-red.'[9]

The fires passed the Vassiltchikovs by but the raid claimed the lives of 1,500 people that night. The attack was a new and appalling experience for Berliners. One of Missie's colleagues in the foreign ministry, Hans-Georg von Studnitz, arrived with his wife in the city after a few days away with friends in Pomerania just after the raid finished. The population, he wrote in his diary, had 'lived through an indescribable experience and survived what seemed like the end of the world.'

Their train stopped in the suburbs. They set out to try and reach home by foot but were forced to give up. 'The air was so polluted with the smell of burning and with the fumes of escaping gas, the darkness was so impenetrable and the torrents of rain so fierce that our strength began to fail us. Our progress was further barred by uprooted trees, broken telegraph poles, torn high-tension cables, craters, mounds of rubble and broken glass. All the time the wind kept on tearing window-frames, slates and gutters from the destroyed buildings and hurling them into the street.'

And this was only on the outskirts. When, the following morning, they finally reached the city centre by underground and emerged at Alexanderplatz, the bombers had long gone but Berlin was still a 'burning hell... all around the destroyed station in the Alexanderplatz the great warehouses were burning fiercely. Further towards the city stood the Royal Palace, the former residence of the Hohenzollerns, in the middle of a tornado of fire and smoke ... we crossed the Spree into the burning banking quarter. The Zeughaus, the university, the Hedwigskirche and the National Library had all been reduced to ashes ... the Tiergarten looked like some forest battle scene from the First World War.'[10]

At the edge of the Tiergarten stood a huge flak tower and reinforced concrete shelter which could hold up to 18,000 people. Even those inside could feel the ferocity of the attack. The tower received a direct hit and, according to Konrad Warner, 'the massive building was shaken to its foundations. The light went out and suddenly there was a deadly silence.' When he finally emerged after the all-clear, his coat was set on fire by the blizzard of sparks.[11]

The two consecutive attacks had created far less devastation than had been done to Hamburg. It was, however, to turn out to be the high point of the campaign. Bomber Command went back fourteen more times before the end of the Battle of Berlin but with nothing like the same success.

The poor results came at a high price. On the last trip of the month, on 26/27 November, twenty-eight Lancasters were destroyed and fourteen more crashed on landing. On 2/3 December the German controllers identified Berlin as the target in sufficient time for the area to be swarming when the bomber stream arrived. This time, a total of forty bombers were lost.

The American journalist Ed Murrow, famous for his broadcasts from Britain during the Blitz, accompanied 619 Squadron commander

BOMBER BOYS · 213

'Jock' Abercromby on the trip. He described the experience in a powerful piece of reportage which went out on his *This is London* programme. It was an eventful night for Murrow who did not hide the intense fear he felt over the target. He told his audience that 'the thirty miles to the bombing run was the longest flight I have ever made. Dead on time . . . the bomb-aimer reported "target indicators going down". At the same moment the sky ahead was lit up by bright yellow flares. Off to starboard another kite went down in flames. The flares were sprouting all over the sky – reds and greens and yellows and we were flying straight for the fireworks.' The bomber he was in, D-Dog, 'seemed to be standing still, the four propellers thrashing the air but we didn't seem to be closing in.' Then, without warning 'D-Dog was filled with an unhealthy white light. I was standing just behind Jock and could see the seams of the wings. His quiet Scots voice beat into my ears: "Steady lads, we've been coned." His slender body lifted half out of the seat as he jammed the control column forwards and to the left. We were going down. Jock was wearing woollen gloves with the fingers cut off. I could see his fingernails turn white as he gripped the wheel. And then I was on my knees, flat on the deck, for he had whipped the Dog back into a slashing turn. The knees should have been strong enough to support me, but they weren't, and the stomach seemed in some danger of letting me down too . . .' As the bomber flipped over Murrow glimpsed what was happening on the ground. 'The cookies . . . were bursting below like great sunflowers gone mad . . . I looked down and the white fires had turned red; they were beginning to merge and spread just like butter does on a hot plate.'

Berlin, he said later, 'was a kind of orchestrated hell – a terrible symphony of light and flame. It isn't a pleasant form of warfare.' The men he flew with spoke 'of it as a job.' Before he left Woodhall Spa he looked into the briefing room where 'the tapes were stretched out on the big map all the way to Berlin and back again. A young pilot with old eyes said to me "I see we're working again tonight."'

And so the labour went on, dangerous, dispiriting and without any obvious signs of progress. The authorities were eager to emphasize the importance of the work and the value of the sacrifices. The anonymous editor of the 115 Squadron news-sheet stressed that Berlin would be the target 'until the place is wiped out. It is the HQ of nearly everything that matters in Germany – Armaments, Engineering, Foodstuffs, Administration. Berlin is the "London of Germany". Until Berlin is Hamburged Jerry's mainspring is wound up.'[12] Freeman Dyson, a civilian scientist at Bomber Command headquarters, wrote afterwards that 'the boys in the Lancasters were told that this Battle of Berlin was one of the decisive battles of the war and that they were winning it. I did not know how many of them believed what they were told. I knew only that what they were told was untrue.' Dyson, who worked in the Operational Research Centre, had studied the bomb patterns from photographs which showed they were being scattered over an enormous area. It was true that Berlin contained a great variety of war industries and administrative centres. 'But Bomber Command was not attempting to find and attack these objectives individually. We merely showered incendiary bombs over the city in as concentrated a fashion as possible, with a small fraction of high-explosive bombs to discourage the firefighters. Against blanket attacks the defence could afford to be selective, with fire-fighters giving priority to dousing fires in factories and leaving houses to burn.' He concluded that with bomber losses rising sharply there was 'no chance that continuing the offensive in such a style could have any decisive effect on the war.'[13]

Dyson's prescriptions were unrealistic. Everyone wanted precision. But the technology could not deliver it. The Harris approach relied on weight of numbers. But as the battle progressed it was clear those numbers were dwindling alarmingly. On the thirteenth trip, during the night of 28/29 January 1944, forty-six aircraft were lost, 6.8 per cent of the force of 677 aircraft that had been sent out. On 30/31 January Harris launched his last attempt on Berlin. The German controllers failed to intercept the stream on the way in but the fighters eventually caught up, hounding the bombers throughout the return flight. One Halifax and thirty-two Lancasters were shot down.

Bomber Command was bleeding, but there was little to show for its sacrifices. It was inflicting pain on Berlin, but with nothing like the intensity needed to produce any serious collapse of morale. Many of the bombs were wasted. The sprawling city could soak up a huge amount of violence. Reports showed that for all the damage done to the built-up areas and though the centre of Berlin was effectively flattened, many of the bombs so painfully and expensively delivered were falling into open country.

The level of dread felt by the crews when they heard they were going to Berlin mounted. Michael Beetham's crew found themselves back in the Big City the night following their debut. On their return they found that their Lancaster's flaps were not working and were forced to divert to the emergency landing strip at Wittering. Two nights later they were ordered to Berlin again. On the way back they were told Skellingthorpe was fogged in and they were to land at Pocklington. That too was covered in low cloud so they switched to its satellite, Melbourne. At least three aircraft were lost trying to land there that morning. One ran out of fuel and crashed into a farmhouse, killing five of the crew and a widow and a forty-year-old female lodger who were living there. Another ran off the runway and got bogged down, to be hit by another bomber as it landed. All survived. Beetham got his team down but as they were being driven by a WAAF back to the base they heard over her radio two crews who were trying to land being told to head their aircraft out to sea and bale out.

The odds against the crew surviving seemed infinitesimal. 'We were beginning to think that's only four operations and we've got thirty to do,' Reg Payne, the wireless operator, remembered. So it continued. On 3 December on a trip to Leipzig they were badly shot up by a Ju 88. On 29 December, on their way yet again to Berlin, a thirty-pound incendiary bomb dropped from an aircraft above crashed through their wing. Luckily the fuel tank was already empty.[14]

Yet even these experiences did not match the night of 30/31 March 1944. The target was Nuremberg, one of the alternative destinations chosen to keep the German controllers wondering whether or not Berlin was the target. Bright moonlight was forecast. Such conditions offered great advantages to the defender and it was expected that the operation would be cancelled. But a weather update predicting high cloud along the route and clear conditions over the target persuaded Harris to press ahead. There was further confusion when a Mosquito from the Met Flight returned from a reconnaissance trip to report that the reverse was likely. There would be no sheltering cloud on the way, but plenty over Nuremberg itself. Despite this up-to-date intelligence the order to stand down never came, and 795 aircraft were dispatched. The Germans were not fooled by diversionary raids and fighters were waiting along the route, picking up the stream as it reached the Belgian border. They followed it through the moonlight all the way to Nuremberg and back again. Altogether ninety-five bombers were lost, nearly 12 per cent of the force. Hardly any damage was done to the city. The wind forecast was wrong and upset navigational calculations so that 120 bombers attacked Schweinfurt, fifty miles to the north-west of the intended target, though again to little effect.

Looking out of the astrodome, Reg Payne could see 'aircraft being shot down all around us ... we could even see the aircraft registration letters it was so clear.' They were painfully aware they were leaving condensation trails in the clear night sky and dived to lose them but it was no good. 'The fighters had a field day.'

The Nuremberg catastrophe was the last disaster in a losing battle. The losses could not continue. Nuremberg marked the end of the Battle of Berlin. Harris maintained to the last that if the Americans had joined in, his claim that the war could be finished by bombing alone would have been vindicated. But it was clear even to him that to continue under the prevailing conditions would mean disaster. The night-fighters controlled the sky. Between November 1943 and March 1944 1,047 British bombers were destroyed. During that period the number of aircraft available for operations varied from about 800 to just below 1,000. That meant that the German air defences disposed of the entire bomber strength available at the start of the battle. The bombers, which never had the ability to defend themselves, were losing even the capacity to evade. In the words of Noble Frankland, 'the tactical conditions of daylight had invaded the night.'[15]

Harris admitted defeat in early April. The battle had cost twice the number of aircraft he had told Churchill it might be necessary to lose as the acceptable price of victory. The sacrifice had not 'cost Germany the war'. He laid out the harsh lesson he had learned in a letter to the Air Staff. He wrote: 'the cost of attacking targets in Berlin under weather conditions which gave good prospects of accurate and concentrated bombing is too high to be incurred with any frequency.'

Belatedly, he turned his attention to some of the technical faults that had contributed to the heavy losses. The bombers' chances would improve, he said, if the gunners were better armed. He also pointed out that visibility from the turrets was abysmal. Even if improvements were made overnight this was unlikely to redress the imbalance significantly. It would have to wait for the advent of the protection that long-range fighter escorts could provide before the mortal threat of the Luftwaffe's night-fighters receded.

Long before Harris's change of heart, some of the crews had started to lose faith. This was reflected in the increased rate of 'early returns' when aircraft turned back because of real or imagined technical difficulties. Out of sixty-six sorties flown by 115 Squadron in the first three weeks of December, eleven crews turned back without reaching the target area. This compared with the figures for May during the Battle of the Ruhr, when there were only two aborted missions. The tendency was particularly marked in squadrons equipped with Halifaxes which had shown themselves to be specially vulnerable to night-fighters. The decision to load yet more bombs on the Lancasters, slowing them down and making them less manoeuvrable, thereby depriving their pilots of their main defensive advantage, also produced displays of indiscipline. Some captains took to dropping part of their bomb load in the North Sea on the way out to give themselves a better chance of evasion. The lengthening tail of the creepback over the bombing area was another sign that nerves were fraying.

But the great majority of the crews never wavered and persisted with their duty, even though there was little sign that their efforts were worth it. There were, however, limits to courage, as the men leading the campaign were obliged to remember.

12

The Chop

Fear of the chop loomed over everyone. Even the outwardly nerve-less like the Australian Dambuster veteran Dave Shannon felt its shadow. He and Leonard Cheshire were about to board their aircraft one evening, Germany-bound, when Cheshire remarked on the wonderful sunset. 'I don't give a fuck about that,' said Shannon. 'I want to see the sunrise.' The great question was the extent to which that dread could be controlled. Bomber crews had an intimate relationship with death, which stalked their careers from the first months of training. Non-combat crashes accounted for 15 per cent of overall fatalities. The pointlessness of these losses made them stick in the mind. Reg Payne remembered how, having survived the worst of the Battle of Berlin, he was sent on a fighter affiliation exercise over Yorkshire. A Canadian pilot was flying alongside his skipper, Michael Beetham, and two extra gunners joined the crew. When the fighter made its mock attack the Canadian put the bomber into a screaming corkscrew. As they dived at 300 mph the port outer engine caught fire. Beetham ordered the crew to jump.

There were ten men aboard. Beetham, the Canadian and the navigator slipped easily through the front hatch. At the back of the aircraft, though, there was chaos. Payne struggled rearwards from his wireless operator's desk to find five men huddled around the side exit. The bomb-aimer had already jumped but the others clung to the fuselage, each urging the other to go first. Don, the flight engineer, was already doomed. As it was only a training exercise he had not bothered to bring his parachute. The others were paralysed with fear. Their last position had been over the Humber estuary. It was February. Spread below them was a thick, grey blanket of cloud with no way of knowing if sea or land lay underneath. Finally Jock

Higgins, the mid-upper gunner, lunged for the door 'but instead of going out like you should do rolling up in a ball with your back to the slipstream so as to miss the tail, he stepped out and hit it.' For a moment it seemed that the tailplane would slice him in half then his parachute opened and 'flipped him off as quick as lightning like flicking a fly.'

Payne went next. As he plunged through the cloud he tugged frantically at his rip-cord with no result, before realizing that he was pulling the wrong handle. He looked up to see one of the stricken bomber's blazing wings 'coming down like a leaf'. Fred Ball the rear gunner, with whom Payne had endured so much, and the two extra gunners, 'didn't get out . . . they just didn't [manage] to do it.'[1]

Crashes such as this were especially bruising to morale. Lives had been spent for nothing. The mortality rate at OTUs, which were often equipped with clapped-out and underserviced aircraft, was particularly high. In the six months Doug Mourton spent as an instructor at Wellesbourne, fifteen aircraft and crews were lost. 'An OTU should be a safe enough place,' he wrote, 'but actually we were flying with dodgy crews in dodgy aircraft . . . Wellington 1Cs which were very old and obscure.'[2]

Training accidents often provided the crews with their first sight of a dead body. Corpses were curiously absent from the war the crews were waging. Guy Gibson's nerves were rattled by the sight of a Wellington which crashed-landed one snowy night and burst into flames. The following morning Gibson and his friend Dave Humphries went to look at the wreckage. 'As we got closer we could smell that unpleasant smell of burnt aircraft, but when we got really close we could see quite clearly the pilot sitting still at his controls, burnt to a frazzle, with his goggles gently swaying in the wind hanging from one hand. Without a word we began to retreat and were back in our operations hut within a few minutes.'[3]

In the air, death was often instantaneous. A cannon shell or a lump of molten flak would hit the bomb bay and the aircraft and those inside it were blown to pieces. There were also times when individual members were killed in a fighter or flak attack while others survived. The swing of the scythe was impressively arbitrary.

Reg Fayers described in a frank letter to his wife the death of a young sergeant pilot called Wittlesea, 'a nice kid with bags of enthusiasm,' who was flying second dickey. They were on their way back from Nuremberg. Fayers was visiting the Elsan toilet when they ran into flak. H-Honkytonk 'was thrown around the sky and me with it, until Steve got her out of this nasty stuff which had been our worst yet.' A large chunk of shrapnel hit the port outer engine which promptly caught fire. 'At the same minute, Witt said: "I think I've been hit, skip. I think I'm going to pass out." . . . By the time we were out of the flak, Lew found Witt to be unconscious – no more than five minutes at most. It took several more minutes for Lew and Phil to get Witt back to the rest position and find the wound and treat him. Anyway I think Witt was already dead. He died very soon anyway, and there was so much blood about he must have died from the loss of it, and the shock of course.'

The crew were too preoccupied with nursing the damaged aircraft home through an area thick with night-fighters to brood much on the death. Fayers recorded his surprise when informed that Witt was dead: 'I wrote in the log "second dickey died." It was nothing more than that.' They eventually landed safely at Ford, an emergency aerodrome on the Sussex coast. The following day they went to examine 'Honkytonk' and discovered that 'the piece of flak fragment that killed poor old Witt was no more than an inch and a half across. It came thru the nose of the kite by Tom's right hip, up thru two pieces of metal, right thru my seat – upon which I was not sitting by the grace of god.' Fayers' trip to the Elsan had probably saved his life. Wittlesea had been correspondingly unlucky. The shrapnel had hit an important artery in his thigh and he bled to death. As Fayers reflected, 'I don't think there's more than a breath of wind or a feather's weight between life and death.'[4]

The spirit of death was everywhere. The crews accorded it an awed, mediaeval respect. To them, death was The Reaper and they sensed when one of their number had been brushed by his bony fingers. Brian Frow's writings do not show him to be a fanciful man but he recorded how, when waiting on long winter nights in the ante-room for ops to begin, he came to recognize 'the chop look'.

Tail End Charlie.

It was a very real feature and whether it was true or not we believed it. Some aircrew would spend time playing snooker, cards or reading. A few just sat and pretended to doze; but sometimes their faces lost colour and they would nervously flex their muscles. If approached they would talk in raised voices and they invariably missed the 'aircrew supper' of eggs, bacon and beans. They could be seen visiting the [lavatories] too often and a few would sit outside the telephone call box trying to get through to their friends or relations, but forgetting that all 'off station' calls were banned during alerts, and that the phones were cut off. These were some of the symptoms of the 'chop look'. We believed that anyone who had it was aware that he was near to death; he seemed to have been informed by some extraterrestrial power, be it God or intuition.

Frow noticed it in his friend 'Shack' Shackleton, who like him was nineteen years old. 'He had gone through training with aplomb and was a popular and lively figure. One night . . . we had received a postponement of take-off and were sitting around in the mess, waiting. I saw to my horror that Shack had the dreaded symptoms, but I was unable to comfort him. By now we had completed four successful operations without serious incidents so Shack had no specific reason to be suffering from nerves.' At eight o'clock operations were scrubbed and Frow and his friend relaxed. Two days later Shackleton was assigned to an attack on the *Scharnhorst* in Brest docks and failed to return.[5]

Everyone had a similar story. Don Charlwood remembered 'a particularly coarse but good-natured Australian' known to everyone as 'Bull' approaching him as he prepared to set off for Turin. A trip to Italy was generally regarded as a 'piece of cake' given the anti-air gunners' reluctance to stay at their posts during raids. Crews marked each mission over Germany or France by painting a bomb on the nose of their aircraft. Italy merited only an ice-cream cone.

> 'Listen son [Bull said], you're not going tonight. If any-thing happens to me, could you get my personal belong-ings home to my mother?'
>
> I looked with astonishment at his ruddy face, taken unawares by the sudden change in him.
>
> 'I suppose the Air Force would do it, but you know the way it is.'
>
> I stammered, 'They say the target's easy – '

'I know all about that son, but I've got an idea. Anyway, you'd do that for me?'

'Of course.'

But that Turin could claim 'Bull' I refused to believe.

Charlwood woke the next day to see a van removing 'Bull's' belongings from the hut opposite.[6]

Not all premonitions turned out to be accurate. Cy March remembered how 'before going on a particular operation, I felt all day long that this was to be my last trip. All aircrew have had that feeling I suppose. We turned on to the runway for take-off and there, in a field was a dead tree, with a dirty great black crow sitting on one of its branches, just like a horror film. My blood turned to ice. We got the "green" and off we went. It was one of the easiest ops we ever did.'[7]

The knowledge of your own fragile mortality was all-pervading. Edwin Thomas displayed a touching emotional reticence in the many letters he wrote to his mother throughout his brief RAF career. He was anxious not to upset her by revealing the dangers of his job but occasionally even he could not keep death out of the picture. 'My dear mother,' he wrote on 24 September 1942 from RAF Harwell. 'I have arrived safely at this huge camp and am settling down in the sergeants' mess . . . when I first arrived in the dormitory I pointed to an empty bed and said "is this anyone's?" "No," came the answer. "He's missing."' Three weeks later he described running into a friend whom he had met during training. 'He and I shared a room and it is very interesting to hear news of the boys I knew – most of whom appear to have gone for a burton.' Just before Christmas he asked if she remembered him mentioning 'my old friend Wee Baxter from Blackpool. He was killed in a night crash last Tuesday, poor old chap. Only last week we were talking about prangs and he said "I shall be all right, I have a good pilot." They say that only the good die young . . .'

It was not long before he joined their number. He arrived finally at 78 Squadron at Linton-on-Ouse at the end of March 1943, two and a half years after joining up. At last all his training was going to be put to use. 'Our crew are to do our first op tonight,' he wrote. 'Do not worry because this squadron has a fine reputation and loses few kites. We have been waiting the last few days for this job and all feel very bucked and excited (note the steady hand).' This was one of the last raids of Bomber Command's spring diversion to the Atlantic ports and it went off smoothly. 'The whole business was little different from an ordinary crosscountry night flight ... we arrived there nine minutes ahead of the bombing time so we had to circle it until we could bomb. The flak was said to have been light by the veterans but there was sufficient to keep us weaving and turning.'

Thomas knew very well that a trip to France was not the same as a trip to the Ruhr. Nonetheless, it was an enormous relief to have finally been tested in battle, no matter how gently, and his letter to his mother of 8 April was cautious but optimistic, talking about a possible twelve days' leave in four or five weeks' time. 'This will suit our purpose admirably because Pat, the rear gunner, will be twenty-one in May and is going to have a GRAND PARTY. I have never in all my two-and-a-half years in the RAF had so much time to spare. I inspect the wireless equipment of our kite in the morning and sign as having done so and if no ops, I buzz off to York in the afternoon with the crew.'

Thomas loved dancing and claimed to have worn out his shoes in the dance-halls of York. He asked his mother to send a pair from home, 'as soon, soon, soon as you can. I don't want to be deprived of my favourite enjoyment. I will reward your kindness by saving some more sweets and a tin of orange juice.' It was his last letter. Thomas's Halifax, K-Kathleen, disappeared on the night of 16/17 April while attacking the Skoda works at Pilsen.[8]

Empty beds had the same gloomy effect as the empty chairs at breakfast in the messes of the Royal Flying Corps on the Western Front. The RAF's administrators were keen to remove evidence of losses as quickly as possible. Sergeants were issued with a haversack to carry their wash kit which hung on numbered hooks at the mess. Reg Payne remembered how 'they would put up a notice in the mess saying will all members remove their [haversacks] from the pegs from 11 o'clock until 1 o'clock.' He passed by the mess just after the deadline had expired to see 'them throwing all the ones that were left into a wheelbarrow. They [belonged to] the ones who'd gone missing.'[9]

The loss of friends was confirmed by the doleful letters FTR – Failed To Return – chalked up on the crew blackboard. The rules of survival meant that grief had to be curtailed. 'The first time I lost a good pal, one I'd trained with, I felt very, very sad,' Roy MacDonald remembered. 'I went out into York determined to get absolutely blotto. I can't remember how much I drank but I remained horribly, stone-cold sober. But after that you just said, "well that's tough," and forgot them.'[10]

Surviving meant overcoming odds that, it was all too apparent, were stacked toweringly against you. From the beginning it was clear that the crews would have to be given some hope that they were, nonetheless, beatable. The Air Ministry worked on devising a limit on the amount a crew would have to fly before being switched to non-operational duties. Initially the line was drawn at 200 hours, which, it was thought, would allow a 50–50 chance of survival. There was an obvious objection to this yardstick. Because of the difference in flying speeds, those manning twin-engined bombers would only have to do thirty trips to reach the limit whereas those in the heavies would have to do forty. In August 1942 Harris's office made an interim ruling that crews would have to complete thirty operations before they were 'tour expired' and eligible to move on to a six-month stint instructing at a training school. This became official policy on 1 May 1943. Anyone who completed a first tour was not expected to do more than twenty on a second. Pathfinder Force crews were set a single continuous tour of forty-five sorties.[11]

It was the squadron commander who decided what constituted a completed sortie. Their interpretation of the rules could vary from a degree of sympathy that in some eyes approached laxity to a rigidity that bordered on the inhumane. By the middle of the war most COs were veterans who had completed a tour themselves and their attitudes were conditioned by their own reactions and behaviour. The keenest commanders were likely to regard any failure as an indication of slackness or loss of nerve.

Early returns, 'boomerangs' in RAF parlance, when a crew turned back because of a fault in the aircraft, were rigorously investigated. Pilots who had experienced genuine mechanical failures prayed for the trouble to be identified in order to avoid the suspicion that they were shirking, and to have another precious operation to count towards their thirty.

The establishment of a limit on operations showed an awareness in the upper reaches of the RAF of the weight that the crews were being asked to carry. But their concern stemmed from practical as much as humanitarian considerations. If the best and keenest airmen were allowed to continue until they were killed it would rob the organization of experienced, and perhaps inspirational, leaders. The point of nursing men through a first tour was so they could do a second, or even, some argued, a third. 'Those men who return for their second tour are immensely valuable,' a squadron commander told investigators from the RAF's Flying Personnel Research Committee. 'They are experienced, well-trained and teach the others. They usually come back as officers making valuable Flight Commanders or seconds in command.' Even so there was a limit to what anyone could do and it was the responsibility of senior officers to impose it. Otherwise a good man was likely to feel bound by duty to push himself on until he was broken or dead.

'Percy' Pickard, the seemingly imperturbable, pipe-smoking star of *Target for Tonight*, survived seventy bombing trips and numerous missions dropping agents into France before being given command of 140 Wing. This was made up of three Mosquito squadrons and was tasked with low-level bombing in daylight. It was an unfortunate appointment. Night bombing was very different from precision daylight raiding and Pickard was, it appeared to those around him, worn out. Charles Patterson who flew with him, regarded him as a 'splendid character. But it was quite plain to me that he should never have been allowed to go on. He was a nervous wreck . . . he was obsessed with getting on operations . . . but his brain was really too tired to really sit down and tackle the detail . . . it was quite obvious that he should have been rested, no matter how much he wanted to go on.' Pickard's wing was in 2 Group which was commanded by Basil Embry, who liked taking risks himself and did not mind ignoring the rule book. He had been shot down over Dunkirk in 1940 and captured, but escaped and made his way back to England via Spain and Gibraltar to fight again. As an Air Vice-Marshal he was considered too great a security risk be allowed back on operations. He nonetheless continued to take part in attacks flying under the pseudonym 'Wing Commander Smith'. He could hardly refuse Pickard's entreaties to get back into action. Patterson thought it a stupid and wrong decision. 'A man who'd made a staggeringly splendid contribution to the war was denied his future . . . Embry ought to have recognized that after [so many] trips on light bombers there was no basis on which to start off a completely new career on low-level daylight bombing.'[12] Pickard's fame was such that senior French Resistance figures asked for him to lead a special operation in early 1944 to breach the walls of Amiens jail where dozens of their members were held awaiting execution. Operation *Jericho* was a success and 258 prisoners escaped. Pickard's Mosquito was shot down leaving the target and he and his navigator Bill Broadley were killed.

Later in the year the most illustrious name in Bomber Command kept what had seemed like an inevitable rendezvous with violent death. Guy Gibson had become a 'professional hero' as a result of the Dams Raid, in the words of his biographer Richard Morris. He was adopted by the prime minister and went with him to Canada in the late summer of 1944. There he embarked on an exhausting programme of speeches, dinners and press conferences, playing up the strong comradeship between Canadian and British aircrews and trying to persuade America in general of the value of the strategic air campaign. On returning to Britain, with Churchill's support, he sought and won the nomination for the Conservative seat of Macclesfield in Cheshire.

But these were diversions. During 1944 he became increasingly restless with his safe, largely desk-bound new job and strained to get back on operations. Eventually his wish was granted. On

19 September, he made his debut as a bombing controller, directing a raid on the twin towns of Mönchengladbach and Rheydt, on the German-Dutch border. Gibson was flying a Mosquito, an aircraft with which he was unfamiliar. The marking was erratic and the bombing confused. After leaving the target area his aircraft ploughed into a polder near the Dutch town of Steenbergen. The Mosquito exploded in flames. He and his navigator, Squadron Leader James Warwick, were incinerated. Gibson was twenty-six. In common with several of the legendary airmen of the First World War, whose complexity and charisma he shares, his end was mysterious. The cause of the crash was never discovered.

As well as accepting that there should be a restriction on the length of a tour, those at the top also understood that there was a limit to the losses that the organization could endure. This calculation was not a simple matter of manpower and resources. It was a question of effectiveness. If the campaign was to be pursued with the maximum aggression, what percentage of wastage could be sustained without a drastic fall in efficiency and morale? The proportion of aircraft missing from 1940 to the end of 1944 fluctuated from 1.8 per cent to 4.4 per cent of sorties dispatched. But during periods of intense activity such as the Battle of Berlin, losses could climb much higher. In January 1944, 11.4 per cent of the Halifaxes from 4 Group sent to Germany failed to return, a disaster that had resulted in them being withdrawn from operations against German targets.

Bomber Command planners concluded that 'the higher the loss rate the lower the level of experience and the lower the operational effectiveness.' In other words, fewer veterans and more freshmen meant poorer results. Poor results and high losses were damaging to morale. It was efficiency rather than spirit, though, that was the main concern. A paper from the office of the director of bomber operations concluded that a strategic bomber force would become relatively ineffective if it suffered operational losses in the region of 7 per cent over a period of three months' intensive operations, and that its operational effectiveness might become unacceptably low if losses of 5 per cent were sustained over this period.[13] The definition of ineffectiveness was never spelled out. It appeared to mean a degree of carelessness, recklessness and absence of judgement that meant that the crews were more of a danger to themselves than they were to the enemy.

During the first period of Harris's command, from the end of February to the end of May 1942, the overall rate stood at 3.7 per cent. During the Battle of the Ruhr period it climbed to 4.3 per cent. But these were the figures for all operations and all units. Against specific targets and among individual units, levels could be much higher. The losses of aircraft attacking Berlin during the battle reached 6.3 per cent. Five squadrons, 75, 434, 620, 214 and 623 suffered appalling rates of between 15 and 20 per cent.

On these sort of percentages, the chances of survival were pitifully small.

It was officially calculated that with a loss rate of 8 per cent, only eight out of a hundred crews would finish a tour. The figure dropped to less than three crews if the figure rose to 11.4 per cent. Whatever the statistics the cold reality was that in 1942 less than half of all heavy bomber crews would survive their first tour and one in five would make it through a second. In 1943, only one in six could expect to survive one tour, and one in forty a second.[14] The question of odds obsessed the crews and was the subject of endless debate. Optimists argued that the risk remained the same for each trip. Pessimists claimed that the laws of probability determined that it increased with every flight. Experience taught that some targets were less hazardous than others. The statistics bore this out. Bombing Germany was around four times more dangerous than bombing France.[15] Yet, as the death of 'Bull' over Turin had demonstrated to Don Charlwood, there was no such thing as a safe destination.

Nor, it seemed, did the skill of the captain and the expertise of the crew seem to make much difference. In January 1944 Dr Freeman Dyson at the operational research section at Bomber Command HQ made a statistical study of survival factors. An earlier report had confirmed the official doctrine that a crew's chances of living increased with experience. 'Unfortunately,' Dyson wrote later, 'when I repeated the study with better statistics and more recent data, I found that things had changed.' His conclusion was 'unambiguous'. The decrease of loss rate that came with growing experience, which had existed in 1942, was no longer present in 1944. There were many individual cases of experienced crews nursing home badly-damaged bombers that novice crews would have been unable to fly. But they 'did not alter the fact that the total effect of all the skill and dedication of the experienced crews was statistically undetectable. Experienced and inexperienced crews were mown down as impartially as the boys who walked into the German machine gun nests at the Battle of the Somme in 1916.'[16]

There were technical improvements which might have increased the survival rate. But no one in the upper reaches of Bomber Command seems to have paid them much attention. The provision of parachutes and the extensive escaping drill that was taught during training promoted the hope that even if you were shot down there was a realistic chance of surviving relatively unharmed. The truth was that the likelihood of emerging alive from a doomed aircraft was less than one in four. Of the 4,319 men aboard the 607 heavy bombers shot down attacking Berlin in the Battle, only 992 (22.9 per cent) survived. The odds altered depending on what aeroplane you were in. Lancasters, despite their reputation for general flying safety and reliability, were nonetheless difficult to escape from. The number of men surviving from a seven-man crew averaged 1.3 compared with 1.8 for a Stirling and 2.45 for a Halifax. The Hally enjoyed several features that increased crew safety. The escape hatches were easily accessible. The wireless operator and the navigator were in the nose of the aircraft, close to the forward escape hatch. In the Lancaster and Stirling they and the upper gunner were in the mid-section and had to claw their way along the fuselage past bulky equipment battling the dynamic forces of a plummeting machine to get out. To get to the rear door, they had to negotiate the main wing spar which ran across the body of the aircraft. This was difficult enough in normal clothing. Fully dressed and burdened with Mae West and parachute harness it was virtually impossible.[17]

For the first years of the war pilots received some measure of protection from the steel plates fitted behind their seats. Later, as loads increased, they were sometimes removed, apparently to improve lifting capacity. Ken Newman 'never saw bomber pilots so angry before or since', after the move was announced in the summer of 1944.[18] Little was done to investigate the merits of flak jackets, such as those issued to American airmen. The survival rates of the Americans were significantly better than those of Bomber Command.

Dyson and his colleagues at the operational research centre thought hard about reducing casualties and came up with what they thought was a promising proposal. It was clear that the bombers' .303 machine guns offered little or no protection from night-fighters. Why not rip out the two main gun turrets and their associated hydraulic machinery? This would lighten the aircraft's weight and improve aerodynamic performance, add fifty miles per hour to its speed, and increase its manoeuvrability. Even if this did not significantly reduce aircraft losses it would definitely save lives, as gunners would no longer be needed. The proposal was passed up the line. The process of bureaucratic filtration, however, 'eliminated our sharper criticisms and our more radical suggestions . . . the gun turrets remained in the bombers, and the gunners continued to die uselessly until the end of the war.'[19]

After the German defences, the biggest enemy facing Bomber Command was the weather. The determination of Harris and his commanders to maintain a high tempo of aggression meant that operations often went ahead when to the eyes of the crews the conditions were unacceptably dangerous. The quality of weather forecasting was also extremely variable resulting in situations like that on the night of 16/17 December 1943 when twenty-nine Lancasters were lost and 148 men were killed trying to land in thick fog on returning from Berlin. To Ken Newman, who was finishing his training at 1656 Heavy Conversion Unit, Lindholme at the time, it seemed that 'the fog should have been forecast and the attack aborted. We all strongly suspected that the weather forecasters had been ignored or over-ruled by the top brass. The atmosphere was such that we who were waiting in the wings for our turn to operate against Germany rapidly came to the conclusion that the

Commander-in-Chief and his staff at Bomber Command – and Churchill come to that – regarded us in much the same light as the dyed-in-the-wool generals of the First World War regarded their soldiers – in a word, expendable.'[20]

Yet for all the towering dangers of fog, flak and night-fighters, there was no discernible pattern to the way that death made its choices: Newman himself marvelled at how he had completed a full tour of thirty operations including eighteen to Germany and several others against heavily defended objectives and had 'returned with my Lancaster undamaged with not even a scratch on the paint.'[21]

The crews recognized the unpredictability of it all in the name they gave to what they did. 'We nearly "diced" last night,' Reg Fayers wrote to his wife on 7 October 1943. 'It always happens the same night we come back from leave, but fortunately it was scrubbed.' Two weeks later, looking forward to a promised leave he predicted that 'we shall almost certainly "dice" again before then, and I'd rather we did. Too long between ops can be bad, and anyway we want to get them finished.'[22]

The temporal horizon extended no further than the next trip. 'Useless business, this, thinking about the future,' Guy Gibson wrote, and he was right.[23] 'It was pretty obvious that a lot of us were never going to return,' said Bill Farquharson. 'I was going to do all I could to stay alive but the chances were against me and I realized this.'

A Canadian in his squadron, 115, went as far as to keep a book on who would not be returning. 'He used to say, "Do you know Bill, you're on the chop list tonight?" and I'd say, "Oh am I? Jolly good Bob. What are the odds?" . . . anyway, chaps complained about it and he had to stop it. He [replied] that there was nothing wrong with it. We know some of us are not going to return. It was his way of overcoming [his] anxiety about not returning.'

Some men ticked off each trip in their diaries or in their heads as one step closer to safety. Farquharson preferred not to think about it. 'I really tried not to count. You can't help it though – another one off. You had to treat every trip in exactly the same way, no matter how easy you might think it might be . . . you didn't let up on anything as far as I was concerned and neither did the crew.'[24]

Everyone shared the warm but illogical conviction that whatever might happen to the others, they were going to beat the odds. Whatever Dyson's research might say, there was great comfort to be had in exercising a rigorous professionalism so that death if it came was due to fate rather than inefficiency. Harry Yates believed that a rough pattern developed in the way a tour progressed. 'A tour was a construct of three aspects,' he wrote, 'each distinct, each characterized by a potentially lethal weakness. In the beginning, of course, was naivety. A few hours flying together at OTU and Finishing School barely qualified as preparation for the real thing. From the moment a sprog crew arrived on station it had to learn – before the lesson was driven home by the enemy. There was plenty of help at hand. The path to survival was well-trodden even though not everyone reached its end.'

The dozen or so ops in the middle of the tour, he thought 'tended to coincide with the assumption that this learning period was over. The log book was filling up. The enemy and Lady Luck had done their worst. One was not blasé about being shot at but had reached a certain, internal accommodation with it. Instead of operating at maximum vigilance throughout, there might . . . perhaps . . . occasionally be a tendency to cut corners or relax a little. But *might* and *occasionally* were enough. Even that was complacency and it invited the Reaper along for the ride.' Towards journey's end aircrew had survived and surmounted these hazards. They were secure in the knowledge of their own expertise. 'But then came the even more insidious danger of staleness. It was all too easy to weary of the sheer repetition of operational life. The months of Battle Orders and Briefings were bound to pall, along with the pills to keep you wide-eyed or to knock you out; the ops scrubbed on the tarmac and others re-ordered because of scattered bombing; and always, the pals known but briefly and who, in the relentless drive to mount the next op, somehow went unmourned.'

Of these three killers, he believed, 'the cruellest was naivety, but the most undeserved was this business of going stale like old bread.'[25]

Before the thirty-trip limit came in some commanders had already noted the tendency of crews to get sloppy when they thought they saw safety beckoning. One wing commander reported that 'if ever I hear a man say "this is my last trip" either I don't send him on the trip or I tell him he has another dozen to do, then send him twice more and unexpectedly take him off.'[26]

The confidence that mounted with the accumulation of operations was never robust enough to displace fear. Indeed as the end of the trip approached it was common to feel a gathering anxiety that at the last moment the prize of life would be snatched away. There were many stories of crews going missing on their last but one mission. Fear is unsustainable for protracted periods. It waxes and wanes, not always in direct proportion to the current level of peril. Everyone felt it. Most extraordinarily, almost everyone managed to control it. The first thing to do was to acknowledge its existence. David Stafford-Clark, one of the few trained psychologists to work as a medical officer on a bomber station, observed that it was acceptable to show fear. '[Men] could say "I'm scared shitless" and that was fine.'[27] This frankness was echoed in one of the songs that raised the roof of mess and pub in many an eastern county town, sung to the tune of 'The Long and the Short and the Tall'.

> They say there's a Lancaster leaving the Ruhr
> Bound for old Blighty's shore
> Heavily laden with terrified men
> All lying prone on the floor . . .

The most powerful antidote to terror was the greater anxiety of losing control in front of one's colleagues. The Mosquito pilot Charles Patterson listened with mounting alarm as his commanding officer briefed him on a mission that appeared to have only the slimmest chance of success. He and his navigator were to fly alone over Magdeburg and return via Berlin and Rostock to obtain an up-to-date weather report in advance of a major raid that evening. The aircraft would be pushing its range to the limit. As there were no other daylight operations scheduled, that day his lonely Mosquito presented the sole target on offer to the entire might of the Luftwaffe.

'To show how bad it was . . . the squadron commander said he was sorry that he'd had to send me on this. But it had to be done. Somebody had to do it. And he looked at me and said with a twinkle in his eye "and you're not married you, see. Which is a factor we have to take into account."'

As he crossed the Suffolk coast climbing to reach his operational height of 25,000 feet he 'began not to feel myself, and then this feeling got worse . . . I thought this is awful . . . it had crossed my mind [something] which I couldn't control, was taking me over.' He considered turning back but was immediately struck by an even more unpleasant sensation. 'The thing that came to my mind was that if I went back I would have to say to Eddie [the CO] when I landed, and he said "why have you come back?" – I would have to say, ". . . because I don't feel well . . ." I suddenly saw in my mind clear as daylight . . . him standing in front of me while I said it. And the thought of that was so appalling that I just kept going on climbing.' The feeling of nausea turned out not to be panic at all but anoxia caused by a disconnected oxygen pipe. Patterson reflected later that 'the interesting thing was that such was the force of Eddie's influence over his pilots and his crews that it was purely the thought of him that made me keep going, even when I was running out of oxygen at 25,000 feet.'[28]

Nor did anyone want to be thought of as having let down those who kept them in the air. That meant the entire base. 'Aircrew were regarded on the station as pretty special,' said Michael Beetham. 'When you went off on operations masses of people would be down at the end of runway cheering and waving you on your way. Your ground crew would get round and make sure that everything was right on the aeroplane and be really looking after you to see that everything was perfect . . . How could you chicken out really? . . . that was a driving force. You were being made something special. It's something you had to live up to and you feared letting them down more than you feared the German defences. I regarded it that way and I found it very uplifting.'[29]

Ultimately, though, it was the respect of the crew that mattered most. In David Stafford-Clark's experience a crew member might decide halfway through the tour that he was going to 'go LMF'. Then 'the crew would say stop talking rubbish. We're all going to finish this together. And then the end of the story is that they all do finish together but maybe they only finish together because on the next trip they're shot down. But leaving the crew meant letting the side down. Somebody else has to come in. It is very, very disruptive and traumatic. It happened very, very rarely.' It did, however, happen.[30]

13

Crack Up

One day early in 1945 the crews of 150 Squadron were ordered to the parade ground of their base at Hemswell and told to form three sides of a square. As they stood to attention a sergeant was marched into their midst by the station warrant officer. The sergeant had been found guilty by a court-martial of avoiding his duty. His punishment was a period of detention and reduction to the ranks. According to Dennis Steiner who was there 'the Adjutant read the sentence and when he got to the words "reduced to the rank of aircraftman" the SWO who was standing a pace behind the sergeant, took a took a pace forward and ripped off his sergeant's chevrons which had already been unpicked and lightly tacked on. At the end of the sentencing, he was made to double off the square, no doubt to a period of misery.' It was, Steiner, thought, 'a most humiliating performance for everyone'.

The prisoner's story was pitiful. At the end of his limits of endurance, he had tried to get extra leave by telephoning the squadron office from a public telephone by the main entrance of the base, pretending to be his wife's doctor and warning that she was seriously ill. The sergeant was immediately given leave but on returning tried the subterfuge again. Suspicions were roused and he was watched and caught making another fake call.[1]

Jack Currie witnessed a similar ceremony at Wickenby after two Canadian gunners were found guilty of desertion, having failed to turn up at a pre-op briefing. 'The runaways eventually returned to face the inevitable court-martial, and it was ordained, perhaps *pour encourager les autres*, that the sentence be pronounced before us all.' On a cool, grey morning the full complement of the base was mustered by flights and squadrons on the parade ground. 'The

Station Commander made his entrance, wearing his peaked cap with the "scrambled egg" instead of the usual faded forage cap . . . the drama of the day began.' The miscreants were marched on to the parade ground from the left flank. In a formal, toneless voice, the adjutant read out the charges and the sentence of the court.

'The ensign,' wrote Currie, 'stirred limply on the staff. At the rear of No. 3 Squadron there was a quickly stilled disturbance as a fainting aircraftman was led away. As silence fell again, the Station Commander marched to one of the offenders and, with sure, quick movements, ripped the chevrons from each sleeve and the brevet from the breast. The gunner was a tall, aquiline fellow who might have stepped from a page of Longfellow's *Hiawatha*. He stood erect and motionless, staring straight ahead. The grey-blue sleeve showed darker where the tapes had been. The other gunner stood with shoulders bowed, and would not raise his eyes. He flinched at the Station Commander's touch. It was a dreadful moment.'[2]

Such ceremonial degradations were unforgettable and intended to be so. Yet courts-martial were used only rarely to maintain discipline. They were messy and time-consuming. By the time the proceedings began, witnesses had often been posted away or were dead. Usually they were fellow-airmen who detested the idea of ratting on a comrade.

It was, anyway, impossible to put on trial every member of Bomber Command who displayed signs of weakness. The existing martial law contained in the Air Force Act was much too heavy an instrument to deal with problems which, as the RAF had been forced to recognize from the earliest days, were inherent to combat aviation.

In the First World War both the Royal Flying Corps and the Royal Naval Air Service had accepted that pilots could break down under the stresses of their work. Rest homes were set up in the stylish Channel resort of Le Touquet where officers could recover after being ordered there by the squadron medical officer. There was a consensus among early researchers, some of whom had direct experience of the air war, that psychological pressures were as powerful as physical strain. When a man broke down, as he invariably would if he kept on long enough, it was a normal reaction to an abnormal situation. Fear, and its consequences, were the natural response to the unique rigours of aerial combat.

By the start of the next war, this commonsensical analysis had given way to a new view, expressed by men fluent in the theories of modern psychology. This maintained that character was the most important factor in how an individual coped with the mental buffeting of war. For all the modernity of those who framed it, it was a regressive perspective but it came to dominate the RAF's approach to psychological casualties. It was laid out in an Air Ministry pamphlet circulated among medical officers just before the start of the war. It restated the opinion that stress was cumulative and that 'everyone has a breaking point'. However it tended to blame character defects, rather than the accumulation of fear, for psychological collapse.[3]

'Morale [it read] is of the greatest importance both in the maintenance of efficiency and in the prevention of breakdown. It depends largely upon the individual's possession of those controlling forces which inhibit the free expression of the primitive instinctive tendencies. It is based upon the sentiments acquired during education and training. Its essence is the ability to live up to an ideal, to face dangers and difficulties with confidence and tenacity of purpose, and to be able to sacrifice personal interests and safety in the course of duty.'[4] In other words, good morale would overcome the base desire to run away. It could be inculcated by the right upbringing and reinforced by service discipline and values. But essentially it was a matter of character. Strong characters displayed patriotism, tenacity, and self-sacrifice. The weak were vacillating, undependable and ineffective.

In a well-organized selection and training programme such types should have been identified and discarded long before they reached a squadron. The RAF training programmes by the middle of the war were indeed thorough and efficient. Nonetheless, some men deemed unsatisfactory still got through. The question was how to deal with them.

Despite the reversion to Victorian notions of the paramountcy of character, the system had some elasticity. It acknowledged the omnipresence of fear and was subtle enough to perceive that orders were carried out with varying degrees of enthusiasm. From early in the war the RAF tried to devise a method for deciding who was unable to fly because of a genuine psychological condition, and who was simply unwilling. The next step was to form a plan for patching up the former and getting rid of the latter.

Most of the work on aviation psychology was done by two men, civilian specialists who had joined the RAF medical service in 1939. They were Charles Symonds, who became the senior consultant in neuropsychiatry and rose to the rank of Air Vice-Marshal, and a younger practioner, Denis Williams. In a key report, which appeared in August 1942, Symonds and Williams set out the findings of their investigation of psychological disorders in flying personnel of Bomber Command.[5] Much of the evidence contained in it came from questionnaires and interviews with station and squadron commanders and medical officers.

They started off by making a disinction between flying stress and the effects that arose from it. The former was defined as 'the load of mental and physical strain imposed upon a man by flying under war conditions'. The effects varied depending on 'the weight of the load, and the mental and physical stamina of the individual'. When the load grew too heavy to carry, the strain could be manifested in signs of 'fatigue, anxiety, or inefficiency' and in any number of other ways.

Commanders and medical officers were instructed to keep their charges under constant observation. It was a complicated task. The guidelines for spotting signs of deterioration and the variety of recorded symptoms were highly detailed and sometimes contradictory. Following the official advice also required a reasonably close knowledge of the personality of the man in question for any alteration in his manner to be noticed. Bomber squadrons contained up to 200 airmen. They were subdivided into crews, often hermetically sealed social subdivisions. There was the further barrier created by commissioned and non-commissioned rank. It was hard for commanders to know all of their men well, though the best of them, and the more conscientious medical officers, tried.

The symptoms fell into four categories: changes in appearance, talk and behaviour, loss of keenness for flying duties, loss of efficiency and alcoholic excess. Strain changed people in different ways. One general rule seemed to be that sufferers began to behave in a manner that was in complete contrast to their normal conduct. 'A quiet man will become sociable and garrulous,' observed one medical officer, 'and a normal man quiet, solitary and moody.' In others, their usual demeanour became sharply exaggerated. 'The change in behaviour has no particular direction,' a station commander reported. 'They are apt to be a bit more extreme in their behaviour one way or the other.'

Essentially, any behaviour that appeared out of the ordinary, and life in a bomber squadron allowed considerable latitude, was a ground for concern. The signs ranged from 'making weak remarks around the mess and roaring with laughter at them' to 'becoming irritable, sarcastic, truculent and out for trouble.' In contrast, 'unusual quietness, with a desire for solitude' was equally worrying, especially if the subject had previously been a good mixer. 'He ceases to be one of the party. He may remain in it without interest, or keep drifting away, starting a game of shove-halfpenny, but soon losing interest in even that. He breaks off a conversation and . . . later becomes unoccupied and lacks all initiative.' They tended to sit around in armchairs, staring blankly ahead or dozing. They looked 'tired and haggard, pale, worried, tense and nervy or miserable and depressed'. Undue reference to the events that had wrought these changes also signalled danger. 'He talks about the people who have been shot down in the searchlights. In discussion in the mess he enlarges on the casualties and in his mind leans toward the dangers rather than concentrating on the job in hand.'

This sad condition of loneliness and anxiety was characterized by a station commander as a 'state of alarm'. With it often came an increased consumption of cigarettes and alchohol. Most of the crew members smoked and drank. Getting drunk was a natural and recognized antidote to the strain of the job as well as the most common means of celebrating survival. It took some doing to stand out.

These were the off-duty symptoms. During operations there were other generally agreed portents of trouble. Investigators put them under the heading of 'loss of keenness' and they started at the pre-op briefing. It was noted that 'a keen man will react to the announcement of a "heavily defended target for tonight" with immediate professional interest, but if he is suffering from stress he will show his lack of keenness by immediate preoccupation with the defences.' He might start asking 'unnecessary questions' about the sortie or appear half-hearted in the mess. On the other hand there were others who 'overcompensate and appear wildly enthusiastic, emphasizing their keenness too forcibly'.

It was in the air that the trouble became fatal. There it became categorized as 'loss of efficiency'. This state produced 'foolish errors of judgement, or gross carelessness, leading to bad landings or crashes.' Over enemy territory 'carelessness or recklessness may lead to catastrophe.' This observation, as the report admitted, had to be theoretical as the deadly consquences of the mistake meant that no one was likely to be alive to bear witness to what had actually happened.

If an aircraft suffered repeated damage but made it home it was taken as evidence that the pilot's judgement was going. 'He forces himself to go in regardless of risks because he is afraid that his nerve is getting shaky.' In the case of a navigator, he may 'make silly mistakes . . . gives wrong fixes or sets the wrong course . . . he may go to pieces over the target.'

On the other hand, returning without a scratch might also be evidence of shattered nerves. Early returns were regarded as one of the surest indications of the state of morale both in individuals and squadrons. Even in the best-maintained aircraft it was inevitable that once in a while a crew would be forced to abort its mission because of mechanical failure. However the fault had to be serious and real if the captain were to avoid arousing official attention. Commanders were on the lookout for defects which were 'trivial or imaginary' including 'minor engine troubles, such as a fall in revs or oil pressure, turret trouble, or difficulty with the intercom.' The decision to turn back was the captain's and it was on him alone that the responsibility for doing so fell. 'Once they occur they tend to be repeated, a different reason being found each time.'

Different commanders took different approaches to the problem. Some ordered a full, potentially humiliating investigation if an aircraft returned twice without reaching the target. It was the practice of one to check the trouble himself if a fault was reported before take-off. If he found all was well but the pilot was still reluctant to fly, he would stand him down for further investigation and ask a spare pilot and his men to take over. Another went around each crew before take-off to ascertain they were happy with the condition of their aircraft, thereby making a 'boomerang' all the harder to justify.

Failing to reach the target without good reason was an extreme example of 'inefficiency'. Over the target it could manifest itself in other, equally undesirable ways. The investigators recognized that shredded nerves might result in recklessness. But they could also lead to excessive caution which diminished the crew's contribution to the raid. Some pilots would drop their bombs hopelessly high, while the so-called 'fringe merchants' would scatter their cargoes before they reached the aiming point.

Such nervousness emanated from fear of death. But those suffering it seemed to die as frequently than those who did not. There was no accurate way of telling. Dead men could not speak. But it seemed logical to one medical officer that 'if . . . carelessness, recklessness and loss of judgement result from excessive stress, there must surely be an abnormally high casualty rate in the aircrews who, through one member, have become inefficient.' Symonds and Williams also judged that shattered nerves increased the likelihood of death, particularly among those who never gave any formal indication, oblique or direct, that they were suffering. This 'sort never report sick. They show their signs and symptoms in the mess, but they keep on flying and in the end write themselves off, because they have become inefficient through loss of judgement.'

The other 'sort' were those who felt their spirit weakening, though they were unwilling initially to acknowledge this directly in front of authority. According to one MO they 'report sick with some trivial complaint which has no real physical basis. After a talk if you ask them why they have come to sick quarters they will say that they are afraid or that they panic in the air.'

Sinusitis, visual defects, airsickness, even boils were employed to avoid flying. It was only when the condition had been cured or discounted that the patient admitted his fear. It was then up to him to choose whether to return to flying or cry off with all the dire consequences that entailed. The report found 'the result of the decision is usually unsatisfactory.' Those that went on soon cracked. Those who gave up were lost to the effort for ever as surely as if they had been killed.

A larger category did report sick but refused to admit they felt any psychological strain, even though examination suggested this was the root cause. Base doctors noted a higher incidence of such cases if a big operation was in the offing, even among 'very good men'. The most common symptoms were discomfort, nausea, mild dyspepsia and diarrhoea. These, it was felt, were literally 'a visceral response to impending danger'. Some medical officers told their patients frankly that their illness was a product of fear. This, in many cases, at least initially, had the effect of reinforcing resolution.

It was unusual for these men to assert that they could not carry on with operations. 'They all exaggerate the point that they don't want to come off flying. But later, if they are kept on, they may say they do not think it fair to the rest of the crew that they should carry on, because they are afraid that they may let them down.'

Commanders and medical officers were more impressed with those who openly admitted their fear or revealed that their nerve had gone. By doing so they had demonstrated strength of character and consequently the chances of returning them to operations were better. 'The man who comes up complaining of inability to carry on is the honest type,' one respondent said. 'There is more chance of getting him back to flying than the others.'

The medical officers making these observations were, by peacetime standards, little qualified to do so although they did receive some psychiatric training on joining the service. Psychiatric and psychological studies were underdeveloped in Britain at the start of the war. Although the military had recognized that psychiatry could

A sight to inspire fear. A flak battery opens up as an attack goes in.

not be ignored in maintaining morale, the tendency in some quarters was to regard its terminology as jargon that described existing conditions which could more easily be diagnosed by observation and commonsense. In the experience of David Stafford-Clark, one of the few medical officers who had specialized psychiatric knowledge, 'psychiatry was regarded in those days as an extremely cranky operation.'

MOs were expected to know the men they were treating. When ops were on they sat in on the briefing, waved the crews off and were waiting for those who returned when they arrived for the post-attack interrogation. They were encouraged to mix with the crews off duty in mess and pub. The aim was to 'think squadron and live squadron every minute of the day,' but not in such a way that made them appear to be snooping.[6] Separate messes created an obstacle for the conscientious MO and several suggested that the system should be scrapped in favour of an aircrew club that all could attend. To get round the problem, one squadron medical officer arranged for crews to come to the sick bay for ultra-violet treatment, during which he would strike up conversations aimed at winning their confidence and learning their concerns. Another organized 'informal talks on oxygen, equipment and quasi-medical affairs, ostensibly for education, actually for observation and personal contact.'

Medical personnel were also expected to go on the occasional operational trip. Stafford-Clark did so regularly. 'I decided that once in a while, the person that they would turn to when their morale was shaky should participate in what they were doing . . . I found it absolutely terrifying [but] one of them was kind enough to say "it was a great comfort to have you with us, Doc."'[7] The station medical officer at Wyton, Wing Commander MacGowan, was at forty an old man by RAF standards. He nonetheless took part in many operations, including several to Berlin. He told Freeman Dyson that 'the crews loved to have him go along with them. It was well known in the squadron that the plane with the Doc on board always came home safely . . . at first I thought he must be crazy. Why should an elderly doctor with a full-time staff job risk his life repeatedly on these desperately dangerous missions? Afterwards I understood. It was the only way he could show these boys for whose bodies and souls he was responsible that he really cared for them.'[8]

The quality of medical officers varied considerably. There were those like Stafford-Clark who understood that dispensing reassurance, understanding and sympathy was at least as important as doling out sleeping pills and amphetamines or acting as a military GP. Then there were the likes of Jack Currie's MO at Wickenby who was approached in the ante-room during a drunken sing-song by a Canadian crew member whose nerve had long gone. He was 'shaking horribly in every limb; his head spasmodically jerked sideways and, every few seconds, his left eye and the corner of his mouth twitched. He placed a trembling hand on the doctor's arm and croaked: "I'll fly, Doc. Tell them I'm fit to fly. I was pretty bad this morning, but I'm OK now." The MO, raising a tankard, glanced at him.

'"Yes, you look all right to me."

'"Gee, thanks, Doc." [The Canadian] staggered away, alternately grimacing and twitching, and the choir, refreshed, struck up again . . ."[9]

The RAF went to considerable trouble to establish whether there was a medical explanation for a man's inability to carry out his duties. Nonetheless, it also maintained that there were airmen whose failure to perform was due to weakness of character rather than any illness. The bureaucratic formula referred to them as those 'whose conduct may cause them to forfeit the confidence of their Commanding Officers in their determination and reliability in the face of danger.' There were two categories: 'the man who is maintaining a show of carrying out his duties,' and, more worryingly, the 'man who has not only lost the confidence of his Commanding Officer in his courage and resolution but makes no secret of his condition and lets it be known that he does not intend to carry out dangerous duties.'

The ministry letter dealing with what it was clear even at the time of writing in April 1940 would be a persistent problem, acknowledged that such men might be suffering from a genuine medical condition. It made a soothing reference to the possibility that with encouragement and tactful handling they might once again become useful squadron members. But, it went on, in a passage that was to resonate throughout the rest of the war, 'it must however be recognized that there will be a residuum of cases where there is no physical disability, no justification for the granting of a rest from operational employment and, in fact, nothing wrong except a lack of moral fibre.'[10]

LMF was born. Essentially it was a device to punish an offence which fell outside the conventional military crimes of cowardice or desertion. The designation was controversial from the outset. The RAF's chief medical consultants, including Symonds, objected to the terminology, though his suggestion that it should be replaced with the phrase 'lack of courage' hardly seemed more scientific.

Making the judgement was extremely difficult. Symonds himself admitted that there was no clear line between an 'anxiety neurosis' and a normal emotional reaction to stress. He nevertheless concluded that 'in the interests of morale, a line must always be drawn.'[11] The process was thorough and complicated. Cases came to light in several ways. A squadron commander might notice a lack of determination and reliability in one of his men. Alternatively a man might report to him that he was unwilling or unable to carry on his flying duties. In both cases the suspect would be referred initially to the medical officer. Often it was the medical officer himself who learnt of an impending problem when someone reported sick with real or imagined ailments that prevented him from flying. It was then up to him to determine whether or not there was any physical or nervous reason to explain the subject's condition. If the MO felt unwilling to pass judgement the patient was passed on to a specialist, consultant or one of the twelve Not Yet Diagnosed (Neuropsychiatry) centres set up by the RAF early in the war.

The guidelines struggled to be fair. They emphasized that it was 'highly important . . . to eliminate any possibility of medical disability before a member of an aircrew is placed in [the LMF] category.' A medical diagnosis made life simpler for all concerned and some MOs were willing to oblige in order to spare a man the ignominy of being thought a coward. Subjects found to have physical or nervous problems were treated on the station, sent on leave, admitted to hospital or passed on for a more specialized examination. The vast majority of those who were removed from flying duties were stated to be suffering from 'neurosis' rather than cowardice. The proportion was roughly eight to one. Between February 1942 and the end of the war, 8,402 RAF aircrew were thus diagnosed, a third of whom were from Bomber Command. In the same period there were 1,029 cases of LMF.[12]

Medical officers were not qualified to categorize a man as LMF. Nonetheless the initial diagnosis could be crucial. A man who was found fit for flying duties was automatically open to the charge of LMF. If inadequate medical cause, or no cause at all was found, the matter returned to the hands of the CO who, after interviewing the individual and consulting his record, decided whether or not he was lacking in moral fibre. His report was then passed up the line to the Air Ministry. The punishment for LMF was shame. Officers and NCOs alike were remustered as Aircraftman Second Class, the lowest RAF rank. They lost their entitlement to wear the aircrew brevets they had laboured so hard to win. They were segregated from their fellow airmen and quarantined in Aircrew Disposal Units.[13]

The LMF procedure was designed as a deterrent. Wing Commander Jimmy Lawson, who was closely involved with its administration, admitted in an internal review that 'the intention was to make the chances of a withdrawal, without legitimate reason, as near impossible as could be . . . if withdrawal had been an easy matter without penalty, this would have undermined the confidence and determination of some of those who continued their duties loyally and effectively.'[14]

Official guidelines put great emphasis on the need to act quickly. LMF was considered to be contagious by RAF bureaucrats and squadron commanders alike. Cheshire was brisk and unemotional about LMF. 'I was ruthless with "moral fibre cases",' he said later. 'I had to be. We were airmen not psychiatrists. Of course we had concern for any individual whose internal tensions meant that he could no longer go on; but there was the worry that one really frightened man could affect others around him.'[15] Peter Johnson's technique with LMF cases was to 'try to shuffle them as rapidly as possible off the station via the "trick cyclist" . . . who could produce some medical grounds. It wasn't the pleasantest of tasks. You always remembered that these men were volunteers who had failed, not conscripts who had revolted.'[16]

Breaking down was felt as an enormous personal failure by those to whom it happened. It was a tragedy as powerful as any encountered in the life of the crews and they recognized it as such. Jack Currie remembered at the beginning of the Battle of Berlin coming across a newly-arrived sergeant pilot who was 'a casualty neither of flak or fighters, but of an enemy within himself. He came back early from the mission ... and gave as a reason the fact that he was feeling ill. Next night he took off again, but was back over Wickenby twenty minutes later. Again he said that he had felt ill in the air. I had seen the crew together in the locker-room clustered protectively around their white-faced pilot. They may have thought that some of us would vilify him, but no one except officialdom did that. We knew what was wrong: the so-called lack of moral fibre, and most of us had felt that at times.' But most did not succumb. In the battle of fears, the greater terror of letting down your comrades almost always prevailed. Currie felt only sympathy. 'Goodness knows what hell the wretched pilot lived through – the fear of showing cowardice is the strongest fear of all in most young men.' All the years of training, all the hazards that marked the journey to an operational squadron, counted for nothing. The pilot 'soon ... disappeared, posted to some dread unit especially established to deal with such unhappy cases.'[17]

One 115 Squadron pilot spotted the signs of collapse in his wireless operator even though their tour was well advanced and the end in sight. 'When we were in the air he started to speak out of turn. He said "I'm not very happy with this wireless set, sir ..." I said don't worry about it. He said you shouldn't go on without a working wireless. I said well I am ... he kept this up and I said I want you to forget about it, I'm the skipper of this aircraft. We're going to complete this trip. But by this time he'd already got the rest of the crew a bit concerned ... I told them all to shut up and I said to this other chap if I have another word from you I'll have you arrested when we land ... it was all quiet after that. We got back and we landed and we had a good trip.' The pilot had the wireless checked. There was nothing wrong with it but he did not report the matter. 'I had a word with him and he admitted that he was wrong. I said to him you need a rest. I spoke to the squadron commander and they sent him off for a rest and he came back again later [and completed his tour]'.[18]

Despite the official reluctance to identify *prima facie* cases of LMF there were some circumstances that made action inevitable. A blank refusal to fly could not be overlooked. Flight Sergeant X appears to have made his aversion to operational work very clear long before he was posted to 103 Squadron at Elsham Wolds in the summer of 1942. After a short while he wrote to his commanding officer stating that 'owing to complete lack of confidence, I ask to be relieved of aircrew duties and be reverted to ground duties.' He had, he explained, volunteered as a pilot [in July 1940] but had been selected instead as an air gunner. During flying he suffered from catarrh and eye trouble and had injured his back in the gym. He had asked to be remustered and had hopes of being commissioned to serve as a trainer on the Link flight simulator. He was surprised when he heard he was being posted to 103 Squadron. In addition to his medical complaints he was 'a married man with three children [which] adds to my dread while in the air.' He would, he concluded 'rather be doing ground duties with complete confidence than flying in mortal fear.'

It seems strange that someone so clearly lacking enthusiasm should ever have reached an operational squadron. His commanding officer wasted little sympathy when submitting his recommendation. 'I consider [wrote J. F. H. du Boulay] that this NCO has been drawing aircrew pay without earning it since enlistment and that he is a coward with no qualifications for a commission in any trade, or NCO's rank. As a Flight Sergeant his example is deplorable and I request that he may be removed from this Squadron immediately. I strongly recommend that he be deprived of his Air Gunner's badge, reduced to the ranks and made to refund part of the pay which he has received without earning it since his enlistment.'[19]

This was an open and shut case. Sergeant X appeared to belong to that group of men identified by David Stafford-Clark who had passed the point where they cared what anyone thought of them. That of Sergeant Y, a wireless operator with 150 Squadron, which occurred at the same time, was more complex. He too, the official correspondence reported, announced that 'he has completely lost confidence in himself and no longer wishes to continue operational flying.' Searching for reasons to explain his loss of nerve his commanding officer reported that he had crashed-landed when his aircraft ran out of fuel returning from his first op but no one had been injured. That had been to Lille, a relatively easy target. Since then he had been to Essen four times and carried out one mining trip. In his report Wing Commander E. J. Carter, the 150 Squadron CO, remarked that 'at no time has Y been subjected to any particularly bad experience.' Yet Essen in the summer of 1942 was one of the most dangerous destinations. Y had carried out four operations in eight days at the beginning of June. They were all launched between 4.35 and 6.35 in the evening. Given the summer light they might as well have been carried out in broad daylight.[20]

He would seem to have suffered a classic reaction. The crews themselves had noticed that pessimism and optimism came in cycles. The same appeared to be true of fear. Symonds and Williams reckoned there were three critical periods in a tour and the first six ops were the toughest. Their reporters observed that 'between the third and sixth trip there is a great likelihood of "waverers" reporting that they cannot go on with their duty. There was striking agreement in the story. "In the first few trips he sees what he is up against, in the next he makes an effort, but by the sixth he has thrown his hand in." He usually manages the first three. He is invariably an unsuitable individual and the outlook is usually hopeless.' Another critical period came around the twelfth to fourteenth operation, when the dangers of the business were appallingly clear but the end of the tour stretched dismayingly into the distance. In such cases men 'with explanation and encouragement control their fear, and nearly all go back to complete their tour.' Some who had endured a particularly hard run tended to flag when there were only five or six trips left to go and the finishing line was in sight. These, the specialists recommended, if rested, would go back to fulfil their duty. The same was true of those who had been shaken up by a particularly nasty experience such as a bad crash or a forced landing in the sea.[21]

The need to deal with nervous cases was recognized by the crews. As Harry Yates pointed out, 'no crew could afford to have one of their number snap on board and plunge everything into hysteria and chaos.' But despite all the official thought that went into the subject, manifest in the dense thickets of procedure, there was still a widespread belief among those doing the fighting that the system was insensitive and sometimes unjust. They knew better than anyone the difference between a coward and a man who had reached the limits of his courage. They also resented the calculated humiliation of men who, whatever their failings, had volunteered to serve at the axe-edge of the war.

An instructor who served with Doug Mourton at the OTU at Wellesbourne refused to fly with a partly-trained crew when Harris drafted in OTU personnel to make up the numbers for the Cologne 'thousand' raid. He reasoned that having survived one tour 'he did not want to get killed with a crew who were not very proficient.' When Mourton returned from the operation his friend had disappeared.

> He had been found guilty of LMF ... the punishment would have been that he would be stripped of his sergeant's stripes and crown and sent to another station. The marks where his sergeant's stripes had been removed would be perfectly obvious and everybody would know what had happened to him. Besides this he would have been given no trade and as a consequence would be given all the tasks of an air force station, such as washing up, cleaning out latrines etc. It was quite a severe punishment for somebody who, just on one occasion, had refused to fly. And he would have been quite happy to have been posted to an operational squadron as part of an experienced crew.[22]

No one seemed to know what happened to LMF cases after they disappeared from sight. Where to put them was a continuing problem for the authorities. Initially they were sent to the RAF depot at Uxbridge but their proximity to airmen in training was thought to be bad for morale. Later they were posted to the Combined Aircrew Reselection Centre at Eastchurch in Kent where the same objection was encountered. There was a further move to the Aircrew Disposal Unit at Chessington in Surrey. There they were isolated from other airmen and treated humanely. The regime was intended to improve their self-esteem, restore their confidence and rebuild their belief in the war effort through 'motivational' lectures with titles like 'What Shall We Do With Germany?' and patriotic films. Under the benign eye of the commander, Squadron Leader R. I. Barker, they visited cathedrals and zoos and attended a weekly dance in the drill hall.

When Chessington was taken over by Balloon Command there was a final move to Keresley Grange near Coventry, where on 8 May 1945, the inmates trooped to the local church for a service of thanksgiving for victory in Europe.

The war was barely over before the term LMF became an embarrassment to the RAF and it was dropped in 1945. The numbers of people accused of it have never been firmly established. A scholarly recent study of the subject has calculated that an average of 200 cases of LMF were identified each year in Bomber Command.[23] Given the stresses of their occupation the figure seems very small. It can be seen, from one side, as an indication of the stigmatizing power of the charge of cowardice. More importantly it is a tribute to the remarkable steadfastness of the vast majority of those who flew with Bomber Command.

14

Home Front

When the crews touched down at the end of a mission they were returning to a monochrome world of flat fields, dank huts, drab food and weak beer. The memoirs of the pilots of the Battle of Britain are suffused with the sunshine of the summer of 1940. In the letters and diaries of the Bomber Boys it seems to be always cold and dark, no matter what the season. Life on bomber bases was often dismal and primitive, far removed from the elegance and comfort enjoyed by the pre-war RAF. A lucky few were installed in well-equipped stations that had been built to the highest specifications in the nineteen-thirties. The majority lived in the cheap, temporary constructions thrown up all over East Anglia, Lincolnshire and Yorkshire as the campaign got under way. The pre-war bases looked like giant architect's maquettes with their neat brick rows, hedges and flower beds. In wartime even a permanent base like Wyton in Huntingdonshire (now Cambridgeshire) was transformed, as a civilian visitor noted, into an ugly sprawl of 'endless puddles, barracks, warehouses full of bombs [and the] rusting wreckage of damaged equipment not worth repairing.'[1]

The RAF spent lavishly on maintaining its front-line aircraft. It was miserly when it came to the welfare of its front-line troops. They were housed ten to a Nissen hut, thirty-six feet long by sixteen feet wide corrugated iron humps which had no insulation. The only heat came from a coke-burning stove and in the bitter winters of the war years they became an icy purgatory. The men slept on iron bedsteads under rough blankets, whose meagre warmth had to be supplemented by the addition of a greatcoat when the temperature dropped. They washed in distant ablution blocks reached along muddy pathways in water that was seldom more than tepid. These privations did not extend to the 'penguins', the non-flying base adminstration staff who often lived in greater comfort than the crews they were supposed to look after.

Bad conditions caused resentment and chipped away at morale. Shortly after arriving at his Heavy Conversion Unit at Wigsley near Newark in Nottinghamshire in the autumn of 1943 George Hull sent a gloomy letter to his friend Joan Kirby. 'I seem to have fallen decidedly into the soup or what have you in being posted to this station,' he wrote. 'Even the name is obnoxious. Wigsley, ugh! Pigsley would be more appropriate yet I doubt whether any pig would care to be associated with it. The camp is dispersed beyond reason. If I never had a bike I doubt if I could cope with the endless route marches that would otherwise be necessary. Messing is terrible, both for food and room to eat it. Normally we queue for half an hour before we can even sit, waiting for it. Washing facilities are confined to a few dozen filthy bowls and two sets of showers an inch deep in mud and water.

Hull and his companions tried to alleviate the misery by heading to the nearest pub each evening and returning 'three parts cut'. At Wigsley, Hull's disillusionment with the RAF touched bottom. 'Don't for a moment . . . imagine that I want to be associated with the above nonsense' he wrote, a reference to the RAF crest at the top of the headed notepaper, which he had scored through with four angry lines.

Holme-on-Spalding-Moor, which sat on the plain between the River Humber and the city of York, was notoriously uncomfortable. James Hampton, who served with 76 Squadron, declared that 'on no other Royal Air Force station, before or after, did I ever encounter such intolerable living conditions.' On arriving at his Nissen hut in August 1944 he found it completely empty of furniture. Previous inhabitants had fed it all to the stove when the coke ran out. The only fittings were shelves, provided to store personal possessions, which the authorities had sensibly decided to have made out of asbestos. One wash house had to do for 400 aircrew, who queued up for the sixteen tin bowls and a few showers.[2]

But stoicism and resignation were Bomber Boy virtues. The men grumbled, but at least they were alive. With that in mind, they could put up with almost anything. Dennis Field found Tuddenham, in Suffolk, with its widely-dispersed sites and intermittently heated water, no different from any other pre-fab station he had been on. But it was 'Utopia compared with the jungle, desert, Italian mud or Arctic Sea.'[3] Newly installed at Holme, Sergeant Reg Fayers described his new quarters to his wife. The wash house was 'tastefully decorated in yellow, brown and rust with a discarded thrush's nest stuck up on one of the pipes . . . so I washed in clean soft water – why does cold water seem so much more clean? – and sang my bloomin' head off . . . then in my boudoir wear – wellingtons, pyjama trousers, tunic dressing gown of tender RAF blue with a navigator's badge rampant and oil stains magnificent I paraded into my study to write good morning to my wife.'

Fayers's 'study' was a corner of his Nissen hut, which, he reported, 'is just about the nearest we airmen get to "home" . . . Out of [the] roaring night and with ground mists at dawn garlanding the morning and welcoming our return we come tiredly and competently down to egg and bacon and this – a bed . . . faithfully waiting in the corner of a corrugated tunnel, MY bed because my two kitbags stand by it, my three-year-old slippers proudly inscribed FAYERS on the left and 963752 on the right, stand under it and my tunic hangs from . . . one nail.' It was 'a place to sleep . . . a place for dreams; that's my home darling.'[4]

Fayers was a romantic. There was another way of looking at things. Don Charlwood remembered the lowering experience of returning to Elsham after a mid-winter leave and opening the hut door to be met by 'the smell of last night's fire, of dirty clothes and unwashed bodies . . . gunners were asleep in shirts that appeared to have been welded to their bodies by the dirt of weeks.'[5]

Communal living shrank the boundaries of privacy. It was only rarely that a man could be alone. Frank Blackman, who described himself in a letter to his girlfriend Mary Mileham as 'somewhat lacking in the boisterous aspects of manliness', sometimes found the public nature of air force life intolerable. On 8 July 1943 he settled down in his room at East Moor in Yorkshire to write to her but was almost immediately interrupted. Even though he was an officer, he shared a room with three Canadians. 'The first has just come in and as usual when he has had a few beers is so talkative that he keeps on without stopping for more than a yes or no to keep him company. As I write now he is giving me a dissertation on flak, fighter belts, searchlights and relative losses of aircraft etc. . . . I've no doubt that unless I'm rude to him which I fear I shall be very shortly he will finish up on navigation – which is his final subject when all else fails. By the time he quietens down the other two will be in and then goodbye to all peace. They've been in to York and one at least will be tight.' The disturbance did not necessarily end when sleep descended. One of Blackman's roommates had been 'having nightmares and has kept us in fits of laughter after the preliminary shock of being woken up at about 3 a.m. [by him] hollering his head off.'[6]

A room of one's own, even one so basic as that allotted to Ken Newman at Lindholme after he received his commission, was the peak of gracious living. It was 'simply but adequately furnished, with a built-in wardrobe and a basin with hot and cold water. Better still there was a WAAF batwoman to make the bed and clean the room as well as polish my shoes and buttons. It felt like heaven in comparison with the sergeants' barrack room and particularly the Nissen huts that I had been living in . . .'[7]

As front-line warriors the crews might have reasonably thought they were entitled to the best food available. Their diet, though, was little better than that endured by civilians. They counted themselves lucky to sit down to bacon and eggs before they took off and again when they landed. Additional luxuries were rare. When not flying they lived on Spam and dried eggs, sausages and lumps of nameless fish. They filled the gaps with bread, smeared thinly with margarine and fishpaste or jam. To supplement the shortages of fresh produce there were plates of vitamin capsules to which the airmen were expected to help themselves.

To guarantee a share of this sparse fare you had to arrive early. Breakfast in the sergeants' mess at Holme started at 7.30. By 7.45

the meagre supplies of cereal and milk had run out. Tempers were short at the start of the day. The aircrew sergeants were allocated an area that was far too small for their numbers and they often had to wait until a table became free followed by a further delay until a harassed waitress was able to serve them. The permanent staff sergeants had a separate dining room which, the crews noted with bitterness, was rarely more than half full.

The Canadians were appalled at what they were expected to eat in British messes. At Abingdon, Ralph Wood had his first encounter with brussels sprouts, 'a kind of minature cabbage, eaten boiled. At our mess the cook must have boiled them and reboiled them until they emerged a sickly green gob . . . Small wonder that we looked forward to a snack in the village where we had the big choice of Welsh rarebit . . . beans on toast, or fishpaste on toast.'[8]

Letters home throb with a sensual yearning for peacetime food. The occasional parcels of treats sent by family and friends were received with rapture. 'Darling,' wrote Reg Fayers to Phyllis, 'I'm eating myself to death in a lovely orgy of pears, grapes and apples.' Bernard Dye felt it worth recording in his diary on 9 January 1944 the simple entry: 'received two oranges and two lemons'.[9] Doug Mourton befriended a worker at a farm near his Driffield base who supplied him with buckets of chitterlings, a doubtful mix of pig liver and stomach lining, which he would never have touched in peacetime. Mourton was extremely resourceful at scrounging. The British crews were envious of the lavish food parcels, packed with luxuries like tinned cheese and butter, received by the Canadian crews. He and his friend Jock noticed that when a new consignment arrived a list of recipients was pinned up at the local post office. 'Jock and I would look down this list and when the names corresponded with people who had been killed we went [in] and claimed the food parcels. We would then cycle back . . . and excitedly open the parcels, which contained tinned meat, chocolates and other items that were very hard to come by, indeed non-existent in England . . .'[10]

Even in the depths of wartime, luxury was available if you could pay for it. George Hull's friend Joan Kirby who was serving with the

Above The price of total war. Rubble and corpses, Berlin, January 1944.

Below The husk of a city. Cologne at the end of the war.

Exhaustion and relief as a 90 Squadron crew is debriefed after a raid on Berlin.

'Someone to idealize
and love':
Mary Mileham.

'You ask if I believe one has any
control over one's destiny . . .
much as I would like to believe it,
I don't.' Frank Blackman.

George Hull
'felt his Englishness
with a poetic intensity'.

Top left The 'winsome Wren', Joan Kirby.

Left Frances Dowdeswell in her WAAF days.

Top right Denholm Elliot and his bride
Virginia McKenna on their wedding day, 1954.

Tony Iveson in 1943.   Don Charlwood.   Ken Newman.

Reg Fayers. A wry self-portrait for his wife.

Above Tony Iveson (*second right*) and some of his crew in front of their battle-scarred kite after a rough trip.

Below Setting off for Hamburg, July 1943. John Maze, tall and fresh-faced, is third from the left. Willie Lewis is second from the right.

Above The well-hidden soft side to Arthur Harris, seen here with his wife Jill and daughter Jackie.

Left Ruthless yet humane. Leonard Cheshire personified the Bomber Boy paradox.

Below An intellect as cool and hard as marble. Charles Portal (*left*) converses with US Eighth Air Force Commander Ira C. Eaker.

Above 'Precision bombing': a B-24 Liberator in a daylight raid. Often the results were little different to Bomber Command's area attacks.

Right Pressing on: a doomed B-17 Flying Fortress drops its bombs over Berlin.

Below A Grand Slam bursts on Arnsberg Bridge on 19 March 1945. By the end of the war, Bomber Command was at last approaching the accuracy and efficiency that was claimed for it from the outset.

Cyril March and crew. Left to right are Cy, Des and Ken (back row) and Terry, Bug, Ray and Cliff (*front row*). 'Sitting on the tail plane of Lanc, notice gremlin on Des's head'.

To the crews it was just another op, but the Dresden raid became a grim symbol of the bombing war.

The longed-for peace. VE Day crowds outside the Saracen's Head, Lincoln, where Bomber Boys drank, laughed and courted.

WRNS at the HMS *Cabbala* shore base in Lancashire reported to her family that she had 'been having some nice food lately. Not at Cabbala I hasten to add but at the Midland in Manchester on Sunday, namely hors d'oeuvres, lobster, cream sauce etc. brandy trifle and cream, coffee and drinks.' Her host at the hotel was a 'Yankee named Bob. He's a really nice chap for a change and as long as we keep on being hungry at the same time and he's still got some money he suits me.' Such largesse was way beyond the pocket of a British airman. Bomber Boys were more likely to experience the sort of dates that Dennis Field took his future wife Betty on in Cambridge, where she was studying at Homerton College. On fine evenings they would spend pleasant hours wandering along the Backs. But 'on cold, wet and dark nights it meant joining a queue in the hopeful expectation of seeing a film. It did not matter what was on because it would be warm and dry inside. Alternatively, after a long wait we might get a couple of seats in a café and make beans on toast and a cup of tea last as long as possible. The only other possibility was to shelter under a dripping tree in the park and admire the view in the blackout. The glow of cigarettes, the nearest equivalent to a brazier, from neighbouring elms showed that we were not alone in our predicament.'[11] It was unsurprising that the Yanks stirred envy and hostility in the breasts of their British counterparts.

Among the bleak, utilitarian infrastructure of Bomber Command there were a few outposts of graciousness. After the horrors of Wigsley, the operational station of Coningsby was a sybaritic dream to George Hull. 'We've struck oil at last,' he announced to Joan. 'Coningsby the Beautiful, Coningsby the Comfortable.' The Nissen hut days were over. He was 'lording it in a double bedroom which contains a deal table and radiator' with a fellow-crew member, Jack Green. Suddenly Bomber Command life was not so bad. 'The food is eatable (so far),' he wrote, 'and the hours are reasonable. Hurrah for the RAF.'

The Dambusters Squadron, 617, was fortunate enough to be located at Woodhall Spa, south-east of Lincoln where wealthy Victorians and Edwardians once went to take the waters. On the edge of the town stood a house called Petwood, built at the beginning of the century in half-timbered neo-Elizabethan style by the Maples furniture-manufacturing family. It was there, in a low-beamed, oak-panelled parlour that 617 established its officers' mess. A photograph taken in 1943 shows a smiling Guy Gibson standing on the terrace alongside fellow officers, gins and tonics and 'half cans' of beer in hand. This was the sort of life many trainee airmen imagined they might enjoy when they finally reached an operational squadron. In most places the facilities on offer would turn out to be far more basic.

Most stations had a cinema which showed up-to-date films. There were attempts to raise the cultural tone with serious plays and concerts. Bomber Command was a rich social mixture and there were some who appreciated these occasions. Michael Scott, a schoolmaster before he joined up, listened to at least one piece of classical music virtually every day of his short career as well as devouring every book he could find. His cultural intake is listed, touchingly, in the pages of his Charles Letts Office Desk Diary. In four days in January 1941, during his flying training, he listened to Schubert's *Alfonso and Estrella* Overture and C Major Symphony, Bizet's Symphony No. 1, Haydn's Symphony No. 97, Schubert's Unfinished Symphony, Tchaikovsky's Suite in G, Humperdinck's *Hansel and Gretel* Overture and Schumann's Symphony No. 4. He also managed to read three books.

Many of those who kept diaries had literary ambitions. The life of a writer held a surprising appeal to the men of action who volunteered for Bomber Command. When at the end of the war the restless Leonard Cheshire was looking for something to do his first thought was that he should become an author. Scott found space in his limited off-duty time to work away at short stories. On the first day of 1941, he listed his hopes for the New Year. 'I would like to know where I was going to stand on December 31st,' he wrote. 'Let us look forward in a spirit of hope. In twelve months I hope to be back home with 500 hours [of flying], a demobilized Flying Officer about to return to schoolmastering. To have flown is one of the greatest joys of my life, but I want to return to my life's work.

I hope to have thirty short stories in my notebook, two of them published and a novel half-finished.'

The entries in Scott's diary get shorter and shorter as his training progresses and the prospect of action grows nearer. The literary references and nostalgia for his old life at Cheam prep school dwindle and there is a mounting tone of excitement. The last entry, for 18 May reads: 'A very heavy day, all formation flying. I found this very hard work at first, but it was a bit easier towards the end. We went over to Wotton to join up with 21 and 89. Apparently we are to do a show on Tuesday morning with fighter escort. May the Gods be with us! Formation flying is the most companionable of pursuits.' Six days later he was reported missing after he failed to return from a sweep over the North Sea on 24 May. It was his first operation. He left behind a poem, written just as spring broke in the countryside he loved.

> Why do I weep the follies of my kind?
> Larks are still merry, sing the birth of day
> Eagles still soar their proud majestic way
> The April coppices are primrose-lined
> Why do I weep?
>
> Why do I weep this man-made frenzied strife
> Mountains still sweep to heaven their rock-scarred crests
> Lakes are still blue as sunlit amethysts
> Nature is changeless, Earth is full with life
> Why do I weep . . .'[12]

The Australians cultivated a reputation for hard-living philistin-ism. Don Charlwood and his well-read, thoughtful friends rather contradicted the image. In the evenings he would as soon listen to a classical concert on the radio as go to the bar. His friend Johnnie Gordon was a 'scholar of Latin and Greek who read *Oedipus* and *The Medea* because he "liked the murders in them" [an] accomplished violinist who "knew nothing about music but enjoyed the noise it made."'[13]

Even so, it could not be said that high culture was a major preoccupation among the crews and those who supported them. One night George Hull tried to forget the horrors of Wigsley at an orchestral concert put on at the base by RAF musicians. 'It was pretty good,' he wrote to Joan, 'although there was rather an interruption when I "ordered" two WAAFs and an airman outside for making a lot of unnecessary noise.'[14] Sometimes the entertainment was the best the country could offer. One night Robert Donat, Edith Evans, Joan Greenwood and Francis Lister, who worked for ENSA six weeks a year as their contribution to the war effort, arrived at Holme to perform a play by George Bernard Shaw. To the fastidious eyes of Reg Fayers, the reactions of the ground staff present somewhat lowered the tone. 'Everyone was darned grateful for the show they'd given us, especially under rather trying circumstances,' he wrote. 'Shaw's wit and ideas are hardly written for a gang of erks whose literary standards are mostly pornographic or James Hadley Chase.'[15]

The democratic, popular nature of Bomber Command meant that undemanding literature and light music held more appeal than the rather earnest entertainments preferred by Hull and Fayers. Hadley Chase's *No Orchids for Miss Blandish* was perhaps the most widely-read book of the war. Soldiers, sailors and airmen loved this pulp thriller whose *risqué* passages marked a new frontier of daringness in popular literature. It earned the prim disapproval of George Orwell who claimed it bordered on the obscene. To its many readers in uniform it provided a merciful diversion from the boredom interspersed with anxiety that characterized service life.

The music that affected them most were the bittersweet ballads and dance tunes that summoned thoughts of distant homes and longed-for girls who held the promise of happiness and fulfilment but who might never be seen again. The potency of these songs and melodies was at its most emotionally devastating just before ops. John Dobson, the 218 Squadron sergeant pilot who took part in the disastrous Berlin operation of 7 November 1941, remembered how before they set off, the mess echoed to the sounds of the crews' favourite records. 'Even the swingiest of them could almost evoke tears from the listener as it is impossible not to be moved by the most blatant passage of jazz when it tangibly recalls a memory that had been stored away in the innermost recesses which men who fear death keep hidden away for ever. I remember one very vividly, it began: "I dreamed that my lover had gone for a moonlight walk, I spoke to the moon, but the moon wouldn't talk."[16]

To those who went out in bombers at night, the moon was a powerful presence. Its waxing and waning set the rhythms of their lives. They flew in its light. The sight of it hanging mysteriously in the purple blackness filled even the most unfeeling airman with wonder. It was beautiful and it was treacherous. It helped them on their way as the bombers trundled towards their targets, but it also swept away the darkness that shielded them from the night-fighters. It was easy to see why *No Moon Tonight* was an unofficial anthem of Bomber Command.

The messes provided the station's social hub. There, off-duty airmen could go for a quiet drink or a full-scale piss-up as the mood took them. The RAF took a relaxed view about alchohol consumption. Harris felt the need to justify the frequent mention of drink contained in Guy Gibson's memoirs. 'It may well be that references to "parties" and "drunks" in this book will give rise to criticism and even to outbursts of unctuous rectitude,' he wrote in the introduction. 'I do not attempt to excuse them if only because I entirely approve of them . . . remember that these crews, shining youth on the threshold of life, lived under circumstances of intolerable strain.' Anyway, he argued, the booze-ups were 'mainly on near-beer and high rather than potent spirits.'[17] This was not strictly true. Wartime restrictions meant that the beer available in the NAAFI and local pubs was notoriously flat and watery. But whisky was available and gin, which when mixed with lime cordial was supposed to have a liberating effect on the morals of WAAFs.

As Harris acknowledged, parties were a necessary part of Bomber Command life. On some occasions drunkenness and high jinks were almost obligatory. George Hull described to Joan a typical Saturday-night dance at Coningsby. 'Many people were drunk or merry (your humble servant was not among them although he drank all night at someone else's expense!). The Station Warrant Officer did an Apache dance with a redhaired bit of stuff from the orderly room. Two Squadron Leaders played rugger with a squashed bun and finished up under the billiards table. Two F/Sgts fought a bloody battle on the stairs over something they had both forgotten. We shot horrible lines to the girls we had invited from Boston, two of whom missed the bus back and spent the night in the WAAFs' quarters. The Group Captain danced a beautiful solo tango with his wife (despite his bulk) and even the Air Officer Commanding had a good time.'

Ken Dean, the flight engineer in Hull's crew and still only eighteen years old, could not stand the pace and had to be helped to bed by George and Jack Green. 'He insisted on kissing us both four times before going to sleep and this morning was filled with alcoholic remorse.'[18]

As the Coningsby dance showed, the best commanders understood it was important to occasionally reveal a less dignified side. One of the most evocative photographs of the war shows Wing Commander John Voyce, a popular and notably courageous officer in 635 Squadron, in black tie and braces leading a chorus of a mess favourite entitled 'Please Don't Burn Our Shithouse Down'.[19] Charles Patterson remembered one squadron commander from 2 Group who had to be replaced 'after an unfortunate accident . . . not a very gallant accident for such a gallant man. He fell out of the first-floor window of Weasenham Hall which was our mess after a party and had to be carted off to Cambridge hospital.'[20]

The licensed boisterousness was thought to build the team spirit which sustained the whole business of bombing. The well-oiled good fellowship that pervaded air force life could be overwhelming to a quiet men like Frank Blackman. He complained from Topcliffe to his girlfriend Mary that his attempts to concentrate on a classical music broadcast on the radio in the mess had been defeated by a dozen officers, 'mug in hand and obviously having huge fun but nevertheless making such a disturbance that music was out of the question for the three or four of us who would have liked to listen.

And these were not all your heathen Canadians but partly English squadron leaders and Flight Lieuts of the type you might personally meet anywhere.' Frank was obviously sensitive to teasing about his high-mindedness, asking 'do you not see how much more childlike are these bluff playmates than those of us who rely perhaps more upon intellect for interest and amusement?'[21]

But people like Frank Blackman were in a minority. Most members of Bomber Command were too young to be very worldly and most came from unsophisticated backgrounds. It was just as well. The bomber bases were located in parts of the country where the opportunities for pleasure were limited. Bomberland lay in the eastern half of England. It started where the pregnant belly of East Anglia juts towards the Lowlands and Germany, and stretched northwards to Lincolnshire and Yorkshire. It is a land of watery steppes and huge skies. Martha Gellhorn thought it looked 'cold . . . and dun-coloured. The land seems unused and almost not lived in.' George Hull was not impressed. 'It's flat,' he wrote, 'monotonously flat, petering out to a forlorn seashore grudgingly giving way to the sea. Windmills are the distinctive feature, great brick towers of placidity with their sturdy sweeps turning as they have done for two hundred years.'

Where the ground rises it exposes itself to the easterly winds slicing in from the North Sea. It is scattered with well-preserved small towns and villages, full of fine buildings reflecting the area's mediaeval wealth. The industrial revolution largely passed it by. The county towns are rich in old-world charm. But historical tourism was not what most of the airmen had in mind when they left the base to look for fun.

They were looking for a cinema, a dance-hall, a pub. Cities like Lincoln, York, Nottingham, Norwich and Cambridge had enough of each to cope with peacetime demand but were stretched by the influx of men in blue. On off-duty nights they would set off by bus or bike to the nearest town or metropolis, full of the romantic optimism of youth. The provincial streets and dingy bars held the prospect of fun and even romance. That, at least, was how the evenings started.

Don Charlwood described a night out in Scunthorpe, a popular destination with the Elsham airmen. It was typical winter weather. Cloud had settled on the low fields and the wind howled in from the east driving the rain and flocks of seagulls before it. It was a night to get drunk and many were intent on doing so. Ops had been scrubbed and in Charlwood's huts there were deaths to mourn. Two of the occupants had failed to return the previous night. The authorities had laid on buses. 'As we clambered in at the back, hurrying to get out of the rain, a dim blue light was switched on. It blanched the faces of twenty or thirty men who had begun singing with steaming breaths . . .'

They stopped at the Barnetby crossroads to pick up a dozen rain-soaked WAAFs, then raced towards Scunthorpe through wet, invisible countryside, the tyres hissing on the roads. The delights of the town were limited. 'One could get drunk at the "Crosby", or see a floor show and get drunk at the "Oswald" or dance and get drunk at the "Berkeley". And in the event of missing the bus back, it was always possible to stay the night at Irish Maggie's and return to camp by train in the morning.'

When the bus light was switched on, Charlwood realized he was sitting a few seats away from his friend Keith Webber. Scunthorpe was sunk in darkness. They groped their way through the Stygian streets to the Berkeley. 'We stepped out of the rain and darkness into the sudden brilliance of a large dance floor. RAF men, Poles, Americans, Canadians and Australians circled and swayed under a pall of tobacco smoke.'

They were vying for the attention of a far smaller number of WAAFs and local girls. The serious drinkers withdrew from the competition and clustered at the bar. The buses left again at 10 p.m. The one Charlwood boarded was packed solid and he found himself hanging out of the back. As it lurched off 'the singing increased in volume. Sometimes three or four different songs were being sung together, the most tuneless now shouted to the skies . . . with each expulsion of the singers' breaths, the smell of regurgitated beer became stronger.' As the journey lengthened, the distress of the drinkers mounted. The bus stopped by the WAAF camp.

Leading from the front: WC John Voyce.

'Somewhere among the tangle of bodies a voice shouted hoarsely, "Lemme out. I gotta get out or I'll bust!" . . . a dozen men stumbled to the roadside.' Finally the bus reached Charlwood's hut. He and Webber stepped out of the fog of stale beer, cigarette fumes, perfume and wet coats into the icy night. The rain had stopped and the skies shone with frigid brilliance. The clear weather did nothing to lift their spirits. It meant that tomorrow, ops would be on for sure.[22]

The nights out described by George Hull were rather more sedate. 'The crew ambled into Lincoln on Wednesday evening,' he wrote to Joan. 'We [didn't have] much money so after a few beers and eyeing a few doubtful-looking women, we went to a local dance-hall for a session. Now only a few us can dance much, [I'm] amongst the majority, so we looked over the place, met a great many old friends from other stations, and contented ourselves with a waltz or so, a shuffle, and a cycle home – sans lights.'

The important thing was to get off the base. The nearest pub provided a welcome taste of the civilian lives they had left behind. While based at Tuddenham in Suffolk, Arthur Taylor and his crew headed whenever they had the chance for the Bull, a pub at Barton Mills. It was a 'comfortable and roomy Georgian coaching inn . . . there was a cheerful air about the place and it became the haunt of RAF personnel as it was situated close to three aerodromes. There was a good fire going when it was cold and the air was full of cigarette smoke, loud talk and laughter. To get off your bike on a black night and enter this building was a heartening experience.'[23] Jack Currie and his crew frequented a similarly welcoming pub on the northern boundary of their base in Derbyshire. There, they were 'privileged to share . . . the landlady's favours, which included the use of her kitchen for bacon, eggs and sausages after hours, and the company of her daughters. The eldest of these was a big, untidy, cuddlesome girl whose efforts to keep her relations with us on a sisterly basis weren't always successful.'

The pub had a piano, as most did in the days when jukeboxes were still a novelty. 'For the last half-hour or so before closing time . . . downing the clear, bitter ale they brew beside the Trent, we liked to sing . . . while the village postmistress pounded an accompaniment. Her repertoire was limited to hymn tunes and a few songs of the day, of which we favoured "Roll Out the Barrel", "Bless 'em All" and, for the Australians' sake, "Waltzing Matilda".'[24]

The ability to play the piano was a great social advantage. Before he was killed, an Australian sergeant, J. A. Bormann, left behind a list of eighty tunes he could bash out in mess and pub. It includes 'Over the Rainbow', ''Till The Lights of London Shine', 'Blackout Stroll', 'South of the Border', 'Beer Barrel Polka', 'Rose Marie' and 'Lily of Laguna'. These songs are old and new, sentimental and rousing, upbeat and slow but they all have one thing in common – a melody that even the tone-deaf could sing along to.

The men clustered around the piano were doing a job that would harrow most hardened veteran, but in many ways they behaved like the adolescents they had so recently been. George Hull reported that he and the crew had 'discovered a wizard pastime . . . we call it "scrub riding". On our way to and from the mess we miss the road, turn into a muddy barren field, dive into ditches, over the plank crossing a stream and crash the wire-netting into the mental home for aircrew. Funny isn't it what you have to do for a bit of excitement. Tonight we did it in the dark – most of our cycles returned safely, but ditchwater dun half taste peequleeah.'[25]

Writing from his training camp at Yatesbury, Wiltshire, Edwin Thomas described to his mother the evening's entertainment. 'The main attraction in the ENSA concert tonight in the camp theatre is George Formby. Tomorrow night we are all going on a binge to celebrate the end of the course – and I expect it will end with a terrific pillow fight about eleven o'clock.'

At this time Thomas was a few months past his twentieth birthday but still rooted in the pleasures of childhood. 'I had fun last Wednesday at our Wing Dance which Tony and I gatecrashed,' he reported home. 'We buttonholed a cross-eyed LAC who was standing outside the NAAFI canteen, and he advised us to try to make our entry by a door at the back of the building marked "Corporals". We took this advice but the door wouldn't budge an inch. We battered at the bally thing for ages then it finally "gave" with a noise that seemed almost to bring the building down. It had been held fast with a chair. We entered a small room in pitch darkness, barking our shins, laughing and crashing into one another. We found another door leading into the Sergeants' Cloakroom. We plucked up courage, put on a bold front and simply walked through into the dance-hall. Of course, most of the WAAFs were bagged by then . . . but we enjoyed ourselves. We drank cider and NAAFI beer. The latter is as flat as a pancake, and doesn't deserve the name beer.' Edwin's innocence appears to have survived untarnished until he was killed.[26]

It is easy to imagine what lay behind all the drinking and the boisterousness. The crews, as Harris had pointed out, were facing imminent death. It was natural that they should want to fill their lives to the brim during whatever time was left to them. The privations of air force life meant that the opportunities for sensual enjoyment were limited. This was particularly true of sex. Wartime had loosened the strict limitations on sexual behaviour imposed on most of society by the *mores* of the 1930s. But the number of women who were willing to engage in brief, non-committal encounters was still very limited, especially in the provincial, unsophisticated towns where the airmen went to unwind.

At work they were surrounded with females, the women of the WAAF, who made up a large proportion of the ground staff of the bases. The fact that they had joined up rather than being drafted for war work suggested an adventurous nature. But their tendency to independence did not necessarily indicate a free-and-easy moral approach. Most of the WAAFs were women of their time. They believed in love and found it hard to imagine sex without it. If they succumbed, it was in the expectation that marriage would follow.

There were, of course, exceptions, who earned the disapproval of their more strait-laced peers. Pip Beck, a radio telephony officer at Waddington had little time for a colleague called Jane who was 'a different type entirely' from the other WAAFs. She had 'short bleached-blond hair and eyebrows plucked to a thin line and pen-cilled black; deep blue eyes with black mascaraed lashes; eyes, as rapidly became evident, wise in the ways of men.' It was her habit to bring her embroidery to the watch office and work on it on a quiet evening. She would spread her 'hanks of coloured silk about the desk – and wait. Sooner or later an aircrew officer would appear, and Jane would add a stitch or two to her pattern and flash her blue eyes in his direction. After a brief word with the FCO [Flying Control Officer] – his excuse for the visit – he would slip into a chair beside her and chat for a while, then leave. This was followed by a discreet exit on Jane's part – and no Jane for a while.'

One night an exasperated senior officer had had enough. Pip was startled to hear a senior officer 'say, in great indignation, "what does she think this is – a bloody knocking shop!" I hadn't heard the expresssion before but was wary of asking what it meant. I had the glimmering of an idea.'[27]

The best hope for those seeking casual sex lay with the 'saloon bar sirens' who frequented the pubs of Bomberland. Some were bruised women whose husbands were away at the war or dead or imprisoned. They offered the prospect of a few free drinks and some laughter and companionship. 'A few of the ladies were pretty but most were just acceptably plain,' Brian Frow wrote. 'All were out for a good happy time with the chaps, whose days in most cases were numbered. Some did, some didn't and many just teased.'[28]

There was another category of females, much disapproved of by clean-living young men like George Hull, whom he came across in the pubs of Lincoln, 'young girls of seventeen and eighteen, offering themselves for the price of a dance ticket or a glass of port.'[29]

The desire not to die a virgin was very strong. Willie Lewis, despite many dates, had yet to lose his innocence when he was informed by a Canadian gunner that an ATS girl who Lewis had spotted him with in a Lincoln pub the previous night was 'a certain bang'. When he ran into her a week later he decided to act. 'Plump and slothful in her brown uniform she sat with a companion in the corner of the snug sipping a half-pint of bitter.' Lewis's target was called Betty. He complimented her on her hair even though it was 'fuzzed about her ears in an untidy fashion' and offered her and her friend Eva a drink – a short, he insisted, because he hated buying women beer.

They accepted two gins. It turned out that Betty's husband, like Willie, was a flight engineer. Fortunately he was thousands of miles away in India. As the small talk dwindled Lewis asked Betty if she wanted to fit in a dance at Bridgen's dance-hall before it closed. According to his slightly fictionalized account, Betty was enthusiastic.

'"Yes," she said. "I'd like a dance. You don't mind, do you, Eva?"

'"You're always doing this to me, Betty," snapped the other girl. "This is the last time I'm going to come out with you."

'As soon as they got outside they started kissing. When they finally reached Bridgen's it was full up. "What shall we do now?" she said. It was an idle question, answered as she spoke, for they had already started in the direction of the East Gate, and were under slow progress, kissing, and cuddling, every few yards, towards the town playing fields.'

It was drizzling and the fields were sodden. They took refuge in an air-raid shelter. Lewis gallantly spread his coat on the dank concrete floor. After it was over they lay there 'locked together, dozing, until the clock struck twelve in the main square.'

He walked her back to her ATS billet where they hugged for a final time. '"Wait here a moment, Willie," Betty whispered. "I've got a photograph of my husband in my room. I'll go and get it. It's quite possible you might know him."'

Lewis was appalled at the thought. He hurried away before she returned. He knew he ought to feel ashamed. Instead the experience had 'filled his thoughts with joy. "I am a man at last," he said to himself. "I am a man at last." And those words danced a pulsing, happy, feeling in his mind on the journey back to the 'drome.'[30]

This was perhaps not the most sophisticated introduction to sex. If you were in search of something more refined it was better to visit London. Jack Currie took advantage of a short leave to go there with his rear gunner, Charlie Lanham. They lunched at Australia House and took the train to Maidenhead where they stayed at Skindles on the river. The following day Currie played cricket for his old boys' side, then they took the Metropolitan Line into town for an evening of fun. Lanham had laid on a couple of girls for the evening. The first came to meet them at their Sloane Square hotel. 'She walked into the . . . bedroom, swinging her wide hips and her long, coarse hair. Lanham introduced us, and her soft, cool fingers rested in my hand. She raised her pencilled eyebrows and looked me up and down, still undulating slowly.

'"So you're his skipper, that I've heard too much about. OK let's see you skipper something, like a drink maybe?"

'"What will you have?"

'"A fainting fit if I don't sit down soon. And Scotch on the rocks . . ."'

This vampish repartee delighted Currie as Lanham was quick to notice. '"What did I tell you Jack? Isn't she a beaut? Come on, let's hit the town."'[31]

It took considerable courage to flaunt sexual differences in this fiercely heterosexual society. 'Rory', a mid-upper gunner at Wickenby felt strong enough to do so, perhaps because his toughness was never in doubt. Currie described him as 'neat and well-groomed, with a face like that of a contented cat. He spoke with a lisp and a lilting, feminine diction, and he used scented soaps and lotions.

He occasionally dabbed his nose with a small, silk hankerchief. However he was well advanced on his second tour of operations, and he wore a DFM ribbon and a wound stripe, so his manner escaped the abuse which it might have otherwise attracted, in the aggressively masculine society in which he moved.'

One night in the mess Rory was describing the damage a German bomb had done to the *objets d'art* in his London flat during the Blitz. Among the listeners were 'several robust Australians whose aesthetic interests it would not be too harsh to term philistine, embracing as they did little beyond the world of sport and "Sheilas".'

Rory's usual good humour collapsed under the weight of prolonged Australian mockery. He threw himself at his two biggest tormentors and had to be restrained. Peace was restored after the philistines apologized and Rory allowed them to buy him a gin and lime.[32]

Gay airmen were more likely to keep their preferences to themselves and pretend to be heterosexual. Drink, though, had a way of dissolving the deception. Willie Lewis remembered an occasion when an American crew that had been rescued from the Channel after ditching spent the night with his squadron on their way home. 'The three officers were made very welcome in the officers' mess, and we stood shouting, and howling, through the usual list of nice songs, and then filthy ones, and back to nice ones again. And then the incredible happened. One of our chaps continued to keep holding the hands of one of the Americans. And yet I'd never thought he was a nancy boy before . . . The American was terribly distressed . . . We grabbed our man and took him back to his bedroom and said "Don't come back." And that was that.'[33]

The British airmen may have had the good fortune to be fighting from their own country. But that was not the same as being at home. In Bomberland, the natives were not always friendly. Some of the locals resented the influx of airmen and women, and the disruption that they had brought in their wake. Farmers complained about the damage to their crops and disturbance to their flocks caused by the arrival of Bomber Command. This attitude was resented by the men who were risking their lives on their behalf. Returning to Wigsley from a night-time cross-country training flight Hull and his crew 'got the wind under our port wing and and ran off the runway at a hell of a pace, passing the end of the runway lights at a fairly good speed and finally leaving through a vegetable field near a farmhouse to come to rest with about sixty yards of fencing wrapped around the fuselage. We were a bit shaken but soon hopped out. A few short minutes later out came the farmer and grumbled that we had made a mess of the vegetables. "Next time," he said, "someone will hit the farm." My God! The damn audacity. We could easily . . . have been seriously injured at least if the 'plane had turned over, yet all he could think about was his measly cabbage patch.'

This was not his first run-in with ungrateful civilians. 'Yesterday evening,' he wrote to Joan on 17 November 1943,

> we got a rare evening off and cycled into Lincoln . . . a garage attendant . . . as good as told me to get the hell out of the way while I was fixing a flickering rear lamp. The hate I've been storing up for the last fortnight came to the boil. I rather let rip with my opinion of Lincoln and his garage in particular . . . Admittedly we are a little boisterous in Lincoln on occasions – it's a case of letting off steam or bursting – but I think a little toleration on the population's part is required. Would you believe that in certain cafés the RAF are pointedly refused service when the place is crowded or civilians are waiting also? I've experienced it often, but rowing with the staff has little effect – they tell us we should only use the canteens.[34]

The aircrews often had a fractious relationship with local policemen who seemed to take a perverse pleasure in picking on them for petty infringements of the blackout.

For most of the British airmen, joining the RAF was their first experience of spending a long time away from home and when leave was granted, home was the first place they headed. The question of leave caused more frustration than almost any other aspect of RAF life. It was supposed to come every four weeks or after every six ops but the rules were often altered. It was granted, then snatched away, wrecking carefully-laid plans and nascent romances. When it finally arrived it was often disappointingly short. A '48' in most cases left barely enough time to go anywhere given the snail's pace of wartime transportation. When the opportunity to return to the world they left behind did come it was a strangely disconcerting experience. By the time they reached their squadrons they had spent around two years in a parallel society that duplicated many of the functions of family life. The small minority with wives and children could plunge into a brief, blissful respite of love-making and domesticity. For the rest, re-entering the past could be dislocating. The comforts and rhythms of civilian life seemed odd and the old, familiar faces seemed altered. They found themselves talking about comrades whom those at home had only read about in letters and places they had only heard of from the radio. The confusion wore off eventually, but usually just before the return to base loomed.

The question they asked themselves, as they walked the familiar streets to their front doors, was how much to say of what they had seen and done. Granted a welcome seven days' leave after completing eight ops, Harry Yates made his way from Wolverton station to his home in Stony Stratford and decided he would tell his mother nothing. 'She would not have thanked me if, in the quiet of the evening when she was alone in the house, she had cause to ponder corkscrews and scarecrows, flaming onions and blue master beams.' His father, however, was anxious for every detail, as were the regulars in the local pub, The Case is Altered. There, he discovered, he was a celebrity, not least for having flown low over the village, a 'beat up' in RAF parlance, on a couple of occasions to show off his piloting skills. The 'regular clientele of crib and dart players and grizzled old characters who would nurse a pint of mild for an entire evening was a bit short on recent operational experience. They gave us no privacy or peace . . .' They were proud of their local hero and bought him drinks all evening.[35]

Bernard Dye left a laconic account of a six-day leave in February

1944, detailing the homely pleasures that after the dreadfulness of operational flying must have tasted as sweet as anything the peacetime world could offer. On Friday the eleventh he recorded he 'had tea at Arnold's with Trevor, Charlie and Jimmy. It was like old times.' The next day he 'went to the pictures with Mum, Dad and David. Went to the ATC social. Had a good time.' On Monday he 'had a good day in Yarmouth.' On the fourteenth he 'went to the pictures with Geoff and Grace.'

Then it was back to Mildenhall and stark reality. Four days after returning from leave and his crew were chalked up on the battle order for Stuttgart. 'Navigator and bomb-aimer refuses to fly,' he wrote. 'We were all ready in the kite to take off. [They] were then put under armed escort & put into clink, expect it will mean a court-martial for them.' The crew was subsequently reformed and posted to 622 Squadron at Lakenheath.[36]

The overseas crews had no homes to go to. Some of them were taken under the wing of kindly locals or invited back to the families of their British colleagues. Others drifted to London where places like the Kangaroo Club offered homesick men a whiff of Australia or at least the chance to get drunk with different fellow-countrymen. The Canadians had the Beaver Club in Trafalgar Square. Ralph Wood would start his London leaves there before setting off to pubs like the Captain's Cabin and a favourite RCAF watering-hole in Denman Street in the West End called the Crackers Club. Then there were afternoon dances at the Hammersmith Palais where 'young girls were plentiful . . . too young to work, but not too young to dance.' Nightlife for all servicemen was centred on Piccadilly Circus where 'about the only civilians you could see were the prostitutes, and they were numerous. They were called the Piccadilly Commandoes.'[37]

Leave was unsettling. The airmen were desperate to reconnect with the world they had left. Harry Yates, back home in Stony Stratford, took comfort in 'discussing the (for me) entirely irrelevant goings on along the street or in McCorquodale's print works or the church, the hostelries or any of the odd corners that blessed our town with its singular character and its sense of continuity.' Coming home after the manic world of the bomber base was 'like taking a four-weekly moral bath and I was ever sorry when the moment came to leave.'[38]

Contact with home could induce a desperate nostalgia for a universe that, even if they survived, had gone, banished by the annihilation of innocence that went with their work. George Hull reminisced in a letter to Joan of departed bank holidays, 'good old Hampstead on a Whit Monday, gay colourful caravans and sideshows with their bedlam of cries, steam organs and laughter. Brass bands murdering overtures in the distance, couples strolling arm-in-arm through leafy lanes, picnics in the woods with cold chicken salad and bananas and cream, tongue sandwiches with sliced, sugared tomatoes, honey and biscuits, flasks of tea and coffee. Good days taken so much for granted.'[39]

The first letters and diary entries written by airmen after their return are touched with melancholy and regret. They had caught a glimpse of the life they would lose if they went the way of so many of their friends. And the biggest loss of all would be the chance to find lasting love.

15

Love in Uniform

Love flourished in wartime. Doubts and inhibitions withered in the heat of instant attraction and the knowledge that time might be short. Starting a romance was relatively easy. The problem was how to keep it going. The road to happiness was blocked by many practical and bureaucratic obstacles. Bomberland was a conglomeration of backwaters and was badly served by trains. Unless your girl was in Lincoln or Norwich or York, you faced a long and erratic journey getting to see her on leaves. Speaking on the phone was almost more frustrating than not speaking at all. The maximum length of a trunk call was six minutes and it could take hours to get a line. Often one party or the other would find themselves tongue-tied as they struggled to find the words that would make the most of the brief opportunity. At least the mail worked. It was a reasonable assumption that letters written one day would arrive the next, no matter where they were coming from or going to. But they too brought their problems. It was tricky conducting a love affair by correspondence. Feelings were pitched high and the words often tumbled on to the paper, unrevised. Burning sentiment might have cooled in the grey light of a Lincolnshire morning, or a cautious or hesitant remark seem ungallant after a few drinks in the mess. Either way it would take another letter and another delay for the first impression to be corrected.

Frank Blackman fell for Mary Mileham in the early summer of 1943. He was a flying officer with 429 RCAF (Bison) Squadron and she was working at the Admiralty in London. They came from very different backgrounds. She was the eldest of six children, the daughter of a prosperous solicitor who lived in bourgeois comfort in Boxmoor, Hertfordshire. There was enough money to send all the children to fee-paying schools and to St Moritz to ski in the winter.

Frank Blackman's father had been killed in the First World War and never saw his son. His mother worked as a housekeeper to provide for her two boys. He wanted to become a doctor but had to settle for training as a pharmacist. Before joining the RAF he had a post with a big pharmaceutical company and lived in a flat in London where he took care of his mother. Mary's family had servants. Frank was the son of one. 'In peacetime in no way would we have been on the same road,' Mary wrote later. 'But in war it is different. We became friends as we were both on an escape path and the companionship was comforting to us both.' Mary was recovering from 'a long unsatisfactory relationship'. Frank was seeking some relief from the 'fire of landing in a bomber squadron'.

According to Mary he was 'a gentle person', 'well-informed' and 'knowledgeable'. He was sensitive and literate, knew some German and Russian and was teaching himself Italian. She considered herself 'wild', loved the country and sport, but was 'academically completely dim'.[1] This made no difference to Frank. In the ten months they knew each other, Mary and he wrote to each other constantly, sometimes twice a day. For Blackman, the relationship became the central point of his precarious life. 'Forgive me,' he wrote one June night shortly after he had spent a leave with her, 'if just for one moment before I close I send you again my love and tell you – as I began to do on the phone before people started coming through the hall – that as a direct result of that one short week the whole tenor of my existence seems to have altered. Life is now an infinitely sweet thing and the thoughts of all the things we have yet to do or see and hear – music, holidays, fun in crowds and joy alone – are the things which my mind turns constantly towards . . . blast this war darling.'

At that point their story was only a few weeks old. They appear to have first met properly on 26 May 1943 when Frank visited her office at the Admiralty. He recorded the encounter in verse.

> I bless the day I wandered in
> To see you – and still full of doubt
> Asked bashfully to take you out
> For truth to tell I always knew
> I'd like to come to mean to you
> No mere acquaintance but a friend.[2]

The following day they went for a drink. Two days later they had supper together. On 1 June they saw *Arsenic and Old Lace* and dined at the Waldorf. Just before he returned to Blyton where he was in the throes of converting to Halifaxes, he took her to meet his mother. After that they spent every leave together. Letters and phone calls flew between them during the long spaces apart. Mary's correspondence has not survived but she kept all of Frank's letters. They brim with gratitude and delight. 'Life has come to mean much more than all the year that went before,' ran one of his couplets.

Love breeds optimism. In the beginning, Frank allowed himself to believe that he might survive. One summer morning, sitting in a garden in the grounds of East Moor, the squadron base, he wrote her a letter while he waited to hear whether or not ops were on that night. 'In such surroundings on such a lovely day, one's thoughts turn to the sweet things of life,' it said. 'Truly this moment is so peaceful that the prospect of the next hours seems like an evil dream.'

The romance was proceeding at a hectic wartime pace, but he, at least, did not care. 'Don't worry Mary about the rushing of fences,' he reassured her a few days later. 'I do have sense in this matter – nevertheless I don't think any of us can be quite happy without some little dream tucked away in his mind, even in self-deception. Without it existence for most of us would be a barren experience. Probably most of us has his idea of the sought-for peace. Mine could not be complete without – indeed depends on – someone to idealize and love.' He believed he had found in her 'that tiny sheet anchor upon sanity and faith' that would enable him to keep going.

Frank's love affair seems to have become more real to him than the 'evil dream' of flying over Germany at night. He wanted the nightmare to end as quickly as possible, and his waking life to begin properly. In the middle of June he was alarmed by a rumour that the squadron might be posted 'to the Middle East which God forbid.' The relative safety of the Mediterranean theatre held no attraction if it meant he was away from Mary. Yet weighed against the optimism was a fatalism that he had learned from cold experience. 'You ask if I believe one has any control over one's destiny,' he wrote. 'Darling, much as I would like to believe it – I don't.'

Frank and Mary were baring their souls to each other on the basis of a very short acquaintance. Sometimes it worried her. 'I hope that you don't quite mean it when you say sometimes you are writing to a stranger,' he fretted. 'I understand the feeling that must go through your mind. Nevertheless, I do hope and believe that we are beginning to understand each other.'

The next proper leave was a long way away. Frank recorded gloomily that 'with the present rather grievous losses in the squadron I see our 48s receding further and further in the background.' The Battle of the Ruhr was at its height and 429 Squadron had lost seven aircraft, nearly a third of its strength, in the previous few nights in major attacks on Krefeld, Mülheim and Wuppertal.

He suggested she come north to visit him, even though there was a high likelihood that he would be flying most nights. At least she would be able to watch him depart. He gave her directions to the airfield. 'If you care to walk along the road past the telephone box and turn right you will come to the edge of the 'drome and can, if you want to, see us take off. If you do, I can't wave to you exactly – but you can be sure that that mile between us will be positively sizzling with telepathic activity.' On 25 June she travelled to York then north to East Moor, near the village of Sutton-on-the-Forest. Frank was indeed on ops. Despite its recent mauling the squadron was detailed for an attack on Gelsenkirchen in the Ruhr. The raid was not a success and losses were heavy. Thirty aircraft failed to return, more than 6 per cent of the force.

Mary arrived too late to meet him before he left but was able to watch him take off and stayed up all night to see him safely home. After he woke they enjoyed one of the days they had fantasized about. 'Frank came round just before lunch,' she wrote in her abbreviated diary. 'Lunched, walked sunbathed dinner talked early to bed.'[3] He had arranged for her to stay with a Mrs Skinner who lived near the base. The following day he picked her up in the morning. They had a blissful Sunday before going into York for dinner. He put her on the 9.30 train and she arrived back in London at 3 a.m.

The visit reinforced his desire 'to get this business done.' In the days after her departure he flew operations by night and wrestled with his feelings by day. On Wednesday 30 June he wrote that he had 'been trying to analyse my own state of mind since the weekend. I'm not being really introspective about it – I've been too busy for one thing – but emotions have been so mixed that I had to give it some thought.' On Monday he had been 'excited – perhaps even intoxicated and much of this has survived.' But overlaying this elation was 'a strong feeling of resentment that so much sweetness is so near and yet so far. I think this last day or two – since you opened once again my eyes to such boundless happiness – I have hated this war more . . . than at any time since it began.'

The righteousness of the fight seemed of lesser importance than the fact that he was in love for the first time. He now knew what he wanted and was sure he could attain it 'but for this wretched stupid war.' Viewed in this light, Frank saw little that was noble about his work. What lay ahead were 'possibly months of bitter, destructive, death-dealing labour.' He was 'not able to hate enough to feel otherwise.' He was suddenly gripped by fear, but 'not of dying. That must be . . . usually at least, thank God, oh so simple – but fear of losing the good things of life.' And by far the most important of these was Mary Mileham.

By the end of July the Battle of the Ruhr was over and Harris turned his attention to Hamburg and then Berlin. The squadron converted from Wellingtons to Halifaxes. Its losses declined dramatically and only thirty-seven men were killed in the last five months of the year, seven fewer than had died in three nights in June.

Mary went to see Frank again at East Moor early in August and spent a 'lovely weekend'.[4] Back in London she visited his mother and was waiting for him when he came to London on leave on

14 August for a few days. In September he had a '48' and they spent it together dining one night at Quaglino's.

On 22 October she made the arduous journey north again to visit him at his new base, Leeming, in Yorkshire. Afterwards he wrote to Mary in some confusion. 'You know, Mary that I cannot yet ask you to marry me. Indeed if I did you would be afraid to say yes – being far, perhaps, from knowing your own wish. Yet Mary you must know that I wish it above all things and I am supremely happy even in the hope and anticipation of it.' By that stage they had spent only seven short spells of time together. Frank's hesitation appears to have been selfless. He wanted her to be his wife. But he knew that the squadron's good luck could not last for ever and the chances remained high that if they did marry, Mary would soon be a widow. Despite the time they had spent together, which was considerable by wartime standards, she seems to have been much less certain about her feelings and more hesitant about committing herself. Her emotions were tender. As well as the 'unsatisfactory' romance she had lost her brother Denys, a fighter pilot who had fought in the Battle of Britain, who was shot down over the Channel in April 1942. Nonetheless they showed every sign of being a couple on the two leaves that Frank took in London in what was left of the year. They played bridge, visited his mother and ate out at the Liaison-Slavia Club and the Argentina.

On 20 January 1944 Frank had a week's leave and came to London. For once he did not call her immediately, provoking in Mary a pang of suspicion. 'Out with his other girlfriend?' she wondered in her diary. No one reading his love-struck letters could believe him capable of any romantic deception. The more likely explanation is that he felt his first duty was to attend to his mother. He rang on the twenty-second and the following day they went to the country and spent the afternoon playing bridge. On the last night of their leave they went to dinner at the Argentina then to the cinema to see *Jane Eyre*. 'Felt disturbed,' Mary wrote in her diary.[5] The following day he dropped by her office to say goodbye and took the train north to Leeming.

Frank always kept his hope warm, searching for positive signs in the swirling confusion of the war. Late in October 1943 he had written that 'the beginning of the end is in sight . . . with the Soviets doing these incredible things . . . there is no doubt that a point is coming when tremendous air armadas will operate day and night with at first great losses perhaps – but with an effect that may finish the war without invasion.' He was well aware of his ignorance of the big picture. 'I have no knowledge of these things at all of course,' he admitted. But it was 'obvious that this is the next step – and God help the Hun.'

His prediction was already coming true. As he wrote, the Battle of Berlin was beginning and 429 Squadron were part of it. On the snowy night of 19 February 1944 they went on one of the bloodiest raids of Bomber Command's war. Altogether 823 aircraft set off. The target was Leipzig. Frank's aircraft was among the force of 255 Halifaxes. A diversion towards Kiel aimed at drawing away the German night-fighters was unsuccessful and the bomber stream was under attack all the way to the target. The wind was stronger than forecast and pushed the bombers along so fast that many got there early and were forced to orbit until the Pathfinders arrived. Four bombers were destroyed in collisions and twenty shot down by flak. Leipzig was covered by cloud and the Pathfinders had to mark blind. Immediately there 'was a wild scramble as several hundred bombers came in from all directions, anxious to bomb quickly and get out of the area.'[6] The raid was considered a success in that more than 50,000 Germans were bombed out. But the price was appallingly high. Bomber Command recorded its worst night of the war to date with seventy-nine aircraft lost. Almost 15 per cent of the Halifaxes that reached enemy territory never returned. Many had turned back before crossing the enemy coast. Thereafter Halifax IIs and Vs, the older types, were withdrawn from operations to Germany. The raid had been a disaster.

Frank's Halifax was shot down by a night-fighter near Berlin. All on board were killed. It was Mary who received the telegram telling her that he was missing. He had listed her, rather than his mother or elder brother as his next of kin. Then came a last letter, postmarked 21 February and presumably posted by a comrade. There is no indication of when it was written. After the passion and enthusiasm of his other letters the tone seems flat and stilted and there is a feeling of resignation behind the unconvincing optimism.

> Well Mary, dear.
>
> This will tell you if something unfortunate has happened. I shall hope in due course to be writing to you again either from some Oflag or other – or with any luck from England on return.
>
> In the meantime it is hard to know what to say. You have meant so much to me – and been so very charming to me during these last few months that it is hard to say 'Goodbye' even if only for a while.
>
> God bless you darling and thank you again – a million times. Lots of luck and my deepest and sincerest wishes.

Despite the chaos of wartime, Frank and Mary had at least managed to have something like a fulfilling courtship. They had met and flirted, fallen for each other, though he clearly more heavily than she. They had shared rich experiences leaving memories that lasted Mary the rest of her life. They revealed themselves to each other with a rare frankness and traded more sincere endearments than many couples do in a lifetime.

George Hull's relationship with Joan Kirby was less satisfying. He met her at the funeral of her brother who had been killed in a training accident in July 1943. George had made friends with John Kirby in Canada where they were both training to be navigators.

He was brought up in Stepney, east London, the only son of Jack and Margaret Hull. As a boy he was interested in science and once rigged up an electric sign that flashed 'Happy Christmas' to visitors when they stepped on the doormat. George belonged to a category of young men who grew up in the nineteen-thirties that was particularly well represented in the ranks of Bomber Command. He came from an ordinary background and received an ordinary education. But the walls of deference were crumbling, a process that was hastened by the war, and he was eager to plunge into the world of

'Silver wings in the moonlight / Flying high up above
While I'm patiently waiting / Please take care of my love.'

high culture that had previously been the domain of the wealthy.
He loved good books and good music as well as the ordinary pleasures of the British male. His idea of a perfect evening was a visit
to the Proms followed by a few pints and a game of darts. He

had, Joan remembered, a strong social conscience. 'He was a great believer in social justice,' she said. 'He would have been a leader in some form.' His initial ambitions were simple enough. If he got through the war alive he planned, like Frank, to be a pharmacist. He was, in a quiet way, a patriot who felt his Englishness with a poetic intensity. Nazism represented everything that repelled him and he had joined the RAF Volunteer Reserve as soon as the war began.

George disguised an attractive naivety behind a show of sophistication and pragmatism and there was enough of the lingering legacy of Victorianism in his make-up for him to affect a dislike of overt displays of feeling. 'He was a very jolly sort of chap,' Joan said, 'an optimist full of plans for getting the war over and getting on with life. Yet he had a very serious side to him and was quite unsentimental. I got a bit mawkish one time, I remember, and he more or less said, don't be ridiculous. Sentiment is fine but sentimentality is not.'[7]

Coming from George this was mildly hypocritical. His letters vibrate with emotion. The correspondence began after he and his friend Philip Kitto, known to everyone as Mac, travelled back with Joan when she returned to her WRNS base, HMS *Cabbala* at Lowton near Warrington after her brother's funeral. The journey was fun and lifted some of the gloom imposed by John's death. His loss seemed particularly pointless. His aircraft had been diverted from his home base at Wigsley to another airfield after a training exercise and crashed on landing. The Kirbys were a tight-knit, dutiful English middle-class family. Mr Kirby was in charge of the Air Raid Precautions area. His wife was a hardworking Red Cross nurse. The death cast a shadow over the family's happiness which never quite cleared.

Being with her brother's best friends cheered her up. 'What do you think? – George and Mac came right the way up here with me,' she wrote home. 'I was terribly pleased because instead of the horrible journey I anticipated, it was very pleasant. You would have laughed to see us; we were sitting around a desolated refreshment room on one of the platforms with my sandwiches and three cups of tea trying to work out how to get through the barrier without paying.'[8]

On 8 July the long pursuit began. He was, he wrote to her, waiting for his new crew to finish off their training and for once had some time on his hands. 'With a bit of luck and a cunning tongue, I may be able to pop up and see you for a weekend – that is if you get any time to yourself during Saturdays and Sundays.' George was completing his training at Bruntingthorpe in Leicestershire, not so very far from Warrington. But this apparently simple ambition turned out to be maddeningly difficult to achieve.

As George schemed to make a rendezvous, Joan was getting acquainted with a new and exotic species of servicemen; the Americans. One Sunday in the middle of July, dressed up in her new uniform she 'went to an American Red X dance in Warrington. The dance itself was awful – it was an afternoon affair but we got taken to tea at the American Club and had "Coke" which John used to talk about so much.' At the end of the month the prospect of leave was once again dangled tantalizingly in front of George, and then whipped away. 'Well it happened again,' he wrote to her. 'I don't know what you are thinking about all this but I would have given a week's pay not to have had to send that telegram on Friday evening. I felt sure I would get that "48" this weekend. All Friday morning I talked to the rest of the navigators about asking for a "48" until they could think of nothing else. The course leader was approached and he saw the OC of our flight. The decision was rather vague. "Perhaps, eh. We'll see." At 10 a.m. that morning we found ourselves building a road with picks and shovels under the impression that if we did enough we might get it. Needless to say nobody really believed it. That's a common instance of official craftiness.'[9]

While George fumed, Joan was making the most of the rich social opportunities available to an attractive young woman in a country crammed with men in uniform who were starved of female company. Returning by train from a leave spent at the family home in Oxhey near Watford she and her friend Jan 'met some Americans – I've got a date with a Captain McClees on Friday – wrote me a complicated phone number and got me a table and carried my bag and said "please ring me up tomorrow as I can't ring you." . . . I might go – be fun for a few weeks – he's a doctor so he should be alright, but he's married!'

Joan did indeed go out with the captain, three times in a row. 'He takes me out to dinner etc. & is quite nice,' she wrote to her family on 17 August. 'Unfortunately he's going south this week but wants to see me on my leave in four weeks' time & all kinds of things. I came back . . . laden up with cigarettes etc., it's really quite amusing.'

Nearly two months after their first encounter, George and Joan had still not managed to meet. 'I hope we can see something of each other within the next few weeks,' he wrote plaintively. 'I am eager to see this winsome Wren in uniform.' When he did finally get some leave he went to London to see his family but was able to keep his memories of Joan fresh by visiting her parents at 'Shirley', the Kirbys' house. 'I went to see your folks on Friday evening,' he wrote. 'Mac came along too. Your Dad met us at Carpenters Park around five thirty and we walked to Shirley.' They then set off to the Load of Hay, the local pub which was to lodge in George's mind as a symbol of the cosy Englishness that comforted and sustained him. There, he was 'as usual beaten in two darts matches' and settled down to drink pints for the rest of the evening.

George had something far more significant to report but modestly left the news to well down the page. 'Did I tell you that I did my first ops trip last week? Well I did! We made a good job of it apparently. As you can guess we had our doubts at the beginning but soon we were on our way and I was too busy to think about anything but navigation.' This appears to be a reference to a raid on a long-range gun battery at Boulogne on 8/9 September 1943 in which crews from Operational Training Units took part. It was a relatively easy debut. Little damage was done to the emplacements but no aircraft were lost.

By now Joan was finding the novelty of Americans was wearing off. She wrote home to complain about a dance at the American Red Cross in Warrington. 'Jan went out with a Yank. I had one as well but didn't fancy going out with him. They bore me. All they talk about is themselves non-stop with just enough breaks now and then to say "gee I like your legs" or "how far is your camp from here honey?" Makes you sick!'

Towards the end of October, George finally managed to be reunited with the girl who had haunted his thoughts for nearly four months. Joan wrote to her parents with the news. 'On Saturday afternoon I was waiting at the local bus stop about 1.15 p.m. for a bus to the station when a Warrington bus stopped at the other side of the road and who should get out but George! Evidently he and his bomb aimer – Ray [Stones] – had mizzled off from camp Friday night and come up to Manchester where Ray lives. He had taken a 100–1 chance & come to Lowton to see if he could see me. By tremendous luck I had just ignored a lorry as being too dirty and was still in the queue with Jill. We went to Chester and had a very nice time . . . it's a lovely old town full of old-fashioned tea places etc. We had a look round for a present for Jan, then had tea, then went to the pictures, then went to a lovely hotel called "The Blossoms" for dinner.'

Joan had arranged to go to Liverpool that Sunday to visit a ship but put it off in order to meet George in Manchester. 'He was terribly pleased to see me and marched me off to "the most palatial place in town" viz the Midland Hotel where you pay 2/6 to wipe your feet. We were safely ensconced in a corner of the lounge with a silver teapot when Jan drifted in. Her date had let her down so she made for the Midland and us. George rang up Ray who was out to tell [his mother to tell him] to come down town . . . the boy's train went at 5.30 p.m. so we went to the station and met said bomb-aimer there – a very nice boy indeed – and saw them off midst great giggles & kisses and promises of "be up next weekend." Jan and I killed ourselves laughing and then went and had a lavish dinner at the Queen's. The coffee was 2/- a cup so we left it & went down to the YM[CA] for a cuppa tea!! We laughed all the more then – Queen's to the YM!'

George, by now, was completely smitten. 'You may not believe this but the last two days were the best I've spent ever,' he wrote on his return. Even desolate Wigsley, which lay under a thick autumn mist seemed 'easier to endure now'. The mood did not last long. Less than a week later he was missing her badly and taking out his frustration on Bomber Command. 'I hate the RAF, this camp in particular. I hate the job we do, not for myself but for those who are lost in the gamble.'

By the middle of November his crew were making their final preparations before starting their full operational tour. 'Tonight is a special occasion,' he wrote to Joan on the thirteenth. 'It's the first night for eight in a row that we can get to bed at a reasonable hour. We've flown twenty-five hours in three days! Both night and day. We ought to be on a squadron in a few days, then you can really sing "Silver Wings in the Moonlight", say a prayer or two and get worried.' The weather had got even worse. He was writing the letter 'huddled over the radio in the mess waiting to be told to get airborne. It's hellish cold, there's about five hundred bods, about a square foot of glowing coals and there's more heat from my cigarette than from the fire at this range.'

The approach of operations coincided with the news that Joan would soon be moving on from Warrington, a thought that filled George with anxiety. 'One of the chief reasons for my being completely cheesed is the realization in my more pessimistic moods what with going from the Manchester area after Christmas and our leaves never coinciding we are unlikely to be seeing each other at all again – grim isn't it, or don't you think so?'

Death was edging closer all the time. The names of those he had trained with in Canada were starting to appear on the casualty lists. 'Do you remember my raving about John Beebe, one of the Winnipeg and Harrogate boys?' he asked her. 'He is posted as 'missing' on his thirteenth 'op'. Two more went the same way last week. God! How right you are on the world's unnecessary suffering.'

George finally reached 207 Squadron in mid-December, 1943. The Battle of Berlin was at its height. Like many, he found that after all the training it came as something of a relief to finally be fighting and the anxiety was overcome by the professional satisfaction of doing what he set out to do. 'Strike One!' he wrote exultantly to

Joan. 'Hull opens his offensive on Germany. Last night bombers of considerable strength Bombed Berlin – you can surely guess the rest!' His squadron had been part of a force of 483 Lancasters which struck the capital on the night of 16/17 December. Little industrial damage was done. Most of the bombs hit houses and railways, killing more than 700 people.

It had been a hard night. The bomber stream flew straight, without diversions, and night-fighters harried them all the way to Berlin and over the target area. Twenty-five Lancasters were lost. When they returned they found heavy cloud smothering many of the bases. Another twenty-nine Lancasters either crashed or were abandoned by their crews. Nearly 150 men were killed in the confusion. Altogether 283 men died on the raid, a casualty rate of 9.3 per cent. George's squadron had got off lightly. Only one aircraft belonging to 207 Squadron was shot down, the victim of a night-fighter. Two of the crew were killed and five subsequently reported to be prisoners of war.

Ten days later the good mood had worn off. By now he had three squadron operations under his belt, one to Frankfurt and another trip to Berlin on the night of 23/24 December. Two days after Christmas he wrote that the holiday had been 'a mixture of work and play, Noel over Unter Den Linden . . . we were so damned tired on our return after close on thirty-six hours without sleep that we were fit for nothing.' He felt curiously dispassionate about the raids. 'I cannot say that I have much emotion. I appreciate their extreme danger but also their necessity. It has a cancelling-out effect. Physically they call for all you have. On return I feel wretchedly tired and depressed and to sleep through a glorious morning when I should like to be walking through the countryside in the crisp, clean air depresses me further.'

George surveyed the coming year in a mood of cold realism. He had grown very close to the Kirby family during his visits to 'Shirley' and 'The Load'. He had put Mr Kirby's name on his 'death form' as someone who was to be informed in the event of bad news. Later he changed his mind and took it off, reckoning that 'it would be unfair to ask him to be subjected to what might amount to a great shock . . . he's had enough already.' He now accepted that his feelings for Joan were not, at least for the moment, reciprocated. She was, he told her semi-facetiously, the third woman in his life, coming after his 'kite', A-Able, and his mother. Joan was the 'girl from whom I draw inspiration to give battle against those who violate peace and God's wish to succour humble mankind. If fate deems me unfortunate in unrequited love then that is [fate's] will.'

The chances of their meeting again were about to become even more remote. At the end of January Joan learned where she was to be posted next. She was going to a Fleet Air Arm base at Machrihanish on the Mull of Kintyre and 'one of the loneliest parts of the Scottish coast you'd ever find.' This was unwelcome for a number of reasons as she explained in a letter to her family. She would be unable to get home for the weekends as she had at Warrington and only one of the friends she had made at HMS *Cabbala* was coming with her. Worst of all it meant 'leaving all my boyfriends, viz Bob and Dennis (my sailor) and getting further away from George.'

Joan was in great demand. Bob was the American who had bought her lobster at the Midland Hotel in Manchester. She had received, she reported 'a proposal . . . last Monday night!!! Of course I'd never marry him but it wasn't altogether a shock. The poor lad will be so miserable at me going so far away from him but I think it's a good thing as I didn't love him a scrap. Poor Dennis too will be disappointed, he's out on a trip on his corvette now but should be in port again next Friday.' And then there was Flight Sergeant Hull. 'Won't George be disappointed? Poor thing, every time we make any arrangements they are always upset. It seems like fate, doesn't it?'

George felt the same way. 'I am sure you feel quite bad enough without me adding to your unhappiness,' he wrote on 27 January 1944 from London where he spent his leave with his family as well as making his regular visit to the Kirbys. 'It seems like a plot to prevent us meeting, apart from the stolen weekend in Manchester – for which I thank God for giving me such an opportunity. We have consistently crossed each other's tracks but never coincide. Perhaps if I ask to be transferred to the Far East our chances would improve. Cheerio pet, keep that chin up. We won't always be unhappy.'

When his leave was up his mother and father saw him off at King's Cross. George found the parting upsetting. 'Nothing tries me so much as the pseudo cheerfulness that we all present to each other during those last few hours: Dad talks hurriedly about "when you come home again" and Mother's organization and preparation would be just the thing for a Polar Expedition. Then in the last few minutes remaining we say goodbye with lightness that certainly finds no echo in our hearts. Mother stands bravely at the gate striving to hide those tears . . . King's Cross . . . a long, boring journey, and the familiar face of a Station Policeman who assumes the role of jailer for another six weeks of uncertainty.'

Joan's worries about Machrihanish did not last long. On the ferry to the Mull of Kintyre she was 'entertained by two sub-lieutenants – one a radio officer at Campbeltown who wanted me to meet him tonight but I wasn't having any.' The other, a Fleet Air Arm pilot called Bill was 'just her dream man'. He reminded her of her brother John, who had always been the ideal she sought, 'tall and a bit thin with a thin face and sandy-coloured hair, not really good looking but ooooo! He's terribly cynical on top because he was shot up over Salerno and they won't let him fly at sea any more but underneath he's grand.'

Clearly Joan was concerned about the effect that the guilelessly reported news of her busy social life would have at home. She sent a letter bursting with frank pleasure at the joy of being an optimistic and pretty young woman enjoying every minute of the new freedom that the war had brought in its wake. 'Really and truly I am fed up as hell. Bill is flying most nights so I can't even see him, but we had a lovely time last week. We walked our shoes off almost going up the hills and among the heather!! Happy days – I'm not a flirt Dad, you can't help liking them, they're such good fun and so crazy. I love them all a little.'

She had just received George's latest letter, telling of his visit to the Kirbys. 'He does like coming up to Shirley doesn't he – it's his second home almost, The Load being the third. I wish I could come

home for a day or two. I'd love to stroll up to The Load this evening.'
Mrs Kirby had clearly been intrigued by the elbowing of Bob. 'How
did I convey to Bob that I didn't love him mummy? Well I just told
him!! I told him I liked him an awful lot but I didn't love him the
way he loved me – I couldn't marry him! He talked a bit about
"love coming later" but I know different by now and I wasn't having
any! I feel terribly sorry for him as he's going through hell I know
but callous though it seems I can't do anything about it. He'll just
have to go away and forget me. It's been done before.'

Whether or not he knew about the new developments in Joan's
romantic life, George's pursuit remained as dogged as ever. He sent
a plaintive letter from Coningsby. 'It does seem that Fate takes a
hand in all our plans but my reaction is to fight her,' he wrote. 'I
could get a great deal fonder of you if I saw you more often –
I remember that weekend in Manchester all too vividly – and perhaps it would not be fair. Not fair to me because it disturbs my
peace of mind, unfair to you because what little interest you may
have in me might be one day a grief to you equal almost to that
which you have lately suffered. I don't want to labour the question
of danger in this job like a little tin hero but I do want you to know
that what I said . . . about the girl who inspires me still holds. What
I really mean is that when I think of you I want to hold on to life
with both hands and get out of the War somehow and live in
certainty – a dangerous idea when it is for people like you that
I will fight this to the end.'

Joan appears to have given a cautious response to this declaration
for in his next letter he accepted that it would better to take things
more slowly. 'Thank you for the many sweet things you talk about
in your letter,' he wrote. 'I appreciate your feelings and reluctantly
agree with them. I had already made my mind up before I wrote
that letter I would not trespass on your feelings to the extent of
making a major issue of it. It is, as you suggest, a strange thing
that our correspondence during the last months has developed an
understanding. It's such a limited medium for thoughts, things
could hardly go beyond the present stage. I doubt whether writing
less often would have much effect. For my part I should miss your

frequent letters more than anyone else.' He now seemed resigned to the unlikelihood of their meeting in the near future. 'Since . . . only a miracle of chance could bring us together we simply must mark it down to the debit side of the War . . .'

By now 61 Squadron, with whom George had flown most of his operations, was firmly in the front line of the Battle of Berlin. All together, it dispatched 242 Lancasters on twenty raids on the Big City. By the middle of February, as Bomber Command was heading for defeat, George wrote that he was 'very tired, cold, hungry, thirsty and deafened.' He had just returned from a huge raid on the night of 15/16 in which forty-three aircraft were lost. 'When I think back to what happened over there last night I am sure that this morning we are living on borrowed time!'

George was now flying so often that there was little time for writing letters. As the flow of correspondence slackened Joan started to become alarmed. 'I'm terribly worried about George,' she wrote home on 11 March 1944. 'He's never left it as long as this ever between letters & it's now over a week since I heard. I'm sure something must be up. So sure in fact that I sent him a telegram but so far haven't heard a word back. I don't know what to do next. Maybe I'm worrying needlessly but there's something strange going on I'm sure.' Her concern prompted both her mother and father to send letters of their own to Coningsby, asking if anything was the matter.

The following day George wrote to say he had received the telegram and two letters. 'I am very sorry to have caused you so much anxiety but there was nothing I could do about it. We have flown day and night in all weathers on all sorts of missions during the past few weeks and had barely enough sleep quite often, let alone spare time. I am afraid a satisfactory explanation would entail telling more than I am permitted to talk about – I ain't trying to be all mysterious like, it's a fact.'

The war and his determination to fulfil his part of it had pushed all other thoughts aside. His doubts melted in the heat of the fight and his criticisms of the RAF were forgotten. He told her proudly how he and his comrades had been honoured with one of the photographs showing spot-on bombing that Harris signed and awarded as a prize to successful crews. The squadron had been switched temporarily to French targets. The moonlit night before, they had taken part in a smallish raid directed at four factories and George's crew were expecting another aiming point photograph. 'I believe we are earning our keep,' he wrote with satisfaction. He was trying not to think about the leave that would soon fall due. 'It looks like the twenty-fourth more or less for certain. I am so fed up with haggling that I do not really care if we go on leave or not.'

That was the last letter. Six days later George and his crew were part of a force of 846 aircraft that took off for Frankfurt. The marking was accurate and the city suffered heavily. Some 420 civilians were killed and 55,500 bombed out. The damage to Bomber Command was light. Only twenty-two aircraft were lost, 2.6 per cent of the force. It was some time before it was discovered how George met his death. After taking off from Coningsby at 19.17 hours on 18 March nothing more was heard of the aircraft or crew. An investigation by the Missing Research and Enquiry Service discovered that their Lancaster had been hit by anti-aircraft fire and crashed into the outskirts of Biegwald Forest near Frankfurt. All on board died but only George and Jack Green were allotted identifiable graves. They were buried first at the Frankfurt Main Cemetery by the German authorities. After the war their bodies were moved to the Bad Tölz British Military Cemetery.

George was not as resigned about his lack of progress with Joan as his last letters suggest. A few days before he was killed he telephoned Mr Kirby to say that he thought he might be able to make it back for Joan's birthday which was on 20 March. He had some important news. '[He] said that he was going to ask me to marry him though things hadn't got to that stage,' Joan recalled. She was at home when the telegram came. She thought at first that it was yet another disappointing communication from George announcing that his leave had been cancelled. Jack and Margaret Hull telephoned and came to Shirley at the weekend and the families grieved together for their lost sons.

It was only later that Joan came to really appreciate the magnitude of the loss. 'Reading those letters it stands out a mile . . . he never really had a chance to press his case.' When his effects were collected a wedding ring was found in one of his pockets.[10]

The bomber stations were emotional incubators. There was no attempt to integrate wives and families into the social structure of the base. Spouses were seen as a nuisance and a distraction. Shortly after Harris took over he banned all wives from a forty-mile radius of their husbands' bases. The order came through when Guy Gibson had just taken over 106 Squadron at Coningsby. Only those airmen who already lived out were exempted. There were only four in the squadron. Gibson, who was married himself, approved. 'This was the best news I had heard for a long time. You cannot fight a war and live at home.'[11]

Yet on the stations, men and women lived and served side by side in a proximity that would have seemed unimaginable to the generation who had fought the previous war. Romances were inevitable. Some were uncomplicated boy-meets-girl stories. Others were not. Fidelity, it has been said, is the second casualty of war. Frances Scott was one of only three WAAF officers on a Cambridgeshire bomber station. Their presence was resented by some of the older male officers but appreciated by everyone else. In their brief time at the base, she felt they had 'showed we could offer companionship and sympathy as well as friendliness, and perhaps a deeper relationship to a chosen few.'[12] The bomber crews were unlike any men she had encountered before. 'Most of the men who flew looked older than they were. It seemed as though they suddenly changed from adolescents to mature men, missing the carefree years of the early twenties.'

In December 1943 she was setting off with a group to a dance at a neighbouring station when they were joined by a twenty-eight-year-old wing commander called Clive with a DFC ribbon on his tunic. He 'spent most of the evening talking and dancing with me, brought me back in his car and – we fell in love.' They spent Christmas at the base. The celebrations started with a dance in the mess on Christmas Eve. Regulations forbade the WAAFs to wear civilian clothes. They tried to brighten up their severe 'best blue' uniforms with silk stockings and the lightest footwear they could get away with. Clive was a 'looker' and knew it. He had a 'generous supply of black hair, giving a rakish air. His face was long with high forehead, beneath which deep set, dark blue eyes looked out on a world which offered him danger, disillusionment, love. His mouth was firm and he had a dark moustache . . .'

Clive was president of the mess committee and one of the hosts of the evening but he often 'left his guests for longer than he should. We ate and drank and laughed and found each other.' When everyone had departed they ended the evening in front of the dying fire, wrapped chastely in each other's arms. The following day there was a service in the station church, a simple wooden hut. Afterwards the officers served Christmas dinner to non-commissioned men and women before retiring to their own mess for a buffet lunch. Somebody produced some mistletoe and one of the officers urged Clive to give Frances a kiss. This remark 'though made in fun, had an unintentional effect on some of those present who put the proverbial "2 and 2" together and tongues wagged, male tongues and malicious tongues for Clive was not popular at that time on the squadron.'

That night there was a dinner in the mess which went on until the early hours. Clive took her back to the little sitting room which served as the WAAF officers' mess. It was out of bounds to male visitors after 11 p.m. but they ignored the rules, sitting on the floor by the fire and drinking wine. Clive seemed subdued. It turned out he was on ops the following day. As a senior commander he was not expected to go on every trip but that did not reduce the agony of anticipation. '"I suppose you think wing commanders with DFCs don't know fear?"' he asked her bitterly. He appeared thoughtful and on the point of saying something important. 'He seemed to want to talk, to get at something in his life that puzzled him, and it put a shadow across his face. "If only there was something more to come back to," he said, "something to hold on to like so many of the [others] have."'

Frances's spirits rose. She began to hope that there could be more between them than an awkward infatuation. She decided to reveal her feelings. She had known him for just forty-eight hours but already felt she loved him, and told him so. Clive's tender expression turned 'to a gloom bordering on anger'. Frances immediately regretted her boldness and tried to reassure him. She understood his reticence. He was afraid of starting an affair that would only end in pain and grief, if he was killed.

Clive seemed suddenly relieved. ' "Yes," he said, "yes that's it," as if struggling for a reason and glad I had provided it for him. "I shall hurt you if I love you any more and you must not get hurt." But I knew that this wasn't his reason. I was aware of the streak of selfishness, and I knew, as surely as I knew that dawn would come, that I would get hurt, but I let it go at that for it didn't seem to matter.'

In fact it was several days before Clive flew again. They went out for supper one evening to a riverside hotel, the Pike and Eel, at St Ives, Cambridgeshire, where there was good food and wine. Two of Clive's RAF acquaintances from the neighbouring station were there when they walked in, together with their wives. 'Clive spoke to them and introduced me casually and seemed very on edge. They were politely interested and no doubt found ample gossip in our relationship once our backs were turned.'

Frances believed that their liaison aroused particular comment because she was a junior WAAF and he was an important man. She worried that she had got a reputation for 'cold-shouldering any officer beneath the rank of squadron leader,' which was, she felt, 'a malicious untruth.' One night she complained to Clive about the injustice of it. ' "Just because I go about with a wing commander . . ." I stormed, "I am classed as a 'ring-chaser' and flirt of the highest order, and yet, if you were a pilot officer, people wouldn't notice us, it makes me livid, why is it?" "They're jealous, my sweet, I expect," he answered absentmindedly, but I knew that this was not the real reason.'

On the morning of 30 January 1944 Frances woke to find the base humming with activity. Ops were on that night. Clive came to see her in the office where she worked as assistant to the station adjutant. He was an altered man. He stayed only long enough to ensure that she would look after Jasper, his golden retriever, while he was away.

Later, as the orange winter sun sank in the west and the rumble of the engines vibrated through the station she watched Clive and his crew climb into their Lancaster, 'their figures awkward and bulging with the weight of their flying kit.' She got a lift to a vantage point near the runway and watched them take off before going back to sleep. She was woken at 1 a.m. by a phone call telling her the squadron was back. She dressed and ran to the interrogation hut where 'a familiar scene greeted us – a cheery scene, brightly lit, it breathed good news at once. We always knew when they had all returned safely; the CO, MO, and the Padre would smile benignly at us; but if they were awaiting some news they would probably scowl absentmindedly . . . the first crew had arrived, tired, grubby-faced and dishevelled, but with a ready smile for us, who brought them what they most longed for at that moment, tea and cigarettes.'

Clive was some time showing up. Jasper started barking before he reached the door. Frances 'felt a pang of envy as I watched him snuggle close to his master and receive an affectionate caress, which doubtless I would have had under different circumstances.' Clive managed to exchange a few words with her when he slipped into the kitchen where she was making more tea. She saw him the following day at lunch. He had some news. He had just been given command of a squadron based at a neighbouring station. The reason for his promotion, he explained, was that its CO had failed to return the previous night. He 'announced this horrifying news with about as much emotion as if he'd been telling me that cabbages grew in the kitchen garden.' That night he took her to a New Year's Eve dance at his new station. After midnight chimed and 'Auld Lang Syne' had been sung, Clive grabbed her arm to lead her away to a quieter spot. Suddenly, they came face to face with a couple whose faces were familiar. It was one of the couples they had run into at the Pike and Eel just before Christmas. 'How they must have been waiting for this opportunity and how quickly they came to the point. He wore that "it's for your own good" expression on his face, and she was smugly silent. "Hallo Buck, Happy New Year," called Clive, as completely happy and carefree as I had ever known him. I felt wonderfully pleased with life and we had promised each other that a separation of five miles would do nothing to stop our relationship.

'"Same to you," answered Buck . . . "What a pity your wife isn't here, Clive, we four could have had some fun together," he said turning to his wife and regarding me as if I were the direct descendant of a slug.' Clive looked panic-stricken. The 'expression on his face was terrible; he looked like a caged animal looking around frantically for some escape as he mumbled excuses for his wife's absence.'

That explained everything. Frances's first reaction was to walk away but she found herself being steered outside and into Clive's car. They drove for a while in silence. There were tears in his eyes. Then they parked up and he began a long rambling speech, half a defence of his actions and half a declaration of love. He had been married to his wife for only three years but they had already drifted apart. Frances, to her surprise, found herself looking for reasons to believe him. She should, she knew, stop it now, painful though that might be. On the other hand, she reasoned, if she did so, 'he'll soon find someone else.' She told him, somewhat to his surprise, that she would accept the situation and 'be to you what I've been in the past, something for you to hold on to, to live for, and to come back to until we can see another way out.'

Clive had a few days to settle business on the base before he moved up the road. The story was now in the open. Frances went to his leaving lunch which was supposed to be a stag affair, and endured some knowing banter from the CO. She drove with him to the new station, a pre-war base with well-built roads, laid-out gardens and brick buildings with hot water and central heating.

He left her at the WAAF office while he talked to the station commander. When he returned his mood had darkened. Both of them realized that the story was over.

> The coming days were bound to be different; things would not be the same again, no matter how hard we tried. For one thing we would not be bumping into each other several times a day in the casual way we had . . .

I would not know if Clive was flying and I wouldn't be able to see him when he came back . . . Clive's entire position had changed. He had become what was often termed 'A Little Tin God' . . . everything he did and said would be criticized and heard by the whole station. His private life would surely come into the limelight too, especially if there was something like an 'affair' attached to it. This would be unearthed, examined and enlarged by all who indulged in . . . gossip.

Frances decided to go to London for a few days to see her parents. Clive phoned the day after she returned and that evening they went to the pictures. Afterwards he drove her back to her quarters and he sat by the fire while she cooked an omelette on the electric stove. The girls she shared with were absent. Mary, the senior officer, was on leave and Leslie was unlikely to bother them when she returned. But the warm domestic scene was interrupted when Leslie did show her face. She disapproved of liaisons with married men. Frances was unrepentant, telling her, 'I've fallen in love with him and at the moment I don't give a damn if he has ten wives.' Now Leslie had come to deliver a warning. She had been talking to the CO and he had asked what time the WAAF officers ejected their male visitors from their quarters. She replied that they were always out by 11 p.m., as the rules dictated. The CO seemed unconvinced. He hinted that he might spring a surprise visit on the girls one night, to check that the regulations were being obeyed.

It seemed to Frances like a bad omen. The next day, however, her doubts evaporated when Clive called to remind her of a mess party in a nearby aerodrome to which they had both been invited. They spent a 'very happy if somewhat boisterous evening.' She danced with a few old admirers but noticed how quickly they slipped away afterwards as soon as Clive appeared to take her off to the buffet or for a drink. She glimpsed, for a moment 'how lonely and miserable I would be without him.'

Almost immediately the premonition became real. The morning after the dance she was summoned to the CO's office. She was told that she was to leave the base immediately for a new post at Bomber Command HQ in High Wycombe. There was no attempt to disguise the reasons for the order. It was her relationship with Clive. News of it had 'reached the ears of senior WAAF officers who considered it "undesirable".' She would be allowed to say goodbye to Clive. After that she was not to communicate with him in any way. The CO claimed to have tried to stop the posting. But, in the circumstances, he told her, he felt it was probably for the best. At least it would give Clive a chance to mend his marriage. The last meeting was too painful for Frances to record. The next six months for her were the unhappiest time of her four years in the WAAF. She 'missed Clive unbearably, and the busy, warm atmosphere of life on a bomber station.' At HQ she 'worked mainly with women and social life was almost nil.' Eventually the misery came to an end. She was posted to RAF Scampton where she met the man who was to become her husband. When love and war collided, the interests of the RAF were always going to prevail. And in the spring of 1944, Bomber Command was as busy as it had ever been.

16

D-Day Diversion

The approach of *Overlord* gave Bomber Command a new purpose. Its efforts up until the spring of 1944 had been titanic but they had failed to achieve the promised results. The attack on Berlin had been the ultimate test of Harris's theories. But the Big City, though bleeding, was still functioning and the spirit of its citizens was bruised but not crushed.

Bombing France was less dangerous than bombing Germany and the switch to preparing the ground for D-Day was welcomed by the crews. Their primary task was to disrupt the transportation links that would play a vital part in shifting enemy troops around the battlefield once the invasion began. This meant a radical change in their *modus operandi*. They were now engaged in widespread attacks on a number of objectives rather than a concentration of force against one. This change of tactics created problems for the German defences, and particularly the night-fighters. Bombers flying in a stream up to 150 miles long, six miles wide and two miles deep made a big, vulnerable target. Once the radar had located them, the interceptors could harry them almost at their leisure, knowing they had little to fear from their guns. The Luftwaffe now had to juggle its resources to deal with several diverse threats. They had less time to get into an attacking position, for the bomber bases were much closer to the targets they wanted to bomb.

The new conditions meant a significant reduction in losses. Between April and June, Bomber Command flew operations on fifty-seven nights and lost 525 aircraft. This was a considerable improvement on the 1,128 machines, almost all four-engined bombers, destroyed during the Battle of Berlin period when only 18 per cent more sorties were flown. Even when Bomber Command resumed its onslaught on Germany it would never again face such dreadful odds as it had endured during the winter of 1943/44.

Harris thought of the new work as a diversion, but one that he accepted was both inevitable and desirable. The Casablanca and Pointblank directives of a year before had given the combined American and British bomber forces the job of creating conditions for the main Allied invasion of Europe to begin. Harris had largely ignored the spirit of Pointblank. He had chosen to misinterpret the instruction to concentrate on a system of precise war industry targets, in particular both the equipment and infrastructure of the German air force. Instead, he persisted with bombing towns.

As *Overlord* approached, this contrariness could no longer be tolerated. To obtain the tightest possible co-ordination between the key elements in the operation, Bomber Command was placed under the direction of the Supreme Allied Commander, General Dwight Eisenhower. For once Harris was subordinated to an authority that was impervious to his bluster and he came to heel with surprising grace. He may also have felt the need to behave following the manifest failure of the Berlin campaign, which had threatened to destroy his command.

The principal objective was the dislocation of the railways of northern Europe and in particular northern France. Harris doubted whether his men had the ability to deliver the concentration and accuracy needed for the attacks to be effective but he went ahead and ordered their execution. They began in March with raids on marshalling yards at important junctions like Le Mans, Amiens, Trappes and Courtrai. Between the beginning of April and the end of June, a hundred major operations were flown. There were constant attacks against any target that could interfere with the success of the landing. They included the flying bomb launching sites which threatened the forming-up areas across the Channel, coastal batteries, the synapses of the enemy signalling system, ammunition dumps and military camps. For a while German place names were heard only occasionally at briefings. Between April and D-Day there were only twelve major attacks and eight minor ones on German targets. Instead, to the satisfaction of the crews, they were now directed to specific targets which had an obvious bearing on the progress of the war.

The activities of Bomber Command were, for the time being at least, in tune with American perceptions as to how the air war should be fought. Having entered the war first, the RAF naturally assumed that its methods were the best but the pre-war theories about bombing practice had rapidly been chewed up in the jaws of experience. Commanders had begun the campaign in the belief that bombers, flying in disciplined formations, could defend themselves with their onboard armament. According to this thinking fighter escorts, although desirable, were not essential. There were none available in any case. At the start of the war, designers had yet to come up with a machine with the range and speed to accompany and defend bomber fleets on long-distance raids.

The myth of self-protection had been shattered in the winter of 1939 and spring of 1940 when German fighters, flak and radar made it impossible for Bomber Command to operate in daylight. Instead it sought the cover of darkness. Its survival depended on invisibility, and developing equipment and techniques to outwit the German defences. The Germans in turn devised counter-measures and refined their aeroplanes to deal with each new threat, culminating in the high point of their success, the introduction of the radar-equipped night-fighter.

The RAF tried to pass on its hard-won tactical wisdom to the USAAF. The Americans were reluctant to listen. In the first place they had little faith in the value of of night bombing. They had some evidence of its lack of success through the reports of professional observers, the American diplomats and journalists who stayed in Germany until the United States entered the war in December 1941. By the time the first units of the Eighth Air Force arrived in Britain in 1942 they already had in place the foundations of a bomber fleet which they believed fitted their strategic vision of how an air war should be conducted.

The Americans' preference was, as they constantly reiterated, for precision bombing carried out in daylight. The emphasis they placed on this formula seemed at times a reproach to Bomber Command. The implication was that American methods were superior to the indiscriminate nocturnal blunderings of the British. The American approach was meant to be cleaner, both militarily and morally. In daylight, the theory ran, they could see what they were doing. In addition their bombers were equipped with the Norden bombsight, which was believed to be marvellously accurate. With all these advantages they stood a far better chance of hitting their targets and missing innocent civilians than their amiable, but to American minds, misguided allies. This belief turned out to be something of an illusion, though it sustained American thinking for some time.

As for the risks of operating in daylight, the USAAF planners discounted the British experiences of the early war. Their two main aircraft, the B17 Flying Fortress and the Liberator, were well equipped with heavy .50 machine guns firing from five turrets. In theory at least, a tidily-held formation should enable the gunners to provide a field of fire of such breadth, height and depth to deter all but the most foolhardy German fighter pilot. To add to their defences, they had the support of fighter escorts which began arriving in numbers in Britain in the autumn of 1943. Their reach though, was limited. The Lightnings and Thunderbolts could not range more than 300–400 miles from base if they were forced to weave or to dogfight.

The Americans were intent on hitting specific targets which had a direct and unarguable bearing on the Germans' ability to prosecute the war. That meant factories, oil installations, ports, submarine pens and the like. Operations began in the late summer of 1942. Initially they concentrated on objectives in France but in January 1943 moved into Germany itself. In keeping with Pointblank, their particular intention was to fatally weaken German air power by destroying aircraft while they were still in production. This ambition was undiminished by the fact that the aircraft industry was widely dispersed and its factories hard to find. By the late summer they were suffering severe losses but remained convinced that they were nonetheless inflicting serious damage on the enemy. On 17 August

An early version of the American P-51 long-range escort.

1943, the anniversary of the beginning of operations from England, two large groups of Fortresses set off to bomb the Messerschmitt factory at Regensburg and the ball-bearing factories at Schweinfurt, a particular favourite with those who believed in surgical operations to cut out vital components of the machinery of war. The 147 aircraft from Fourth Bomb Wing heading for Regensburg were to carry on after their attack to land in bases in North Africa. Those from First Wing bound for Schweinfurt were to return to England. The two groups were supposed to leave together in order to divert the attentions of the waiting fighters. First Wing were held up by thick ground mist. The delay meant that the chance that the enemy would be confused by the two-pronged assault was lost. The first group crossed the Dutch coast at 10 a.m. in formations of twenty-one. There was barely a cloud in the sky. Two clusters of Thunderbolt fighters met up with them over Holland to provide a patchy escort for as long as their petrol supply allowed.

The ordeal started when Focke-Wulf fighters began attacking the unprotected tail of the stream, south-east of Brussels. At the German frontier, the fuel indicator needles of the Thunderbolts were dipping ominously and they were obliged to turn back. As the Fortresses headed into Germany the attack began in earnest. Relay after relay of Focke-Wulfs and Messerschmitt 109s drove into the formations, often in head-on attacks and one by one the bombers began to burn and fall. An observer riding with the 100th group reported later that 'the sight was fantastic; it surpassed fiction.' A historian of the Eighth Air Force described the battle moving over Germany, 'its course marked by flashes, flames, smoke, the debris of disintegrating aircraft, parachutes and men; the noise indescribable . . .'[1] This running combat went on for ninety minutes. By the time the Americans reached Regensburg seventeen Fortresses had been destroyed. Nonetheless the force, led by the famously aggressive Colonel Curtis Le May, still managed to attack with exemplary determination and precision. On arrival in Africa, Le May cabled London: 'Objective believed totally destroyed.' The belief was justified. The result turned out to be even better than he imagined. Unbeknown to him, the bombs had obliterated a workshop housing the fuselage jigs for a secret jet fighter.

First Wing had met equally ferocious opposition. From Antwerp to Schweinfurt and back it was under continuous attack from a swarm of fighters vectored in from virtually every Luftwaffe fighter base in the West. The bombers beat on with extraordinary bravery and achieved respectable results. The cost of the operation, though, was shockingly high. At the end thirty-six B-17s and 370 crew were missing. Many other aircraft limped home with dead and wounded aboard.

Altogether sixty aircraft were lost. This was more than double the previous high of twenty-six recorded in a raid the previous 13 June. Was it worth it? The claims made by the air gunners suggested it might be. They reported downing an astonishing 288 enemy aircraft. This figure almost matched the entire Luftwaffe force involved in the interception. The figure was later reduced to 148, still an impressive score and one which some senior officers appeared to find credible. The true figure, it emerged later, was twenty-seven.[2]

The Schweinfurt factories continued to exert a fatal attraction for the Eighth Air Force planners. Destroying ball-bearing production would not only do fundamental damage to the German military machine. It would also vindicate the air chiefs' claims. On 14 October 1943 the bombers went back in an operation that was to settle the question of whether air operations could continue as conceived.

A force of about 300 set off from bases in central and eastern England. The German fighters waited for their escorts to drop away before attacking in earnest. Then the assaults were relentless all the way to and from the target. The attack was a success. Three of the five main plants were hit heavily. But so too were the bombers, especially as they ran for home. At the final count, sixty aircraft were lost and five others crashed in England as a result of damage sustained in the fight.

The operation was nonetheless hailed as a significant victory. Portal was particularly fulsome. It could well, he claimed, 'have saved countless lives by depriving the enemy of a great part of his means of resistance.'[3] The lives that were demonstrably saved by the operation, as it turned out, were those of American airmen as a result of the change of tactics that the incident had brought about. The overall losses of 14 October were nearly twice the figure of 5 per cent of the force, considered as the maximum that could be sustained for a protracted period before operations became too costly to endure. The Americans could not mount similar operations on a regular basis without a catastrophic loss of both effectiveness and morale. Despite the extravagant claims of the gunners it was clear that their efforts were having no appreciable effect on eroding the means and the will of the Luftwaffe to resist. Inevitably, as any professional and motivated air force could be expected to do, the Germans had devised tactics that blunted the formations' ability to defend themselves. They had learned to concentrate on one formation at a time, unleashing salvoes of rockets from beyond the range of the American guns so that the pilots were unable to hold station, then swooping in on the dispersed components.

There was clearly an urgent need to think again. In the space of six days 148 American bombers had failed to return home. It was obvious that until they gained control of the air and succeeded in dominating the enemy's skies, they would never achieve their strategic goals.

The American air force staff, despite its proud modernity, was sometimes afflicted by stiffness of thought and an arrogant outlook. Its members could, on occasion, be as mulish as the most conservative French or British general of the First World War, preferring to reinforce failure than to admit error or the fallibility of the rule book. The obvious thing to consider, when it became clear that the British warnings about daylight operations were well-founded, was whether to follow their example and shift to bombing by night. Indeed the idea was explored tentatively in the late summer of 1943 when 422 Bomb Squadron carried out a handful of night operations alongside the RAF. But the experiment was discontinued. The American crews had been prepared for only one task. A shift from daylight to darkness would mean enormous upheaval and the effective discontinuation of the American effort for an unacceptable period. Portal reckoned the process would take two years. The American crews were highly trained in the formation tactics that sustained day bombing. But that was of little use at night. What was needed primarily was an ability to navigate in the dark, which few American navigators possessed. In the absence of that option, intensive thought was given to the question of how the bombers could be better protected. The need for an effective long-range fighter escort was more obvious than ever.

The Americans' occasional inflexibility was counterbalanced by a redeeming national virtue. Faced with a crisis, they could react effectively and fast. In this case the hunt for the solution was greatly helped by the application of British technical ingenuity. Underlying the transformation in the Allies' fortunes was the arrival of a new aeroplane which completely altered the nature of the air war. This was the long-range fighter which could accompany the bomber fleets all the way to distant targets and escort them home again. The value of the long-range escort had long been understood but until the winter of 1943 the technology was not available to provide one.

In the history of aviation no single aircraft tipped the strategic balance as effectively as the P-51 Mustang. Its arrival on the battle-field resuscitated the Eighth Air Force and accelerated the Luftwaffe's terminal decline. The aircraft began life in the most unpromising circumstances. It was designed by North American Aviation in 1940 in answer to a request from the RAF's Air Commission who were desperate to obtain aircraft from any quarter. Britain bought a number. The Americans, whose needs were less urgent, were unim-pressed however. The Mustang was slowish and its performance fell off sharply at altitude. Its optimal height was only 15,000 feet where it strained to reach 366 mph. By the time it arrived at the RAF in November 1941 the aircraft shortage was over and it was shunted off to army co-operation duties. There the Mustang's undistinguished operational career might have ended but for the diligence of some Rolls-Royce engineers. The problem, they decided, was a lack of power. As an experiment they installed their own Merlin 61 engines in five aircraft and put them through air tests. The initial results were unpromising. They decided to persist, modifying the airframe and trying again with a new power plant, a Packard-Merlin hybrid. This technological cross-breeding worked brilliantly. The humdrum genes produced a machine which shattered the existing supposition that long-range and a sparkling peformance could not be combined in the same machine.

The new Mustang went faster as it got higher. At 15,000 feet it could only manage 375 mph. At 35,000 feet it could reach 440 mph. This made it quicker than both the Focke-Wulf 190 and the Messerschmitt 109. Even more importantly, it could turn more tightly than its two main adversaries, thus giving it a crucial edge in the most important manoeuvre in dogfighting. But speed and nimbleness were of limited use without range. By September 1943 Thunderbolts fitted with drop tanks were covering 1,500 miles in test flights, with the extra weight of fuel only marginally reducing performance. This was soon stretched yet further so that by the spring of 1944 they could accompany the Fortresses and Liberators from their bases in the Midlands and East Anglia deep into eastern Germany.

After Schweinfurt, Mustangs began to pour off the production lines. They started operations with the Eighth Air Force in December 1943. Thanks to their arrival, the effectiveness of the short-range fighters was also substantially increased. Until now the Luftwaffe could, if it chose, ignore the presence of Lightnings and Thunderbolts. It was simply a matter of waiting for their fuel to run low and their noses to turn homewards. Then the German fighters had the freedom of their own skies. Now the luxury of waiting for their prey to come to them, unescorted, had vanished. The aerial front line was pushed forward and henceforth they were forced to attack wherever they could, exposing themselves to the attentions of the conventional Allied fighters. The demands the new circumstances imposed also meant that German night-fighter units were now landed with the extra duty of going to the support of their daytime colleagues.

The extraordinary difference the Mustangs would make to the balance of the air war became apparent in a few days in February 1944, which became known as Big Week. Between 20 and 25 February the Eighth Air Force carried out thirteen major strikes against fifteen centres of the German air industry. The 1,000 bombers had with them an almost equal number of fighter escorts. Faced with the destruction of their infrastructure, the Luftwaffe, as General Carl Spaatz, commander of the American strategic air forces in Europe had calculated, had no choice but to come up to meet them. In the fighting, the Americans claim to have destroyed more than 600 German interceptors for losses on their side of 210 bombers and thirty-eight fighters. These figures were of course extremely unreliable but whatever the precise details one thing was undeniable. American operations may not have devastated the German aircraft industry which showed astonishing resilience in continuing to produce machines. But the punishment they inflicted on the existing machines and the men flying in them could not be sustained. The grinding attrition continued through March as the Eighth expanded its operations to Berlin. The American bombers suffered heavily in the process but the huge increase in the number of crews and aircraft pouring into the theatre meant the losses could be more easily absorbed. After Big Week the Luftwaffe's daytime ascendancy was finished and the force in general gradually and inexorably lost control of the skies.

Looking back, General Joseph 'Beppo' Schmid, who commanded the fighter group 1 Jagdkorps from September 1943 to November 1944, recorded that as early as March 'the numeric superiority of enemy fighters had become so great that fighting became most difficult for our own units.' The supply of aircraft and men could not keep up with the losses so that 'the alacrity or fighting spirit of the [airmen] was generally below the average.' Germany was fighting an air war on three fronts, in Russia and the Mediterranean as well as Western Europe, with limited and declining resources. The Luftwaffe pilots were courageous and highly motivated but they were often poorly trained compared with their Allied counterparts. Many of their casualties were caused by crashes. The Luftwaffe General Adolf Galland calculated that in the first quarter of 1944, more than 1,000 pilots were lost from the day-fighter force including some their finest. He concluded that 'each incursion of the enemy is costing us some fifty aircrews. The time has come when our weapon is in sight of collapse.'[4]

The success of the Mustangs raised the question of whether Bomber Command should follow the Americans' example. By switching to daylight bombing the RAF could benefit from the air superiority established by the American escorts and reinforce it with their own short-range fighters. The Air Staff thought seriously about this dramatic change of course. Harris, however, was opposed to the idea. The new American methods retained the tight formation and the defensive field of fire as the basis of its tactics. The great advance was that now each group had the additional protection of a phalanx of aggressive, free-ranging fighters buzzing around it ready to swoop on any enemy aircraft that dared to approach.

Harris argued that the system only worked because of the higher operational ceiling of the American aircraft, which allowed them both to hold station and avoid the worst of the German ground artillery. The British bombers were different. Even the easy-handling Lancasters were incapable of keeping formation at heights above nineteen thousand feet. At that altitude they would be vulnerable to flak and any savings gained from the protection offered by the fighter escort would be cancelled out by losses from ground fire. In any case, if such an important decision was implemented, the preparations needed would mean it would be a very long time before it started producing results. The arguments now seem glib and flimsy. No effort was made to put his assertion to the test. Far greater difficulties had been encountered and overcome. Harris may not have set Bomber Command on its original course. But once established, he followed it relentlessly and distrusted ideas that seemed to take it in a different direction. The shift from night to day was far too radical a change for him to accept without protest. Inevitably, he came up with some suggestions of his own.

His solution was to establish during the hours of darkness the same degree of air superiority that the Americans had achieved by day. Harris had been appealing for a force of long-range night-fighters to support his command since the summer of 1943 but had been consistently turned down by the Air Staff. Harris believed that Mosquitoes could do the same job as the American escorts and asked that ten squadrons of them should be supplied to Bomber Command. In April 1944, he was allowed three. They proved to be far less effective than their American counterparts. In the seventeen months from December 1943 to the end of the war, the fighter squadrons of 100 Group, which escorted Bomber Command, destroyed less than 270 enemy aircraft. Equipment was part of the problem. The onboard radar they carried had difficulty tracking any aircraft and when it did, could not distinguish between friend or foe.

The Mosquito was many things but it was not a long-range escort fighter. The absence of such a machine from the RAF's front-line force was due, in part at least, to the obstinacy of Portal. From the start of the war he had stuck to his view that stamina could only be increased at the expense of performance and agility. Once a long-range fighter met its German short-range opponent, the German was bound to win. The Americans had tried to persuade him otherwise, even modifying some Spitfires so they could fly the Atlantic. Portal's usually agile mind was unmoved. Pressure to switch to day bombing slackened but it never went away. But in the spring of 1944, the debate was shunted aside by the approach of D-Day.

In March Bomber Command began preparatory operations in France. The targets were small compared to those that it was used to attacking in Germany, and often lightly defended. The emphasis now was on avoiding civilian casualties. Churchill the Francophile was particularly distressed at the thought of spilling French blood, which he feared might 'smear the good name of the Royal Air Force across the world.' But try as they might to spare the innocent, it could not always be done. The civilian death toll proved tragically the argument that even with the best intentions and the greatest care, in a bombing war non-combatants inevitably died.

On the night of 9 April, 239 aircraft, most of them Halifaxes, arrived over Lille, an important road and rail crossroads in northern France. Their mission was to destroy the Lille-Délivrance goods station. There was a full moon. The bombs devastated the railway complex, destroying most of the wagons lying in the sidings and tearing up the tracks. But they also fell in the narrow streets housing the *cheminots* who worked on the railways, which lined the yards. The bloodshed was on the scale inflicted in an area attack, with 456 dead and many wounded. In the district of Lomme, 5,000 houses were destroyed or damaged. To those searching through the smoking rubble for loved ones the drone of the bombers overhead did not seem like the sound of liberation. Less than ten days later another sizeable raid was mounted on marshalling yards at Noisy-Le-Sec. Again great damage was done to the complex but again friendly civilians paid for the success with 464 killed and 370 injured.

Despite these horrible but inevitable mistakes, the crews felt uplifted by the work they were doing. The prospect of the invasion cheered everyone. An end, no matter how remote, was at last in sight. Now they really could start to believe that each mission accelerated victory. Their bombs would help to liberate France and save the lives of many of their own soldiers. As the casualty figures declined and the number of operations carried out without loss grew, their hopes rose that they might be there to celebrate victory.

The operations they were engaged in reminded them of why they had joined. There were some spectacular successes that suggested that Bomber Command, for so long a blunt weapon, was at last evolving into a sharp instrument of efficient and useful destruction. On the night of 5/6 April, 144 Lancasters of 5 Group attacked and completely destroyed an aircraft factory at Toulouse. The accuracy of the attack was attributed to the precision of the marking which for the first time had been carried out by a Mosquito flying at low level. The pilot was Leonard Cheshire who had been applying his innovative intelligence and considerable energy to improving bombing accuracy. The problem at this stage was less with bomb-aiming than with marking. Much of the latter was being carried out by Mosquitoes equipped with the *Oboe* blind-bombing radar device, which told the pilot where the target indicator should be dropped. This was an advance on earlier methods but still far from infallible. Cheshire's idea was to cast the Mosquito in yet another role. Using its great speed and nimbleness it would be possible, he claimed, to fly in very low and drop the marker by sight alone, eschewing radar and relying only on the bombsight.

At Toulouse he put his theory to the test. He and his co-pilot Flying Officer Pat Kelly made two passes over the factory before releasing red spot markers. Lancaster crews higher in the sky dropped more indicators, which now burned brightly from the heart of the target. The main force then went in, demolishing or heavily damaging nearly all the buildings in the target area. Even with all the care and skill this was not a surgical strike. Bombs struck about a hundred houses near the factory killing twenty-two.

These successes did not come without cost. On the night of 3 May, a force of 346 Lancasters lead by Mosquitoes went to bomb a German military camp near the village of Mailly, south of Châlons-en-Champagne. The target was well marked by Cheshire but the order for the main force to attack was drowned out by an American forces broadcast and in the delay caused by the confusion German fighters arrived. In the ensuing carnage forty-two Lancasters were lost.

As *Overlord* opened, Bomber Command's might was displayed in the southern skies of England. On the night of 5/6 June, the inhabitants of the south of England looked up to watch an apparently seamless carpet of bombers rolling overhead towards the beaches and cliffs of Normandy. Harris had amassed more than a thousand aircraft, Lancasters, Halifaxes and Mosquitoes, laden with bombs to pulverize the coastal batteries sunk into the dunes behind the tranquil, low-built fishing villages that for centuries had managed to avoid Europe's swirling wars. The weather favoured Hitler. Only two of the ten targets, Ouistreham and La Pernelle, were free of cloud. The rest were bombed blind using *Oboe*. In the course of the night 5,000 tons of bombs were dropped, the greatest quantity in the war so far. A thousand bombers were in the air again the following night smashing railway and road junctions to prevent the Germans rushing troops to the beach-heads.

So it went on. The destructive power of the Allies was enhanced by the deployment of a new super-bomb, the Tallboy, another invention of Professor Barnes Wallis whose bouncing bomb had made the Dams Raid possible. It weighed 12,000 pounds and was sleekly designed to drive deep into the earth before exploding, creating an earthquake effect that produced a crater that needed 5,000 tons of earth to fill. On the night of 8/9 June 617 Squadron, led by Leonard Cheshire, set off to attack a railway tunnel near Saumur, in the Loire valley. A German Panzer force was expected to pass through heading towards the Normandy beach-head from its garrison in the south. The area was marked by flares by four Lancasters, then Cheshire and two other outstanding master bombers, Squadron Leader David Shannon and Flight Lieutenant Gerry Fawke, dived in low to place their red spot markers at the mouth of the tunnel. The subsequent bombing was reasonably accurate. The reconnaissance photographs show two direct hits on the railway lines that gouged out enormous craters in the cutting leading to the tunnel. Even greater devastation was caused by a bomb which speared through the roof of the tunnel entrance, bringing down an avalanche of rock and dirt. This took a major effort to clear and the progress of the Panzers to Normandy was, for the time being, halted.

The role of the British and American air forces was crucial to the success of *Overlord*. In the space of a few months Bomber Command had gone from the wretched and harrowing business of pounding cities to the cleaner work of destroying an army in the field. For once they were dropping bombs on an enemy that was wearing uniform. More and more, they were operating in daylight. Between the invasion and the middle of August, 17,580 out of the command's 46,824 sorties were outside the hours of darkness.

Their activities transformed the battlefield. On 18 June they successfully carried out a huge attack on five villages east of Caen which lay across the British line of advance. Twelve days later at Villers-Bocage they obliterated a crucial road junction through which two Panzer divisions were expected to pass on their way to launching a counterattack at the point in the line where the British and American armies met. As a result, the German operation was abandoned. Offering close support to the men on the ground carried inevitable dangers. Confusion, inaccuracy and human error combined to create some black incidents when British and American bombs fell on Allied troops. But given the colossal scale of the enterprise, perhaps the real surprise was that there were not more of them.

The crews now felt an engagement with the battlefield that they had never experienced before. On 30 July, Ken Newman set off to bomb six German positions in the Villers-Bocage-Caumont area which were holding up the American advance. He was forced down to 2,000 feet to get below the cloud. The low altitude made him nervous, and the fact that 'the twenty-four of us from Wickenby were all trying to get into the same small airspace at the same time and I had to keep moving the aircraft around to avoid a collision.' But then the markers went down and he witnessed a phenomenon which he 'had never seen before, or ever saw again. We were so low that I was able to see the pressure wave of every exploding bomb – a bright red ring expanding rapidly outwards like ripples on the surface of the water.' Newman decided to risk staying low to witness the spectacle and the navigator and wireless operator came forward to share the experience. It was 'exciting to see the hundreds of Allied tanks, their crews waving madly at us . . . I waggled our wings in acknowledgement.' At that moment 'we all felt that we had done something to help our Army colleagues in Normandy and wished them every good fortune.'[5]

Despite the care taken over civilian casualties the bloodshed continued. On one particularly appalling occasion, the catastrophe was due to incompetence rather than accident. On 5 September, Bomber Command was sent to Le Havre. The retreating Germans had left garrisons in several Channel ports with orders to hold them for as long as they could stand and fight. When Harry Yates and his crew heard that 75 Squadron were on the raid their first reaction was relief. They had expected to be briefed for Dortmund, a particularly daunting target in their experience. By comparison 'a brief excursion to occupied France was a cakewalk.'

They were further cheered by the assurance that the raid 'would trigger the liberation of Le Havre and save the lives of countless British soldiers.' The local population had been warned by leaflet drops to vacate the town. The only ones underneath their bombs would be the diehard German soldiers. Later Yates was to reflect on the 'total trust we put in the facts as they were presented to us. I doubt if anybody had a single insubordinate thought about them or about the safety of the local populace. Our competence did not extend to such matters. That was the preserve of high-flying staff officers at Bomber Command and the Group HQs.'

The operation went off smoothly. The bombs fell with remarkable accuracy. In the Plough and Harrow, the Mepal local, that night Yates and his crew all 'thought the same. It was a job well done. We wouldn't be going back.'[6]

It fact the intelligence had been disastrously wrong. Few Germans were left in the target area. Much worse, the French population were concentrated in the old part of town, the district in which most of the 6,000 bombs that were dropped fell. Three thousand men, women and children died.

As well as their contribution to the success of the Normandy landings the crews were also helping to make the Home Front safer. Throughout the high summer they flew missions against V1 flying bomb sites and stores, reducing the Germans' ability to bombard London and other British cities. The sites were small and hard to hit and despite the enormous expenditure of effort the Germans still managed to launch bombs in significant numbers long after D-Day. By 15 July, 2,579 had fallen on England, about half of them on London. The determination of the crews, British and American, to stop them was measured by the casualties. About 3,000 airmen were killed in attacks on V-weapon targets. Leonard Cheshire's last operational mission was against a site at Mimoyecques on 6 July. After that he was ordered to take a rest, along with three other leading 617 Squadron officers, all of them veterans of the Dams Raid.

They were withdrawing from a battlefield that was becoming decreasingly dangerous for airmen. As the Allied beach-head widened, German day-fighters faded from the Normandy skies. On some days major operations on land and in the air proceeded without a German aircraft being seen. Bomber Command continued to suffer casualties. Flak was still lethal, especially over the ports. Ralph Briars, a gunner with 617 Squadron, was happy to note that there were no fighters near Le Havre when they went to drop Tallboys on the E-boat pens on 14 June. 'Target quiet until a few minutes before dropping,' he wrote in his diary. 'Then they let loose bags of light and medium flak . . . as bomb left, flak hit starboard inner engine and top turret, gunner OK, engine had to be feathered.' The danger, he recorded with satisfaction, was worth it. 'U-boat pens, twenty-five feet thick, were hit. Good bombing.'

There were still night-fighters to worry about. During a number of operations mounted against synthetic oil plants in Germany during June, July and August, the normal levels of losses obtained. But overall the trend was heartening. During the period the casualty rate fell to a level that the crews would have considered trifling six months before. Only 1.6 per cent of the force dispatched were lost. Nonetheless, that still amounted to 727 aircraft.

Germany had fallen to the back of the minds of the Bomber Boys during their welcome French diversion. Only one major operation had been launched against a German city, when Stuttgart was laid waste in three nights in late July. But as the nights lengthened and the Allies moved eastwards, the respite drew to a close. Once again Bomber Command turned back to its task of destroying the Reich.

17

Tallboys and Tirpitz

The great advances in methods and technology Bomber Command had achieved meant it was now able to strike targets that had previously eluded it. At the top of this list came the battleship *Tirpitz*. In the autumn of 1944, it was lying in Kaa Fjord in northern Norway, threatening the vital Arctic convoys that supplied the Soviet war effort. It was the most powerful warship in the Western Hemisphere. It could steam at nearly 40 mph and was armed with eight fifteen-inch guns, twelve six-inch guns and about eighty flak guns. In the course of the war it had survived more than thirty aerial attacks, largely thanks to its heavy armour, which seemed proof against the bombs of the Fleet Air Arm and RAF. In September, two squadrons, 9 and 617, were ordered to the Soviet Union to launch their attack. The trip made an interesting diversion for Ralph Briars, who left with 617 from Woodhall on the evening of 11 September, crossing Norway and Sweden and landing at an island airfield near Archangel. The crews were put up in an old river steamer. While they waited for suitable weather, they were fed on eggs and spam. Mutual incomprehension did not stop them making friends with the Russians, who swapped their cap badges for cigarettes. The authorities laid on entertainment for the three nights they were there; films, concerts and dances. The movies were earnest sagas with interminable battle scenes. The dances were better. The band could even play 'The Lambeth Walk'.

It was all very different from Woodhall Spa. They were looked after by local staff who lived in primitive huts around the airfield. The women were baffled by requests for hot water to shave in. The men spent much of the time playing cards, breaking off occasionally to supervise their wives' labour as they lugged away logs that floated down the river and chopped them up for firewood. The crews found the Russians 'kindly, generous hosts' and good sportsmen, too. They played football and the base side trounced them seven–nil.[1] On 15 September the weather cleared and the Lancasters, loaded with 12,000-pound Tallboy bombs and 'Johnny Walker' mines designed to blow up under the battleship's hull, took off. Tony Iveson remembered seeing the battleship clearly outlined, 'black against the cliff and the snowy mountains, but at the same time I saw the smoke generators start up all round the cliffs and by the time we got to bombing height there was just a sea of cloud beneath us.' The *Tirpitz* was badly damaged but still afloat. Two months later the RAF went back again. By now the *Tirpitz* had moved to the sheltered waters of Tromsø on the west coast of Norway. One attempt at the end of October was thwarted by low cloud. On 12 November they tried again. The thirty Lancasters of 9 and 617 squadrons that mounted the attack had been specially modified so as to be able to reach Tromsø from Lossiemouth in the north of Scotland. All armour plating as well as the mid-upper and front gun turrets were removed. They were also fitted with improved-performance Merlin T24 engines. Loaded with a Tallboy, they were just capable of making the twelve-and-a-half-hour round trip.

Tony Iveson and seventeen other 617 Squadron crews were set to take off at 2 a.m. They lined up while the hoarfrost was swept from the wings then 'off we went, up past the Orkneys and the Shetlands to about 65 north, seven east when we turned towards Norway.' As dawn came up he 'saw another Lancaster, silhouetted, so I formated on him.' It was his CO, James Tait. They headed for a lake that had been designated as the rendezvous point. As they circled it, 'Lancaster after Lancaster came out of the dark western sky and joined us.' Tait fired a Verey light, the signal for the last leg of the operation to begin and they set off for Tromsø. As morning broke 'it was absolutely gin clear. You could see for miles and below the white-topped mountains and the blue, blue sea.' Their first thought was that the conditions could not have been more perfect for bombing. Their second was that they were equally favourable for the German fighter unit that was believed to be stationed in the area.

When they arrived, the *Tirpitz* appeared to have been taken by surprise. There was no smokescreen. It was a Sunday and many of the crew were ashore. Iveson and the rest of 617 Squadron dropped their bombs within the space of four minutes from 15,000 feet. Their Lancasters were fitted with a new, computer-assisted bomb-sight. The Tallboys fell away 'on a beautiful, steady course. After the fourteenth bomb they weren't able to plot any more because there was so much smoke and muck around.' The accuracy was extraordinary. There were two direct hits on the battleship and three near misses. Within six minutes of the first strike she was on her side. Within eleven minutes she had capsized but was unable to sink completely because of the shallowness of the water. Nearly a thousand sailors were killed or injured out of the ship's company of 1,900 men, including the captain and most of the officers. The attackers suffered only one casualty. A Lancaster of 9 Squadron, which arrived shortly after 617, was damaged by flak but landed safely in Sweden. The German fighters that Iveson had feared took off too late to intercept the bombers.[2]

By now the Tallboys were a key element in Bomber Command's arsenal, allowing them to hit important strategic targets with devastating effect and at reduced risk. Unlike the 'cookie' which resembled a giant oil-drum, the Tallboy looked like a proper bomb. It was twenty-one feet long, made out of special steel casing, and was shaped aerodynamically with four stabilizer fins that made it spin on its axis as it fell. It was designed for deep penetration, so that on detonation it set up a ripple of shock waves that destroyed the target from its foundations.

Tallboys had been dropped first by Leonard Cheshire and David Shannon in their celebrated attack on the railway tunnel at Saumur during the Normandy landings. Their effectiveness was demonstrated again on the night of 23/24 September against the Dortmund–Ems canal, a vital waterway. The banks of both branches of the canal were breached and a six-mile stretch of it was drained. Most of the damage was done by bombs dropped by 617 Squadron. Ralph Briars took part in the raid and his diary entry for the night is a reminder that although the Luftwaffe was severely weakened

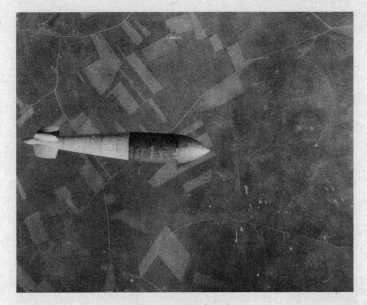

A Tallboy, seconds after release.

Bomber Command's operations were very far from being risk free. 'Had first shaking when two kites collided off coast,' he wrote in his diary. 'Queer things, red, green and yellow flares, enormous flak bursts, kites going down without combat – no tracer used by fighters, I guess. Spot fire just under cloud, had several tries to bomb, but it became covered just before release so we brought it back. Felt tired and shaken on return, curse the darkness.' Reading this entry many years later he thought he detected in it 'just a hint of bother'. It revealed, he suspected, the advent of 'the Twitch', which he had noticed in airmen who had been flying too long.[3] Fourteen Lancasters, more than 10 per cent of the force, failed to make it back from this operation.

By the end of 1944 the Allied airforces had achieved virtual mastery of the skies of Europe. But despite the efforts of the bombers against the German aircraft industry, it was still managing to function, and at a remarkably brisk pace. In September the production of single-engined fighters reached a new high. By the end of the year the overall number of aircraft had climbed to 3,300. As Germany by then had a much smaller area to defend, this force, in theory at least, could be used with more concentration and therefore with more effect.

These statistics disguised the hopeless situation facing the Luftwaffe. There was no shortage of aircraft. But there was a desperate lack of fuel to propel them and men to fly them. As summer faded, the shortage of petrol made a mockery of the abundance of equipment. In August 1944, Germany was still managing to meet 65 per cent of its aviation spirit needs. By February 1945 the figure had fallen to 5 per cent. Starved of fuel, ground down by relentless attrition, the Luftwaffe could no longer exert any control over the direction of events in the air or on the ground.

It seemed obvious that the Allies' air power would best be used in trying to turn off the fuel tap completely. This was how the Americans saw it. They had been bombing oil targets since March. Bomber Command also had dedicated much of its energy during the Normandy campaign to hitting synthetic oil plants in the Ruhr. Oil had been a favourite target of RAF planners since the start of the war, and continued to be until they were persuaded that the difficulty of finding and hitting installations and the losses this entailed outweighed the results. Now the tactical landscape held far fewer perils.

The new approach was spelled out in a directive of 25 September 1944. It listed, in order of priority, Bomber Command's targets. The first was the 'petroleum industry, with special emphasis on petrol (gasoline) including storage.' Next came the German rail, river and canal systems, followed by tank and lorry factories.

The emphasis on oil had the approval of Portal and the Air Staff. It did not please Harris, whose independence had been restored after Bomber Command was detached from Eisenhower's control in September. The new realities appeared to have done nothing to modify his belief that the continued bombing of cities was the fastest way to end the war. He had always derided the 'oily boys' who preached that cutting the fuel pipeline was the key to victory.

There had been many occasions when he had enjoyed the satisfaction of being able to point out that their theories, however logical, were easier to expound than to put into practice. Now the goal seemed within reach. Harris, though, remained deeply and aggressively sceptical.

He was, he recorded in his memoir, 'altogether opposed to this further diversion, which, as I saw it, would only prolong the respite which the German industrial cities had gained from the use of the bombers in a tactical role [i.e. in the Normandy campaign]. I did not think we had any right to give up a method of attack which was indisputably doing the enemy enormous harm, for the sake of prosecuting a new scheme the success of which was far from assured.' He admitted in retrospect that, as it turned out, the offensive against oil was a 'complete success', and shamelessly claimed credit on behalf of Bomber Command for its contribution to the result. Nonetheless, he was determined to have the last word. The advocates of the strategy may have been right, he argued, but they were right for the wrong reasons. At the time he had raised his objections, 'it was [not] reasonable . . . to expect that the campaign would succeed.' What the Allied strategists had done was to 'bet on an outsider, and it happened to win the race.'[4]

Like it or not, the oily boys had carried the argument. Harris hated losing, but he knew the advantages of a tactical withdrawal. He proceeded against a list of oil targets but managed by imaginative interpretation of the directive to carry on battering cities at the same time, achieving, he boasted, 'a destruction rate of two and a half a month'. He also maintained his aversion to day operations, even though they were now both effective and comparatively trouble-free, and seemed to order them only reluctantly.

The Luftwaffe, though apparently dying, was still capable of causing lethal damage with its last kicks. On 16 December the German army launched its desperate counter-offensive through the Ardennes. On New Year's Day 1945, the Luftwaffe made its contribution to the action. Somehow it scraped together more than 750 fighters and enough fuel to get them into battle. The operation was mounted in complete secrecy and there was astonishment when they arrived at seventeen Allied airfields in the Lowlands and France. They destroyed 150 aircraft and killed forty-six people, most of whom were working on the ground. It was an impressive act of defiance but in the long term achieved nothing. The German losses were disastrous; 270 aircraft lost and 260 aircrew killed. Adolf Galland regarded this as the last gasp of his beloved air force. 'The Luftwaffe received its death blow at the Ardennes offensive,' he wrote.[5]

Even before this catastrophe German aircraft were decreasingly seen in the skies. On their way to Cologne at the end of October 1944, Harry Yates and his crew in S-Sugar were startled to see an unfamiliar silhouette flash in front of them, climbing out of nowhere at an impossible speed and angle. It was an Me 262 jet, one of the few that the Luftwaffe managed to get airborne. This was the only visual sighting of any German aircraft by 75 Squadron in the forty-six sorties it had flown in the previous four days. The main enemy now was flak. Shortly before this encounter and just as they approached the target Yates watched the end of two aircraft ahead of him in the stream. 'One of them carved a fiery trail down into the cloud. There seemed to be a reasonable chance that one of them would get out. The other . . . took a direct hit in the bomb bay and in the blink of an eye was a ball of shocking white and orange, expanding violently outwards across a large area of sky and then petering out into a sickeningly slow drift to earth.' He looked away, reflecting that 'sometimes the cynical view was right. It was all a matter of luck. Every kite had its bomb doors open. One small splinter of flak hitting S-Sugar's cookie or incendiaries would bring the same end to us.'

As they went into the bombing run they 'entered a furious hailstorm of red-hot metal. An instant later there was an explosion between us, unseen but no distance away.' The aircraft convulsed and Yates felt something solid and fast-moving smash into it. The Perspex panel above the pilot's seat blew out, blasting freezing air through the fuselage. Yates felt a 'flood tide of fear'. The thing he dreaded was finally happening to him. But the Lancaster flew on unperturbed and Yates's pounding heart subsided.[6]

Bomber Command's work rate was extraordinary. In the last three months of 1944 it dropped 163,000 tons of bombs and would drop even more in 1945. This deluge would have been even heavier if the munitions could have kept up with demand. The thought, energy and sacrifice of the early years had produced a creation of terrifying power and efficiency. Harris was determined that it should go on being put to the use for which he believed it was intended.

Despite the 25 September directive, 53 per cent of Bomber Command's effort in the last three months of 1944 had gone into flattening cities. Oil targets accounted for 14 per cent while the rest was expended on railways and canals, enemy troops and fortifications and naval and other objectives. Some of the targets were old Bomber Command favourites. So far they had escaped total destruction. But now, in its new might, the RAF was returning to finally cross them off its list. On the night of 6/7 October it was Bremen's turn. It had been visited on the first night of the war when a handful of Whitley bombers scattered a harmless cargo of leaflets over its rooftops. It was attacked about seventy times thereafter and had been the objective of a 'thousand' raid. This time only 262 Lancasters took part, dropping 1,021 tons of bombs. What was left of Bremen's war industry went up in flames, including the two Focke-Wulf factories. Sixty-five people were killed and 766 wounded, a low figure that suggests that most people had fled. Bremen was effectively dead. The bombers had no need to go back again.

The name of Essen had once induced dread in the crews. Now they could attack it with virtual impunity and did so in two huge attacks thirty-six hours apart at the end of October. By now incendiaries did not always make up the bulk of the bomb loads. In some towns, it was reckoned that everything that could burn, had burned in previous raids and high explosive was more effective. By the time the raids were over, Essen had ceased to be an important centre of war production, though this was not the end of its ordeal.

These attacks were easy to justify. Germany had patently lost the war yet still could not bring itself to surrender. Every extra day meant more Allied casualties. The attacks on oil targets were proceeding but the beneficial results were not yet visible. Anything that persuaded Germans of the hopelessness of their situation was worth doing. In the Ruhr, which lay in the path of the Allied armies, dogged workers and their directors were continuing to try to make weapons for a struggle that had already been lost. Operation *Hurricane* was devised by the Allied planners to address that problem. Its purpose was spelled out in a directive of 13 October 1944 to Harris. It read: 'In order to demonstrate to the enemy in Germany generally the overwhelming superiority of the Allied Air Forces in this theatre . . . the intention is to apply within the shortest practical period the maximum effort of the Royal Air Force Bomber Command and the VIIIth United States Bomber Command against objectives in the densely populated Ruhr.' The object was, in the words of the official history, 'to cause mass panic, havoc and disorganization in the Ruhr Valley, to disrupt the immediate German front-line communications by driving the railheads back east of the Rhine and to demonstrate to the Germans the futility of further resistance.'

This was not intended to replace oil targets as the principal object of the American and British air forces' attentions. However it did mark a further advance in another plan which had been under consideration as the Allies pondered how to use their massive superiority to its best advantage.

Portal had asked the Air Staff in July 1944 for their thoughts on how the bombing war should proceed. They had ceased to believe that bombing on its own could create a decisive collapse of German morale. However a 'blow of catastrophic force' delivered at the right moment, and taken in conjunction with defeats on other fronts, might persuade the population that there was no further point in holding out. That right moment would only come when Germans generally believed that the Nazi system was collapsing and total defeat was imminent. The object of the attack would not be to destroy Germany entirely but to preserve what little remained. In other words, it was to hasten surrender rather than induce defeat. An orderly surrender would avert the risk of the breakdown of central military and civil authority with all the problems that would create for the invading Allies. The memorandum gave a cautiously optimistic appraisal of the effects of a 'catastrophic blow' against Berlin, which as the centre of government and the home of 5 per cent of the population was the obvious target. But it also suggested that 'immense devastation could be produced if the entire attack was concentrated on a single big town other than Berlin and the effect would be especially great if the town was one hitherto relatively undamaged.' This proposal, which became known as the *Thunderclap* plan, was passed on to the Chiefs of Staff. It was received unenthusiastically by their planners who did not feel it 'likely to achieve any worthwhile degree of success' at that time. They did, however, recommend that it should be placed before the Chiefs of Staff when conditions seemed more promising.

In the meantime Harris went about implementing *Hurricane*, starting with a massive raid on Duisburg. He put together more than a thousand bombers, accompanied by a fighter escort. The Americans sent 1,251 heavy bombers and 749 fighters to Cologne. They attacked during the day and saw not a single Luftwaffe fighter. That night yet another 1,000 RAF aircraft went back to Duisburg. The raids did not have the effect wished for by the *Hurricane* planners and the town would be bombed several times more before the war was ended.

Such was the wealth of Harris's resources that he could also mount an attack on Brunswick the same evening. This was the fifth raid on the town that year and there was no need of another. Bomber Command was running out of urban targets. Its attentions were now turned to places that had not previously seemed worth attacking. Until now Bonn, a small well-preserved town on the banks of the Rhine, had been left alone. It had no importance to the German war effort or to Allied plans. That changed when Air Vice-Marshal R. Harrison, the commander of 3 Group, requested permission to raid it. Some of the Lancasters in Harrison's force had been fitted with a new radar blind-bombing device called G-H, which in theory enabled bombing to continue even in the worst weather.

The conditions on 18 October were cloudy enough to test this proposition. Harrison sent 128 Lancasters to Bonn accompanied by

Mustang and Spitfire escorts. They flew in 'vics' of three, each formation headed by a G-H equipped aircraft. Only one German fighter was seen on the journey but its pilot prudently veered away. The raid was a success. It was an exaggeration to say, as one post-operational report did, that the attack 'practically wiped out the town'. But it had certainly done severe damage. The university and many public buildings were burned out. The house in which Beethoven lived and composed was saved by the heroism of its caretakers. Seven hundred houses were destroyed and many more damaged; 313 people were killed. The bomb damage was easy to assess. As Bonn had never been targeted before there was no previous wreckage to obscure the picture when the reconnaissance photographs came back. This, it was believed, was one of the reasons why it had been chosen.

Towns which presented any kind of threat or hindrance to the Allied advance were now in peril. Freiburg, on the banks of the upper Rhine near the French border, had never been attacked by the RAF before. It had no industry to speak of but was the site of a minor rail junction. At the pre-op briefing, Ken Newman and the rest of the crews were told that 'it had not previously been regarded as a worthwhile target but it had an important railway junction. Moreover . . . it had been reported that the town was full of German troops poised to repel any Allied attempt to cross the Rhine in that area.' Allied troops were approaching from the west. Freiburg was protected only by light flak batteries. About 350 aircraft attacked on the night of 27/28 November. They dropped 1,900 tons of bombs which failed to hit the rail junction. They fell instead on the main town, killing 2,088 civilians. Another 858 were reported missing. The soldiers in the town were either well-protected or few in number. Only seventy-five of them were killed. On the run into the target, Newman had seen 'no opposition whatsoever'. The highlight of the trip for him was the St Elmo's Fire which flickered over the propellers as they crossed the Channel for home.[7]

Anything that lay in the Allied path could now expect annihilation. The historic town of Heilbronn was even more militarily insignificant than Freiburg. It had the misfortune to lie on a main north–south railway line. On the night of 4/5 December, 282 Lancasters of 5 Group dropped 1,254 tons of bombs in the space of a few minutes. The density of the bombardment produced a firestorm which devoured the wooden-framed buildings and killed 7,000 people.

During the autumn and winter Harris once again came under pressure to broaden the scope of Bomber Command's attacks. Sir Arthur Tedder, the Deputy Supreme Allied Commander, argued for an integrated approach so that 'various operations should fit into one comprehensive pattern.' That meant attacks on everything that kept the German war effort going; oil, yes, but also road, rail and river communications and 'political targets'.[8]

Portal supported his view. It was translated into a directive from the Combined Chiefs of Staff on 1 November 1944. Again it listed the petroleum industry as the first priority with the German lines of communication as the second. 'Important industrial areas' were only mentioned in third place. This left little room for imaginative interpretation.

The directive could be seen as an implicit criticism of Harris's singular approach. That was certainly how he took it. Until now he had taken care to avoid a head-on confrontation with Portal. He appears to have reckoned that as long as Bomber Command kept up a reasonable rate of attacks against oil, he would be left alone to pursue his course of wiping out Germany's largest cities.

In doing so, he was flouting the wishes of every commander with a say in how the air war should proceed. Harris, though, was undeterrred. His reply to the directive was brusque and unapologetic. He repeated his conviction that targeting individual objectives could never be as effective as area attacks. The dramatically changed situation which gave the Allies command of the air seemed to have had no effect on his prescription of blanket destruction. It only needed the obliteration of twelve more cities, including Berlin, for the job to be done. 'Are we now to abandon this vast task . . . just as it nears completion?' he demanded.[9]

This sort of disagreement was intolerable at a crucial stage of the war. If it was allowed to persist the great advantage of air superiority could be dissipated and the opportunity to bring a swift end to the war squandered. Portal, with his customary combination of steeliness and emollience, moved to deflect his turbulent subordinate from a collision course.

'I have, I must confess at times wondered [he wrote in a letter of 12 November] whether the magnetism of the remaining German cities has not in the past tended as much to deflect our bombers from their primary objectives as . . . tactical and weather difficulties . . . I would like you to reassure me that this is not so. If I knew you to be as wholehearted in the attack of oil as you have in the past been in the matter of attacking cities I would have little to worry about.'[10]

This smooth rebuke produced some results, but they were only temporary. The proportion of operations against oil targets climbed from 6 per cent in October to 24 per cent in November. Harris had responded to the tug on his chain. But he had by no means changed his mind, and did not pretend that he had. On 12 December he wrote a sulky letter to Portal deriding the scientific experts of the Ministry of Economic Warfare for their faith in 'panacea targets', his favourite term for specific industrial targets such as the famous ball-bearing works at Schweinfurt whose destruction they claimed would hasten German defeat.

Portal replied in a tone of weary disappointment. Harris's belief that oil was another 'panacea' was to be regretted. 'Naturally,' he wrote, 'while you hold this view you will be unable to put your heart into the attack on oil.' The exchanges went on into the New Year with Portal struggling to get his subordinate to do what he was told. It was no good. Harris was immovable; he brought the dispute to a head in mid-January 1945 when he offered his resignation. In his letter he declared he had 'no faith' in selective bombing and 'none whatever in the present oil policy'. But he protested that despite his misgivings he had never failed 'in any *worthwhile* efforts to achieve even those things which I knew from the start to be impracticable, once they had been decided upon.'[11]

The temptation to call his bluff must have been enormous. Portal resisted it. In his reply he blandly accepted Harris's assurance. 'I am very sorry that you do not believe in it,' he wrote 'but it is no use my craving for what is evidently unattainable. We must wait until after the end of the war before we can know for certain who was right.' He went on: 'I sincerely hope that until then you will continue in command of the force which has done so much towards defeating the enemy and has brought such credit and renown to yourself and to the Air Force.' Thus Portal not only missed his chance to sack Harris. He had also guaranteed him tenure of his job until the end of war.

How was Harris able to get away with this extraordinary behaviour, which bordered on insubordination? In his time at the head of Bomber Command he had achieved a gilding of prestige that shone as brightly as that emanating from Montgomery and approached the aura of glory that surrounded Churchill himself. He had arrived at the head of Bomber Command when it was sunk in failure and was beginning to be tainted by despair. His effect on the organization had been extraordinary. His aggression and sense of showmanship restored in the crews a faith in their own abilities and a sense of worth about what they were doing. He impressed the public with his obvious confidence and pride in his command's achievements. Harris had a strong understanding of what propaganda could do for him and his men in the internal bureaucratic battles he fought with as much ferocity and tenacity as he showed towards the Germans.

He was helped by his proximity to the prime minister. Whether Churchill liked him or not was questionable. But in the end it did not matter. Far more importantly he trusted him and judged him to be the man to do the job. The qualities needed to pursue the biggest bombing campaign ever seen in history were not necessarily attractive or endearing. The task required an ability to inure oneself to death, whether that of an airman or a German civilian. It needed someone who could take in minutes, decisions that merited a year of reflection, and once taken, stick to them, even when the initial evidence suggested that they might be wrong.

Harris was able to do these things. He belonged outside the normal confines of time and place. Those around him, his staff and his family, maintained loyally that there was a warm and affectionate side to Harris. If so, it is hard to discern in his writings and his actions. The crews who never saw him had a better understanding of who he was. To them, he was remote and unemotional, untouched by the climate of sentimentality that flourished in wartime as a respite from the uncertainties and harshness of existence. That did not mean that they did not trust him or respect him. But nobody would say they loved him.

Portal's reaction was probably inevitable. Sacking someone of Harris's standing at that stage of the war would have disrupted the smooth running of Bomber Command at a crucial period in the campaign. It was still an unfortunate decision. Harris had outlived his usefulness. He had never, as Webster and Frankland drily pointed out, been famous for his farsightedness.

'Sir Arthur Harris's prestige did not depend on a reputation for good judgement,' they wrote. 'He had, after all, opposed the introduction of the incendiary technique, the creation of the Pathfinder Force and the development of the bomb with which the Möhne and Eder dams were breached. He had confidently supposed that the Battle of Berlin could win the war, and he had declared that Bomber Command would be operationally incapable of carrying out the French railway campaign. In all these, and many other judgements, he had been shown to be, or at least by his superiors been supposed to be, wrong and he had repeatedly been overruled, in theory if not always in practice.'[12]

Despite all Portal's pleading and cajoling, Harris continued to direct most of Bomber Command's efforts against cities. In the remaining months of the war, it devoted only just over a quarter of its energy to attacking oil targets. Attacks on cities, however, made up 36.6 per cent of its effort. In that time it showered 66,482 tons on built-up areas, drenching them in high explosive in a literal demonstration of overkill that often brought minimal military advantage.

It was an irony that the raid that did most to damage the reputation of Bomber Command after the war was far easier to justify than operations such as those against sleepy, mediaeval backwaters like Freiburg and Heilbronn.

The attack on Dresden was one of the most carefully considered of Bomber Command's war. It had its origins in the *Thunderclap* plan of August 1944 which the official historians judged could 'be regarded, if only indirectly, as the title deeds' of the operation.[13] By the time it was back on the table for consideration the Allies and the Soviet Union had moved even closer to victory, though how long the end would be in coming was impossible to predict. The operation was carried out in the belief that a major attack on a city that had hitherto escaped serious bombardment would significantly hasten the end of the war. It was essentially devised to create mayhem in the German front-line areas as they faced the Russian offensive developing in the east.

What was needed, Portal wrote to his deputy Norman Bottomley at the end of January 1945, was 'one big attack on Berlin and attacks on Dresden, Leipzig, Chemnitz, or any other cities where a severe blitz will not only cause confusion in the evacuation from the East but will also hamper the movement of troops from the West.'[14] The object was to destroy infrastructure and create panic, forcing non-combatant men, women and children on to the roads, creating conditions that would stop German soldiers getting to and from the battlefield. It was not a pretty idea. But by this stage of the war it was well within the boundaries which the Allies, and those in whose name they were fighting, thought acceptable.

18

Götterdämmerung

On the morning of Monday, 13 February 1945, Roy Lodge, a twenty-one-year-old bomb-aimer with 51 Squadron and the rest of his crew learned that they were on operations that night. Their job was to mark a target that was as yet unannounced. 'The normal preparations for an op went ahead,' he remembered. In the afternoon they heard where they were going. 'The CO addressed us with, "Gentlemen, your target for tonight is . . . Dresden," and the curtain over the map was drawn aside.' The news caused some whistles and groans. It was the depth of winter and 'Dresden seemed to be halfway across the world, an eight-and-a-half-hour trip there and back.'

Lodge, a Cambridge undergraduate before volunteering, read afterwards that some of those who took part in the raid had experienced beforehand 'a sense of foreboding as though they felt some terrible act was about to be committed.' For him and his crew, however, 'Dresden was just another target, though a long, long way away.'

The normal routine had differed in only one respect. Unusual detail was given about the purpose of the mission. 'We were told that the Russian armies advancing towards Dresden had been held up; that Dresden was the main base for the German army on that front; that though normally it was not an important industrial town, it would be crammed with German troops and transport; that the Russians had asked Bomber Command to help break German resistance.'[1]

Until now Dresden had escaped serious bombardment. But it had been in the Allies' sights for some months and its attraction as a target had increased as the Russian advance ground westward. During the second half of January, Soviet troops crossed Poland

and breached Germany's eastern border. Germany was now fighting hard on two fronts inside its own territory.

The Allies gave urgent thought to how their air power could be used to clear the way for the Red Army. It was apparent that the speed of the Soviet advance would have a decisive effect on the length of the war. The view of the influential Joint Intelligence Committee (JIC), where all the main intelligence services came together, was that the assault on oil targets should remain the main priority. But they also proposed that a major effort should be made to come to the aid of the Russians. Portal shared their opinion.

The Russians' progress was by no means assured. Their advance was threatened by the arrival of German reinforcements from the west. A JIC assessment had predicted that almost half a million men could be moved from Germany's rapidly shrinking territories to reinforce the Eastern Front. For Hitler, stemming the tide from the east was the overwhelming priority. Of all the Germans' many enemies it was the Russians who struck real terror into their hearts.

Churchill was eager to hear the RAF's ideas for hounding the Germans as they were pushed back. He considered Berlin and 'other large cities in East Germany' to be 'especially attractive targets'. On 27 January, Portal issued orders to Harris and Bomber Command to prepare for an attack. Portal considered that an all-out assault on Berlin would not produce decisive results. His pessimism was justified a week later when the Americans took on that task. Almost a thousand Fortresses bombarded the capital in daylight in what was effectively a classic area attack. Over two thousand tons of bombs were dropped, half of which were incendiaries. Huge destruction was done to the fabric of the city and nearly three thousand people were killed. But there was no surrender and Berlin staggered on.

In view of the prime minister's preferences, it was placed on Bomber Command's target list. The cities of Dresden, Leipzig and Chemnitz were also added. A few days later, the Vice-Chief of the Air Staff, Sir Douglas Evill, told the Chiefs of Staff Committee what the RAF were planning. His report placed great emphasis on the potential for exploiting the disruption caused by the large number of evacuees streaming westward through Berlin, Dresden and

Leipzig from the German and German-occupied areas that were falling before the advancing Soviet troops. The administrative problems in dealing with them were 'immense'. The strain on the authorities was doubled by the need to handle the military reinforcements arriving to shore up the crumbling Eastern Front. 'A series of heavy attacks by day and night upon those administrative and control centres,' he wrote, 'is likely to create considerable delays in the deployment of troops . . . and may well result in establishing a state of chaos in some or all of these centres.'[2] Such operations would serve the dual purpose of speeding the Russians' progress westwards as well as perhaps fulfilling the objective mooted in *Thunderclap* of creating sufficient panic and despair to persuade the German nation that further resistance was futile.

On 4 February, four days after this assessment was delivered, Churchill, Stalin and Roosevelt met in the ballroom of the Livadia Palace, the summer residence of the Tsars near Yalta in the Crimea, to discuss the war's next, crucial phase. On the subject of bombing, the Red Army made a request for air action to hinder the enemy from moving troops to the Eastern Front.

Four days later this had been translated into the basis of an order. On 8 February, the Air Staff's targets committee informed Bomber Command, the US Strategic Air Force Command and Supreme Headquarters Allied Expeditionary Force (SHAEF) that 'the following targets have been selected for their importance in relation to the movements of Evacuees from, and of military forces to, the Eastern Front.' On the list were Berlin, Dresden and Chemnitz. But it was Dresden that was to be dealt with first.

The crews, on the whole, were pleased to be doing something to help their Russian allies. The members of the newly-formed 227 Squadron heard about it at the afternoon briefing from their CO, Wing Commander Ernest Millington, who went on to become a Labour MP. In the audience was Freddie Hulance, who had just completed eight operations as a pilot. 'He announced with some relish,' he said later, 'that the target of Dresden had been nominated at the Yalta conference by the Russians who wanted support for their front, which was then about 100 miles to the east.'

Hulance 'got a certain amount of satisfaction about supporting the Russians.' They had 'born the brunt of the land forces offensive at the time and suffered the worst casualties ... not that I in any way had Communist feelings, but they were allies, doing a good job, bringing the war to a more hasty conclusion.' The rest of the squadron, he believed, felt the same way.[3]

The Americans had agreed to help and were scheduled to open the attack on 13 February but the operation was scrubbed due to bad weather. In the end, Bomber Command did most of the work, dispatching 796 Lancasters and nine Mosquitoes in two separate raids that came three hours apart.

The first wave of 244 bombers, all from 5 Group, took off shortly after 6 p.m. Despite the weakness of the Luftwaffe night-fighter force they took a tortuous route, turning first towards the Ruhr, then along a jinking path designed to keep the German defences constantly guessing as to where they were heading. These deceptions meant the journey was 500 miles longer than the direct route.

The 5 Group Pathfinders began marking at 10 p.m. local time. Green marker flares were dropped to define the bounds of the city centre, followed by a thousand white magnesium flares to illuminate the ground. Then Mosquitoes swooped down to 2,000 feet to deliver 1,000-pound target indicator canisters whose red flares lit up the aiming point. The planners had chosen the stadium of the city's most popular football club, just to the west of the River Elbe, as the focus of the attack. There was nothing to put the markers off their aim. Most of the city's limited anti-aircraft artillery had been moved to sites deemed to be more important and there were only ten night-fighters stationed in the area.

The main force Lancasters came in at different heights and slightly different approaches to create a zone of destruction that fanned out south and east of the aiming point. The 400 tons of bombs they dropped were a mixture of high explosive which blew down walls and blasted away roofs, and 4-pound incendiaries which set the ruins alight. As the last of the 5 Group aircraft turned away towards home, the fires seemed to be taking hold well.

Roy Lodge was in the second wave of 529 Lancasters. He was still a hundred miles from the target when the glow from Dresden became visible. 'As I drew closer I saw the cause of the glow,' he wrote. 'Ahead was the most enormous fire. Ahead, and then below us were great patches, pools, areas of flame.' Lodge's crew had been detailed to further mark the target but it hardly seemed necessary. 'We added our own long line of flares to those already across the target . . . I saw white flashes of bomb explosions and more splashes of sparkling incendiaries. As we completed our run across the target and turned away on our homeward journey, I could see that the pools of flame were joining up into one huge inferno.'

This was not an exaggeration. The attack had created a firestorm that was to engulf the old city centre. The morning brought no reprieve. More than 300 American Fortresses dropped 771 tons of bombs, aiming at the railway yards which had been outside the RAF's bombing area. At the same time, to intensify the chaos, some of their Mustang fighter escorts shot up road traffic. When the ordeal finally ended, according to the latest best estimate, between 25,000 and 40,000 people had been killed.[4]

The scenes the crews had witnessed were impressive but not necessarily indicative of enormous loss of life. Looking back, Lodge chiefly remembered he and his comrades as afterwards feeling 'tired, of course, excited by what we had seen and done, awed by the enormous destructive power that we had demonstrated.' But it did not seem to him that they had taken part in 'an especially historic event'. Bill Farquharson, who was flying with 115 Squadron, arrived in the middle of the main force when the target was already ablaze. 'At the time it didn't strike me as being a heavy raid,' he said.[5]

Dresden was unusual only in that it went off so well. It was, as it turned out, a disastrous success. The death toll was on a par with that resulting from the first firestorm, created some eighteen months previously at Hamburg, which was regarded at the time as a great victory. But by the time the war was over Hamburg was only a memory to a few non-Germans. The horror of Dresden was still fresh and raw when the last shot was fired. Such a devastating act so close to the dawning of peace seemed particularly brutal and gratuitous. How could killing on such a scale be justified when the end was in sight? The simple answer was that the end was not in sight. No one could know when the war would finish and in the middle of February 1945 there was no indication that the Germans would not fight on until the death of the last Nazi.

Even while fires still burned in the ruins of the old city, unease was mounting about the raid. On 17 February a report by Associated Press, the main American news agency, from Supreme Allied Head-quarters stated that the 'Allied Air Chiefs' had made a decision to 'adopt deliberate terror bombing of German population centres as a ruthless expedient to hastening Hitler's doom.' It cited recent attacks on 'residential sections' of Dresden, as well as Berlin and Chemnitz as evidence that the campaign was already under way. This dispatch was widely distributed and broadcast and though quickly suppressed it made a strong impression. It was especially disturbing to American audiences who had received continual official assurances that their air force was a precision instrument which was applied only to select targets. The stir the story created was thought sufficiently damaging to merit a clarification from the US Secretary of War, General George C. Marshall, who issued a counter-statement emphasizing that the attack on Dresden had taken place at the request of the Russians.

The controversy, initially at least, made little impression on the crews. They were anxious to press on. Although the final date of the war was unguessable it was clear that the Germans were beaten. There were odd, cheering signs that lifted their spirits. Flying over Sweden, Dennis Steiner and his crew were buoyed to see below them lines of tracer hosing up in the form of a V for Victory sign.

When a crew finished a tour they could now reasonably hope that they would not have to do another. Harry Yates's thirtieth op was a trip to a place he had never heard of before, Vohwinkel in the Ruhr, where the target was the marshalling yards. Crews were specially apprehensive on their last trip. The loss rate may have dropped to just below 1 per cent. But inside a squadron, the deaths of friends and comrades were as real and painful as ever, and despite the weakness of the Luftwaffe, people were still dying.

Essen, May 1945.

At the briefing before Yates's final trip, the route map was heavily spattered with red blobs indicating the whereabouts of flak batteries. Over the target they met sustained and accurate anti-aircraft fire which disrupted the bomber stream, breaking up its coherence. They 'rocked through the dirty air, anxious like everybody about our proximity to other kites.' The bombing was ragged and the high wind further diluted the concentration. The bombs missed the rail junctions, even largely failed to hit the town.

Yates and his friends did not care. 'We came away with joy and

relief bubbling up as irresistibly as champagne from a shaken bottle
. . . no words were wasted on the bombing we had just witnessed.
The time had come to celebrate the fact of being alive.' As they
headed home 'a party atmosphere swept through the aircraft. We
crossed Holland at 5,000 feet while the boys bawled a gloriously
crass ditty into the intercom. The coffee came out.' His New Zealander navigator, Bill Birnie, proposed a toast: 'To us.' Yates offered
his own. '"To our future," I said, realizing as I pronounced the word
that I had not allowed myself such unqualified optimism for the
last twenty weeks.' They came to a halt at the end of the runway at
Mepal to 'wild, triumphant cheering.' Yates had climbed aboard his
aircraft 'proud of who we were and what we were doing.' This was
how most of the men in Bomber Command felt.[6]

Peter Johnson was one of the few who had contemporaneous
doubts about the morality of carrying on the bombing. By March
1945 he was commanding 97 (Pathfinder Force) Squadron. On the
sixteenth he woke up in his room at Coningsby feeling that the 'smell
of victory was in the air.' Operations were on that night and he
assumed that he would be marking an oil target in eastern Germany
or Czechoslovakia. At the briefing he learned that they were in fact
going to Würzburg, which had not until then been subjected to a
major attack. He asked the squadron intelligence officer what was the
significance of the target and was told 'nothing very much'. There
were 'no big factories', just 'a bit of a railway junction'.

Johnson was too busy making preparations to give the matter
much thought. He and his crew, using sophisticated blind-bombing
techniqes, would be first on the target, dropping primary indicators.
Soon after, magnesium flares would light up the bombing area for
seven or eight minutes allowing Mosquitoes to swoop in low and
mark the exact point for the bombing force to aim at. By now they
could be reasonably assured of success. His group had 'perfected an
elaborate method of bombing towns [that] ensured that bombs
were evenly distributed over the target area and conducive, with the
huge numbers of incendiaries used, to the production of a firestorm
. . . this was the treatment we were to mete out at Würzburg.'

Johnson was a believer in the virtue of Bomber Command and

the necessity of the strategic bombing campaign, for which he had specifically volunteered. He had been untouched by the murmurs of doubt that had from time to time emanated from churchmen and the benches of parliament. 'Such criticism,' he thought, 'had come from quarters unable or unwilling to suggest new or alternative policies to win the war and they had cut little ice with the general public and went unnoticed in Bomber Command.'

Johnson had been unconcerned by the Dresden operation which he had not flown on but had helped to plan. It was, he thought, 'a potent blow in assisting our Russian allies who had borne so much of the burden of war and suffered so appallingly from German atrocities in their homeland.' But as he lay uneasily on his narrow bed that afternoon awaiting the Würzburg operation he found it 'difficult to justify the deliberated destruction of a small city whose military value to the enemy seemed negligible.' The victims would certainly include some prominent Nazis. The majority though, 'would be the young and the old, many of them refugees from other disasters, non-combatants in the truest sense.' As the minutes slipped away towards H-Hour he found he 'simply could not shut my eyes to this, nor could I convince myself that "success" in our attack would make the slightest contribution to bringing the war to an end nor to saving casualties among our armies on the continent.' Johnson decided he wanted none of it. But how could he find a way out? As squadron commander he could choose whether to fly or not. But if he felt the mission was wrong he could hardly, with a clear conscience, order others to carry it out. In addition, to refuse to give the necessary orders would constitute mutiny, followed by a court-martial, severe punishment and disgrace, and penury for his family. It would shock the squadron and possibly deflate their morale. When he finally made up his mind, the deciding factor was fear of being accused, or at least suspected, of LMF. The point he was trying to make would be blotted out by the stain of cowardice.

Sick with misgivings, he took himself to the final briefing, conducted by Air Vice-Marshal H. A. Constantine, who had taken over 5 Group in January and was anxious to make an impression. He stressed that 'the war was not over and the task of Bomber Command was as important ever.' When Constantine asked if there were any questions, Johnson spoke up. Was there, he wanted to know, any special reason for the attack? ' "I've said it's an important railway centre," he said (it wasn't), "and also there are thousands of houses totally undamaged sheltering tens of thousands of Germans. I hope that will not be the case tomorrow, which will be another nail in the enemy's coffin." '

Constantine's hopes were satisfied and Johnson's fears realized. The Würzburg raid was devastating. More than 1,100 tons of bombs were dropped in a little over a quarter of an hour, landing with exemplary accuracy. The authors of Bomber Command's war diaries noted that 'Würzburg contained little industry and this was an area attack.' The historic heart of the city was burned out. Nearly nine tenths of its buildings were destroyed. The number of dead was never decided. It lay somewhere between four and five thousand.

By now Bomber Command could wreak blanket destruction virtually at will. This had been demonstrated ten days after the Dresden raid when it visited Pforzheim. Hitherto the town had not been considered important enough to attack. On the night of 23/24 February, it dropped about 1,800 tons of bombs, a huge quantity, on a compact area measuring three kilometres by one and a half. In the resulting crucible, according to the local official report, 'more than 17,000 [a quarter of the population] met their death in a hurricane of fire and explosions.' This was probably the third heaviest air raid death toll in Germany during the war after Hamburg and Dresden.[7] To the crews though, it was just another raid. They were told at the pre-operational briefing that it was being targeted because it contained a factory making clockwork mechanisms that were used by the Luftwaffe.

The raid stoked up hatred and rage against the RAF. Three weeks afterwards seven British airmen who had baled out after being shot down were marched through Pforzheim on their way to a prisoner of war camp. They were settling down for the night in a school building in a village outside the town when a mob turned up outside. They had been sent there by a senior Nazi official in Pforzheim, Hans Christian Knab, in a 'demonstration of public outrage.'

Three of the airmen managed to run away but the remaining four were dragged to a cemetery and shot dead. One of the three escapees was recaptured and held in a police station. A Major Niklas of the Volksturm (home guard) turned up and demanded he be handed over. The police complied. The prisoner was given up to a crowd that had gathered outside and was beaten, then shot by a member of the Hitler Youth. The two other airmen survived to give evidence in the subsequent military trial. Knab and Niklas were hanged.[8]

As the end grew closer, disquiet mounted at the conduct of the bombing campaign. It was Dresden that marked the stealthy change of heart. The first indication of how the aircrews would be regarded by the post-war world came from the pen of Churchill. On 28 March 1945 he sent a minute to Portal and the Chiefs of Staff Committee which questioned the usefulness of further area bombing. It is remarkable in its frank acceptance of the real purpose of such operations. It also shows a politician's worldly appreciation of how certain acts of war were likely to be viewed once the smoke had cleared from the battlefield. 'It seems to me [he wrote] that the moment has come when the question of the bombing of the German cities simply for the sake of increasing the terror, though under other pretexts, should be reviewed. Otherwise we shall come into control of an utterly ruined land.' This was common sense. Continuing to knock down German houses at this point merely added to the Allies' post-war headaches. It was they who would have to look after the welfare of the defeated nation. He might have added that flattening towns made the job of the advancing armies harder as the rubble provided cover for the defending forces.

But hidden in the middle of what was a workaday communication was a sentence that bore no relation to the surrounding subject matter. 'The destruction of Dresden,' Churchill wrote, 'remains a serious query against the conduct of the Allied bombing.'[9] With these charged words the prime minister signalled the arrival of a controversy that is still alive today.

This statement was disingenuous and hypocritical whichever way it was looked at. As the official history pointed out, it ignored the fact that Dresden had happened six weeks before, when the situation had been much more uncertain. The plan of attacking important cities in eastern Germany had been approved at all levels the previous year and had Churchill's enthusiastic backing. This was consistent with his attitude of the previous four years, whereby he had been firmly supportive of Harris's dogged mission, whatever doubts he might have from time to time as to the utility of the violence. Now he appeared to be changing his tune.

It did not take much imagination to foresee the trouble ahead. Once the war was over the world would have the chance to see what strategic bombing had done to Germany. It would shock even the most fervent advocate of revenge. Some of it was, as Churchill had admitted in the minute, terror bombing. Yet the official position was that the Allies had been engaged in no such thing. As recently as early March, Richard Stokes, the Labour MP who had persistently and bravely questioned the conduct of the campaign, had once again returned to the subject. Was terror bombing, he demanded of Sir Archibald Sinclair, the air minister, the policy of the RAF? Sinclair replied with what now seems spurious indignation. 'It does not do the Honourable Member justice to come here to this House and suggest that there are a lot of Air Marshals or pilots or anyone else sitting in a room trying to think how many German women and children they can kill,' he said.[10]

On the evening after Churchill's minute was written Portal suggested to him that he should think about it again. The prime minister took the hint and withdrew it, substituting a few days later a few mild sentences repeating his concern about the usefulness of continued area bombing but making no mention of Dresden. 'We must see to it,' he wrote on 1 April, 'that our attacks do not do more harm to ourselves in the long run than they do to the enemies' immediate war effort.'

The Air Staff was now anyway agreed that area bombing had outlived its usefulness and that 'at this advanced stage of the war no immediate additional advantage can be gained from [attacks on] the remaining industrial centres of Germany.' They wished though, to reserve the right to bomb towns near the front if German resistance revived and to strike at population centres in Thuringia if the Nazi leadership made a last stand there.

In the event, no such action was needed. Germany was tottering towards total collapse and the main work of Bomber Command was done. For the remainder of the war the force would mainly be used helping the army and blowing up roads and railways in and around Leipzig and Halle on the German line of retreat.

On 16 April Portal sent a message to Harris that he suggested should be turned into an order of the day. The last paragraph stated that 'henceforth the main tasks of the strategic air forces will be to afford direct support to the allied armies in the land battle and to continue their offensive against the sea power of the enemy which they have already done so much to destroy. I am confident that Bomber Command will maintain in these final phases of the war in the air over Europe the high standard of skill and devotion that has marked their work since the earliest days of the war.' With these words the strategic air offensive against Germany effectively came to an end.[11]

The last area bombing raid of the war had taken place the day before. Five hundred Lancasters and twelve Mosquitoes closed in on Potsdam, the imperial and military town west of Berlin. It was the first time that big bombers had entered the area since Harris had called off the Battle of Berlin in March 1944, when it was realized that they were no match for the German night-fighters. Now they could do as they pleased. The aiming point was a barracks in the centre of the town, once the home of the old Prussian guards regiments. The bombs fell all over the place and as far afield as northern and eastern districts of Berlin. Up to 5,000 people were killed, possibly because many neglected to take shelter thinking, when they heard the air-raid sirens, that the attack was bound for the capital. This was the raid that so impressed Portal when he drove through the ruins a few weeks later and felt both awed and depressed at what had been done on his orders.

The last heavy bomber raids of the war took place on 25 April. One was aimed at Hitler's Bavarian retreat at Berchtesgaden and the SS barracks nearby. Freddie Hulance, who had been at Dresden, took part. The two operations could not have been more different. Berchtesgaden was a fine example of aerial warfare, precisely applied. Setting off from Lincolnshire, Hulance felt relief that the end of the war seemed only days away, but also apprehension. The target was believed to be one of the most heavily defended in the Reich. All together 359 Lancasters and sixteen Mosquitoes of 1, 5 and 8 Groups were involved. For most of the crews, it was their last operation of the war. There was scattered cloud when they arrived over the Bavarian Alps. 'We were briefed that we shouldn't bomb unless we could see the target,' he remembered, '[then] quite suddenly the cloud cleared as I was approaching it so we bombed.' Hulance watched the ordnance slanting down towards the SS barracks which was 'pretty well saturated. There was only one building unscathed.' The crews had been told they would be blowing up the Führer himself. But Hitler was not at home.

Thirty-nine airmen died on operations that day. Most of them were killed during an attack on the coastal batteries on the Friesian island of Wangerooge, in a series of mid-air collisions between friendly aircraft. It was a reminder, if anyone needed one, of the precarious nature of life in Bomber Command.

The last German civilians died when sixty-three Mosquitoes attacked Kiel on the night of 2/3 May. It was feared that ships were waiting to carry troops to Norway to carry on the fight. Bombs fell on the town and eighteen people were killed. Flying Officer R. Catterall, DFC and Flight Sergeant D. J. Beadle were lost carrying out a low-level attack on an airfield. Shortly afterwards the remaining German soldiers left town and Kiel was declared an open city. After carrying away what they could from the central stores, the citizens went home to await the arrival of British and Canadian troops.

The war ended just before Bomber Command dropped its millionth ton of bombs. The final figure was 955,044 tons. The USAAF had delivered a further 395,000 tons. The American troops arriving in the Ruhr valley in April 1945 entered a vast ocean of rubble from which protruded the twisted girders and tortured metal that were all that was left of the factories, foundries and workshops that powered the German war machine. It was destruction on a cosmic scale.

There had been sixty large towns and cities on Harris's target list. All of them now had been substantially damaged and many almost completely destroyed. Three quarters of Hamburg was razed, 69 per cent of Darmstadt and 64 per cent of Hannover. A third of sprawling Berlin was flattened: 6,427 acres. That compared with the 400 acres of London that the Luftwaffe laid waste. In the infamous raid on Coventry, they had devasted a hundred acres. In Düsseldorf, a town of similar size, Allied bombing had wiped out an area twenty times as large.

Hidden underneath the desert of brick and dust lay the unburied dead. The figure of around 600,000 came to be accepted as the number of German civilians killed by bombing. A post-war enquiry by the German Federal Government's statistics office, published in 1962, put the total as 593,000.[12] The exact number will probably never be known. After heavy raids civil defence workers often piled up the human remains, doused them in petrol and set them on fire to reduce the risk of disease. Whole families were wiped out leaving no one to report their deaths. A further 67,000 were killed in France by air attack according to recent research. In Italy, more than 60,000 are thought to have died.

The number of combatants killed in the bombing was low. The German dead were mostly women, children and the old, those who were left at home when the men of fighting age not needed to run the factories went off to the war. Thus, for every 100 male casualties in Darmstadt, there were 181 females. Many in Britain were prepared to accept the argument that any German adult engaged in war work could be regarded as having placed himself or herself in the firing line. But no definition of what constituted a legitimate target could include children. In Hamburg, 7,000 of the dead were children or adolescent. This slaughter of the young was repeated in numerous urban centres big and small, in roughly the same proportions.

In Freiburg, in the Breisgau region, 252 boys and girls under the age of sixteen were killed, 19 per cent of the total civilian death toll.

The old died alongside the women and children, and for the same reasons. When the air war came to Germany they found themselves in the front line. In some cities they made up 22 per cent of the dead. There were many others who lost their lives because of grotesque bad luck. A substantial number of the victims were forced workers from the countries that the Allies were fighting to liberate.[13]

German history provided a comparison for death on this scale. Official figures claimed that 800,000 people had died directly or indirectly as a result of the Royal Navy's maritime blockade during the First World War. Included in the figure were the 150,000 who, it was claimed, perished as a result of undernourishment which lowered their defences against the influenza epidemic that ravaged Europe after the war.

But it was the sort of death the victims had suffered that gave the tolls their awesome quality. Death by malnourishment or disease came in stages. It was slow and organic. Death by bombing came in several forms, all of them horrible. It was violence distilled into its most nightmarish form. By the end of the war, raids had been compressed into a few horrific minutes. In Pforzheim there was just over a quarter of an hour between the first bomb falling and the last bomber departing, leaving behind a town whose centre had been turned into fire and smoke and glowing ashes. The lucky ones died immediately, from crashing masonry or the effects of blast. The less fortunate burned up, or, cowering in a shelter or cellar, suffocated as the fire consumed the oxygen in the air leaving only carbon monoxide.

The crews had mostly had few doubts about the justice of what they were doing and little sympathy for those they were doing it to. It was nonetheless a relief when, in the last days, Bomber Command was given tasks that gave life rather than took it. Operation *Manna* was launched to bring relief supplies to western Holland. The population was approaching starvation and many old people had already died. It began at the end of April and lasted until the German surrender. In that time, Lancasters and Mosquitoes flew nearly 3,000 sorties, dropping 7,000 tons of food into an area that was still under German occupation.

Another operation, *Exodus*, brought particular satisfaction. By the end of the war there were 75,000 British servicemen in German prisoner-of-war camps. It was remembered that after the previous war it had taken nearly two months before all PoWs were repatriated. The RAF offered its Lancasters to speed up the process. Leaflets were dropped over a number of camps telling them to stand by to be liberated. Between 26 April and 7 May, 469 sorties were flown without accident. Each Lancaster could take twenty-six passengers. Many were too shattered by their experience to show much gratitude. Peter Johnson flew a batch from Brussels and stood with the crew at the foot of the ladder to welcome them back home. 'They were tired and still numb from their freedom. Many were emaciated from lack of proper food. It was queer that not one of those that I brought back said "Thank You" to the crew.'[14]

Among the the PoWs were 9,838 airmen from Bomber Command, some of whom had been incarcerated since the earliest days of the war. Given the destruction that the aircrews had inflicted on the Reich, the Germans' treatment of their British and American charges was surprisingly mild and respectful. They could, undoubtedly, be ruthless when needed. No one would forget the mass murder carried out by the Gestapo in March 1944 of fifty PoWs from Stalag Luft III captured in the aftermath of the Great Escape. But unless prisoners looked for trouble, their main enemies for much of the war were boredom, frustration and the psychological chafing caused by enforced communal life.

The Germans quickly established a system of processing captured airmen. The experience of Geoffrey Willatt, whom we last heard of baling out on the night of Sunday, September 5/6 after his Lancaster was shot down by a night-fighter on the way back from Mannheim, was typical.[15] He was the only one of the crew to survive. He was soon picked up and taken to Dulag Luft, an interrogation centre near Frankfurt through which most captured aircrew personnel passed.

RAF intelligence officers painted a lurid and not unattractive picture of what could be expected there. The camp was supposed to be an oasis of leisure and luxury, where flighty women and peacetime comforts were employed to loosen the captives' tongues.

The truth, he noted in his diary, bore 'no resemblance whatsoever' to what he had been told. There were 'no parks, no booze, no women, no dances.' The intelligence was proved right in one respect however. Many prisoners reported being interrogated by sympathetic officers who spoke perfect English and startled them with questions such as 'and how are Wing Commander Gibson and Wing Commander Cheshire?' just as they had been warned.[16]

Geoffrey was then packed with other RAF prisoners into a cattle truck, whose capacity was labelled '40 hommes ou 8 chevaux' and taken by train to the place where he would spend the next eighteen months. Stalag Luft III, carved out of a pine forest at Sagan, about a hundred miles south-east of Berlin, was the hub of the prison system. When he arrived at the North Compound there was a crowd waiting to look over the new arrivals. Some shouted delightedly as they recognized old comrades but 'mostly [they were] silent, looking at us in the way old prisoners look at new ones (poor b—ers, but lucky devils to have come so recently from home).' They were a motley bunch dressed in 'anything from full uniform to loin cloths, and looked incredibly fit with brown bodies and beards.'

By now Stalag Luft III had expanded considerably. In North Compound there were fifteen sleeping huts, fifty yards long, partitioned off into twenty-four rooms. Each held up to six men who slept in bunk beds. Geoffrey made quick character assessments of his fellow-inmates. The British all seemed good types. An American navigator who had been flying with the Canadians, however, was 'inclined to be self-centred and with an all-embracing prejudice against anything English. The less said the better.'

Geoffrey had nightmares at first, reliving the terror of being shot down, but soon recorded that 'usually I sleep like a log.' He learned the camp patois. They, the inmates, were 'kriegies', taken from the German word for war prisoner. The guards were 'goons' and the English-speaking staff who tried to mingle and snoop were 'ferrets'. He learned, too quickly, the established routines of the captive's life. He was among men 'from nearly every country in the world, Holland, Norway, India, S. America, Denmark, Poland, Czecho-Slovakia.'

It was the custom to walk in twos around the circuit by the side of the warning wire, ten yards from the perimeter fence. Stepping over the wire invited a shot from a watchtower. Too many circuits were 'apt to accentuate the position of the wire and the smallness of the camp.'

As he grew accustomed to camp life he found that 'kriegies are influenced enormously by 4 things in this order – mail, weather, food and news, and it's extraordinary how our spirits are up or down all in a moment.'

The flow of mail was erratic but somehow the system worked. There would be nothing for days on end, and then a welcome flood. Geoffrey was able to keep in touch with his wife Audrey. Her first letter arrived on 11 November. 'Marvellous feeling,' he recorded. 'I can actually see her writing and the paper she wrote on.'

Reg Fayers, who ended up in Stalag Luft I near Barth on the Baltic coast, after being shot down on the night of 25/6 November 1943, received a steady stream of letters from his beloved wife Phyllis. The news of the films she had seen and the mundane goings-on in their home town of Sudbury in Suffolk provided a heartening glimpse of the longed-for life going on hundreds of miles away across the wire.

'Darling it's evening time and everywhere is smelling so perfect,' she wrote on 30 July 1944. 'I wish we were walking round Brundon [a local beauty spot] or even sitting here together with all our favourite records . . . darling I love you so very much. Why should this war have to come now?' There was no doubt in her mind that sooner or later the reunion would come. On 7 October she mentioned the latest movie she had seen, *A Guy Named Joe*, starring Spencer Tracy and Irene Dunne. 'I loved every minute of it,' she wrote. 'We shall just have to see it when you come home. Darling how are you after all these months? Do you still look the same and talk the same? You will never really change will you? I wished so much that you were with me this morning . . .'

There were plenty of opportunities to indulge the British preoccupation with the weather. It was sometimes extreme and often uncertain. Geoffrey was able to sunbathe on 1 November. There was more sunbathing early in April the following year but the false spring was followed by a snowfall. 'Who said the English climate is unpredictable?' he wrote. In the winter the huts were dismal. There was one stove to a room and barely any coal, which had to be eked out with potato peelings and tea leaves. The cruel east wind stripped the felt from the roof letting in the rain. One night Geoffrey and his room-mates dragged their beds into the corridor to escape the drips and slept in their clothes to keep warm.

Food was restricted to one Red Cross parcel per man per week, supplemented by meagre German rations. The cooking was centralized. Each room was given thirty-five minutes' use of the one small stove and two pots. Monty, one of Geoffrey's room-mates, had volunteered to be chef. 'Little knowing what we were in for we accept,' he wrote. 'We take it in turns to be "Joe" for a day, peeling potatoes, washing up, sweeping out, fetching hot water etc. Not very irksome in itself but tiresome when Monty criticizes all the time . . .' Food theft was a shameful crime. 'This month's bombshell,' wrote Geoffrey in September 1944. 'Someone in the room is "fiddling" bits of food. We seem to be short of milk, margarine and other things . . . This all sounds petty but is of real importance when every little scrap of food must be rationed out.' The culprit was eventually caught red-handed and expelled from the room.

The potential for getting on each other's nerves was enormous. Bad weather meant they were cooped up together, 'leading to increased friction'. Most of it, he believed, was 'caused by one person who has no sense of give and take & issues anti-British propaganda at every pore' – presumably the American navigator. His conduct drove the others 'out of the room on every possible occasion to lectures on Art, Music, Architecture, Literature & concerts in unheated lecture rooms.'

Anything that relieved the boredom was welcomed. They played football, rugby and cricket. They tried to learn languages and study for the careers they hoped to follow when the war was over. They read enormously from the libraries provided by the Red Cross and mounted dramatic productions. Sagan had a theatre which put on a stream of often ambitious shows. There was a prodigious amount of talent in the ranks of the kriegies. Denholm Elliott, the RADA student turned wireless op who was shot down in the North Sea in September 1943, ended up in Stalag VIII B, near Breslau in Upper Silesia. On learning of the theatrical possibilities he approached 'a chap called Stanley Platts who later became a professional after the war . . . he used to talk "lake thet" in a rather sepulchral voice. I said to him "excuse me but I am a student from the Royal Academy and I wondered if . . ."' Platts offered him an understudy role in the Patrick Hamilton play *Rope*. Soon he had all the parts he could want, including Macbeth, and Eliza Doolittle in *Pygmalion*. Female roles were something of a speciality. He also played Viola in *Twelfth Night*. The Germans could not have been more helpful. For the latter production they lent the prisoners costumes from the Breslau Opera House. All this activity was designed to dispel the most lowering aspect of camp life. 'The unpleasant thing about being a PoW was the uncertainty,' Denholm Elliott recalled afterwards. 'When would one be released? In six weeks or sixty years. One didn't know.'[17]

Prisoners were remarkably well connected with the outside world. They listened to the BBC on home-made radios, and interrogated the friendlier goons who also supplied them with German news-papers. News of the progress of the war created wild mood swings. By April 1944 Sagan was humming with rumours of the impending invasion. Fantastic bets were struck about the date. A sergeant pledged he would allow himself to be thrown into the communal latrine if the landings did not come before a certain date. There was a craze for table-rapping séances to seek the spirit world's advice on when liberation would come. Already they could see evidence of the Allies' progress in the far-off flashes from the air raids on Berlin.

For once it seemed that the veteran kriegies' predictions that they would 'all be home by Christmas' would come true. But Christmas 1944 came and went and they were still there. Geoffrey sang in the camp choir's production of *Messiah*. The festivities were over-shadowed by news of the success of the German offensive in the Ardennes. Nonetheless they managed to put together a feast of tinned turkey, sausage, and Christmas pud and 'cheer up momentarily'.

In mid-January their spirits received a real lift when they heard that the Russian offensive was gathering pace to the east. Soon they could hear the guns in the distance. On the evening of 27 January the order was given to evacuate the camp. One ordeal was over but another was beginning.

At 1 a.m. Geoffrey and his fellow prisoners passed through the camp gates and out into the freezing snow. They piled their Red Cross provisions on to makeshift sledges, which began to break up within a few hundred yards. They trudged through the night, passed by streams of refugees and white-clad troops heading towards the sound of the guns. The few guards with them abandoned any pretence of discipline. Kriegie and goon were facing the future together.

The civilians in the fearful villages they passed through seemed 'amazingly friendly'. Geoffrey, who had learned German in captivity, overheard two women discussing the prisoners as they passed. 'The older one said, "I do feel sorry for them but they *are* terror-bombers." The younger one answers, "yes but they are a lot of nice-looking young men."' The Red Cross coffee and chocolate and the cigarettes they brought with them could be traded for almost anything that was available. They slept in barns and one night in a bomb shelter.

The greatest danger seemed to be not from the Germans but from the Allied aircraft which droned frequently overhead, sometimes shooting up trains and traffic. The Russians were coming and everyone knew it. At one point, as they trailed westwards, away from the direction of the advance they watched 'small groups of old men dig pathetic little gun pits and sit in them,' waiting fatalistically for the enemy. After six days' march they were put on cattle trucks which hauled them off to another camp at Tarmstedt, near Bremen. They stood in the freezing slush outside for three hours before they were let in. It was a surreal moment. 'A few hysterical voices can be heard shouting "open the bloody gates!"' he recorded. 'Fancy shouting to be let *in*' to a prisoners' camp.

Geoffrey and his fellow-prisoners had to endure another forced march before liberation. When it finally came they were billeted in the farm buildings of a large estate not far from Lübeck. They shared it with Polish female slave workers aged from twelve to seventy who had been living and working there in appalling conditions for five years. When he woke up on 2 May the guards had gone. He ate a breakfast of egg and chips in glorious sunshine and with the sound of approaching gunfire in the background. 'Unmistakably this time tanks on both sides of us,' he wrote. 'German soldiers of all kinds start straggling along the road – all going to give themselves up . . . they are tired & bedraggled and some of them are armed but most have thrown their guns away. We give them cigarettes and they give us their belts, badges, food etc. Their chief feeling is relief that it is all over . . .'

A rumour began that British tanks were at the edge of town. At last 'a Bren carrier rushed into the camp and the Kriegies go mad. We shout, cheer and clamber all over it, shaking the crews' hands . . . we are prisoners no more . . . the wireless on the Bren carrier starts up. The driver answers "tank 19 speaking. Am in village & at PW camp. Over to you, over –" Yes. Over to you, over the English Channel & *home*.'

In the strange anarchic interlude between the Germans abandoning their posts and the arrival of their liberators, some had the chance to see the nature of the enemy they had been fighting. The Germans had seemed amiable enough to Geoffrey Willatt. Reg Fayers saw another side of them. When the Russians arrived at his camp on 2 May the inmates set out to explore the surrounding country. When they returned they told each other what they had seen. There were two concentration camps nearby. 'Thirty thousand have reputedly gone thru it,' he wrote. 'The other one, eight thousand. On two potatoes, watery soup, one seventh of a loaf, forced labour worked hard until they were useless, then they were gassed. Our army doc was, he said, almost sick when he entered rooms where living skeletons sat around tables too weak to move, to get out of their own excreta . . . the bodies stayed there, decomposing, bloated. One thousand were supposed to have been drowned in the creek on one barge. And so on . . .' All the prisoners shared his disgust. 'This has been going on within a few miles of us. Any humanitarian feelings for the German plight now is banished by all this.'[18]

Back in England the crews celebrated VE day in the way that they knew best. Dennis Steiner and his comrades went into Gainsborough to their favourite pub, the Woolsack, where they 'made a thorough nuisance of ourselves. We "borrowed" a builders barrow and loaded it with WAAFs and toured the town, on the way removing convenient bunting that had decorated the streets . . .' The following day the mayor of Gainsborough arrived to reclaim the town's decorations. Negotiations were conducted in the mess where he was 'well and truly entertained and had to be driven home, having lost all interest in his bunting.'[19]

There had been a hundred nights like it but this time there was an altered quality to the fun. There was something that was lacking, something whose absence was very welcome. For the first time in nearly five years, the thought that this party might be the last no longer hung over the celebrations. Cy March was on leave and in bed with his wife Ellen when they heard a tremendous crashing at the door. He 'went out and asked what the hell they thought they were playing at.' The neighbours told him the news. 'I can't explain the relief I felt,' he wrote later. 'No more flak or fighters, biting cold, sleepless nights.' The following night he celebrated in the local pub, all the time time wishing 'I had been on the station with all the boys.' When he got back to Syerston he took the ground crew on an aerial 'Cook's Tour' of the places they had contributed to bombing. The flight took eight hours. 'We flew quite low at times and you could see the crowds milling about in the towns, all as chuffed at the war's end as we were I suppose. One thing stuck in my mind. We flew over the Black Forest and it must have been a forester's cabin, but he and his wife and little girl were at their door waving like mad. Yesterday's enemies, I thought, just like families at home after all that.'[20]

19

Forgetting

Eight days after the end of the war Harris issued a special order of the day to Bomber Command. It was a tribute to his men and women, thanking them for all they had done for him, the country and the free world. 'To those who survive I would say this,' it ran. 'Content yourself and take credit with those who perished that now the "Cease Fire" has sounded countless homes within our Empire will welcome back a father, husband or son whose life, but for your endeavours and your sacrifices, would assuredly have been expended during long further years of agony.' He went on to list their many feats and finished by declaring his pride in having been 'your Commander-in-Chief through more than three years of your Saga . . . Famously have you fought. Well have you deserved of your country and her Allies.'[1]

The nation's thanks, though, were slow in coming. Bomber Command was both the symbol and the instrument of Britain's defiance of the Germans throughout the war. It provided an antidote to despair and sustained the hope of victory and peace. In the early years, Britain suffered serial defeats. But in the air it seemed different. Every night the bombers went out into the darkness, the searchlights and the flak to show the world that though the struggle against the Germans might appear futile, there was still someone prepared to wage it. Hearing the throb of friendly bomber engines overhead, listening to the radio bulletins or reading the reports in the papers, the nation could comfort itself with the thought that their injuries at the hands of the Luftwaffe were being repaid. With the arrival of new aircraft, new crews and new equipment and techniques, the attack ceased to be symbolic. By the middle of the war British bombers were inflicting terrible destruction and pain on the enemy.

At the end, their now enormous power helped to crush the last sparks of vitality out of Hitler's empire.

The main job carried out by the crews was amongst the worst that warfare could devise. There was little satisfaction or glory in bombing cities. Yet that was what they had been asked to do and that is what they did, unflinchingly for the most part and at enormous cost to themselves. Yet when it came time give thanks and honour to the living and the dead the official voice was muted.

Churchill broadcast his speech announcing Victory in Europe on the afternoon of 13 May. All over the country, in NAAFI and mess, sitting room and pub, citizens and servicemen clustered round the wireless to hear the prime minister thank all who had secured Britain's survival and eventual triumph. Everyone received their share of praise: the Royal Navy for keeping the sea lanes open, the Merchant Navy who gallantly manned the convoys, the Army whose victories in North Africa paved the way for the reconquest of Europe. The crews listened eagerly as he reached the part played by the RAF. He began by eulogizing Fighter Command and its victory in the Battle of Britain, asserting again that 'never before in the history of human conflict was so much owed by so many to so few.' He predicted that the name of Dowding, its commander, would 'ever be linked with this splendid event.' He spoke of the danger posed by the Germans' V weapons and the RAF's role, along with the domestic anti-aircraft batteries in suppressing them. They had not completely destroyed the menace, however. The credit for that went to the Allied armies who 'cleaned up the coast and overran all the points of discharge.' Otherwise, he went on, 'the autumn of 1944, to say nothing of 1945, might well have seen London as shattered as Berlin.'

The Bomber Boys leaned forward to enjoy their share of the praise that seemed to be coming next. But that was it. Churchill passed on to survey the post-war scene. The strategic air campaign might never have happened. As the speech ended and the radios were switched off, the airmen were left with the uncomfortable feeling that all their mighty effort, all the fear and sorrow, the stresses and sacrifices, had not been been considered worth mentioning.

The peace celebrations had barely begun but the victors were already constructing their version of history. The war had been a triumph for morality and civilized values, of light over darkness. The presence of Bomber Command loomed awkwardly over this legend. From then on, the political establishment colluded to keep it to the margins of the story. The intention seemed to be to avoid any mark of distinction that would draw attention to what Bomber Command had actually done. Harris complained to Portal that neither he nor any member of his staff was invited to any of the surrender ceremonies. When it came to awarding medals, care was taken not to identify the strategic bombing offensive as a distinct campaign. Those who served in other campaigns such as such as those in Africa, the Far East and France and Germany, were awarded their own star. Despite intense lobbying from the Air Ministry the official line held firm. These were awards for overseas service. Bomber Command had been fighting from home and would have to be content with the Defence Medal, given to all who were engaged on the home front. The aircrew, and the men on the ground who supported them were entitled to the 1939–45 Star, but that was issued to everyone. This provoked a protest from Sir Arthur Street, Permanent Undersecretary of State for Air, who represented the RAF on the Treasury committee which oversaw the grant of honours. The Star he, wrote 'is to be distributed universally . . . altogether it will not be a very worthy distinction for the aircrew of Bomber Command.' They did receive the Aircrew Europe Star. But the citation for this award was phrased with diplomatic precision. In an early draft it was described as decoration for those who had taken part in 'strategical bombing and fighter sweeps over Europe from the United Kingdom.' Later the distinction was dropped and it was given simply for 'operational flying from the United Kingdom bases over Europe.'[2]

Harris was infuriated at the perceived insult to his men. His anger was increased by his belief that it was Churchill, whom he counted as a friend as well as his most prominent supporter, who was behind the decision. On 1 June, he wrote a bitter letter to Portal and Sinclair declaring that 'if my Command are to have the Defence Medal and no "campaign" medal in the France–Germany–Italy–Naval War then I too will have the Defence Medal and no other – nothing else whatsover, neither decoration, award, rank, preferment or appointment, if any such is contemplated or intended . . . I will not stand by and see my people let down in so grossly unjust a manner without resorting to every necessary and justifiable protest which is open to me . . .'[3]

Only a fortnight after this outburst, Harris did accept a knighthood, awarded to him in the King's Birthday Honours, feeling he was unable to reject it because it came from the sovereign. The other giants of the RAF war effort, Portal and Tedder, were ennobled. The absence of a peerage excited conspiracy theories among Harris's supporters, which he was inclined to encourage. The truth was that a peerage was subsequently offered in late 1951, when Churchill returned to power. Harris decided his battle to obtain a special medal for his men was unwinnable. He declined a peerage, preferring the less cumbersome problems of duty and style presented by a baronetcy.

Why was the political establishment so reluctant to honour those who, for the duration of the war, had been cherished by the public and lionized by the government? And why was the embarrassing post-war silence when it came to marking Bomber Command's achievements not more of a public issue than it was? Harris had objected to the award of the Defence Medal on the grounds that the business of Bomber Command had been *offence*. This distinction lay at the heart of the problem. The moral rectitude of the Fighter Boys had been unquestionable. The Battle of Britain was as just a war as it was possible to fight. The pilots were defending their homes and loved ones from a cruel enemy who rejected the values of civilization. The Bomber Boys could argue that they were protecting Britain by so preoccupying the Luftwaffe that it did not have the means to continue its air offensive. But few saw this as their real purpose.

Bomber Command's task was to attack the enemy in their own homes. The British people had lived under the shadow of aerial bombardment ever since the end of the First World War. In the winter of

1940–41 they experienced the reality. They appreciated, at the time, the retribution that was delivered on their behalf. But once the war was ended they had no great desire to be reminded of the deeds that had been done in their name. That amnesia, inevitably, extended to those who had been carrying them out. Harris had summed it up with his usual harsh shrewdness: 'People didn't like being bombed and therefore they didn't like bombers on principle.'

Even those who had taken part in the campaign were filled with awe at what they had done. In May Peter Johnson was summoned by Harris to Bomber Command. 'The C-in-C drove me to his house, Springfield, for lunch wih him and Lady Harris,' he remembered. 'The journey in his Bentley, often at nearly 100 mph through Buckinghamshire lanes, was as alarming as anything on operations.' Harris offered him a post in the Bombing Research Unit being set up to gauge the level of destruction to Germany and particularly to its industry. It was small and inadequately staffed and Johnson believed its pupose was political as much as practical. 'Bert Harris knew that the Americans had an enormous bombing research unit and would be likely to claim all the credit.'[4]

He started work in the Ruhr and his first call was on what remained of Krupp's. He had already looked down on the scenes of devastation from the air. The view on the ground was even more impressive. 'Driving through Essen,' he wrote, 'I had my first close-up view of a bombed German city. As we progressed slowly down the pitted and cratered roads and streets leading to the centre of the town, the full horror of what I had seen from the air three weeks before came through to me. Every street, virtually every building, was gutted, the empty window frames showing the bare and blackened interiors, with twisted and charred remains of beds and furniture often hanging over into the streets.'

His chief, Air Commodore Claude Pelly, was similarly struck when he arrived in the Ruhr. 'There is a deadly silence, which creates a deep impression on the visitor's mind,' he reported home.[5] Johnson saw few people in the towns and most of them were old. 'Dressed mostly in black, they walked slowly, their heads bowed. The pall of their defeat was all around them and they seemed as desolate as their ruined houses.' Johnson wondered where these scarecrows lived. The answer was in cellars underground. Some of the workers who remained had lived like this for three years.

The scarecrows were finished. But there were more resilient Germans who were already pressing forward to stake their claim in the new order. Johnson was guided around the ruins by a Herr Singer, a loyal Krupp's functionary. He arrived in a large chauffeur-driven Mercedes and spoke good English. Total defeat had not crushed his spirits. 'He aimed to show that Krupp's was much more than just a firm, it was an institution which for him, outshone all the others in the Ruhr and Rhineland . . . Governments might come and go, but . . . Krupp's would last for ever.' This was the kind of German that the Allies needed to help relieve them of the burden of reconstruction. Singer, as it turned out, was right and Krupp's did indeed rise from the ashes.

The firm had kept good records. This diligence allowed the team to produce a comprehensive report. It was clear that until March 1943, the many raids launched against Essen and Krupp's had had little effect on production. That came as no surprise. The area's real ordeal began with the Battle of the Ruhr. Bomber Command launched six major raids on Essen between March and July. Two more heavy attacks were carried out in the spring of 1944. The team concluded that in the period March 1943–April 1944, Krupp's had suffered a loss of 20 per cent in output. Johnson, who flew in the battle, knew that 'this was far below what we had been led to expect by British Intelligence at the time.'

The bombing had produced some apparently spectacular benefits, such as knocking out the locomotive shop in the first raid of the Battle, and the destruction of its heavy shell-making capacity in July. But the successes were specious. Train engines and shells could be made elsewhere in the factories of the conquered territories.

After six months' hard research the team arrived at a dismaying conclusion. Over the years bombs might have destroyed or badly damaged 88 per cent of Essen's housing and killed up to seven thousand people. But in that time, the town's contribution to the war had not been substantially reduced. Essen had been defeated in the end. But that end had not come until March 1945 when the war had been substantially won. In the crucial period up to the autumn of 1944, by which time the defeat of Germany was not in doubt, Essen and Krupp's, by bravery and ingenuity, had continued to give valuable assistance to the war effort. Johnson reluctantly 'had to face the fact that no German unit had gone short of the essentials for making war because of our efforts.'

The population had suffered but they had endured. There had been breakdowns in electricity, telephones, water, gas and transport but they had been coped with. Food had been rationed but the supplies had held up almost to the end of the war. It could not even be said that morale had suffered badly. Johnson made careful enquiries. His questions met with much equivocation as the sur-vivors were anxious to disassociate themselves from the Nazi Party. However he came to the conclusion that morale had remained unaffected and had even improved until the end of 1944 when it was becoming clear the war was lost. Even then, there was a strong determination among the population to carry on, sustained in part by the Nazis' manipulation of fears of what would happen to them if the Allies arrived. The work of the *Terrorflieger*, which lay all around, gave the strongest evidence of what they were capable of. In the end, he concluded, patriotism and a sense of duty were more powerful motivations than fear, just as they had been in Britain. He might have added that the presence of a regime that could be as cruel to its own as it was to its enemies also helped to maintain discipline and cohesion.

Johnson left Essen in a state of deep depression. 'It seemed that all that had been done in the long and often terrible summer of 1943 had been in vain. All the agonies and casualties, the numbers of the dead and missing aircrew . . . the civilian men, women and children we had killed in Germany by our rain of bombs, all this had been for nothing.'

This view started to take hold soon after the war was over, gaining ground steadily until by the late 1970s it had become for many a sort of dim truth. Anti-nuclear campaigners claimed that by launch-ing the strategic air campaign, politicians and soldiers had crossed a moral Rubicon which had prepared the way for the use of weapons of mass destruction.

Any criticism, no matter how well meant, was unwelcome to Harris. When the official history of the strategic air offensive appeared in 1961 it brought him little comfort. It ran to four volumes and was a model of thoroughness, incisiveness and fairness. It was sympathetic and respectful towards him, taking his part in at least one of the major controversies with the Air Staff. Before publication, the authors offered to send him a draft so that he could comment, if he wished, in an unofficial capacity. Harris declined. Surely, he argued, he should have been consulted in his official role as commander-in-chief of Bomber Command. This entirely missed the point of the work which both its commissioners and authors were determined would aim for the highest peak of objectivity.

The authors believed that Bomber Command's 'contribution to victory, was, indeed a great one, though in direct terms at least . . . long delayed.' The initial attacks up to the spring of 1942 were little more than a nuisance to the Germans although they provided a great uplift to British morale. The persistence of the attacks also forced the Luftwaffe on to the defensive, which severely reduced its ability to bomb Britain. As Bomber Command's strength grew and its attacks strengthened it soaked up more and more of Germany's resources. The labour of huge numbers of German workers and foreign slaves was wasted clearing up the mayhem created by the big area attacks. Great effort was devoted to providing anti-aircraft defences and searchlight batteries for the homeland, which might otherwise have been expended on the Eastern Front. The constant attentions of the British and American bombers also hampered weapons research, severely reducing the Germans' chances of waging chemical or biological warfare.

In the last year of the war the Command, together with the USAAF, had succeeded in almost completely destroying vital segments of the oil industry, as well as virtually obliterating the communications system. These results had a decisive effect on the outcome of the war. No airman could object to these positive judgements. It was when the authors came to discuss the events of March 1943 to March 1944 that the picture grew more cloudy. The great area offensive, the authors concluded, 'did not produce direct results commensurate with the hopes once entertained and at times, indeed, feared by the Germans themselves.' Huge areas of many of Germany's great towns had been laid waste 'but the will of the German people was not broken or even significantly impaired and the effect on war production was remarkably small.' The fact was, the German economy 'was more resilient than estimated and the German people calmer, more stoical and much more determined than anticipated.' The authors' judgement on the economic effects, which stemmed from the research of the British Bombing Survey Unit, has since been convincingly challenged.

In their conclusions the authors were not attempting to make the case for those who had pressed for the selective approach rather than area bombing. 'Precision' attacks alone would not have achieved any better results. The best that could be said for the combined effort was that it had sapped some of the reserve within the German war economy and caused some factories, notably those making aircraft, to be scattered elsewhere. This made them more vulnerable to air attack later on.

Webster and Frankland's study was recognized as a landmark in military history. It was calm, finely calibrated and honest. It gave credit where it was due but did not flinch from awkward conclusions. Its judgements did not settle any arguments. But it was foolish to insist that there was only one way to fight a war. Harris did insist, however, and went on doing so until he died.

He ignored the subtleties of the authors' analysis and chose to see it as a polemic aimed against him and his men. He claimed they had presented the bombing campaign as a costly failure, an assertion they had never made. The fact that Frankland had flown thirty-six missions as a Bomber Command navigator and had been awarded a DFC did not impress him at all. He told questioners that 'he wrote it as a junior officer, and there was never a junior chief officer who didn't know better than a commander-in-chief how the show should be run.' Later though, he was to relent and pay tribute to Frankland and his work in war and in peace. By the time Harris died he had come to believe that no matter how much he might try to enlighten post-war audiences his life's great work was now seen as 'an expensive luxury' and an exercise in 'carrying out war against the civil population'.

There were few public voices to defend area bombing let alone to vaunt its achievements and inevitably his was the loudest among them. Periodically, when an anniversary or the appearance of a new publication revived the controversy, he went in to fight for his reputation and, more importantly, that of his men. There were many attempts to 'set the record straight'; by which he meant to bend public perception to his own version of events. They were expounded in a tart autobiography, Bomber Offensive, which bristled with criticism of his fellow wartime commanders. Any slight on himself or his men provoked a vigorous counter-attack with all the verbal violence he could muster. Harris's loyalty to those who served under him was deep and genuine. Just before he attended a dinner of 'Bomber Command Greats' at the RAF Club in 1976 he gave an interview to a researcher from the Imperial War Museum. He was in poor health, suffering from pneumonia. His doctor had advised him not to go, but Harris 'told him I was going to that show if I went on a stretcher.' He was determined, he said, 'to get the proper amount of credit awarded to my fellows who made such a tremendous contribution towards winning the war, a fact which has been acknowledged by the enemy and the senior British Army Commanders but not otherwise.'[6]

It was a difficult task, made more so by his own extravagant promises of what bombing could achieve. He claimed that the strategic air offensive could deliver victory on its own. Anything less than victory was therefore, by his own yardstick, a failure. Even so, Harris never deviated from his opinion that the bombing campaign had been a spectacular success. To support this view he leaned heavily on the evidence of Albert Speer, the German Minister of Wartime Weapon Production for much of the war. Harris seems to have admired Speer and harboured no doubts about his veracity as witness. 'He knows exactly, and better than anyone, what effect the bombing had,' he said. The old antagonists appear to have developed a mutual fascination. They corresponded after Speer's release from Spandau prison and Harris expressed a wish to meet him though the encounter never took place. Speer sent Harris a copy of *Inside the Third Reich*, his masterpiece of self-justification. According to Harris 'he said, in his own words, in the inscription of . . . the book itself, that the strategic bombing of Germany was the greatest lost battle of the war for Germany, greater than all their losses in their retreats from Russia and in the surrender of their armies at Stalingrad.'[7]

Harris's use of Speer's opinions was selective. During his post-war interrogation he said he found the attacks on city centres 'incomprehensible' and considered that 'area bombing alone would never have been a serious threat.' Civilian morale, he maintained, 'was excellent throughout, and resulted in rapid resumption of work after attacks.'[8]

In the forty-odd years of his life that remained to him after the war Harris never saw any reason to modify his views. The furore over Dresden did not impress him and in the IWM interview he defended the operation in characteristic terms. 'People are apt to say "oh poor Dresden, a lovely city solely engaged in producing beautiful little china shepherdesses with frilly skirts."' In fact, the city was the last viable governing centre of Germany as well as the last north–south corridor through which German reserves could move to reinforce resistance to both the Russian and Allied advances. What, he wanted to know, was so special about Dresden anyway? Why did no one talk of Lorient and Saint-Nazaire, which were 'destroyed to an extent where the German admiral in charge . . . said not so much as a cat remained alive to prowl the midnight ruins?' Harris suggested his own answer. 'One can only conclude that the reason is that it was ordered by the Navy and not the Air Force.'

The RAF was only doing what the senior service had been practising for centuries. 'People . . . think that when civilians get killed by bombers that it's something brand new. It's not new at all. No navy ever had a strategy except war against a nation as a whole; blockade, deprive the opposing nation of everything that made continuation of living impossible, deprive them of food as well as materials.' It was, he pointed out, 'very successful in the First War. In the 1914–18 war it was reputed to have killed about 800,000 Germans. You don't hear any criticism about that.'

He denied that Bomber Command had ever aimed 'particularly at the civilian population. We were aiming at the production of everything that made it possible for the German Armies to continue the war.' As for what constituted a legitimate human target, Harris had no doubts that munitions workers were fair game and should 'expect to be treated as active soldiers. Otherwise where do you draw the line?'[9]

Harris, as he often complained, had come to be thought of as the man chiefly responsible for the strategic bombing policy. The fact that he was its most vocal defender only intensified this identification in the public's mind. Some who were at least equally answerable avoided the post-war debates and spared themselves the hostility and opprobrium. Portal, whom Harris himself credited with being the prime mover in launching the bomber offensive, proved particularly agile in avoiding the tentacles of the controversy. In the early and middle phases of the air campaign he had been as enthusiastic as anyone in his advocacy of area bombing, only moving away from the policy once *Overlord* had changed the strategic landscape. The war was barely over when, addressing pupils at his old school, Winchester, he said he felt the need to correct 'two curious and widespread fallacies about our night bombing.' The first, he went on, was 'that our bombing is really intended to kill and frighten Germans and that we camouflaged this intention by the pretence that we would destroy industry.' This, as Portal knew better than anyone, was misleading. The intention had been to do both.

Now he told the boys that 'any such idea is completely and utterly false.' By the time he spoke the rough death toll was already known. This carnage, he maintained, 'was purely incidental and inasmuch as it involved children and women who were taking part in the war we all deplored the necessity for doing it.'[10] This struck Peter Johnson as 'hypocrisy of a fairly high order'. In a bombing war of the sort waged by the RAF innocent death was not incidental. It was inevitable. Whatever he subsequently said, Portal had even, at one point, actually thought it desirable. It was his name on the minute in November 1942 arguing the benefits of killing 900,000 Geman civilians and seriously injuring a million more.[11] Yet Portal entered the peacetime world in a shower of praise and garlanded with honours.

Harris's frequently repeated views provided his men with a set of ready-made defences when the subject of bombing came up. It is impossible to characterize the feelings of 125,000 men. But there were certain common strands of thought that ran through the reflections of the crews as they looked back on what they had done. Among the crews there were many thoughtful people, and most of them felt able to justify their actions. Surviving the experience did not induce a mood of harsh self-contemplation.

The Bomber Boys were fighting a new and never-to-be-repeated type of war. Their campaign was open-ended. It was not like a soldier gaining an objective or a sailor sinking a ship. With the advance of aerial photography their achievements became visible. But what did a rash of pockmarks in the ground and a sea of roofless houses mean to the progress of the war? To give some value to the great effort expended, the heavy losses and the great risks endured they had to believe that each trip brought the end at least an inch closer.

Even the least sensitive had some notion of the effect of their arrival over a German town. It was not hard to imagine the tension as the sirens sounded, the terrified scurry to the shelters, the din of the flak guns, the earth-trembling explosions, the smell of falling plaster and the sound of babies crying.

To give meaning to what they did they had to believe they were achieving something and that the good they were doing outweighed the bad. Some might insist that they had no concerns beyond their own survival. That was true during the duration of the operation. But on the ground there was plenty of time in which to think. It was impossible not to consider the bigger picture. Bomber Command had attracted the bravest and the brightest, forward-looking men with questioning and above all positive minds. There were few cynics inside the Lancasters and the Halifaxes. If staying alive was your first priority, why would you join Bomber Command?

So had it all been worth it? It was something that could only be asked of the living. The question of what Bomber Command had contributed to the war effort was, as Webster and Frankland had shown, complicated and never likely to be settled. The crews could comfort themselves with the unarguable fact that the campaign had seriously undermined Germany's defences and accelerated the Allies' victory. Discussion about the way force was focused, and whether different decisions would have produced quicker and better results was barren in the end. There were no lessons to be learned. Area bombing became obsolete with the first nuclear explosion.

By far the bigger issue, one that was never to go away, was the query that Churchill had raised over Bomber Command's conduct of the war. To many Bomber Boys the controversy was baffling and dismaying. They had carried out their orders with extraordinary selflessness and were now being asked to feel shame for actions for which they had once been praised. They had answered the public desire for retribution. This did not mean a measured response, proportionate to what Britain had suffered, but punishment that was relentless and merciless and that would stop the Germans from ever doing what they had done again. When it became clear exactly what the Germans had been doing, Bomber Command's slide from favour seemed all the more unjust.

There is no doubt that they felt slighted, even betrayed. Being the men they were these sentiments were submerged. The ordinary crew members were not inclined to make a fuss in public. But behind closed doors their true feelings could emerge. A speech by Marshal of the Royal Air Force Sir William Dickson, at 5 Group's first postwar reunion, thirty years after the war ended, gives an idea of their sense of hurt and a frank appreciation of what they saw as their own worth. Dickson, who had served on the Joint Planning Committee, was in a good position to put their achievements in the context of the whole struggle. Why, he asked, had the reunion been arranged after all these years? It was partly due to 'a growing feeling that time is moving on and that it is now high time . . . to celebrate the group's spirit and achievements.' But, he thought, 'it may also have something to do with a growing resentment and indignation, shared by the whole Air Force and many outside it, towards some who belittle the strategic air offensive against Germany. Some of these little people try to turn the truth upside down to sell their books or for some vested interest. We particularly resent the argument that the offensive was ineffective and caused needless casualties.'

The role given to Bomber Command after 1940, was 'a vital part of our grand strategy'. Those who criticise Bomber Command, he said, 'completely fail to appreciate the war situation or to put themselves in the place of those who bore the frightful responsibility for the conduct of the war. We were facing an enemy who was waging . . . unlimited war to gain his ends. In unlimited war it is a fight to the death between the whole of each nation. The alternative is surrender. The whole of the German nation was mobilized to destroy our nation and the Russian nation. Germany was all powerful on land, but the war-making potential of German industry was [its] Achilles' heel. Thanks to the foresight of Trenchard, and those who built on his ideas both here and in America, we had the means to attack that heel.'

Dickson then reeled off the list of the Bomber Boys' achievements. Their mission began to have decisive effect, he reckoned, early in 1942 when intensive operations forced the German High Command to concentrate on the air defence of Germany and give up hope that they could rebuild their bomber fleet and launch a new Blitz on Britain. The priority given to defending the Reich meant that outside it, the Allies eventually achieved air superiority. Without that superiority, the campaigns in Africa and Italy could not have succeeded as they did and *Overlord* would have been impossible. It also meant that on the Eastern Front, the German army was deprived of the air support to which it had been accustomed in its western campaigns. If they had the might of the Luftwaffe behind them, Russia would have been defeated. 'That,' he declared, 'should be sufficient answer to those who question the importance and achievements of the strategic air offensive.'

But there was more. Towards the end of the war, the weight and accuracy of the air offensive was such that it was close to accomplishing the Casablanca directive – the destruction and dislocation of the German military, industrial and economic system. It so weakened the enemy's military system that even with all their fighting skill, the Germans could not hold up the advance of the Allied and Russian armies. 'The Strategic Air Offensive,' he judged, 'had in fact brought about the utter defeat of Germany, and if it had not been maintained with great determination by all concerned in it, Germany must have won the war.'

There was a word about the criticism of civilian casualties. 'That criticism should not be pinned on the air offensive,' he maintained. 'It should be pinned on the horror of war itself, especially on unlimited war in which there are no non-combatants and there is no front line.' Compared with the twenty million deaths caused by the German invasion of Russia, 'the civilian casualties caused by the air offensive were astoundingly small. They were a regrettable but unavoidable necessity because the German war making potential was essentially the prime military objective of Allied strategy.'

This was a formidable array of achievements. Why then was the celebration of them so muted? Dickson had one explanation. 'It is hard,' he said, 'to convey by spoken or written word, the military glory of air operations . . . of course there were conspicuous operations which hit the headlines and stirred the nation. But neither the public then or today have any real idea of what was involved in bomber operations.'[12]

Noble Frankland had another. It was partly the fault, he believed, of the government's propagandists. 'The handling of Bomber Command by the official public relations experts had particularly unfortunate consequences,' he wrote. 'Apart from the general glossing over of all failures and the constant exaggeration of all successes . . . there was a more or less constant concealment of the aims and implications of the campaign that was being waged. Attacks on great towns were announced, but somehow or other, especially when questions were asked, the impression was given that specific targets such as armament factories and the like were being aimed at. The damage to the residential and central areas, which were in reality the main aim of the area attacks, was ascribed to what could unfortunately not be avoided if the factories and so on were to be hit.'

The result was that from an early stage in the war the impression was created that Bomber Command had the skill to target a weapons plant or some other plainly worthy target when in fact it could not. When, as occasionally happened, it was admitted that the town itself was the target, the impression was created that this had been chosen in preference to an objective that everyone would recognize as legitimate. Frankland concluded that 'from what one can only assume was a fear of moral indignation, moral indignation was created and in time more than moral indignation. The ultimate reaction was a deep feeling of shock, in the sense of surprise.'[13] It was Frankland who gave the crews the best justification for their war. 'The great immorality open to us in 1940 and 1941,' he told the Royal United Services Institution in December 1961, 'was to lose the war against Hitler's Germany. To have abandoned the only means of direct attack which we had at our disposal would have been a long step in that direction.' This sound judgement was gratefully repeated by his comrades many times in the subsequent years.

There was no great desire among the public for reminders of what had been done on its behalf. Once the reality of the war started to fade there seemed something incongruous and disturbing about the bombing campaign, something unBritish. Britain owned a great empire but its citizens like to think that it had been acquired without violence. They regarded themselves as mild and peaceable people who only took up arms when someone provoked them beyond endurance. Germany had certainly done that. But had the reaction been disproportionate?

Bomber Command was never taken to British hearts in quite the way that Fighter Command had been. It was too large for one thing and its aircraft too gargantuan. Fighter Command was of a

Noble Frankland.

cherishable size. The Spitfire was a very British aircraft. It was neat and agile without being flashy. It was small but it was powerful, like Britain itself. The Lancasters and Halifaxes were giants.

The entertainment industry sensed the public coolness. During the war there had been a series of films celebrating the Command. Movies like *Target for Tonight* (1941) which showed Britain wreaking righteous and specific vengeance on Germany and *The Way to the Stars* (1945) were great successes. The handful of post-war films tended to concentrate on the emotional damage done to the crews by their experiences rather than the damage they did to the enemy.

In the case of *Appointment in London*, which appeared eight years after the war, this owed something to the fact that the men who made it knew the reality of what they were portraying. Aubrey Baring, one of the producers, won a DFC as a fighter pilot and had gone on to fly in the Pathfinder Force. The screenplay and music were written by John Wooldridge who was a much-decorated PFF Mosquito pilot. The film starred Dirk Bogarde as Wing Commander

Tim Mason, the disciplinarian leader of a Lancaster squadron which had been sustaining heavy losses, and was set at the opening of the Battle of Berlin. Mason is on the edge of a breakdown having completed ninety operations yet is obsessively determined to carry on. The character was thought to owe much to Guy Gibson, who was Wooldridge's friend.

The best-known film about Bomber Command was *The Dambusters* which came out in 1954. Here was a subject that could wholeheartedly celebrate the skill and heroism of Bomber Command for feats which were untainted by controversy. The same was true of *633 Squadron* (1964). It was based on a novel which portrayed a fictitious Mosquito squadron in the summer of 1944, attacking a factory at the head of a Norwegian fjord which manufactured fuel needed for the Germans' V2 rocket programme. There was nothing showing fleets of bombers dropping hundreds of tons of high explosives on densely packed cities, let alone the terrible consequences on the ground.

As the years passed, Bomber Command faded from the public memory. The time of the bombers was short. In 1918 they seemed like the future of warfare. By 1946 their day had passed and would never come again. Monuments to their transience lay all over the northern and eastern counties of Britain. The runways of hastily-built aerodromes were ploughed up and the concrete carted away for hardcore. Beet and barley reclaimed the soil. Survivors returning to their old bases found only the odd humpbacked Nissen hut or hangar converted into a store or barn, or a decaying watchtower standing in the middle of a field to stir their memories.

In 1958 Don Charlwood went back to Elsham Wolds. The cement was peeling from the brick gate pillars and the guardhouse was in ruins. But from fifty yards away the mess still looked inhabited. 'I walked through the rain,' he wrote 'and went in at the open door, all at once anticipating the smell of beer and bacon and wet greatcoats, the sound of voices. But down the long room lay ploughs and harrows and bags of superphosphate ... I stood very still. Somewhere hens were clucking and rain gurgled off the roof. There were no other sounds at all. Something in the room eluded me; a deafness shut me from messages on the dusty air. I walked quickly into the rain, groping for understanding of our silenced activity, the purpose of all the courage and devotion I had once seen.'[14]

The old stations made an evocative image. The film *Twelve O'Clock High* opens with an American veteran returning four years after the war to his old base, which like Elsham has reverted to farmland. Cows graze next to the weed-infested landing strip where a tattered windsock hangs. The story that follows is set in 1942 when the American air force had just begun operations. It describes the fortunes of a bomber group which is suffering heavy losses and is undergoing a crisis in morale. The treatment is frank about the disillusioning effect of losses on the men and their commander. But essentially the film is a celebration of the Eighth Air Force and its achievements, which in the eyes of the makers were among the great American military successes of the war. The film, starring Gregory Peck, appeared in 1949.

It was produced by Darryl Zanuck, one of the great Hollywood powers of the time. It was, like all his productions, made in the expectation of commercial success. Film-makers later in the century were cautious about making movies about recently ended wars. *Twelve O'Clock High* did well at the box office. It was one sign that Americans had no qualms about the air war. A clue to the reason for their equanimity is contained in the film's opening credits, which declared: 'This motion picture is dedicated to those Americans both living and dead whose gallant effort made possible daylight precision bombing. They were the only Americans fighting in Europe in the fall of 1942. They stood alone against the enemy, and against doubts from home and abroad.'

The American insistence that they were engaged in precision bombing proved to be a magic shield against criticism. The truth was, as Frankland pointed out, that whatever they said they were doing, the effects were often much the same and the difference between an RAF area attack and a USAAF 'precision' attack could be minimal. As a senior American air force officer joked at a post-war seminar on the campaign, the RAF carried out precision attacks on area targets, while the USAAF carried out area attacks on precision targets. Nor did the American scruples extend to operations in Japan where the fire-bombing of Tokyo brought the principle of area bombing to perfection.

The Eighth Air Force suffered none of the criticism that was aimed at Bomber Command after the war. Its leaders went on to what were the most important military posts of the Cold War era, commanding the strategic bomber fleets that would wage a nuclear war. To some extent, the fact that the American air force had dropped two nuclear bombs on Japan made the debate on the validity and morality of its activities in the European theatre redundant. The American Second World War fliers continued to be honoured and their actions explained in sympathetic films like *Memphis Belle* which described the lives of one Eighth Air Force crew.

In Britain though, the controversy was never laid to rest. New books and documentaries kept the embers of the debate smouldering. As long as Harris was alive the arguments would continue. During the war he had been a remote figure to his crews and to many of those he worked with. In peacetime they began to feel protective towards him. On his ninetieth birthday he received a message from veterans of 12 and 626 Squadrons, once based at Wickenby, which must have warmed his leathery old heart. 'Few of us met you in those days,' it ran, 'but we hope you were aware that your messages which were read to us in the briefing room stirred many a young heart and strengthened many an apprehensive young airman . . . We are grateful for all you have done to remind those who would prefer to forget, what we did and what we achieved and of the enormous cost.'[15]

He spoke at many Bomber Command veterans' dinners, always delivering the same message to his 'old lags' of all ranks: that they had never been given proper recognition for their decisive part in the defeat of Hitler. As long as he was alive, for good or bad, he was determined to go on making their case. During the war he had never had the time to engage in much human contact with his men. He made up for it in peacetime. After each reunion he would, as Michael Beetham remembered, 'sit late into the night with a word for everyone and outlasting most.'[16]

Harris's last great public appearance was on 4 September 1982 at the Guildhall in London to honour his presidency of the Bomber Command Association and to mark his ninetieth birthday. The evening ended with Hamish Mahaddie reciting to a spellbound hall Noel Coward's 'Lie in the Dark and Listen'. He died at his home beside the Thames at Goring on 5 April 1984, a few days before his ninety-second birthday. The presidency of the association passed to Michael Beetham, by now a senior RAF officer. 'The vilification that went on of Bert Harris was deeply resented among all of us,' he said. 'We were determined to do something about it.' St Clement Danes in the Strand is the church of the RAF. A statue of Lord Dowding, the chief of Fighter Command during the Battle of Britain, already stood before it. Beetham and and a group of other veterans decided that Harris deserved a statue of his own.

The plan was announced in September 1991. Harris was seven years dead but his reputation was as incendiary as ever. Enough time had now passed for Germans to feel they had a say in the matter. The mayor of Pforzheim was the first to protest followed by his colleagues in Cologne, Hamburg and Dresden. An attempt was made to enlist the support of the City Council of Coventry with which Dresden was twinned. The German media seized on the story and Harris's detractors in Britain publicly repeated their condemnations and criticisms. The statue was unveiled by the Queen Mother on 31 May 1992. It was, as was pointed out, the fiftieth anniversary of Harris's first spectacular, the thousand-bomber raid against Cologne. The monument cost £100,000, most of which came from ex-Bomber Boys or other past and present members of the RAF. A large group of protesters stood behind police cordons as the Queen Mother performed the ceremony. During it, a lone Lancaster flew overhead. After the ceremony was over and the crowds had dispersed, someone daubed the dull, eight-foot-high bronze with red paint. 'That was quickly cleared up,' Michael Beetham recalled. 'What I found was the most touching thing was that the following day there was a wreath from the people of the East End, in gratitude. That did more for morale than anything. They were the people who suffered and they were grateful.'[17]

The statue, like the man it represents, is open to different interpretations. Harris stands upright, his chest jutting forward and his eyes staring confidently ahead. Is it the pose of a supremely arrogant man, faithful to his own blind vision whatever the cost? Or does the stiff way he holds himself show something more admirable; fortitude, and the determination to carry out a terrible but necessary task?

The elderly men standing in the early summer sunshine fervently believed the latter. They came from all walks of life. When the war was over there was little room in the ranks of the RAF. Not many wanted to stay on. They were volunteers, civilians in uniform who had joined up to serve their country and were eager to go back to the world they had left six extraordinary years previously. A bomb-aimer's or navigator's brevet won no favours when looking for jobs. The world was full of servicemen with good wars behind them. One wing commander with a DFC could only find a job working front of house at the Odeon, Swiss Cottage.

When it came time for the Bomber Boys to say goodbye to each other, the partings were painful. Each crew was a social patchwork stitched from men of every class and background. Fear, mutual dependence and the chemistry that had attracted each to the other during crewing-up, welded them into a nucleus, bound together by respect and a form of love.

In the first decade or two of peace they drifted apart. But in late middle age as mortality once again beckoned, many felt the need to look out their old comrades. Early in 1985 Dennis Steiner learned that 170 Squadron which had shared Hemswell with his squadron, 150, were to dedicate a memorial at the base to the crews who had not returned. Through the 170 Squadron association he was able to get back in touch with three surviving crewmates and they were reunited at the service. They found each other stouter and somewhat worn by time but they could still see their old companions behind the lined faces and grey hair. Hemswell was closed and run down but intact. Like naughty schoolboys they managed to get in by forcing a side door and wandering through the old rooms, dusty and forlorn and haunted by memories.

Dennis returned to Hemswell again in 1988 for the 170 Squadron annual service with his wife and children. A Lancaster flew overhead as usual but the base was much changed. Two of the barracks blocks housed antiques centres, another was an old people's home and the officers' mess had been turned into a hotel. A market was set in the grounds at weekends. He 'walked around with some disbelief and sadness.' The market was held on the spot where many years before his room-mate had been killed when his aircraft crashed. 'I wonder if,' he wrote shortly after the visit, 'when the Lancaster had flown past in tribute to those who lost their lives, people paused in their hunt for bargains and looked up, if they knew why it had flown over and also, if they cared. I think that I shall not return.'[18]

The dead were never far away on these occasions. Between September 1939 and May 1945, Bomber Command lost 47,268 men killed on operations. Another 8,305 were killed in flying or training accidents. Another 1,570 groundcrew and WAAFs lost their lives from other causes. The total amounts to between a sixth and a seventh of all British and Commonwealth military war dead. It is a considerably higher figure than the 38,384 officers from the British Empire lost in the First World War. This toll was considered as a catastrophe, a slaughter of the paladins that blighted the post-war years. The deaths of so many Bomber Boys must be counted as another epic tragedy.

For those who came through, no peacetime experience could match the intensity of those short, terrible months when they flew and fought. The war was always there, stirring into life at the slightest nudge. 'At sixty-six, I sit looking out of my window,' wrote Cy March, forty-five years after it was all over, 'watching seagulls gliding, soaring, side-slipping and wheeling around. I think the old Lancaster could do all that . . . I also sit and watch the sunset, truly a work of God, the sheer beauty of the reds, golds and many other lovely colours. Then I think of the sunsets we created, also beautiful in a terrible way with unearthly colours flickering and brightening, the blue flashes from the cookies, the bright red bursts of flak, lit up by searchlights and fires, all created by man's inhumanity to man.'[19]

Epilogue
WENT THE DAY WELL?

With peacetime the complex human cell structure of Bomber Command dissolved. There was no need for Bomber Boys in the post-war world. They dispersed as rapidly as they had come together, settling down in every corner of the country and beyond, working at every occupation. In my early days, doing holiday jobs, I sometimes came across them in offices and factories. The war was the last thing they talked about. But somehow their experiences seemed to mark them out from the other ex-servicemen in the workforce.

Some of the survivors stayed on in the RAF. Michael Beetham had a distinguished career, retiring after forty-one years in 1982 as Marshal of the Royal Air Force and Chief of the Air Staff. He held the post longer than any of his predecessors. As a member of the Chiefs of Staff committee, he played a crucial role in the direction of the Falklands War. Ken Newman obtained a permanent commission and left, aged fifty, as a wing commander before starting a satisfying chapter of life in school and charity administration.

Most still thought of themselves as civilians and were happy to get out of uniform. Arthur Taylor shed his air force blue for a demob 'overcoat, sports coat, flannels and a pair of shoes', in January 1946. 'I felt,' he wrote, 'that when the war in Europe was over [and] the enemy had been beaten there was no longer any purpose in my staying on. . . I had had the good fortune to serve with some fine people in a fine organization and was pleased to have survived the experience.' He joined the civil service working for the Department of Employment until retiring with his wife in Norfolk, where he passed his time painting, gardening and rambling.[1]

The feat of survival brought no advantages. Dennis Steiner had to wait until July 1946 to be demobilized. He ended his RAF career as a pilot officer and by now was a married man. He went back to the office in Wimbledon he had left as a junior to be told that he would receive the same wages he was on when he joined up. 'I could not have had a clearer indication that the war was over,' he remembered.

Settling down was difficult, especially for someone like Leonard Cheshire who by the end had flown a record one hundred missions. He finished his war looking down on Nagasaki on 9 August 1945 as an atomic bomb exploded over it. In 1948 he offered his Hampshire home to a terminally-ill ex-serviceman who had nowhere to go to die. From this act of humanity grew the foundation that carries his name. It flourishes today in fifty-two countries bringing hope and help to the disabled.

Some were able to take up where they had left off when the war came along. After liberation from a German PoW camp, Reg Fayers returned to Sudbury, Suffolk, and his wife Phyllis, and joined her father in his dairy business. He resumed his old sporting career, playing football for Sudbury Town. Reg and Phyllis had a son and daughter. The family moved to west Wales. Reg took took up farming and wrote a book about it, *The Sheep of Dolgwili*. 'I suppose it was "happy ever after,"' he says now.[2]

The need to write was strong. It had been Don Charlwood's ambition since boyhood. After leaving school in the seaside town of Frankston, near Melbourne, in 1932, he approached the Australian newspaper baron Keith Murdoch for a reporter's job, but was only offered the chance to be a messenger. He managed to sell some short stories while working as a farmhand before volunteering for the RAAF in 1940.

In 1943 Don and his crew became the first in 103 Squadron in nine months to survive a tour. On returning to Australia he worked for thirty years in air-traffic control. He recorded his Bomber Command experiences movingly and perceptively in one of the finest books of the war, *No Moon Tonight*. He has written many others and now lives in happy and honoured retirement in Warrandyte, Victoria. One of the benign side effects of the strategic bombing campaign was that it produced a crop of outstanding literature, as powerful as anything that emerged from the trenches. It includes Jack Currie's *Lancaster Target* and *Luck and a Lancaster* by Harry Yates, classic memoirs which ring with authenticity.

Noble Frankland had a different kind of literary career. As well as writing the official history he became director of the Imperial War Museum and played a large part in the production of *The World At War*, the Thames Television epic, produced in the 1970s and as yet unsurpassed.

Most settled into quiet anonymity. Reg Payne went back to Kettering and a job in an engineering factory and later became a technical teacher in a local college. He took up painting evocative pictures of Lancasters in flight and rural scenes. Willie Lewis went to sea on a trawler, sailing from Hull on gruelling three-week trips to the Arctic Circle. Cy March returned to the mines.

The dead lived their unrealized lives in the memories of those they left behind. The love of George Hull's brief life, Joan Kirby, married and became Joan Hatfield. George seemed to be sitting in the corner of her cosy living room in Christchurch, Dorset, as we talked about him on an autumn Saturday afternoon. 'He was a great believer in social justice,' she said as her husband made the tea. 'Had he lived he would have been a leader in some form. It wasn't until after the war that I realized quite what marvellous material he would have been. . . he was a lovely chap. Hardly a day passes when I don't think of him.'³

Mary Mileham never quite forgot Frank Blackman. She destroyed most of her wartime correspondence but could not bring herself to get rid of Frank's letters. She offered them instead to the Imperial War Museum in the hope that they would give 'some idea of the pain and anguish felt by those flying boys . . . the longing and wishing for peace and love'. Before she died, she wrote to a friend explaining what the relationship had meant. 'It was healing for me to be so needed and some solace to him that I was faithfully there for a few months.' But she felt that 'in peacetime it would not have been any good and had already begun to fade'.⁴ After the war she married Patrick Lindsay who worked as a musical arranger at the

BBC and lived contentedly with him in an old cottage in Hampshire. She died in November 1993.

Frances Scott had a miserable few months after her broken Bomber Command romance. Then she met another Bomber Boy, became Frances Dowdeswell, and settled down to a happy married life.

Peter Johnson carried his doubts about the war he had fought into peacetime. He stayed on in the air force, taking part in the Berlin air lift and serving in the mid-fifties as civil air attaché in Bonn. He worked hard at reconciliation with the people he had once bombed and was a trustee of the Dresden Trust, which contributed to the rebuilding of the Frauenkirche, destroyed in the 1945 attack.

Virtually everyone in Bomber Command had been convinced of the justice of what they were doing while they were doing it. 'I didn't have any feelings of guilt,' Bill Farquharson said, sixty-one years after flying his last mission. 'As Harris said, you sow the wind, you reap the whirlwind. We were trying to save our country from Nazi Germany . . . my generation loved this country. We loved our way of life and we were going to keep it and fight for it. . . The majority of us felt that way.'[5]

Viewed from a Lancaster the moral perspective was clear. 'War is a brutal business,' said Tony Iveson. 'Civilization breaks down and if you're going to win, you [have to] win any way you can. Otherwise you're defeated.'[6] It was an attitude that was shared by those who were facing them. The Luftwaffe night-fighter pilot Peter Spoden felt no animosity towards those he was up against. 'We thought "we are not trying to kill the aircrew. We are trying to get the bombers who are destroying our town". . . . every soldier has to do his duty... it was our duty to shoot them down. It was their duty to bomb the towns.'[7] The passage of time did little to change minds. 'I always stuck up for Bomber Command,' said Reg Fayers in December 2006. 'We did a good job and I was never ashamed of anything we did.'[8] Leonard Cheshire spent the rest of his life comforting the broken, many of them victims of the war. But he was there at the unveiling of Bomber Harris's statue outside St Clement Danes and when he was awarded a peerage he chose to remember Woodhall, the home of 617 Squadron, in his title.

As the years passed and death got closer many felt the pull of the rare intimacy of their wartime lives and sought out their old comrades. They met again in pubs in Lincolnshire and Yorkshire and Suffolk and drove out to look at their bases, many all but unrecognizable save for an old Nissen hut or a derelict watchtower. The dead were never far away and the need to commemorate them was strong. In Britain there is no public day to mark their sacrifice. But many of the dead airmen shot down over France, Belgium, Holland and Norway are still remembered on the anniversary of their deaths by local communities who regard them as liberators and heroes. In September 2006, the small town of Werkendam gave a fitting burial to the crew of a 78 Squadron Halifax that was shot down by a night-fighter and crashed into marshy ground on the night of 24/25 May 1944. The town council raised £85,000 towards the cost of retrieving their remains and raising the headstones. The councillor who led the campaign, Gerard Paans, declared 'we owe our freedom to these brave airmen'.[9]

The Bomber Boys conducted their own rituals of remembrance and raised their own modest memorials. A plaque in Tuddenham parish church in Suffolk commemorates a crew who died flying from the base, which has now melted back into the fields. There are only seven names on it. But the inscription could serve for all the dead Bomber Boys.

> Went the day well?
> We died and never knew.
> But well or ill, Freedom,
> We died for you.[10]

Notes

PROLOGUE

1 Interview with author.
2 W. R. Chorley, *Bomber Command Losses of the Second World War. 1939–40*, Midland Publishing, 2005.
3 ibid, 1945.
4 Jörg Friedrich, *The Fire, The Bombing of Germany 1940–45*, Columbia University Press, 2006.

INTRODUCTION

1 Quoted in Denis Richards, *Portal of Hungerford*, Heinemann 1979, pp. 294–5.
2 Peter Johnson, *The Withered Garland*, New European Publications 1995, pp. 262–3.
3 George F. Kennan, *Sketches from a Life*, W. W. Norton, 2000, p. 121.
4 Harris, IWM, 000931/01.
5 *The Strategic Air War Against Germany 1939–1945. Report of the British Bombing Survey Unit*, Frank Cass 1998, p. 68. The lowest civilian casualty is cited in the survey. The highest is given in Paul Johnson, *Modern Times*, 1983.
6 Interview with author.
7 Lobban, IWM, 88/31/1.
8 Don Charlwood, *No Moon Tonight*, Goodall 2000, p. 131.
9 Harris, Introduction to Guy Gibson, *Enemy Coast Ahead – UNCENSORED*, Crécy 2003, p. 10.
10 James Hampton, *Selected for Aircrew*, Air Research Publications, p. 343.
11 Harry Yates, *Luck and a Lancaster*, Airlife Classic 2001, p. 211.

12 Fayers, *Microfilm copy of letters and diaries*. IWM.

ONE

1 Guy Gibson, op cit, pp. 34–8.
2 The Earl of Halsbury, *1944*, Thornton Butterworth, London 1926, p. 94.
3 In the preface he cites a tract by J. B. S. Haldane, a prominent left-wing academic, to support his predictions. In *Callinicus*, published a year previously, Haldane had also dwelt on the subject of poison gas, an understandable preoccupation with someone who had suffered its effects in the trenches. Unlike Halsbury he suggested some counter-measures to avert the coming catastrophe. In the case of mustard gas, he wrote, 'the American army made a systematic examination of the susceptibility of large numbers of recruits. They found that there was a very resistant class, comprising 20% of the white men tried but no less than 80% of the negroes. This is intelligible as the symptoms of mustard gas blistering and sunburn are very similar, and negroes are pretty well immune to sunburn. It looks, therefore, as if, after a stringent preliminary test, it should be possible to obtain coloured troops who would all be resistant to mustard gas concentrations harmful to most white men. Enough resistant whites are available to officer them.'
4 Titmuss, *Problems of Social Policy*, London 1950, pp. 12–14, 41.

5 Sir John Slessor, *The Central Blue*, Cassell 1956, p. 56.
6 Recounted to Henrietta Miers by Archie Bevan.
7 Letter from Mönchengladbach City Archivist Dr Christian Wolfsburger, 12.9.2006.
8 Sir Charles Webster and Noble Frankland, *The Strategic Air Offensive Against Germany, 1939–1945*, HMSO 1961, vol. I, p. 150.
9 Webster and Frankland, vol. I, p. 47.
10 Webster and Frankland, vol. IV, p. 89.
11 Webster and Frankland, vol. I, p. 154.
12 ibid, vol. I, p. 154.

TWO

1 Memoir of D. R. Field, IWM Department of Documents, 92/29/1.
2 Tim Lewis, *Moonlight Sonata, the Coventry Blitz, 14/15 November 1940*, Tim Lewis and Coventry City Council, pp. 57–61.
3 ibid, p. 63.
4 ibid, p. 82.
5 Kris and Speier, *German Radio Propaganda*, p. 332.
6 John Shelton, *A Night in Little Park Street*, Britannicus Liber 1950.
7 Norman Longmate, *Air Raid*, Arrow 1976, p. 106.
8 Lewis, op cit, p. 128.
9 Longmate, op cit, p. 63.
10 ibid, p. 213.
11 Mass Observation Archive, Sussex University, 6/4/E.
12 ibid.
13 ibid.
14 *The Observer*, 17.11.40.
15 Lewis, op cit, p. 57.
16 MO Archive.

THREE

1 Johnson, op cit, p. 23.
2 IWM sound archive, 8204/03/01.
3 A. R. Taylor, unpublished memoir, IWM Department of Documents.
4 Public Record Office, AIR 29/603.
5 Yates, op cit, p. 15.
6 Brian Frow, unpublished memoir, RAF Museum.
7 Kenneth Jack Newman, unpublished memoir, IWM documents, 06/12/1.
8 IWM, 92/29/1.
9 IWM sound archive, 20926.
10 IWM sound archive, 008901/16.
11 Johnson, op cit, p. 12.
12 IWM, 06/12/1.
13 Ken Goodchild, unpublished memoir, IWM, 98/31/1.
14 Richard Morris, *Cheshire*, Viking 2000, p. 22.
15 Gibson, op cit, pp. 28–30.
16 Interview with author.
17 Interview with author.
18 Bruce Lewis, *Aircrew*, Cassell 2003, p. 117.
19 Interview with author.
20 IWM sound archive, 007372.
21 IWM, 06/12/1.
22 IWM, 94/37/1.
23 Morris, op cit, p. 32.
24 Ralph Wood, 'Seven is My Lucky Number', unpublished manuscript, RAF Museum.
25 Charlwood, op cit, p. 25.
26 ibid, p. 7.

FOUR

1 Webster and Frankland, op cit, vol. IV, p. 30.
2 Interview with author.
3 IWM, 92/29/1.
4 Yates, op cit, p. 59.
5 Denis Steiner, unpublished memoir, IWM, 92/79/1.
6 Hampton, op cit, p. 122.
7 Frow, op cit.
8 Cyril March, unpublished memoir, IWM, 67/281/1.

9 Bruce Lewis, op cit, p. 118.
10 Wood, op cit.
11 Henry Hughes, unpublished memoir, IWM, 99/64/1.
12 Denholm Elliott, recorded reminiscences, IWM, 98/7/1.
13 Interview with author.
14 Charlwood, op cit, p. 17.
15 Interview with author.
16 IWM sound archive, 11587/114.
17 IWM sound archive, 20914/3.
18 Jack Currie, *Lancaster Target*, Goodall 2004, pp. 9–10.
19 Yates, op cit, p. 66.
20 IWM sound archive, 2897/03.
21 IWM sound archive, 20917.
22 IWM, 06/12/1.

FIVE

1 IWM, 94/37/1.
2 PRO AIR, 14/2221.
3 Eric Woods, *While Others Slept*, Woodfield 2001, pp. 57–8.
4 Webster and Frankland, op cit, vol. IV, pp. 128–9.
5 Slessor, op cit, p. 371.
6 Webster and Frankland, op cit, vol. IV, pp. 135–41.
7 ibid, vol. IV, pp. 194–5.
8 Gibson, op cit, p. 195.
9 Slessor, op cit, p. 389.
10 PRO AIR, 21/5. The pilot appealed the verdict and his accuser was killed in action before the appeal came to court.
11 Slessor, op cit, p. 367.
12 John Patrick Dobson, unpublished memoir, IWM, 92/2/1.

SIX

1 Johnson, op cit, pp. 150–151.
2 Arthur Harris, *Bomber Offensive*, Pen and Sword 2005, pp. 88–9.
3 Currie, op cit, p. 91.
4 Interview with author.
5 IWM sound archive, 20926.
6 IWM, 88/22/2.
7 Henry Probert, *Bomber Harris*, Greenhill 2003, p. 204.
8 Wood, op cit.

9 Harris, op cit, p. 83.
10 ibid, p. 85.
11 ibid, p. 105.
12 Quoted in Frederick Taylor, *Dresden*, Bloomsbury 2005, p. 143.
13 Harris, op cit, p. 107.
14 James Fyfe, *The Great Ingratitude*, GC Book Publishers 1993, p. 323.
15 Frow, unpublished memoir, RAF Museum.
16 IWM sound archive, 2897/03.
17 IWM sound archive, 9378/5/2.
18 IWM, 98/7/1.
19 IWM sound archive, 007298/04.
20 IWM, 99/14/1.

SEVEN

1 Quoted in Anja vom Stein, *Unser Köln. Erinnerungen 1910–1960. Erzählte Geschichte*, Sutton Verlag, pp. 111, 116–18.
2 ibid.
3 ibid.
4 ibid.
5 R. M. Ellscheid, *Erinnerungen von 1896–1987*, Stadt Köln, 1988.
6 Quoted in Martin Rüther, *Köln im Zweiten Weltkrieg. Alltag und Erfahrungen zwischen 1939 und 1945*, Emons 2005.
7 Quoted in Bernd Haunfelder and Markus Schmitz, *Humanität und Diplomatie. Die Schweiz in Köln*, Aschendorff Münster, pp. 202–3.
8 Stein, op cit.
9 ibid.
10 ibid.
11 Heinz Pettenberg, *Starke Verbände im Anflug auf Köln. Eine Kriegschronik in Tagebuchnotizen 1939–1945*, Verlag JP Bachem 1981, pp. 162–8.
12 Quoted in Hans-Willi Hermans, *Köln im Bombenkrieg 1942–1945*, Wartberg, Gudensberg-Gleichen 2004, pp. 30, 32.
13 Hans Sester, *Als Junge im sogenannten Dritten Reich*, H-A Herchen Verlag 1986, pp. 47–52.
14 Martin Rüther, op cit.
15 Pettenberg, op cit.

16 Dr P. Simon, *Köln im Luftkrieg. Ein Tatsachenbericht über Fliegeralarme und Fliegerangriffe*, Köln 1954.
17 Stein, op cit.
18 *Die geheimem Lageberichte des Sicherheitsdienst der SS, 1938–45*, ed. Heinz Boberach, Herrsching 1984, vol. 14.
19 Webster and Frankland, op cit, vol. IV, p. 310.

EIGHT

1 Johnson, op cit, p.165.
2 Newman, op cit.
3 IWM, 74/93/1.
4 IWM, 88/22/2.
5 IWM, 93/5/1.
6 IWM sound archive, 209/23/2.
7 IWM, 85/6/1.
8 Hull, op cit.
9 IWM sound archive, 20926.
10 Newman, op cit.
11 Johnson, op cit.
12 IWM, 67/281/1.
13 IWM sound archive, 20917.
14 Yates, op cit, p. 90.
15 IWM, 209147.
16 IWM, 67/281/1.
17 ibid.
18 IWM sound archive, 8901/16/14.
19 IWM, 98/30/1.
20 IWM, 88/47/1.
21 Johnson, op cit, pp. 191–3, 173–4.
22 Parliamentary Debates, Commons, vol. 380, pp. 178–9.
23 ibid, vol. 385, p. 685.
24 ibid, vol. 388, p.155.
25 Quoted in Max Hastings, *Bomber Command*, p. 177.
26 Parliamentary Debates, Lords, vol. 130, pp. 737–46.
27 Parliamentary Debates, Commons, vol. 380, p. 1378.
28 Parliamentary Debates, Lords, vol. 130, pp. 748–9.
29 *The Secret Beast*, quoted in Fyfe, op cit, p. 216.
30 IWM, 88/31/1.
31 Correspondence of Rev. G. Martin, IWM, 93/48/2.
32 IWM sound archive, 2164.

33 Martha Gellhorn, *The Face of War*, p. 166.
34 IWM sound archive, 2170.
35 Terence Rattigan, *Flare Path*, Hamish Hamilton 1942.
36 Currie, op cit, p. 130.

NINE

1 Charlwood, op cit, p. 90.
2 IWM sound archive, 20923/2.
3 IWM, 88/22/2.
4 Johnson, op cit, p. 177.
5 IWM, 80/46/1.
6 Charlwood, op cit, p. 111.
7 Flying Personnel Research Committee, 412 (f) 17.
8 Charlwood, op cit, p. 32.
9 IWM sound archive, 20923/2.
10 Yates, p. 125.
11 Gibson, op cit, p. 174.
12 IWM, 92/29/1.
13 Yates, op cit, p. 101.
14 IWM sound archive, 20926.
15 Woods, op cit.
16 Newman, op cit.
17 John Pudney, *Ten Summers: Poems 1933–43*, Bodley Head 1944, p. 48.
18 Willie Lewis, unpublished memoir, IWM, 67/28/1.
19 ibid.
20 IWM, 67/281/1.
21 IWM, 92/29/1.
22 IWM sound archive, 11587/4.
23 Quoted in Theo Boiten, *Nachtjagd*, The Crowood Press 1997. Pietrek claimed three crewmen managed to bale out successfully. The incident does not appear in British records.
24 IWM, 67/281/1.
25 IWM, 20929/2.
26 Webster and Frankland, op cit, vol. IV, p. 433.
27 IWM, 94/37/1.
28 Johnson, op cit, p. 166.
29 IWM, 94/37/1.
30 IWM sound archive, 20926/2.
31 Charlwood, op cit, p. 44.
32 IWM sound archive, 20923/2.
33 Johnson, op cit, pp. 175–6.
34 IWM, 67/28/1.
35 Currie, op cit, p. 97.

36 IWM, 88/47/1.
37 IWM, 92/10/1.
38 *Militärgeschichtliches Forschungsamt, Das Deutsche Reich und der II Weltskrieg*, vol. 9.
39 PRO WO 235/153.
40 IWM, 98/31/1.
41 Yates, op cit, p. 122.
42 Currie, op cit, p. 86.

TEN

1 IWM, 94/37/1.
2 IWM, 88/22/2.
3 IWM sound archive, 007372/04/02.
4 IWM, 67/281/1.
5 Newman, op cit.
6 IWM, 67/28/1.
7 Interview with author.
8 IWM sound archive, 007372/04/02.
9 Charlwood, op cit, p. 121.
10 IWM, 88/22/2.
11 IWM, 92/29/1.
12 IWM, 94/37/1.
13 Interview with author.
14 IWM sound archive, 007373/04/02.
15 Newman, op cit.
16 *The Second World War Letters of G. J. Hull*, Imperial War Museum Department of Documents.
17 IWM, 67/281/1.
18 IWM sound archive, 007298/04.
19 IWM sound archive, 007372/04/02.
20 Interview with author.
21 IWM, 67/28/1.
22 Charlwood, op cit, p. 53.
23 Newman, op cit.
24 IWM, 94/37/1.
25 Frow, op cit.
26 IWM, 67/28/1.
27 IWM, 88/22/2.
28 Charlwood, op cit.

ELEVEN

1 Webster and Frankland, op cit, vol. IV, p. 155.
2 PRO AIR, 14/3507.

3 Quoted in John Terraine, *The Right of the Line*, Hodder & Stoughton 1985, p. 547.
4 Harris, op cit, p. 176.
5 IWM sound archive, 209182.
6 Webster and Frankland, op cit, vol. II, pp. 201–2.
7 Harris, op cit, p. 187.
8 Interview with author.
9 *The Berlin Diaries of Marie Vassiltchikov*, The Folio Society, London 1991, pp. 97–9.
10 Hans-Georg von Studnitz, *Diarium der Jahre 1943–45*, pp. 137–9.
11 Hans-Dieter Schäfer, *Berlin im Zweiten Weltkrieg*, pp. 144–59.
12 PRO, *Bang On*, 31 December 1943.
13 Freeman Dyson, *Disturbing the Universe*, pp. 19–20.
14 Interview with author.
15 Noble Frankland, *The Bombing Offensive Against Germany*, p. 72.

TWELVE

1 Interview with author.
2 IWM, 94/37/1.
3 Gibson, op cit, p. 127.
4 IWM, 88/22/2.
5 Frow, op cit.
6 Charlwood, op cit, p. 63.
7 IWM, 67/281/1.
8 Letters of Edwin Thomas, IWM Department of Documents.
9 Interview with author.
10 IWM sound archive, 209/23/2.
11 Terraine, op cit, p. 527.
12 IWM sound archive, 8901/16/9.
13 Webster and Frankland, op cit, vol. IV, p. 445.
14 Jonathan Falconer, *Bomber Command Handbook*, Sutton Publishing 2003, p. 51.
15 Hampton, op cit, p. 263.
16 Dyson, op cit, p. 21.
17 Martin Middlebrook, *The Berlin Raids*, Cassell 1988, p. 378.
18 Newman, op cit, p. 110.
19 Dyson, op cit, pp. 25–6.
20 Newman, op cit, p. 70.
21 ibid, p. 184.

22 IWM, 88/22/2.
23 Gibson, op cit, p. 273.
24 Interview with author.
25 Yates, op cit, p. 227.
26 Flying Personnel Research Committee, p. 10.
27 IWM sound archive, 20718/5.
28 IWM sound archive, 8901/16/9.
29 Interview with author.
30 IWM sound archive, 20718/5.

THIRTEEN

1 IWM, 92/29/1.
2 Currie, op cit, p. 114.
3 See Allan D. English, 'A Predisposition to Cowardice? Aviation Psychology and the Genesis of "Lack of Moral Fibre"', *War and Society*, vol. 13, no. 1, May 1995.
4 PRO AIR, 2/8591, AM Pamphlet 100.
5 PRO, Symonds and Williams, *Investigation of Psychological Disorders in Flying Personnel*, FPRC 412(f).
6 ibid.
7 IWM sound archive, 20718/5.
8 Dyson, op cit, pp. 23–4.
9 Currie, op cit, p. 139.
10 PRO AIR, 2.
11 English, op cit, p. 26.
12 Mark K. Wells, *Courage and Air Warfare*, Frank Cass 2000, p. 204.
13 PRO Air Ministry memo, 1 March 1945, S 61141/S7(d).
14 Lawson memorandum, RAF Air Historical Branch.
15 Quoted in Wells, op cit, p. 200.
16 Johnson, op cit, p. 246.
17 Currie, op cit, p. 136.
18 Interview with author.
19 PRO AIR.
20 PRO AIR.
21 Flying Personnel Research Committee, op cit.
22 IWM, 94/37/1.
23 Wells, op cit, p. 205.

FOURTEEN

1 Dyson, op cit, p. 19.
2 Hull, op cit.
3 IWM, 92/29/1.
4 IWM, 88/22/2.
5 Charlwood, op cit, p. 54.
6 IWM, 80/46/1.
7 Newman, op cit.
8 Woods, op cit.
9 IWM, 85/6/1.
10 IWM, 94/37/1.
11 IWM, 92/29/1.
12 IWM, 74/93/1.
13 Charlwood, op cit, pp. 153, 156.
14 Hull, op cit.
15 IWM, 88/22/2.
16 IWM, 92/2/1.
17 Gibson, op cit, p. 10.
18 Hull, op cit.
19 See Lewis, op cit, p. 36.
20 IWM sound archive, 8901/16/14.
21 IWM, 80/46/1.
22 Charlwood, op cit, pp. 59–61.
23 IWM, 99/14/1.
24 Currie, op cit, p. 12.
25 Hull, op cit.
26 Letters of E. G. Thomas, IWM, 67/277/1.
27 Pip Beck, *Keeping Watch*, Crécy 2004, pp. 27–8.
28 Frow, op cit.
29 Hull, op cit.
30 IWM, 67/28/1.
31 Currie, op cit, pp. 73–4.
32 ibid, pp. 163–4.
33 IWM, 67/28/1.
34 Hull, op cit.
35 Yates, op cit, p. 132.
36 IWM, 85/6/1.
37 Woods, op cit.
38 Yates, op cit.
39 Hull, op cit.

FIFTEEN

1 Letters of Mary Mileham. Mileham family papers.
2 Following correspondence taken from Letters of Flying Officer F. H. Blackman, IWM Documents Department, 80/46/1.

3 ibid.
4 Mileham papers.
5 ibid.
6 Martin Middlebrook and Chris Everitt, *The Bomber Command War Diaries*, Penguin 1990, p. 271.
7 Interview with author.
8 Following correspondence taken from Letters of Joan Kirby, IWM, Department of Documents.
9 Following correspondence taken from the Letters of George Hull, IWM, Department of Documents.
10 Interview with author.
11 Gibson, op cit.
12 Frances Dowdeswell, *The Path*, unpublished memoir, IWM.

SIXTEEN

1 Roger Freeman, *The Mighty Eighth*, Cassell 2000, pp. 67–9.
2 ibid.
3 ibid, p. 78.
4 Terraine, op cit, p. 620.
5 Newman, op cit.
6 Yates, op cit, p. 135.

SEVENTEEN

1 Ralph Briars, unpublished memoir, IWM, 67/385/1.
2 Interview with author.
3 IWM, 67/385/1.
4 Harris, op. cit, p. 220.
5 Terraine, op cit, p. 676.
6 Yates, op cit, pp. 179–80.
7 Newman, op cit.
8 Quoted in Terraine, op cit, p. 673.
9 Quoted in Webster and Frankland, op cit, vol. III, p. 82.
10 ibid, p. 84.
11 ibid, p. 93.
12 ibid, p. 80.
13 ibid, p. 55.
14 ibid, p. 101.

EIGHTEEN

1 Roy Lodge, unpublished memoir.
2 Quoted in Frederick Taylor, *Dresden*, Bloomsbury 2004,
   pp. 214–15. The most thorough and lucid work on the subject as well as the most balanced.
3 Interview with author.
4 See Taylor, op cit, pp. 503–9 for discussion of the controversy over the death toll.
5 Interview with author.
6 Yates, op cit, pp. 235–6.
7 Middlebrook and Everitt, op cit, p. 669.
8 PRO WO 235/235.
9 Quoted in Webster and Frankland, op cit, vol. III, p. 112.
10 Quoted in Johnson, op cit, p. 243.
11 Webster and Frankland, op cit, vol. III, p. 119.
12 Statistisches Bundesamt, *Wirtschaft und Statistik*, vol. III, pp. 139–42.
13 Hans Rumpf, *The Bombing of Germany*, Muller 1963, pp. 154–65. The statistics for civilian deaths in France are taken from Eddy Florentin, *Quand les Alliés bombardaient la France*, Perrin 1997.
14 Johnson, op cit, p. 260.
15 Following account from IWM, 88/47/1.
16 IWM, 92/10/1.
17 IWM, 98/7/1.
18 Fayers, op cit.
19 IWM, 92/29/1.
20 IWM, 67/281/1.

NINETEEN

1 Quoted in Henry Probert, *Bomber Harris*, Greenhill 2003, p. 343.
2 PRO, letter from Sir Arthur Street to Sir Robert Knox, 17 January 1945.
3 Probert, op cit, p. 348.
4 Quoted in *The Many*, WH Smith 1995.
5 Quoted in Richards, op cit, p. 335.
6 IWM, 931/01.
7 Quoted in Probert, op cit, p. 410.
8 Webster and Frankland, op cit, p. 375.
9 IWM, 931/01.
10 Richards, op cit, p 339.
11 Terraine, op cit, pp. 505, 684.

12 IWM Documents Department, Misc, 10.202.
13 Frankland, op cit.
14 Charlwood, op cit, p. 218.
15 Quoted in Probert, op cit, p. 411.
16 ibid, p. 411.
17 Interview with author.
18 IWM, 42/29/1.
19 IWM, 67/281/1.

4 IWM 80/46/1.
5 Interview with author.
6 Interview with author.
7 IWM 20/91/8.
8 Conversation with author.
9 *Daily Mail*, 28 September 2006.
10 The lines are usually attributed to the English classicist John Maxwell Edmonds, 1875–1958.

EPILOGUE

1 IWM 99/14/1.
2 Conversation with author.
3 Interview with author.

Bombers

The specifications below are average for each aircraft. Modifications were constantly being made as design and capacity were changed, and the plans overleaf show a precise version ('Mark') of our five most important bombers of World War II.

WELLINGTON
Long-range night bomber

Wingspan:	86 ft
Length:	61 ft
No & type of engines:	2 Merlin X
Crew:	6
Bomb loading:	4,500 lb
Armament:	4 machine guns
Max speed:	255 mph
Average height:	12,500 ft
Range:	1540 miles (loaded)

LANCASTER
Heavy bomber

Wingspan:	102 ft
Length:	69.5 ft
No & type of engines:	4 Merlin
Crew:	7
Bomb loading:	14,000 to 22,000 lb
Armament:	10 machine guns
Max speed:	287 mph
Average height:	1400 ft
Range:	1660 miles

HALIFAX
Heavy bomber

Wingspan:	104 ft
Length:	70 ft
No & type of engines:	4 Hercules XVI
Crew:	7
Bomb loading:	13,000 lb
Armament:	9 machine guns
Max speed:	282 mph
Average height:	13,000 ft
Range:	1260 miles (loaded)

STIRLING
Heavy bomber

Wingspan:	99 ft
Length:	87 ft
No & type of engines:	4 Hercules II
Crew:	7 or 8
Bomb loading:	14,000 lb
Armament:	8 machine guns
Max speed:	270 mph
Average height:	14,000 ft
Range:	2010 miles

MOSQUITO
Fighter bomber

Wingspan:	54 ft
Length:	40 ft
No & type of engines:	2 Merlin 21
Crew:	2
Bomb loading:	2000 lb
Armament:	machine guns or cannon
Max speed:	380 mph
Average height:	21,000 ft
Range:	1220 miles

14 Life-saving jacket stowages
15 Fuel tanks (port and starboard)
16 Fuel jettison pipe (port and starboard)
17 Aileron trimming tab (port and starboard)
18 Formation keeping lamp (port and starboard)
19 Navigation lamp (port and starboard)
20 Pressure head
21 Cable cutter
22 Armoured leading edge
23 Fuel tanks (port and starboard)
24 Dinghy stowage
25 Air bottles
26 Overload oil tank
27 Carburettor air intake
28 Merlin engine
29 Radiator shutter
30 Flotation bags 14 (stowed in roof of bomb cells)
31 Reserve ammunition
32 Navigator (2nd pilot bomb-aimer
   with seat-type parachute)
33 Bombs

1 Tail formation keeping lamp
2 Tail navigation lamp
3 Rudder trimming tab
4 Reserve ammunition boxes
5 Rear gunner
6 Tail turret
7 2 Browning guns
8 Elevator trimming tab
   (port and starboard)
9 Tailplane de-icing mat
10 Tail ballast weights
11 Retractable tailwheel recess
12 Parachute stowage (rear gunner)
13 Parachute stowage (mid gunner)

WELLINGTON II

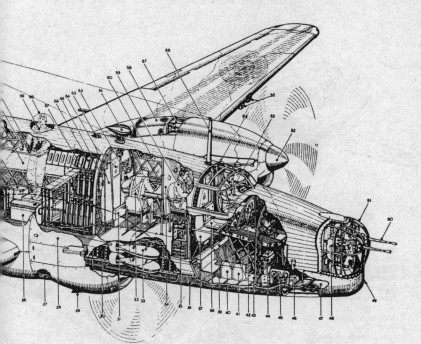

34 Armour plate
35 Main electrical panel
36 Bomb doors (extending aft to
   mid-gun position)
37 Door (sound-proof bulkhead)
38 2nd pilot's folding seat
   (with seat-type parachute)
39 Cabin heating duct
40 Parachute stowage (bomb-aimer)
41 Parachute stowage (front gunner)
42 Pilot's instrument panel
43 Bomb-aimer's cushion (cabin entrance door)
44 Camera
45 Bomb-aimer's control panel
46 Thermometer fairing
47 Bomb-aimer's window
48 Front gunner
49 Forward navigation lamp
50 2 Browning guns
51 Nose gun turret
52 Hydromatic air screws
   (with anti-icing equipment)
53 Pilot (with seat-type parachute)
54 Undercarriage positioning warning horn
55 Retractable landing lamps
56 Aerial mast

57 Oil tank (port and starboard nacelle)
58 Fuel tank (port and starboard nacelle)
59 Wireless operator
60 Navigator's instrument panel
61 D.F. loop
62 Map stowage
63 Upward identification lamp
64 Doors (sound-proof bulkhead)
65 Hand fire extinguisher
66 Oxygen bottles (port and starboard)
67 Reconnaisancre flares
68 Observation dome
69 Navigator (in sextant reading position)
70 Compass
71 Sextant steady
72 Rest bunk
73 Parachute stowage
74 Thermos flasks stowage
75 Mid gun hatch (port and starboard)
76 Elsan closet
77 Mid-gunner's position
78 Flame floats or sea markers
79 Vickers 'K' gun (starboard mid-gun position)
80 Flare chute
81 Fin de-icing mat
82 Rudder mass balance

LANCASTER I

1 Second pilot's seat (folded)
2 Windscreen glycol spray
3 Engine control levers
4 Front gun turret (2 Browning guns)
5 Extractor louver (cabin heating)
6 Bomb aimer
7 Glycol tank
8 Auto bomb sight
9 Glycol spray
10 Bomb aimer's window
11 Air temperature thermometer
12 Pressure head
13 Parachute exit
14 Parachute storage
15 Camera
16 Rudder pedals
17 Control column
18 Navigator's instrument panel
19 Pilot's glycol hand pump
20 Fuel jettison control
21 Intake control
22 Seat adjusting lever
23 Bomb door controlvalue
24 Pilot
25 Pilot's armour plating
26 A.R.I. 5033
27 A.R.I. 5033
28 Navigator
29 T.R.9.F. wireless
30 Navigator's D.F. receiver
31 W.I. operator's receiver
32 Trailing aerial winch
33 T.1154 transmitter
34 Amplifier
35 W.T.operator
36 Signal pistol
37 Hydraulic reservoir
38 Hydraulic hand pump
39 Cabin heating duct
40 Cabin heating inlet

41 B.B.P. plate
42 Oil cooler
43 Radiator (coolant)
44 Header tank
45 Merlin XX engine
46 Oil tank
47 No 1 fuel tank
48 Undercarriage doors
49 Landing wheel
50 Undercarriage jack
51 No 2 fuel tank
52 Flame damper
53 Carburettor air intake
54 No 3 fuel tank
55 B.B.P. plate
56 B.B. cable cutter
57 Navigation lamp

58 Formation keeping lamps
59 Aileron
60 Aileron balance tab
61 Flaps
62 Whip aerial (beam approach)
63 Flare chute
64 Mid gunner
65 Mid lower turret (2 Browning guns)
66 Vacuum flasks
67 Entrance door
68 Downward identification lamps
69 Stepover ammunition chutes
70 Dip-sticks stowage
71 Fireman's axe
72 First aid stowage
73 Dipole aerial
74 Sanitary pan

75 Walkway over tail plane
76 Fixed tail wheel
77 Aerial for A.R.I. 5000
78 Elevator
79 Elevator trimmig tab
80 Elevator balance tab
81 Fin
82 Rudder
83 Rudder trimming tab
84 Aerial for navig. D.F. receiver & T.R.9.F.
85 Rear gun turret (4 Browning guns)
86 Draught proof doors
87 Access ladder
88 Mid upper turret
89 Aerial for A.R.I. 5000
90 Step for upper turret (stowed)
91 Sea markers and flame floats

92 Ammunition chutes
93 Parachute stowage
94 Portable oxygen stowage
95 Ammunition boxes
96 Emergency exit
97 Flare chute extension (stowed)
98 Flap jack cover
99 Reconnaisance flares
100 Back rest for rest seat
101 Rest seat and oxygen crate
102 Dinghy manual release
103 Portable oxygen stowage
104 Armour plate doors
105 Dinghy stowage
106 Control locking gear stowage
107 Bomb handle stowage
108 Observation dome
109 Whip aerial A.R.I. 5033
110 D.F. loop aerial
111 Voltage regulations
112 Aerial for G.P. Marconi
113 Aileron trimming tab

HALIFAX II

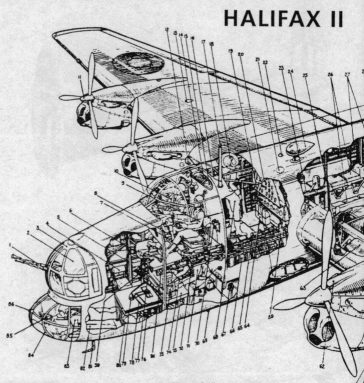

1 2 Browning guns
2 Front gunner's position
3 Nose gun turret
4 Navigator's seat
5 Flexible heating pipes to crew positions
6 Cabin heating
7 Pilot's compass
8 Pilot's panel
9 First pilot
10 Second pilot
11 Airscrews for de-icing equipment
12 Fuel cock controls (pilot operated)
13 Fuel tanks air vent
14 Engine starter buttons
15 Armoured glass
16 Aerial mast de-icing
17 Aerial mast
18 Astral dome
19 Bombs (fuselage bomb bay)
20 Flight engineer's instrument panel
21 Very light signal pistol aperture
22 Upward identification lamp
23 Emergency hand pump
   (hydraulic system)
24 D.F. loop
25 Engine control runs
26 Crew's rest position

27 Handrail
28 Marine distress signals
29 Bombs (in wing bomb bays)
30 Reconnaissance flares
31 Rear escape hatch
32 Dinghy stowage
33 Mid gun turret
34 2 Browning guns
35 Ammunition boxes
36 Ammunition tracks
37 Crash axe stowage
38 D.R. compass
39 Astrograph
40 Tail wheel shock absorber cover
41 Rear gunner's parachute stowage
42 Rear gunner'r instrument panel
43 Rear gunner's rest seat
44 Rear gunner
45 Rear gun turret
46 Four Browning guns
47 Rear identification lamp
48 Rudder tab
49 Rear armour plated bulkhead
50 Entrance door
51 Fuel tanks
52 Oil tank (outboard engine)
53 Aileron tab
54 Formation keeping lamps (port and starboard)

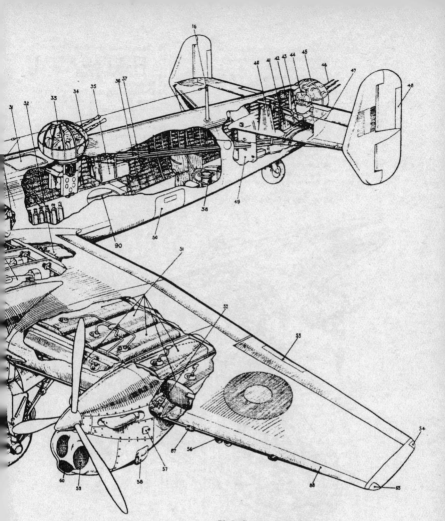

55 Navigation lamp (port and starboard)
56 Retractable landing lamps
57 Access to engine priming cocks
58 Carburettor air intake
59 Cooling system radiator
60 Oil cooler radiator
61 Radiator flap
62 Heater system air intake
63 Oil tank (inboard engine)
64 Flight engineer's parachute stowage
65 Automatic controls
66 Oxygen bottles
67 Spare trailing aerial reel stowage
68 Flight engineer
69 Trailing aerial
70 Controls for emergency flares
71 Radio operator
72 Main electrical panel

73 Radio operator's table
74 R.O. parachute stowage
75 Transmitting and receiving sets
76 Camera
77 Map stowage
78 Navigator's table and chart plotter
79 Navigator's table lamp
80 Navigator's parachute stowage
81 Pressure head
82 Bomb-aimer's prone ramp
83 Bomb-aimer
84 Bomb-aimer's window
85 Bomb sight
86 Forward navigation lamp
87 Cable cutters
88 Armoured leading edge
89 Armour plated bulkhead and door
90 Provision for lower gun turret
91 Navigator's compass repeater

1 Fuel tanks (outboard inter-spar)
2 Fuel tanks (inboard inter-spar)
3 Fuel tanks (rear)
4 Upward identification lamp
5 Fuel tank (leading edge)
6 Aerial mast
7 Aerial mast de-icing equipment
8 Charging and distribution panel
9 D.F. loop
10 Heating system handwheel
11 Airframe de-icing control handwheel
12 Charging cable stowage
13 Oxygen bottles
14 Fuel cock controls
15 Bunk (rest station)
16 Central service accumulators
17 Oxygen bottles
18 Airscrew anti-icing fluid tank

19 Observation dome (stowed)
20 Fire extinguisher
21 Fuselage heating pipe
22 Ground signalling strips
23 Escape ladder
24 Mid-upper turret (2 Browning guns)
25 Flame floats or sea markers
26 Four reconnaissance flares
27 Fuel filler extension
28 Fin de-icing equipment
29 Rudder balance tab
30 Navigation lamp (tail)
31 Rudder trimming tab
32 Rear turret (4 Browning guns)
33 Parachute stowage (rear turret)
34 Elevator trimming tab
35 Tail plane de-icing equipment
36 Bulkhead door

37 Elsan closet
38 Fuselage entrance door
39 Parachute stowage (flare launcher)
40 Parachute stowage (mid-gunner)
41 Four reconnaissance flares
42 Forced-landing flare chute
43 Reconnaissance flare chute
44 Maintenance trestles
45 Maintenance trestle struts
46 Tool roll
47 Ammunition conveyor (to rear turret)
48 Ammunition (rear turret)

49 Reserve ammunition
50 Dinghy stowage
51 Flap
52 Fuel tanks (inboard inter-spar)
53 Fuel tanks (outboard inter-spar)
54 Aileron trimming strip
55 Port formation-keeping lamp
56 Port navigation lamp
57 Twin landing lamps (retractable)
58 Oil tank
59 Carburettor air intake
60 Engine cooling gills

STIRLING I

77 Engineer's instrument panel
78 Bomb in fuselage bomb cell
79 Navigator, 2nd pilot or bomb-aimer
80 Navigator's instrument panel
81 Compass
82 First aid outfit
83 Emergency tool kit
84 Automatic pilot control panel
85 Downward identification lamps (in floor)
86 Camera
87 Gyro azimuth
88 Parachute stowage (bomb-aimer)
89 S.C.I. control panel
90 Ballast weight
91 Bomb-aimer's adjustable platform
92 Bomb- aimer's window
93 Automatic bomb-sight mounting
94 Bomb-aimer's switch panel
95 Navigation lamp (nose)

61 Hercules II or XI engine
62 Constant-speed airscrew (feathering)
63 Oil cooling duct (outboard engine)
64 Cool air duct (cabin heating)
65 Oil cooling duct (inboard engine)
66 Port main undercarriage wheel
67 Undercarriage doors
68 Heating system boiler
69 Bomb in wing bomb cell
70 Carburettor air intake and supercharger
   control handwheels
71 Ration tin
72 Fuel jettison control handwheels
73 Wireless operator's seat
74 Escape and observer-dome hatch
75 Wireless equipment
76 Fire extinguisher

96 Front turret (2 Browning guns)
97 Drift sight stowage
98 Parachute stowage (front gunner)
99 Air bottles
100 Pilot's 1st instrument panel
101 1st pilot
102 2nd pilot's seat
103 Flap control panel
104 Cut-out control levers
105 Carburettor control cock levers
106 Rudder and elevator trimming tab gearbox
107 Compass mounting
108 Flying control locking gear stowage

MOSQUITO IV

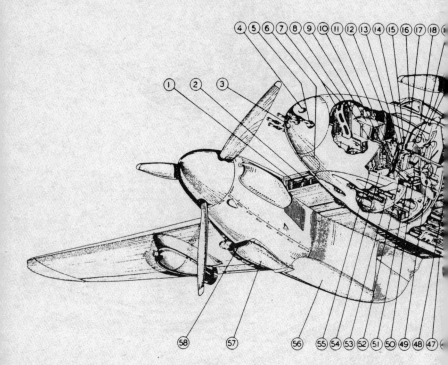

1 Oil cooler	21 Cockpit lamp
2 Coolant radiator	22 Pilot's seat and harness
3 Navigation headlamp	23 Flame-trap exhaust
4 Camera gun spot	24 Outboard fuel tanks
5 Four 303 guns	25 Landing lamp
6 Cover to used cartridge-case chamber	26 500 lb bomb
7 Ammunition boxes and feed chutes for 303 guns	27 Navigation lamp
8 Hinge for gun loading door	28 Resin lamp
9 Inspection door for instrument panel	29 Pitot head (pressure)
10 Folding ladder	30 Aerial for R.1155
11 Ventilator control	31 Tail navigation lamp
12 Compass	32 Tail-wheel (retracted)
13 Control column	33 Oxygen bottles
14 Brake lever	34 Accumulators
15 Firing switches	35 Inboard fuel tanks
16 Sliding window	36 Long range fuel tank bearers
17 Trailing aerial winch	37 Downward identification lamp
18 Emergency exit	38 Bomb winch and hawser
19 Engine and propeller control box	39 Ventral compartment lamp
20 Observer's seat and harness	40 Bomb carriers

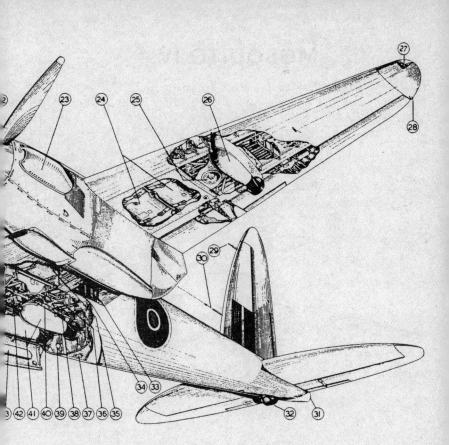

41 500 lb bombs
42 Bomb racks
43 Bomb doors showing trough
    for clearance of 500 lb bomb
44 Central tanks
45 Hydraulic jacks (4)
46 Ammunition boxes and feed chutes
    for 20mm guns
47 Link and cartridge chute cases
48 De- icing tank
49 Elevator trim hand-wheel
50 Pilot's seat adjusting lever
51 Sanitary container
52 First aid box
53 20mm guns (4)
54 Entrance door (starboard)
55 Rudder pedals
56 Undercarriage wheel doors
57 Air intake
58 Ice guard

Acknowledgements

A book like this owes its existence to the generosity of those who took part in the events described. This paperback edition has also benefited from the contributions of readers, many of them veterans of Bomber Command or with relations who served in it, who have put me right on points of fact and detail. I would like to thank everyone who gave so freely of their time and their memories, spoken and written. I owe a special debt to Tony Iveson, Doug Radcliffe and Sir Michael Beetham of the Bomber Command Association for supporting *Bomber Boys*. I am also grateful to the following for allowing me to quote from their memoirs: Reg Fayers, Dennis Field (whose fascinating *Boy, Blitz and Bombers* will shortly be published), Roy Lodge, Cyril March, Ken Newman, Dennis Steiner and Harry Yates. Geoffrey Willat gave me permission to quote from his illuminating book, *Bombs and Barbed Wire, My War in the RAF and Stalag Luft III* (Upfront Publishing), and Mark Briars from the memoir of his late father, Ralph. Thanks to Bruce Lewis for permission to quote from *Aircrew: The Story of the Men Who Flew the Bombers*. Kind permission to quote from Jack Currie's *Lancaster Target* and Don Charlwood's *No Moon Tonight* (both Goodall paperbacks) was granted by Crécy Publishing. Thanks also are due for permission to quote from Harry Yates's *Luck and a Lancaster: Chance and Survival in World War II* (The Crowood Press Ltd, new edition, ISBN 1-84037291-5). New European Publications likewise kindly granted permission to quote from Peter Johnson's *The Withered Garland: Doubts and Reflections of a Bomber*. I have failed in my attempts to contact Arthur Taylor and Doug Mourton, whose memoirs are held at the Imperial War Museum. Please accept my apologies.

I am particularly grateful for the encouragement I received from Edward Hearn of 50 Squadron at the start of my research. Also for the help and hospitality offered by Frances Dowdeswell, Bill Farquharson, Joan Hatfield, Fred Hulance, Philip Mileham and Reg Payne. The great Noble Frankland and his worthy successor Sebastian Cox, Chief Historian of the RAF, were generous with their wisdom. The staff at the Imperial War Museum and the RAF Museum were, as always, friendly and helpful. Arabella Pike, Annabel Wright, Melanie Haselden, Vera Brice and the rest of the team at HarperCollins were the best an author could hope for. A heartfelt vote of thanks, too, to my agent David Godwin. I am grateful to Angelica von Hase for her excellent research on the bombing of Germany. Kate Connolly kindly provided information about the early bombing of Germany. Thanks too, to Felicity Hawkins, Annabel Merullo and Tim Harris for their friendship when the going got tough. I would also like to record my gratitude to my old teacher, Richard Milward, head of history at Wimbledon College, who died last year after a lifetime inspiring generations of boys with his love of history. I cannot thank Henrietta Miers enough. But I will try, in another place in another way.

Index

Page numbers in *italics* denotes an illustration

Abercromby, 'Jock' 213
Adenauer, Konrad 99, 114
air gunners *see* gunners
Air Ministry 52, 101, 226
aircraft 10, 34, 49
  German 205
  heating in 162
  as 'home' 186–7
  loss of in Battle of Berlin 207, 212,
    214, 216, 230, 286, 307–8
  numbers lost on operations 67, 79,
    229, 307, 324
  and safety 231–2
  see also bombers; individual names
aircraft crew *see* bomber crew
Aircrew Europe Star 368
Aitken, Max xl
appeasement 41
Appointment in London (film) 383–4
Ardennes
  German counter-offensive at 331
area bombing 71, 95, 102
  criticism of 140–1
  Harris's advocation of 88–9, 94–5,
    199, 200, 330, 331, 333, 340
  and Portal 14–15, 71, 74, 102, 377
Attlee, Clement 143
Atwood, Sergeant B. E. 186, 187
Australia/Australians 44, 45–6, 52, 263,
  278
Aviation Candidates Board 34
Avro Lancaster *see* Lancasters
Avro Manchester 92

B-17 Flying Fortresses 127, 206, 310
Bader, Douglas xxxii
Bailey, Rob 62
Ball, Fred 220
Baring, Aubrey 383
Barker, Squadron Leader R. I. 255

Barnard, Squadron Leader 103
Bartlett, Les 210
bases, bomber *see* bomber bases
Bato, Joseph 139
Battle of the Atlantic 73, 79
Battle of Britain xxxv, 10, 14, 16, 41–2,
  144, 201, 369
BBC 145
Beadle, Flight Sergeant D. J. 355
Beaver Club (London) 278
Beaverbrook, Lord 27
Beck, Pip 272
Beckers, Albert 120, 121, 122
Beetham, Michael 41, 188, 208, 210,
  215, 219, 236, 387–8, 390
Bell, George (Bishop of Chichester) 142
Bennett, Air Vice Marshal Sir Don 46, 101
Berchtesgaden, bombing of 354–5
Berlin 135, 199–218
  bombing of (1943) 145–7
  bombing of by Americans (1945) 343
  bombing disaster and loss of life
    (1941) 81–5, 86
  bombing of in response to London
    raids 17
  destruction of and impact of bombing
    xxix, 210, 211–12, 215, 356
  drawbacks in bombing 135, 199
Berlin, Battle of (1943–44) 206–14,
  286, 293–4, 298
  aborted missions 217
  aircraft destroyed 207, 212, 214, 216,
    230, 286, 307–8
  Harris's plans for bombing 202
  poor results 212, 215, 216–17, 307
  preliminary raids 206
  problems during 207, 208
Berry, Jim 37, 90, 135, 161, 171
Bettington, Group Captain Vere 35, 37
Bevan, Aneurin 27

Big Week (1944) 316
Bilbey, Freddy 40–1
Billancourt (France)
  bombing raid on Renault factory
    (1942) 87–8, 139
Birmingham, bombing of 21
Birnie, Bill 62–3, 349
Blackman, Frank 156, 258–9, 266–7,
  280–7, 392
blast bombs 159
Blitz see German Blitz
Bochum 110–12
Bogarde, Dirk 384
bomb-aimers 49, 52, 57, 57–9, 60, 157,
  173 see also bomber crew
bomber bases 256–67
  banning of wives from 300
  entertainment and music 264–6, 271
  food on 259–60
  life and conditions xl–xli, 154,
    256–64
  location 267
Bomber Command
  achievement of xxvii, 380–1
  area bombing doctrine 13, 71, 88–9,
    94–5, 102, 113, 199, 200, 330,
    331, 333, 340
  assessment of contribution (1961)
    373–4
  attacks on French ports 104–5
  attacks on V-weapon targets 323–4
  and Battle of Berlin see Berlin, Battle
    of
  Blitz as initial justification for
    campaign xxxiii
  bombing of German towns 13, 113
  bombing of Tirpitz 326–8
  and Casablanca directive (1943) 105,
    199, 202, 308, 381
  change in modus operandi due to D-
    Day invasion preparations 307
  changes in operational procedures
    under Harris 94–5
  controversy over area bombing and
    criticism of 140–3
  criticism of in peacetime xxvii, 372–3
  and Dams Raid (1943) xxxii, 106–10,
    183, 191, 200, 228
  destruction of cities and mounting
    disquiet at conduct of (1945)
    342–52
  and Dresden campaign (1945) 138,

  340–1, 342–3, 344–7, 350, 352–3,
    376
  fading of from public memory 384
  films about 383–4
  first 'thousand' raid against Cologne
    (1942) xxxix–xxxv, 98–100, 113,
    116, 141
  flying in relief supplies 357
  focus of attack on civilian morale
    74–6, 77
  front-line groups 156
  growth of xxxiv
  initial bombing targets and duties
    10–11, 14, 73
  initial weaknesses 4
  lack of recognition of in peacetime
    xxxii, 367, 368–70, 381
  lack of success in first years of war 67,
    73–4, 78, 79–80, 81
  last raids of war 354–5
  liberation of prisoners-of-war 358
  media coverage of operations
    xxxiv–xxxv, 145–7
  morale of 80, 157
  mounting a raid and preparations
    155–64, 160
  new plan for bombing (1941) 77–9
  night-flight raid routine 164–70
  night-fighter escorts 318
  number of airmen killed xxvi,
    xxxviii–xxxix, 389
  number of bombs dropped (1944/45)
    332–3
  oil targets 324, 330–1, 333
  operational loss rate 229–30
  and Overlord operation 320–3
  pattern of raids 170–7
  personnel involved xxxiv
  and Pointblank directive 200, 201–2,
    308
  propaganda value of operations
    xxxi–xxxii, 68, 145
  questioning of achievement
    xxxvi–xxxvii
  role in final phases of war 354
  role outlined in Western Air Plans
    10–11
  shift away from policy of precision to
    policy of annihilation 14–15,
    17–18, 72, 74, 76–7
  switching to daylight bombing
    question 317–19

targets 72, 73, 103, 104, 330, 333, 337

task of disrupting transportation links in preparation for D-Day 307, 308–9, 319–20

total number of bombs dropped 355

Bomber Command Association 387

bomber crew xxxv–xxxvi, 47–66

appeal of Bomber Command and reasons for joining 33–4, 36–8, 41–4

awarding of commissions 54–6

background of 35–6

'crewing up' 60–5, 182–3

dealing with fear 235–7

and death xxxix, 219, 220–6, 233–4

disciplining of 189–90

distinction between commissioned and non-commissioned ranks 187–9

establishment of limit on operations 226–7

feelings about bombing and reasons for fighting 130–40, 155, 378–9, 393

feelings over peacetime criticism towards 379–80

from the Dominions 33, 44–6

issuing of with escape kits 162

leave and visits home 276–9

life and conditions on bases xl–xli, 154, 256–66

love and romance 280–306

lucky charms and superstitions xxxix, 161–2

mounting a raid and preparations 155–64, 160

murder of by Germans on baling out 177–8

night-flight raid routine/experiences 164–81

numbers killed in operations xxvi, xxxviii–xxxix, 389

numbers killed in training 54, 219–20

off-duty nights out 267–71

as prisoners-of-war xxxviii, 358–64

problems encountered on missions xxxviii, 69–70

public and media impression of 144–7

recruitment and selection 34–6, 47–8, 49–50

relationships within 182–6, 198, 388

relationship with locals 275–6

relationship with pilots 195–8

relationship with squadron leaders 193–4

removal of weak links in 185–6

returning to base after raid 179–81

reunions after war 388–9

and sex 271–4

stress and break down of 238–55

survival rate and factors 230–1

training of 47, 48, 50–6, 60, 65–6

uniform 161

see also bomb-aimers; flight engineers; gunners; navigators; pilots; wireless operators

bomber stream 97–8, 172

bombers 49, 56, 77, 86

attempts to ban 8

introduction of four-engined 92–4

myth of self-protection 309

see also individual names

bombing

of civilians and morale question 74–6, 77, 79, 142

controversy over morality of and criticism of xxxi, 140–2

gauging of effects by 'index of activity' 77

moral effect of 8, 15–16, 72, 74

public opinion on area 143–4

psychological effect of xxxvii

Bombing Research Unit 370

bombing run 173–4

bombs 159

blast 159

Grand Slam 93

Tallboy 321, 327, 328, 329

see also incendiaries

Bonn, bombing of 335–6

Bormann, J. A. 270

Bottomley, Air Vice-Marshal Norman 89, 341

Boulton Paul Overstrand 10

break down (of bomber crew) 238–55

and character 240, 248

during First World War 239

and LMF 65–6, 248–50, 251–2, 254–5

off-duty symptoms of stress 241–3

symptoms during operations 243–4, 251

Bremen, bombing of xxvi–xxvii, 80, 333
Brening, Franz 178
Brest 104
Bridgman, Anthony 1
Brize Norton Flying Training School 55
Broadley, Bill 228
Brooker, Ray 64
Brunsbüttel 4
Brunswick, bombing raid on 335
Briars, Ralph 324, 326, 328–9
Buckley, Jack 183
Bufton, Group Captain Syd 101
Burnett, Squadron Leader 194
Butt, D. R. 78

Canada/Canadians 44–5, 52, 278
Capel, Flight Lieutenant 'Cape' 195
Carter, Wing Commander E. J. 253
Casablanca conference (1943) 105, 199
Casablanca directive 105, 199, 202, 308, 381
Cassidy, Jim 62
Catterall, Flying Officer R. 355
Chamberlain, Neville 1, 11
character
    and break down 240, 248
Charlwood, Don xxxviii, 45–6, 57, 154, 156–8, 171, 186–7, 193, 198, 223–4, 258, 263, 267–8, 269, 384–5, 391
Chase, Hadley
    No Orchids for Miss Blandish 264
Chemnitz 343
Cherwell, Lord 78
Cheshire, Leonard 39, 40, 219, 391, 394
    attack on railway tunnel at Samur 321, 328
    background 44
    bombing of aircraft factory at Toulouse 320
    character and qualities 191–2
    and Harris 91
    homes set up xxxii, 391
    improving bombing accuracy 320
    last operational mission 324
    and LMF cases 250
    and writing 262
children
    killed in Germany by bombing 356
Church
    criticism of area bombing policy 142

Churchill, Winston 7, 16, 48, 200, 319, 352
    and attacks on Berlin 17
    and Casablanca conference 105
    and Dresden raid 352–3
    and Harris 202, 339
    questioning of area bombing (1945) 352
    reaction to Bomber Command's new bombing plan 78–9
    victory speech xxxii, 367
    view of bombing issue 78
civilians 12, 15, 381
    bombing of and morale question 74–6, 77, 79, 142
    death toll in Britain 13, 16, 74, 78
    death toll in Germany xxvii, xxxiii, 13, 14, 113, 123, 127, 356–7
    policy to avoid bombing 11
Clegg, Ella Ida 13
Cochrane, Ralph 108
Coleman, Les 24
Cologne 113–25, 335
    anti-Nazi feeling in 114–15
    bunker life 119
    first thousand-bomber raid (1942) xxxix–xxxv, 98–100, 113, 116, 141
    Klostersturm episode 114
    Nazification of 114
    numbers killed in bombing raids 118
    public bunkers and private shelters 117–19
    repression and deportation of Jews 115–17
    St Peter and St Paul raid (1943) 113, 119–25
commissions, awarding of 54–6
Committee of Imperial Defence 6, 7
Coningsby 261, 265–6
Constantine, Air Vice-Marshal H. A. 350–1
corkscrew manoeuvre 167, 172, 205
court-martials 238–9
Cousens, Wing Commander A. G. S. 'Pluto' 186
Coventry 19–20
    bombing of and destruction caused 7, 18, 19, 20–7, 26, 30, 99, 356
    calls for retribution after bombing 30–1
    impact of bombing 77

mood of people after bombing 26–7, 28–9
reporting of bombing by media 29–30
restoration attempts 27–8
weak defences 20–1
Coward, Noël 152
crew, bomber *see* bomber crews
'crewing up' 60–5, 182–3
Currie, Jack 61–2, 90, 152, 174, 180, 238–9, 247, 250–1, 270, 274, 392

Dambusters, The (film) 384
Dams Raid (1943) xxxii, 106–10, 183, 191, 200, 228
Daniell, Raymond 30
Darmstadt, bombing of 356
Dawn Patrol 38
D-Day invasion 307, 308, 319, 320–2, 380
Dean, Ken 266
decoy fires 68
Denain (France) bombing of 137
desertion 238–9
Dickson, Sir William 379–80
Dimbleby, Richard 145–7
Directorate of Bomber Operations 77
Distinguished Flying Cross (DFC) 189
Distinguished Flying Medal (DFM) 189
Dobson, Sergeant John 81–5, 264–5
Dominions 189
  and Empire Air Training Scheme 52
  recruitment of pilots from 33, 44–6
Donat, Robert 264
Dortmund, bombing of 113
Dortmund–Ems canal 328
Dowding 367
Dresden, bombing of (1945) 138, 340–1, 342–3, 344–7, 350, 352–3, 376
Duisburg, bombing of 170, 335
Dulag Luft camp 358–9
Düsseldorf, bombing of 140
Dye, Sergeant Bernard 133–4, 260, 277–8
Dyson, Dr Freeman 214, 230–1, 232, 247

Eaker, Brigadier-General Ira C. 201
Eakins, Rev. T. G. 144
early returns 227, 243–4

Eden, Anthony 30
Eder dam 107, 108–9, 110, 340
Eighth Air Force 200–1, 309, 312, 315, 316, 385, 386
Eisenhower, General Dwight 308, 330
Elliot, Alec 68
Elliott, Denholm 53, 103–4, 362
Elsham Wolds 258, 384–5
Embry, Basil 228
Emery, Neville 'Bug' 64, 184
Empire Air Training Scheme 52
engineers, flight *see* flight engineers
Esbjerg 4
Essen 17–18, 348
  bombing raid on (1943) 148–51
  bombing raids 106, 113, 333, 371
  destruction of 370
  impact of bombing on 370–2
  Krupp factory 69–70, 106, 130, 370–1
Evans, Edith 264
Evill, Sir Douglas 343–4
Exodus Operation 358

Fairbanks, Douglas 52
Fairey Hendon 10
Falgate, Donald 58–9, 166–7
Fallowfield, Geoff 63
Faltham, Bert 84–5
Farquharson, Bill 42, 185–6, 233–4, 251, 346, 393
Fawke, Flight Lieutenant Gerry 321
Fayers, Reg xl, 90–1, 132, 153, 154–5, 182, 187, 221, 233, 258, 260, 264, 360, 364, 391, 394
Field, Dennis 19, 21–2, 24, 36–7, 48, 52, 54, 65, 165, 187–8, 258
Fighter Command xxxii, 47–8, 145, 183, 367, 369, 382–3
fighter escorts
  and USAAF 310, 314–17
First World War 6, 9, 36–7, 239, 357, 377, 389
Fischer, Friedrich 178
flak batteries 170, 205, 246, 324, 332
flak jackets 232
Flare Path (play) 151–2
flares 87
flight engineers 49, 59 *see also* bomber crew
Flying Fortresses 127, 206, 310
Focke-Wulf 190 315

Ford, Ken 64
Formby, George 271
Fortresses 200, 315
France
    attack on ports 104–5
    bombing of transportation targets in
        preparation for D-Day 308, 319–20
    total number of civilians killed 356
Frankfurt, bombing of 67, 299
Frankland, Noble 47, 48, 57, 94, 205,
        217, 374–5, 381–2, *383*, 385, 392
Freiburg
    bombing of 336, 340
    death of young 356
freshman crews 157–8
Frings, Cardinal Joseph 115
Frow, Brian 36, 50, 54, 55–6, 9–100,
        195, 221–3, 272–3
Fruehauf, Hans 22

G-H device 335–6
Galland, General Adolf 20, 317, 332
Gee, Des 64
Gee system 57, 91, 100
Gellhorn, Martha 147–8, *148*, 67
George, King 30–1
German aircraft 205 *see also* individual
    names
German aircraft industry 329–30
German Blitz (1940–41) xxiii, xxxvii,
        16–17, 42, 43, 74, 97, 133
German night-fighters 166, 167–8, 170,
        203–6, 216, 217, 309, 316
Germany
    death toll of xxvii, xxxiii, 13, 14, 113,
        123, 127, 356–7
    impact of bombing on xxix–xxx, xxxiii
    invasion of Low Countries (1940) 12
    radar system 166, 203, 309
    system of decoy fires 68
Gibson, Guy xl, 39–41, 75–6, 91, 145,
        160–1, 190–1, 220, 228–9, 233,
        262, 265, 300, 384
    character 191
    and Dams Raid xxxii, 4, 106, 107,
        108–9, 191, 228
    death 229
    leadership style 190–1
Gneisenau (warship) 73
Goebbels, Josef 97
Goodale, Brian 183
Goodchild, Ken 39, 177, 179–80

Gordon, Johnnie 263
Grand Slam bombs 93
Great Escape 358
Greenwood, Joan 264
Grieg, J. M. B. 145
gunners 59–60, 232 *see also* bomber
    crew

H2S radar 92, 206, 208
Halford, David 193–4
Halifax (aircraft) 10, 47, 49, 65, 86, 92–3,
        94, 162, 207, 229, 231, *383*, *410–1*
Halsbury, Earl of
    1944 (novel) 5–6
Hamburg
    bombing raids on 30, 80, 126–9,
        128, 202, 203, 204, 346
    death of young 356
    destruction of xxx–xxxi, 356
Hampdens 2, 10, 49
Hampton, James 50, 257
Handley Page Harrow 10
Hannover, destruction of 356
Harris, Air Marshal Sir Arthur (Bert)
        xxxix, 88–91, 94–8, 174, 265, 370,
        372, 375–8
    advocate for area bombing and
        bombing of German cities 88–9,
        94–5, 199, 200, 330, 331, 333, 340
    anger at lack of post-war recognition
        of men 386
    attempt to persuade post-war world of
        contribution of Bomber Command
        xxxvi–xxxvii, 375–6
    attendance at reunions 386–7
    autobiography (*Bomber Offensive*) 375
    aversion to day operations 317–18, 331
    background 88
    banning of wives from husbands'
        bases 300
    and Battle of Berlin 202, 207–8, 214,
        216, 217
    and Battle of the Ruhr 105, 106
    'Butch' nickname 89
    changes in operational procedures
        94–5
    character and qualities 71, 89, 91,
        140, 339, 340
    and Churchill 202, 339
    criticism of approach 337
    criticism of Webster and Frankland's
        study 373, 374

death 387
and Eisenhower 308
and first 'thousand' raid on Cologne
    (1942) 97–9
and *Hurricane* Operation 335
knighthood 369
loyalty to men serving under him
    375
and Lübeck and Rostock raids 95–7
ninetieth birthday 386
opposition to Pathfinder Force 100,
    101
as perceived by crews 89–91
and Pointblank directive 201–2,
    308
and Portal 337–9, 340
presentation of campaign as series of
    'battles' xxxviii, 154
prestige of 339
propagandist xxxv
reasons for getting away with
    insubordinate behaviour 339–40
scepticism over emphasis on oil
    targets 330–1, 338, 340
and Speer xxxvii, 375–6
statue of 387–8
style xxxiii
tribute to men 366
on unpopularity of bombers xxxii
on USAAF bombing methods 317–18
use of incendiaries to start fires 95–6
view of alcohol consumption 265
Harrison, Air Vice-Marshal R. 335
Harrisson, Tom 28–9, 31
Harvards 48
Hearn, Edward 41–2
Heavy Conversion Unit 65, 257
Heilbronn, bombing of 336–7, 340
Hemswell 388–9
Henderson, Chic 180
Higgins, Jock 219–20
High Capacity (HC) blast bombs 159
Himmler, Heinrich 178
Hitler, Adolf 39, 114, 131
Hobbs, Flight Sergeant Gerry 177
Hobday, Harold 'Hobby' 107, 108, 109,
    191
Hodder, Group Captain F. S. 176–7
Hoffman, Gauleiter 178
Holland 357
Holme-on-Spalding-Moor 187, 257,
    258, 264

Hughes, Henry 53
Hulance, Freddie 344–5, 354–5
Hull, George 134, 190, 198, 257,
    260–1, 261, 264, 265–6, 267, 269,
    270–1, 273, 276, 279, 287–300,
    392
Hurricane Operation 334, 335–6

incendiaries 32, 94, 96, 127, 159, 340
'index of activity' 77
India 52
Initial Training Wings (ITWs) 51
Inskip, Sir Thomas 10
interwar years 9–10
Iremonger, Sergeant 54
Isbister, James 12–13
Italy 104
    number of civilians killed 356
Iveson, Tony xxvi, 56, 90, 93, 192, 327,
    328, 393

Jagger, Brian 183
James, Sydney 19, 29
Jericho operation (1944) 228
Jews 38
    repression of in Cologne 115–17
Johnson, Edward 34
Johnson, Peter xxix–xxx, xxxix, 33–4,
    38, 86–7, 130, 135, 139–40, 155,
    171, 349–51, 358, 370, 370–2,
    377–8, 393
Joint Intelligence Committee (JIC) 343
Jones, Johnny 137–8
Junker 88s 205

Kammhuber, General Josef 166
Kammhuber Line 166, 203
Kangaroo Club (London) 278
Kee, Robert 41
Kelly, Flying Officer Pat 320
Kennan, George xxx–xxxi
Kiel, bombing of 80, 355
Kirby, Joan 134, 190, 257, 260–1,
    287–300, 392
Kirby, John 287, 289
Kirkpatrick, Wing Commander 82
Kitto, Philip 289
Knight, Flight Lieutenant Les 107, 109
Krupp's 69–70, 106, 130, 370–1

La Pallice 104
'Lacking in Moral Fibre' *see* LMF

Lancasters xl, 10, 47, 49, 56, 86, 93–4, 162, 205, 231, 317, 327, 383, 408–9
Lang of Lambeth, Lord 143
Lanham, Charlie 274
Lawson, Wing Commander Jimmy 250
Le Havre 323, 324
Le May, Colonel Curtis 312
leaflet drops 11
Leander, Zarah 125
leave 276–9
Legge, Flying Officer K. C. S. 145
Leipzig 343
Leslie, Jack 136
Lewis, Bruce 42, 51, 59
Lewis, Willie 136, 137, 163, 164, 173–4, 175, 184–5, 192, 195, 196, 273–4, 275, 392
Liberators 200, 310, 315
Lichtschlag, Carl 13
Lightnings 310
Lille 319
Lindholme 259
Lister, Francis 264
Liverpool, bombing of 25
LMF ('Lacking in Moral Fibre') 65–6, 248–50, 251–2, 254–5
Lobban, Sergeant John xxxv
Lodge, Roy 342, 345–6
London, bombing of 16–17, 25, 95, 324
Lorient 104
love 280–306
Lübeck, bombing of 95–6, 96
Luftwaffe 14, 21, 94, 133, 169, 201, 307, 316–17, 330, 331, 332, 373

Maaka, Flight Sergeant Inia 63
McClachlan, Sergeant 54
MacDonald, Roy 133, 154, 158, 172, 226, 393
MacGowan, Wing Commander 247
Mackay Brown, George 13
Mackintosh, Flight Lieutenant J. C. 68
Maddern, Geoff 186–7
Mahaddie, Group Captain Hamish 63, 100
Malan, 'Sailor' xxxii
Mann, Thomas 97
Manna Operation 357
Mannheim, bombing of 31–2

Manser VC, Flying Officer Leslie 196–7, 197
March, Cyril 50, 51, 60, 63–4, 135, 165, 169, 183–4, 190, 224, 365, 389
Marchant, Hilde 25, 28, 31
Marrs, Eric 42
Marshall, General George C. 347
Martin, Charles 76
Martin, Rev. George 144–5
Mass Observation 26
master bombers 172–4
Maudslay, Squadron Leader Henry 108–9
Maze, John 136–7, 184–5, 192, 195–6
medical officers (MOs) 245–8, 249
Medium Capacity (MC) bombs 159
Memphis Belle (film) 386
Merlin T24 engines 327
Messerschmitt 109s/110s 204, 204, 205, 315
Middleton, Flight Sergeant Rawdon 197–8
Mileham, Mary 280–7, 392–3
Millington, Wing Commander 344
Ministry of Information 76
Möhne dam 106–7, 108, 109–10, 340
Mönchengladbach, bombing of 13
Morris, Richard 228
Morrison, Herbert 27
Mosquitoes 156, 318, 320, 414–5
Mourton, Doug 43, 67, 70, 136, 170, 171, 182, 188, 194, 220, 254, 260
Müllers, Erika 13
Munich, bombing of (1945) 137–8
Murrow, Ed 212–13
Mustangs 311, 315–16, 317

navigation aids 4, 86
    Gee system 57, 91, 100
    H2S 92, 206, 208
    Oboe 57, 91–2, 208, 320
navigators 49, 52, 57, 60, 70, 157, 159, 231 see also bomber crew
Nelson, Wing Commander John 194
New Statesman 145
New Zealand 44, 45, 46
Newman, Ken 36, 38–9, 43, 47, 65–6, 93, 131, 135, 184, 189, 194, 232, 233, 259, 322–3, 336, 390
night flying 11–12, 65
Niklas, Major 352
No Moon Tonight 265

Noisy-Le-Sec 319
Norden bombsight 310
Nuremberg, failure of raid 215–16

Oberon, Merle 52
Oboe 57, 91–2, 208, 320
observers 49
Officer Training Corps (OTC) 55
oil targets 10–11, 72, 73–4, 324,
    330–1, 333, 337, 338, 340, 343
170 Squadron 388
Operational Training Units (OTUs)
    52–3, 60, 220
Orwell, George 100, 264
Overlord see D-Day invasion
overseas crews 278
Oxford Union 41

P-51 Mustang *311*, 315–16
Paans, Gerard 394
parachutes 231
Pathfinder Force (PFF) 63, 100, 100–2,
    113, 156, 226, 340
Patterson, Charles 37–8, 137, 227, 228,
    235–6, 266
Payne, Reg xxxiv, 188, 208, 209–10,
    215, 216, 219, 220, 225, 392
Peenemünde 206
Peirse, Sir Richard 32, 72, 73, 78, 81, 85
Pelly, Claude 370
Perkins, Flying Officer Reginald xxvi
Perkins, Flying Officer Robert xxvi
Pettenberg, Heinz 120–1, 122–3
Pforzheim, bombing of 351–2, 357
Pickard, Charles 'Percy' 48, 227–8
Pietrek, Leutnant Norbert 167–9
pilots 56
    relationship with crews 195–8
    as responsible for crew 57
    second 49
    see also bomber crew
Platts, Stanley 362
Pointblank directive 200, 201–2, 308
Portal, Sir Charles xxix, 17, 70–2, 101,
    313, 330, 334, 341, 343, 354, 369,
    377–8
    advocacy for area bombing 14–15,
    71, 74, 102, 377
    background and character 14, 70–1
    and direct retaliation policy 17–18,
    71
    and Harris 337–9, 340

and morale impact of bombing 15,
    71–2, 74
    and Pointblank directive 201–2
    reply to Churchill's doubts on
    bombing plan 78–9
Potsdam *xxx*
    bombing of xxix, 354
Priestley, J. B. 143–4
prisoners-of-war
    bomber crew as 358–64
    liberation of 358
psychology, aviation 239–40, 241,
    245–6 *see also* break down
Pudney, John 163

Queen Elizabeth 52

radar, German 166, 203, 309
RAF Film Unit 145
Rattigan, Terence 151
Rawlings, Eric 132–3
Red Army 344
Regensburg
    bombing of Messerschmitt factory
    206, 311
Reuter, Ludwig von 39
Rhodesia 44, 52
Riesen, Dr Günther 114
Roberts, Dorothy Courtney 144
Robertson, Pilot Officer 'Robbie' 175
Robinson, Edward G. 52
Roemer, Herr 123–4
Romeike, Franz 14
Rootes, William 28
Rostock, bombing of 95, 96–7
Roth, Albert 115
Royal Canadian Air Force (RCAF) 55,
    156
Ruhr 80, 105
    Battle of the 105–6, 110–12, 113,
    119–26, 217, 230, 283, 371
    destruction of 370–1
    first raid against 13–14
    and Operation *Hurricane* 334
Russians 326–7, 344–5

Saint-Nazaire 104–5
Salisbury, Marquess of 141–2
Sayles, Terry 64
Scharnhorst 73
Schley, Ingeborg 13
Schmid, General Joseph 'Beppo' 317

Schoenenberg, Erna 116
Schräge Musik 205
Schulte, Cardinal 115
Schweinfurt, bombing of 206, 216, 311, 312–13, 338
Scott, Frances 300–6, 393
Scott, Michael 131–2, 262–3
Scunthorpe 267–8
searchlights 170, 171–2
second pilots 49
senior intelligence officer (SIO) 158–9
Sester, Hans 121–2
sextant 70
Shackleton, 'Shack' 223
Shannon, Flight Lieutenant David 108, 183, 219, 321
Shelton, John 23
Shirer, William 76
Sinclair, Sir Archibald 141, 142, 353
617 Squadron 106–10, 261–2, 321, 326, 327–8
633 Squadron (film) 384
Slessor, Sir John 7, 11, 74, 79, 81
Snaith, Leonard 1, 2
South Africa 44, 52
Southampton, bombing of 25
Soviet Union 86, 342–3, 344
Spaatz, General Carl 316
Speer, Albert xxxvii, 203, 375–6
Spitfires 42, 73, 383
Spoden, Peter 203–4, 393–4
squadron commanders 192–4, 226–7, 266
Stafford-Clark, David 235, 236–7, 247
Stalag Luft III camp 358, 359–61
Stalingrad, siege of 200
Star award 368
Steele, T. S. 29–30
Steiner, Dennis 50, 52, 65, 161, 238, 347, 365, 388, 390–1
Stettin, bombing of 113
Stirlings 10, 47, 49, 86, 92, 207, 231, 412–13
Stockton, Norman 145
Stokes, Richard 140–1, 142–3, 353
Strauss, Erich 38
Street, Sir Arthur 368
Studnitz, Hans-Georg von 211–12
Stuttgart 324–5
Sumpter, Len 43, 108, 109, 183, 186, 188–9, 191

Supreme Headquarters Allied Expeditionary Force (SHAEF) 344
Sylt 103
Symonds, Charles 241, 244, 248–9, 253

Tait, James 327
Tallboys 321, 327, 328, *329*
target indicators (TIs) 172
Target for Tonight (film) 48, 383
Taylor, Arthur 34, 110–12, 269–70, 390
Tedder, Sir Arthur 337, 369
Thomas, Edwin 224–5, 271
.303 machine guns 169, 232
Thunderbolts 310, 315
Thunderclap plan (1944) 334–5, 341, 344
Tirpitz (battleship) 107, 326–8
Toulouse 320
training
   of bomber crews 47, 48, 50–6, 60, 65–6
   numbers killed whilst 54, 219–20
transatlantic convoys 73
Trenchard, Hugh 7–8, 9, 15, 16, 74, 75
Tuck, Bob Stanford xxxii
Tuddenham (Suffolk) 187–8, 258, 394
Twelve O'Clock High (film) 385
Twinn, Peter 60, 169–70

U-boats
   attacking of by Bomber Command 73, 104
Uhlenbruck, Gerhard 115
United States Army Air Force *see* USAAF
United States 52
   entry into war 86, 102
   reaction to bombing of Coventry 30
USAAF (United States Army Air Force) xxxiii, 105, 131, 309–17
   attack on ball-bearing factories at Schweinfurt 311, 312–13
   attack on Messerschmitt factory at Regensburg 311–12
   attempt to destroy German aircraft production 310–11
   and Big Week (1944) 316
   experiments in night bombing 314
   and fighter escorts 310, 314–17
   lack of post-war criticism compared with Bomber Command xxxii–xxxiii, 386

little faith in night bombing 309, 310
operations 102, 200–1, 310–11
preference for precision bombing 102,
    200, 201, 206, 309–10, 385–6
total number of bombs dropped 355

V1/V2 rocket attacks 133
Vassiltchikov, Marie 'Missie' 210–11
VE day 365
venereal diseases 50
Villers-Bocage 322
Vohwinkel, bombing of 347
Volmer, Dr Hans 114
Voyce, Wing Commander John 266

WAAFs 272, 300
Walkden, Evelyn 143
Walker, Danny 183
Wallis, Professor Barnes 106, 108, 109,
    321
Wangerooge 355
Warner, Konrad 212
Warwick, Squadron Leader James 229
Way to the Stars, The (film) 383
weather forecasting 232–3
Webber, Keith 268, 269
Webster and Frankland study (1961)
    340, 373–4
Weiss, Franz-Rudolf von 117
Weiss, Stefan 178
Wellingtons 3, 10, 49, 406–7
Werkendam 394
Western Air Plans 10
Whitleys 10, 49, 69

Wigsley
  Heavy Conversion Unit at 257
Wilhelmshaven harbour
  failed bombing attempts (1939) 1–4
Willatt, Geoffrey 138–9, 175–7,
    358–64
Williams, Denis 241, 244, 253
Wilson, Andrew 'Paddy' xxxv
Wilson, Sergeant A. J. N. 144
Window 126, 166, 203, 204–5, 207,
    209
Wingham, Tom 64–5, 135
Winn, Godfrey 56
Winnen, Anne 117
wireless operators 59, 60, 157, 159, 231
  see also bomber crew
Wolverhampton, bombing of 21
Wood, Michael 80
Wood, Ralph 44–5, 52–3, 54, 92–3,
    99, 162, 260, 278
Wood, Sir Kingsley 140
Woodhall Spa 261–2, 326–7, 394
Woods, Eric 69–70
Wooldridge, John 383
Wuppertal, bombing of 113, 136, 137
Würzburg, bombing of 349, 351

Yalta conference (1945) 344
Yates, Harry xxxix–xi, 35, 48–9, 62,
    136, 158, 180, 234, 253–4, 277,
    278–9, 323, 332, 347–9, 392
Yates, Jack 161

Zanuck, Darryl 385

P.S.

Ideas,
interviews
& features ...

About the author

2 Q and A: Louise Tucker talks to
Patrick Bishop

4 Life at a Glance

5 Top Ten Favourite Reads

Read on

7 Have You Read?

8 If You Loved This, You Might Like ...

10 Find Out More

11 Read the first chapter of Patrick
Bishop's new book *3 Para*

Q and A

Louise Tucker talks to Patrick Bishop

For most of your career you have been a war correspondent, and now you also write books, but what did you want to be when you grew up?
Apart from a brief moment when I thought I might be a soldier I always wanted to be a writer. I saw it as a romantic calling that would impress girls and not involve too much work. Both assumptions turned out to be mistaken.

How did your family background influence your choice of career, if at all?
Neither of my parents came from the world of books. My father was a building engineer and my mother a teacher. Both were profoundly interested in books, however, and I, my brother and three sisters were brought up to reverence them.

A real sense of home, and a loyalty to such a place, informs many of the stories in *Bomber Boys.* **Where is home for you, and what does such a concept mean to you?**
The first six years of my life were spent in rural Kent, the scene of much of my first book, *Fighter Boys*. The rest of my upbringing was in suburban South London, parts of which were hit in the Blitz. I have an enduring love for both places and feel a deep attachment to the nondescript streets of places like Morden, Berrylands and the less posh parts of Wimbledon. I feel comfortable there and I think that is what lies at the heart of the concept of 'home'. Most of the Bomber

Boys were fighting for the street they grew up in – not some propaganda concoction of elm trees spreading over the village green.

How and where did you start your research for this book and who was your first interviewee?
I started by talking to one of the great men of Bomber Command, Tony Iveson of 617 Squadron, who was on the raid that sank the *Tirpitz*. One of the joys of research is that you meet remarkable people. I am now proud to have some of them as friends.

Geoffrey Willatt's story about being a POW and the surreal experience of 'shouting to be let *in*' to a prisoners' camp stands out as one of the most memorable stories for me. Do you have a favourite?
I think it would be the tale of Dave Shannon, which demonstrates that even a man of his legendary coolness felt the appalling strain of operational flying like everyone else. Walking with Leonard Cheshire out to their aircraft one evening to fly over Germany, Cheshire remarked on the beautiful sunset. 'I don't give a fuck about that,' said Shannon. 'I want to see the sunrise.'

Were there any differences between writing and researching your first book *Fighter Boys* and writing and researching this?
Fighter Boys was about the Battle of Britain, which was about as morally straightforward a struggle as it is possible to have in warfare. ▶

Author photograph by Ian Jones

LIFE *at a Glance*

BORN

1952, Ashford, Kent

EDUCATED

Wimbledon College;
Corpus Christi College,
Oxford

CAREER

Evening Standard, the
Observer: Northern
Ireland Correspondent,
War Correspondent,
the Falklands, 1982;
Sunday Times: Diplomatic
Correspondent; *Sunday
Telegraph*, *Daily
Telegraph*: Middle East
Correspondent, Senior
Foreign Correspondent,
Foreign Editor, Associate
Editor (Foreign), Paris
Correspondent

◄ The bombing campaign was far more complicated. The story is darker and more terrible, both for those who flew the aircraft and for those under the bombs. One difference in the research was that the long duration of the strategic air offensive meant that there was far more contemporaneous written material to draw from. There is a wealth of diaries and letters and subsequently many veterans felt compelled to record their memoirs.

What has being a war correspondent taught you about war, and peace, and did writing these books confirm or contradict that knowledge?

What I've learned is that war is a complicated and contradictory business. At one level it is simply a matter of destruction, suffering and waste. At another, it provides opportunity and circumstances in which people can behave incredibly well. The enduring fact of modern warfare is that it is always the innocent who suffer most. Also, that fighting rarely produces the desired results.

There is often a distinction made, sometimes to the detriment of journalists, between journalists and writers: do you think that there is a difference?

The best journalists are conscious that they are – to use a hackneyed but apposite phrase – engaged in writing the first draft of history. They are diligent, accurate and aware of context and nuance, and their reporting is a valuable addition to the archive. Others are lazy, sloppy and contemptuous of the truth if it crosses the tramlines of their own or their editors' preconceptions. There is and always has been a lot of this kind of journalism about and in the frantic world of deadlines it is easy to get away with. Good journalists can write good books. Bad journalists venturing into hard covers still tend to write rubbish – just at greater length.

Frances Scott wrote that 'It seemed as though they suddenly changed from adolescents to mature men, missing the carefree years of the early twenties.' Did the stories you discovered ever make you feel that subsequent generations were spoilt in comparison?
Spoilt is perhaps not the right word. But certainly privileged. I am from a generation born in the 1950s and I was brought up to understand the sacrifices that were made on my behalf. Inevitably with time, that comprehension is bound to fade. Having said that, I am pleasantly surprised at the level of awareness amongst the young of what the Second World War was about and the respect that is shown to those who took part in it. When I was growing up the Boer War was only sixty years distant yet it might have happened in the Dark Ages for all we knew about it. The Second World War ended more than sixty years ago, yet it still holds a central place in our collective memory now.

How did those that survived, the rank and file, as opposed to Harris, cope with the public embarrassment about Bomber Command displayed after the war?
They behaved like men of their time. ▶

TOP TEN
Favourite Reads

1. *Sentimental Education*
   Gustave Flaubert

2. *Just William*
   Richmal Crompton

3. *The String of Pearls*
   Joseph Roth

4. *Ashenden*
   Somerset Maugham

5. *The Great Gatsby*
   F. Scott Fitzgerald

6. *A Peace to End All Peace*
   David Fromkin

7. *The Proud Tower*
   Barbara Tuchman

8. *My Early Life*
   Winston S. Churchill

9. *The Canterbury Tales*
   Geoffrey Chaucer

10. *A Hero of Our Time*
    Mikhail Lermontov

Q and A *(continued)*

◄ Whatever private hurt they may have felt at the injustice that was done to them, they kept to themselves. It wouldn't happen now.

At the end of the prologue and in the last chapter you mention the lack of a proper memorial for the Bomber Boys and your hope that the book will 'mark a first step in changing that'. Do you think there is any chance now that a physical memorial will be set up in memory of the sacrifice made?
I would like to think so, but there are large political obstacles that would have to be negotiated. Prime among them is a shared desire by the political establishment not to do anything that might be deemed provocative by our German partners in Europe. There is also the fact that the veterans with their characteristic modesty and restraint do not want to be seen making a fuss.

Human stories, rather than the coldness of statistics, illuminate *Bomber Boys* from the start. Will you continue writing real-life tales or will you be tempted to move into fiction next?
I'm going to carry on writing history but I have recently moved into fiction. My novel *A Good War*, a romantic thriller set during the Battle of Britain and the Normandy invasion, is out this spring. ■

Have You Read?

Also by Patrick Bishop

Fighter Boys: Saving Britain 1940
In the summer of 1940 the future of Britain
and, arguably, the free world depended on
the morale and skill of a small group of
mostly very young men. Their victory
became celebrated as a classic feat of arms.
But it was also a triumph of the spirit in
which the attitudes and outlook of the pilots
played a crucial part. In this highly acclaimed
history, the author reaches beyond the myths
to convey what it was to be a fighter pilot, in
war and peace.

3 Para
When the elite 3 Para Battlegroup were
dispatched to the Helmand Province in
Afghanistan they faced a nightmarish reality:
50 degree heat, few provisions, no water,
fighting an unpredictable and determined
enemy. Their aim quickly changed from
providing security during reconstruction
efforts – to just staying alive. Patrick Bishop
was given exclusive access to this elite
Battlegroup and gives an account of
astonishing discipline, determination and
courage. *3 Para* is an unforgettable portrait of
one of the world's finest fighting regiments.

**Read the first chapter of *3 Para* at the end of
this section**

If You Loved This,
You Might Like ...

Eighth Air Force: The American Bomber Crews in Britain
Donald Miller

A history of the US Eighth Air Force, which flew Liberators and Flying Fortresses alongside the RAF's Lancasters and Halifaxes. Like *Bomber Boys*, it details both the bombing campaigns and the individual experiences, but also shows the effect of hundreds of young American pilots arriving in the quiet of an East Anglia devoid of young British men ...

On the Natural History of Destruction
W. G. Sebald

In this collection of essays published posthumously, W. G. Sebald explores the complete silence in post-war Germany on the subject of the Allied bombing of its cities. With characteristically beautiful writing, he probes the trauma and experiences of a nation that seemed to be choosing to forget its past.

Bomber Command
Max Hastings

A detailed account of Bomber Command's role in the Allied offensive against Germany, written by one of the most well-known writers of British military history.

Band of Brothers
Stephen E. Ambrose
Whether you read this book, or watch the
TV series of the same name, Ambrose's
description of the life of Easy Company,
the 101st Airborne Division, in the Second
World War is unforgettable. Using interviews,
journals and letters, the author takes us
through what it is to be a young US
paratrooper, from the training in Georgia
to their arrival in France on D-Day.

....

Jarhead: A Soldier's Story of Modern War
Anthony Swofford
A memoir of a completely different war, the
1991 Gulf War, *Jarhead* is an unromantic
and cold-eyed examination of both what is
involved in modern warfare and what sort
of person takes part in conflict. Intense,
disturbing and revealing, it has now been
made into a film, directed by Sam Mendes.

....

**Cheshire: The Biography of Leonard
Cheshire, VC, OM**
Richard Morris
Bishop writes that 'Cheshire struck
everybody who came across him as
remarkable in every way; exceptionally
tough, brave and good' and Nehru described
him as 'the greatest man I have met since
Gandhi'. In this biography, Richard Morris
tells the story of a man who not only achieved
great distinction in the Second World War, ▶

The RAF's own very
detailed site, which
includes information on
tactics, personal stories
and links to the Bomber
Command Association.

Another official RAF site,
set up to commemorate
the sixtieth anniversary
of Air Chief Marshal Sir
Arthur Harris being
appointed to take over
Bomber Command.
Lots of in-depth history
and detail about raids,
squadrons and the aircraft
used.

If You Loved This . . . *(continued)*

◄ but also left a legacy that helps millions of
disabled people all over the world.

....

Birdsong
Sebastian Faulks

One of the most lauded novels about the First
World War, and rightfully so, *Birdsong* tells
the story of Stephen Wraysford, who falls in
love with a married woman four years before
the outbreak of war. The relationship is
doomed and when Stephen arrives in the
trenches he is traumatized by the memory of
what he has lost and the fear of what he might
be about to lose. The descriptions of the
Battle of the Somme are astounding. ■

The first chapter of Patrick Bishop's new book, *3 Para*

Day of Days

At about 8 a.m. on the morning of 6 September 2006 Lieutenant Colonel Stuart Tootal rolled out of his cot, pulled on his uniform and boots and set off along the duckboard walkway to catch up on overnight events.

The sun was already high and a pale, malevolent haze hovered over the talcum-powder dust of the Helmand desert. He reached a tent bristling with radio antennae and pushed aside the door flap. Inside it was warm and stuffy. The gloom was pricked with little nails of green and red light, winking from stacks of electronic consoles. It was quiet except for the occasional squawk from the radios. This was the Joint Operational Command, the 'JOC', where the synapses of the battle group he led came together.

Tootal was slight, wiry and driven. He was as interested in the theory of soldiering as he was in the practice, and had as many degrees as battle honours. His enthusiasm for his job was matched by his concern for his men. There would be much to be concerned about before the day was over.

The 3 Para battle group had arrived in Helmand five months earlier. Its task was to create a security zone within which development agencies could get to work on projects to develop an area barely touched by progress and lay the foundations for a future of relative prosperity.

The plan had always been aspirational. The religious warriors of the Taliban, who were struggling to reassert their power in the province, were certain to oppose the arrival of the British.

Everyone had expected some trouble, but not the relentless combat the soldiers were now immersed in. The reconstruction mission had become a memory. 3 Para and their comrades were fighting a desperate war of attrition. Most of them were besieged in bare mud-and-breeze-block government compounds – 'platoon houses', as they had become known – scattered over the north of the province, fighting off daily attacks from an enemy who, despite taking murderous losses, kept on coming. They spent their days pounded by the sun as they took their turn at 'stag', crouching in sandbagged, rooftop gun positions, or standing by

11

to run to their posts when the shooting started. They slept on floors, washed rarely and lived off ration packs and sterilised water. They were gaunt, bony and rough looking. Their sunburned faces were fuzzed with beards, just like those of the men they were fighting.

They were on their own out there. Beyond the walls of the compound and the shattered towns lay tawny, sun-baked mountains and vast stretches of desert, ridged with dry water-courses. The mother base at Camp Bastion was far away and they were connected to it by the slimmest of links, the helicopters whose vulnerability to the insurgents' fire made every sortie heart-stoppingly tense.

The morning started calmly. The previous day, most of the fighting had been around the base at Musa Qaleh, a broken-down fortress in the middle of a ghost town, now inhabited only by men trying to kill each other. It was held by the soldiers of Easy Company, some of whom had been there for thirty-one days. In the morning, the insurgents had lobbed five mortars into the compound from concealed positions in the maze of alleyways and walled gardens that pressed against the walls of the base.

At about 7.40 that evening some of the Royal Irish Regiment soldiers with the 3 Para battle group were on a satellite phone to their comrades at their home near Inverness, discussing the 'big piss-up' that was being organised to celebrate their expected homecoming in a few weeks' time. The call was interrupted by the crash of an RPG (rocket-propelled grenade) smashing into one of the sandbagged 'sangar' defensive positions ringing the platoon house. The blast knocked the four men inside flat and sent a soldier flying down the stone steps, knocking him unconscious. The soldiers in the sangar struggled upright and got on their guns, scanned the ground in front of them for muzzle flashes, and poured fire into the darkness. Green and red tracer flowed back and forth, and the crack of rifles and the throb of machine guns shattered the air.

The Taliban attack was finally beaten off after forty minutes when British and American jets arrived to bomb and strafe the insurgents' positions. Intelligence reported 'many Taliban killed in action'. Before he grabbed some sleep, Corporal Danny Groves, one of the Royal Irish soldiers, wrote with satisfaction in his diary: 'Today was a very good day for the boys . . . The Taliban had attempted to overrun us but instead they received a hell of a beating from the mismatched men of Easy Company.'

And now, another day in Helmand was dawning. At 9 a.m., Tootal's headquarters staff gathered in the JOC for the morning brief. A few incidents had trickled in over the radio net. Just before 8 a.m., four mortars had landed in the base at Now Zad. This was the most remote of the outstations, about fifty miles to the north-west as the helicopter flew from Bastion. Half an hour later, small-arms fire and RPGs were fired at the platoon house at Sangin. This was the normal back-and-forth violence, the metronome tick of aggression and counter-aggression that punctuated every day. There was nothing to distract Tootal from his usual crowded morning of meetings and briefings.

Then, just after midday, the atmosphere in the JOC changed. Reports of casualties started filtering in from Kajaki Dam. The dam was a prize target for the insurgents. The hydroelectric station there generated power for the whole region. The British troops, who lived in sweltering trenches dug out of the stony hills overlooking it, came under regular Taliban attack. But this sounded like something different. The details were sketchy at first. A sniper on his way to spy out a Taliban position had stepped on a mine and was very badly wounded.

Tootal called up his higher headquarters at Kandahar to request a Black Hawk helicopter, equipped with a winch, to lift the casualty out. He was told there would be a long delay. A CH-47 Chinook casualty evacuation helicopter was available. But it did not have lifting gear.

On a patch of barren hillside in Kajaki, a group of men stood rooted to the ground. Beside them lay Lance Corporal Stuart Hale of 3 Para Support Company. The mine had blown off his foot. Corporal Mark Wright was on his position about a mile away when he heard the explosion. He rounded up some soldiers and medics and they ran down the hill to help. They had gone to Hale's side knowing the potential danger they were in. Now they were trying to get him out. They began prodding the gritty sun-baked ground, clearing a path to a spot where the helicopter could get in, then carried Hale on a stretcher to the landing site. Corporal Stuart Pearson turned back along the cleared path. As he bent down to pick up a water container, there was another explosion. Until now, it had seemed that Hale might be the victim of a stray mine, probably left behind by the Russians who had spent years occupying Kajaki. Now the rescuers were hit by a grim realisation. 'We thought, fucking hell,' said Corporal Jay Davis, 'we are in a minefield now. They are everywhere.'

Pearson was only four or five yards away. But every step risked another explosion. He applied a tourniquet and dosed himself with morphine while they waited for the helicopter. It arrived at 1.30, and landed more than fifty yards away across ground that for all anyone knew was thick with mines. There was no question of carrying the casualties to the Chinook. As it lifted off in a cloud of muck and grit, another mine went off, blasting shrapnel into the shoulder, chest and face of Mark Wright.

A medic, Lance Corporal Paul 'Tug' Hartley, moved forward to help. He threw his medical pack on the ground in front of him to detonate any mines in his path. He reached Wright safely. But as he arrived Fusilier Andy Barlow moved back to give him room, treading on a mine that blasted shrapnel into his lower leg. The blast also blew Hartley to the ground and wounded Private Dave Prosser.

All around, men lay bleeding into the dirt. Hunched over the radios, Tootal and his staff had been listening with mounting dismay as the picture grew darker. The only way the wounded and the stranded could escape the minefield was if they were lifted out. Tootal harassed Kandahar for updates on when the winch-equipped Black Hawk would be ready to haul his men to safety. Nearly four hours after the initial request, two Black Hawks arrived. Two American aircrew were lowered into the minefield and, one by one, winched everyone aboard.

When the casualties reached Bastion, Tootal and 3 Para's RSM (regimental sergeant major), John Hardy, were at the landing site to meet them. As the helicopter touched down, they jumped aboard. Six men were stacked across the floor. Three had stumps where one of their legs had been. One was dead. Mark Wright, who had been chatting and joking with his mates during the two and a half hours they had waited to be rescued, had bled to death on the way home. The wounded were hurried away. Hardy and Tootal zipped Wright into a body bag and carried him to an ambulance.

Tootal had been back in the JOC for fifteen minutes when another spate of emergency signals squawked over the radio. There were more wounded soldiers in two of the platoon houses. In Sangin, three soldiers had been hit by mortar shrapnel as they stood in an orchard within the walls of the base being briefed on their tasks for the evening. Mortar fire had injured two more British soldiers and two of their Afghan allies in Musa Qaleh. There was, however, only one Chinook helicopter available to mount a casualty evacuation – a 'casevac'.

The helicopter, with the Immediate Response Team of medics aboard, was ordered to go to Sangin first. One of the wounded, Lance Corporal Luke McCulloch, had been hit in the head and looked close to death. The casevac chopper was flown by Major Mark Hammond of the Royal Marines. The flight took twenty minutes. As Hammond began his final approach, the JOC fizzed with tension. This was when the helicopters were most vulnerable to the Taliban RPGs and heavy machine guns. The loss of a chopper would not only be a human disaster. It would be a huge victory for the Taliban, and could lay the ground for a British tactical defeat. There was already talk in London of pulling out of the farthest-flung platoon houses to minimise the risk of a helicopter being shot down.

As the Chinook swooped towards the landing site, Hammond saw green tracer fire flowing towards him from the fields, thickly planted with tall crops that lay south of the base. Reluctantly, he swung the Chinook away and headed back to Bastion.

He and his crew had been on the ground only a few minutes when they were ordered off again, this time to try to retrieve the two casualties at Musa Qaleh. The base doctor there had warned Tootal that he could keep one of his patients alive only for another six or seven hours. Musa Qaleh was the helicopter crews' most hated destination. The landing site was in the middle of a built-up area full of insurgent firing points. When they reached the town at 8.15 p.m., the Taliban were waiting. One of the escorting Apaches saw two RPGs swish past the Chinook, missing it by 10 yards. To attempt a landing would be suicidal. Again Hammond was forced to return to base. When they arrived at Bastion they found their chopper spattered with strike marks. One round had hit the root of a rotor blade, inflicting potentially lethal damage.

Tootal decided to risk another attempt before the night was over. A replacement was found for the damaged Chinook. Artillery batteries and aircraft were put on alert to batter Taliban positions around the two bases as the helicopter darted in. Hammond, along with his three crewmates and the four members of the medical team, took off for Sangin once more. He brought the Chinook into the landing site low and fast. As it settled in a whirlwind of dust, a Spartan armoured vehicle raced up to the back ramp, where the crew snatched the casualties aboard. The helicopter had barely touched the ground before it was climbing again, chased by streams of green tracer spouting from the Taliban positions. The sound of the engine was drowned out by the ear-battering din as the crew returned the fire from the door guns.

The ambulances were waiting at Bastion to hurry the casualties away to the base hospital. It was too late for Luke McCulloch. The twenty-one-year-old, one of the contingent of Royal Irish Regiment soldiers fighting alongside the Paras, was pronounced dead before he got there.

In the course of the day Mark Hammond had experienced enough danger to last most pilots a lifetime, but he volunteered for a last, risk-laden task. For the second time that night he went back to Musa Qaleh. Tootal had racked up every aircraft available, amassing an escort of Apache attack helicopters, A-10 'Tankbusters' and a Spectre gunship to shepherd the Chinook in. As the chopper arrived, just before 1.30 a.m., the aircraft strafed the Taliban firing points around the base. Despite the barrage, the insurgents managed to launch an attack and bullets cracked around the Chinook as it touched down, picked up the wounded and climbed into the night.

The Chinook finally arrived back safely at 2 a.m. Before he collapsed into bed, Stuart Tootal found time to write up his diary. It had been an extraordinary day, one that those involved in its dramas would never forget. He had spent the previous fourteen hours 'endeavouring to get our wounded out from three different locations. Two died on the way and three have had legs amputated. Some will return to combat and some will not.'

There had been many times since the Paras had deployed when he had turned to RSM Hardy before heading to his cot and said, 'That was a day of days.' But there had not been a day like this one. There had been tragedy, he wrote, but also 'much courage, both by the wounded and those who went to get them. There has been sorrow, sadness, fortitude and even humour. A difficult day, no doubt, but one to be proud of, having seen the way people have behaved.'

His last thought before he dropped into an exhausted sleep was, 'I really don't want tomorrow to be like today but it just might be. It might actually be worse.' ■